My Own Liberator

My Own Liberator

A MEMOIR

Dikgang Moseneke

PICADOR AFRICA

First published in 2016 by Picador Africa
an imprint of Pan Macmillan South Africa
Private Bag x19, Northlands
Johannesburg, 2116

www.panmacmillan.co.za

ISBN 978-1-77010-508-9
SPECIAL EDITION ISBN 978-1-77010-539-3
EBOOK ISBN 978-1-77010-509-6

*While every effort has been made to ensure the accuracy of the details, facts,
names and places mentioned, as an autobiography this book is partly based
on memory. The publisher and author welcome feedback, comments and/or
corrections that could further enrich the book.*

Editing by Alison Lowry
Proofreading by Lisa Compton
Indexing by Christopher Merrett
Design and typesetting by Triple M Design, Johannesburg
Cover design by K4
Cover photograph by Gisele Wulfsohn/South Photographs

Printed and bound by Shumani Mills Communications, Communications, Parow, Cape Town
SW62308

Contents

Dedication

It does not come easily to know to whom one owes a dedication in a tale that divulges remarkable human props and crutches along a long and winding voyage. Is my first gratitude perhaps due to my mother, Karabo Mabel Moseneke, and father, Samuel Sedise Moseneke, who stuck it out with each other until his death and with us, their children, as they nurtured us in a rocky nest of familial affection?

Ought I not acknowledge my primary and secondary school teachers – Mashikwane Susan Moseneke, Marope Susan Thulare, Makhudu Ramopo, Jafta Kgalabi Masemeola, Getz Komane, Eunice Dinalane and Stanley Mmutlanyane Mogoba – who spat at inferior apartheid education, soared above it and gave their all to their pupils for no or little personal profit?

But is perhaps the dedication due to the many stalwarts on Robben Island, who not only helped bring me up but also tutored me on the history and contours of our long and glorious struggle against colonial exclusion and towards a just, inclusive and humane society? They included Robert Mangaliso Sobukwe, Nelson Rolihlahla Mandela and Neville Alexander, at some distance, and closer, John Nyathi Pokela, Zephania Mothopeng, Harry Gwala, Steve Tshwete, Mlamli Makwethu Joe Gqabi, Sedick Isaacs, Selby Ngendane, Johnson Mlambo and Klaas Mashishi.

One may rightly observe that but for my career in law my world would have been markedly different. That is true. Should I then dedicate this life story to my early tutors, who included Mike Meyer, Steven Klagsbrun, Godfrey Pitje, Griffiths Mlungisi Mxenge, Guy Hoffman SC, Marumo Moerane SC and, later, Arthur Chaskalson CJ? If so, how could I look past comrades and members of the Black Lawyers Association and other progressive attorneys, too many to mention, who single-mindedly briefed me as counsel until I earned the prestigious status of senior counsel, was elevated to the High Court bench, was later appointed by President Thabo Mbeki to the Constitutional Court and, in time, served the republic as deputy chief justice?

However, on balance, I dedicate this modest personal memoir to two sets of people. First, to my wife and partner, Kabonina Naomi Moseneke, and my daughter Duduzile, my son Sedise and our departed son Reabetswe Botshelo. *Robala ka kagiso Mokwena*! More than anybody else, Kabo and her children bore the full brunt of the 40 years of my marauding role in the struggle for freedom and the practice of law. They stood by me, tolerated my absence from home and forgave my shortcomings.

In addition, I choose to stake my trust in the future. I consecrate this work to the youth of our land, of Africa and of the world, where radical change is necessary. This is because, ordinarily, young people are deeply intolerant of social inequity. After all is done and dusted, each young person is her or his own liberator in the personal space but so, too, together with others, in the public and social enterprise. No young person, and indeed no generation, may outsource to others the task of achieving meaningful and inclusive freedom, least still to those who wield political or other public power. Each is her or his own liberator.

Foreword

During 2008, I was mindful of the fact that both the then chief justice, Pius Langa, and I would complete our government mandates the following year. In 2009, Chief Justice Langa would have served his fifteen-year term as a member of the Constitutional Court and would therefore have to retire. For my part, I would complete my two terms as president of the republic.

I therefore decided that one of the things I would do before leaving office would be to propose to the Judicial Services Commission that the then deputy chief justice, Dikgang Moseneke, should succeed Chief Justice Langa once the latter had completed his mandated period of service. Unfortunately, this was not to be, as the national executive committee of the ANC decided to 'recall' me in September 2008.

As readers will discover in this memoir, after working for fifteen years as an attorney and an advocate, including as senior counsel, Dikgang decided to go into private business between 1995 and 2001. However, in 2001, I approached him to request that he consider leaving business and accept an appointment to the bench. This view was shared by former President Nelson Mandela, the then chief Justice Arthur Chaskalson and other senior members of the legal community. Fortunately, Dikgang acceded to our requests.

With the approval of the Judicial Services Commission, I appointed Dikgang to a permanent position in the High Court in September 2001 and later, in November 2002, to the Constitutional Court. When Chief Justice Chaskalson retired, I appointed Justice Langa to succeed him and simultaneously elevated Justice Moseneke to the position of deputy chief justice. Both appointments came into effect on 1 June 2005.

At the time we approached Dikgang to persuade him to join the bench, we were concerned about the judiciary's need to be transformed and strengthened, especially in light of the fact that South Africa was a new constitutional democracy, with the constitution being the supreme law of the republic. Accordingly, we were continually preoccupied with the matter of drawing into the judiciary properly qualified people, including and especially as this related to the Constitutional Court.

In July 2003, I addressed a judicial symposium convened by the chief justice to discuss the important matter of the transformation of the judiciary. On that occasion I cited comments that had been made by Alexander Hamilton, one of the most prominent of the founding fathers of the United States of America, concerning the supremacy of the US constitution and other matters. Among other things, Hamilton said:

> To avoid an arbitrary discretion in the courts, it is indispensable that they should be bound down by strict rules and precedents ... [These] must demand long and laborious study, to acquire a competent knowledge of them. Hence it is that there can be but few men in the society, who will have sufficient skill in the laws to qualify them for the stations of judges. And making the proper deductions for the ordinary depravity of human nature, the number must be still smaller of those who unite the requisite integrity with the requisite knowledge.

I then cited the case of the fourth chief justice of the United States, John Marshall, who served in this position for over three decades, from 1801 to 1835. Like Alexander Hamilton, Marshall, a friend of George Washington, had fought as a soldier and an officer in the ranks of the Continental Army during the American Revolutionary War.

History shows that, as chief justice, John Marshall played an outstanding role in terms of defining how the US constitutional democracy should function. This included such important matters as the separation of powers, the relations among these powers, and the role of especially the Supreme Court in ensuring that 'the constitution ought to be preferred to the statute, the intention of the people to the intention of their agents', as Hamilton put the matter of the defence of the constitution as the supreme law of the land.

At the Judicial Symposium, referring to Hamilton and Marshall, I went on to say:

> In this instance, the revolutionaries who had liberated the American colonies from British imperial rule with guns, and replaced feudalism with democracy, took on the responsibility to define and defend the legal order that would define the new society, including the constitution they had drafted and approved.
>
> They [Hamilton and Marshall] were both part of the revolutionary masses that overthrew British rule, and of the new establishment that sat as the legislature, the executive and the judiciary of the new United States of America. Accordingly, Alexander Hamilton could confidently entrust the protection of the people and the constitution to Americans such as John Marshall, a military officer in the American Revolution, elected member of the US Congress, and secretary of state, knowing that they were as much part of the new society that was being born as he was.
>
> And thus do revolutions not only succeed, but also manage to defend themselves, as did the American Revolution.

This memoir tells a detailed story of the upbringing of young Dikgang Moseneke, who was born on 20 December 1947, and describes his early education at schools in and around Pretoria, including at Kilnerton Training Institution, until the apartheid regime closed down this famous school.

Given the political situation in South Africa at the time, it was inevitable that Dikgang would be exposed to people who had committed themselves to the struggle to defeat the apartheid regime. In his case, these were members and activists of the Pan-Africanist Congress (PAC), who inducted him into the politics of the PAC.

Like others among his peers, as well as the black population at large, the young Dikgang was shocked and enraged by the news on 21 March 1960 that the apartheid security forces had committed the Sharpeville massacre, killing scores of unarmed Africans who had responded to the call of the PAC to join the anti-pass campaign. This cold-blooded lethal attack by the state, together with the inspiring report that 30 000 people, led by Philip Kgosana, had marched in Cape Town as part of the campaign, could not but further motivate Dikgang and his peers to join the struggle for the liberation of our country.

Thus it was that they welcomed the decision, which they were told had been taken by the PAC leadership, to launch a popular uprising to overthrow the apartheid regime on the third anniversary of the Sharpeville massacre. Like many among his peers in the Pretoria area, Dikgang, who was then fifteen years old, stood ready to carry out such tasks as would be detailed by the PAC leadership. However, during the early hours of 21 March 1963, Dikgang was arrested at his home in Atteridgeville. His memoir describes how he was charged with sabotage, convicted and then imprisoned on Robben Island.

He writes that his prison card read: 'Prison number 491/63; Name: Dikgang Ernest Moseneke; Crime: Sabotage; Sentence: 10 years imprisonment – hard labour; Date of sentence: 2 July 1963; Date of release 1 July 1973; Group classification: D.' Dikgang also makes the following correct observation: 'The fateful arrest on 21 March was, as the saying goes, a life-changer. It set and dyed my world from then to now. It imposed on me an inexorable path.'

That inexorable path meant that, despite the harsh treatment he received during detention, he refused to betray his comrades and his cause. Nor did the ten years of imprisonment on Robben Island, with all its difficult challenges, persuade him to abandon the struggle.

Rather he prepared himself for the future with great diligence and discipline. Thus did he complete his high school education and obtain two undergraduate university degrees. At the same time, ever sensitive to his own social obligations, he used some of his time on Robben Island to teach a few of his fellow prisoners to read and write.

Upon his release, Dikgang was determined to practise as a lawyer. To do so, he fought to overcome the obstacles set up by the apartheid system, including the Law Society, served his articles, and first practised as an attorney, then qualified and practised as an advocate, later becoming senior counsel.

To improve their effectiveness as attorneys, in 1978 George Maluleke, Willie Seriti and Dikgang Moseneke founded the law firm Maluleke, Seriti and Moseneke. They were later joined by Moss Mavundla. Formed in the aftermath of the Soweto uprising of 1976, the law firm had to defend many of those caught up in the repression that followed the unrest. This included the successful defence of Dr Fabian Ribeiro, who had been falsely accused of aiding and abetting an act of terrorism. Later, as confirmed during the Truth and Reconciliation Commission hearings, apartheid assassins murdered Dr Ribeiro and his wife, Florence. Dikgang also represented Zwelakhe Sisulu when the apartheid state tried, but failed, to force him as editor of the *Sunday Post* to disclose his source of information about comrades who had left the country to join Umkhonto weSizwe (MK).

Before he progressed to practising as an advocate, Dikgang joined with other black lawyers to form the Black Lawyers Association (BLA). The BLA was established with the express purpose of helping those black people who wanted to join the legal profession and doing everything possible to help increase the professional competence of these individuals.

I was fortunate to be part of an ANC delegation that met a BLA delegation in Lusaka, Zambia, in November 1987. Among the BLA delegates were Dikgang's law partners. This interaction confirmed to us that here we had a group of genuine patriots who were ready to honour their own obligations to the people, especially as this related to using their legal expertise to promote the cause of freedom.

After he joined the Pretoria and the Johannesburg Bar, five years after practising as an attorney, Dikgang then worked as an advocate from 1983 to 1995. Fortunately for him, during these years many of the black attorneys briefed him to handle their High Court matters. He also appeared in a large number of political trials. He therefore accumulated a great deal of legal practice experience at this relatively high level of our judicial system, including when he became senior counsel.

Because of the respect he had built up even from when he was only fifteen years old, Dikgang was asked to and agreed to join the team that drew up our country's interim constitution of 1993, under which South Africa held its first democratic elections. Later, he also served in the critically important position of deputy chairperson of the Independent Electoral Commission (IEC) that oversaw the historic elections in 1994. It goes without saying that this IEC carried out its challenging work with great distinction, and earned the gratitude of the people of our country and the rest of the world.

Dikgang has entitled this memoir *My Own Liberator*. In it he says:

> ... the sojourn on Robben Island set me on a course of constantly asking: what are the features of a good society?
>
> Out of all this two cardinal lessons emerged. First, you cannot merely dream about your revolutionary ideals. You have to take real and concrete steps to pursue legitimate goals. The second lesson was that I was my own liberator. The phrase is copied from the inimitable revolutionary thinkers Anton Muziwakhe Lembede and Robert Mangaliso Sobukwe ... [who urged] young people like me to pursue ... freedom in our lifetime.

He also writes: 'I have always seen myself as a freedom fighter and not a politician ... I have made the point that politicians crave for power and influence and sometimes absolute control. They deal in expedience only in order to extend their power. A freedom fighter is animated by ideals of social and political justice.'

Writing about the reasoning behind the formation of the BLA, he says: 'It was important to place the full agency of destroying oppression in the hands of the oppressed people themselves. It was not open to oppressed lawyers to

outsource their push for dignity, equality and freedom. They had to step up
to the plate and become their own liberators.'

It is fortunate that our country had such a liberator as Dikgang, who took
concrete steps to pursue the liberation of our country, and in so doing thus
defined himself practically as his own liberator, animated by ideals of social
and political justice whose realisation would also characterise his own liberation. The consequence of this is that our country inherited an outstanding
personality and character in Dikgang Moseneke, whose youth and adulthood
were inextricably intertwined with the process of the historic transformation
of the country, with him being positioned within this process as a liberator.

Thus do we return to the matter of John Marshall, who, like Dikgang in
South Africa in the struggle against apartheid domination, was part of the
revolutionary masses who overthrew British rule in America, and was therefore deemed to be best placed to defend the resultant US constitution. Like
Dikgang, Marshall was a lawyer and earned a high reputation in this regard.

In 1993 Dikgang, then an advocate, decided to apply to be elevated to the
rank of senior counsel. In this context he writes in this memoir:

> Pound for pound, I had prosecuted a vigorous, diverse and complex
> practice at the Bar, despite the apartheid margins. I had litigated against
> or side by side with most of my peers for over a decade, after a five-year
> stint as a partner in an attorneys' law firm. Add three years of apprentice-
> ship as a candidate attorney and I had a solid eighteen years of exposure
> to legal practice. I had fearlessly presented cases of vulnerable individu-
> als and communities, as well as of political activists of the widest variety.
> Whatever limited business law cases emerged from black businesses, I
> was briefed in most. I had appeared in all courts of the land, including
> the Appellate Division. I was ready for a new phase in my career.

Earlier I cited what Alexander Hamilton said concerning what is required
of judges: 'Hence it is that there can be but few men in the society, who will
have sufficient skill in the laws to qualify them for the stations of judges. And

making the proper deductions for the ordinary depravity of human nature, the number must be still smaller of those who unite the requisite integrity with the requisite knowledge.' Mindful of these requirements, as well as Dikgang's experience, we thus approached him to request that he join the judiciary. We were confident that as a liberator he would defend the victory he had helped to bring about. We knew that he would do this inspired by the values of social and political justice. We were convinced that he would bring into the judiciary the requisite integrity along with the requisite knowledge of the constitution and the law.

Although Dikgang has reserved for a later volume his serious reflection over his years as a member of the Constitutional Court, I am certain that he lived up to our expectations in terms of the discharge of his judicial responsibilities. It was precisely because of this that we appointed him deputy chief justice, which also informed my own resolve in 2008 to nominate him for the position of chief justice, to succeed the eminent Pius Langa.

Naturally, given his pedigree as a liberator, Dikgang poses the challenging question towards the end of the memoir: 'was our democratic transition all in vain?' This question is informed by his deep concern that we have not implemented the required thoroughgoing programmes to bring about the fundamental socio-economic transformation our country needs and for which he engaged in struggle. Thus, despite the progress we have achieved in terms of building a constitutional democracy, among other accomplishments, millions of our people continue to be mired in poverty, with our country characterised by extreme levels of racial and gender inequality.

In this context Dikgang sounds an alarm bell to which the nation must respond. He says: 'The spectre of a stagnant economy yielding widening social inequality, stubborn unemployment, and a growing and poorer underclass is not only stressful but also deeply at odds with our notions of a just society. This threatens to wipe out our democratic dividend.'

This memoir is a fascinating account of the formation of the cadres who undertook the responsibility both to help liberate our country and to attend to its reconstruction and development. From beginning to end it communicates a consistent message about the importance of a value system that gave these cadres the integrity without which they could not truly serve the people.

Dikgang has done the nation an enormous favour by recounting how his parents and extended family, as well as his school teachers, gave him the solid base from which he developed into the outstanding servant of the people he has been. And as his example demonstrates, the need for such cadres who are truly committed to serving the people did not diminish with the victory of the democratic revolution. This is why I am happy to commend this memoir to the younger generations, confident that it will inspire them to emulate the example that Dikgang has set.

It says a great deal that for one who experienced days of despair as a fifteen-year-old political prisoner, the author of this memoir could reflect on his life as follows:

> What a privilege it was to serve our people, and I am grateful that I was able to do my part. I have had the space to work, to think and to write to my heart's content. I have had the pleasure of writing on virtually every big political, social and commercial dispute in our land. I have delivered academic papers at law and justice conferences across our country and elsewhere. I have had the joy of going to law schools in this land and in other lands only to find extensive passages of what I have written taught to young lawyers in training. I have also had the privilege of training young people about the contours of our struggle history and their ever-present duty to guard over the genuine freedom of the people. I have been blessed with extraordinary colleagues, who made judicial collegiality appear natural and inbred. We kept together a remarkable apex court in the marvellous tradition started by Arthur Chaskalson, Pius Langa and the inaugural justices of the Constitutional Court.

It is my hope that others who read and understand this memoir will, in time, have reason to write in similar fashion about themselves, repeating after

Dikgang Moseneke: 'So my life journey has not been in vain, I want to think, and I am grateful for the space my nation favoured me to have, love, cherish and use, and for all the blessings my little efforts brought to me, my family and, hopefully, my country.'

Thabo Mbeki
September 2016

Author's note

After I returned from Robben Island, many people asked me a throw-away question about when I was going to write the story of my life. These throwaway questions just made me chuckle. I thought they were hopelessly ill-timed. Then in my mid-20s, I fancied that, absent some awful divine wrath, my life was yet to be lived. Certain as anything, my 60s arrived – although somewhat more quickly than those of us who get here would imagine. I thought then there was a tale to tell and so I got down to writing. This meant that I had to carry the full load of judicial reading, thinking and writing alongside putting together this autobiography. The days, and indeed nights, turned out long and arduous. I wrote many judgments of the court but also, starting about four years ago, the beginning of my story.

To my surprise but delight, the writing of the autobiography turned out to be a big escape from the judicial toil. Judicial writing tends to be formalistic and imposes a structure informed by legal reasoning. A judge must first absorb and rehash the facts. Then he or she must identify the law that regulates the dispute embedded in the facts. She must then apply the law to the facts. She may have to resort to judicial precedent for guidance on a proper understanding of the law or its application on the facts. At that point, she has to weigh in on the one side or the other of the dispute and, lastly, make a just order of court. Court judgments tend to be cast in that predictable mould.

No, I did not have to do this in the memoir, I thought. I will write what

I like, as Bantu Biko famously asserted. I will write mainly from memory. I will resist structure as to chronology or sequence. I will mix, remix, and match the past and the present, and pray that the reader will come along with me, the protagonist, without being terribly confused. I will choose to tell my life story rather than be smug, clever and judge-like.

I have lavishly drawn from my clan and family history and also from our national history and context. I have relished recalling the small details of my upbringing, the village I grew up in and its magnificent people. I have remembered my childhood and eccentric friends, such as Godi Mboweni, Zwenika Skwinya, Amos Sindane and Tsenene, he who did not know his surname and swore worse than a sailor. I tried to find space for their memory because they were never favoured with the opportunity to rise from and escape the squalor of poverty and exclusion. Up to this day, when I visit my hometown, some would say: '*Heh, die man*, Dikgang – *odese!*' (You know, this man, Dikgang, is an awesome fellow!) That home-grown compliment in local parlance would inevitably cost me a handsome tip to friends who could not scale over the high, barbed fence of deprivation.

I have recounted many stories of Robben Island and the stoicism and joy – yes, joy – of our political incarceration. We as political prisoners beat the oppressive system to the draw. They held our bodies, but our minds and psyches floated out there free, nourished and full of hope for a reimagined future.

I tell the stories of one perspective of the popular uprising in the 1970s and 1980s leading to the treacherous transition towards democratic rule. All are inevitably snippets of shots from where I was standing. They do not pretend to be comprehensive or an exact historical record. The account of the transition is more difficult and its merit is highly contested. I do not engage the debate around the revolutionary efficacy of our kind of transition. I chose to tell where I was and what I did or saw then.

Lastly, this book is the first of a two-part memoir project. My fifteen-year judicial stay was busy and compact. Although I have covered the earlier part of my career here in some detail, charting the beginning of my law practice and also highlighting some of the cases and colleagues that impacted strongly on my life, the fullness and complexity of my judicial life as well as my personal journey cannot be usefully compacted into one volume. My judicial life deserves a separate account. It will favour the reader with a peep into the judicial function in general and detail my personal travails in the judicial service. Hopefully, like this book, it will simultaneously enlighten and entertain.

Prologue

I turned 64 years of age during December 2012 while on holiday at an idyllic resort called Sabi River Sun. It is located in one of the many scenic valleys hugging the Sabi River just before it meanders into the Kruger National Park. Thereafter, it flows inexorably through its gaping estuary into the Indian Ocean. The chalets are rustic but quiet and comfortable, and they are edged by manicured flower beds and lawns. A few muddy dams, including one that is the residence of scores of hippos, complement the tall and thorny indigenous trees rather well. The trees cast shade that keeps out the harsh African sun and their tops sway gently in the breeze. In such serene surroundings, the days are balmy and the pace languid.

The birthday ritual was unassuming. It started and ended around the tiny dinner table in our chalet. My nine- and seven-year-old granddaughters, who bear proudly gorgeous isiXhosa names, Lindokuhle and Zintl'ntombi, sang: '*Ukhule 'khule, Tata, ulingane nendlovu.*' They cheered me on to blow out the candles. 'Cut the birthday cake, Tata; cut the cake!' they yelled and clapped excitedly. Love without qualification flowed abundantly. Unconditional affection is the only stuff grandchildren trade with grandparents. Aside from gentle, or wily, manipulation now and then, they love their grandpas or grandmas only because they are what they are – grandparents.

My daughter Duduzile laid on a three-course dinner, a little feast, which my wife Kabonina and I shared with the family and enjoyed by candlelight,

1

the meal well enhanced by the chattering voices of Kuhle and Zizi. The little girls counted in turns from 1 to 64 and when they got to the end they would shout out loudly, 'Oh Tata, you know what?' I obliged and asked:'What?' 'You are *old*, Tata – very old!' they screamed in unison. Occasionally, my daughter's youngest, fifteen-month-old Lwandle, would join the fun with his unintelligible screams.

How well, I thought to myself, life sometimes presents placid little joys far removed in time and space from the pretentious or empty drudgery on the treadmill of life.

At this ripe age I felt I had earned the place – and the time had come, as I had often told Kabo it would – to tell my little tale; to spin my small yarn; to tell the story in the matchless oral tradition of my forebears, who, around the fireside and under a clear African sky twinkling with stars, passed on the travails, triumphs and traditions of our people and communities. They told tales from and of generations, thus welding kith and kin over ancient times.

Our folklore requires that this be done by recalling one's forebears in their order of lineage and precedence. As you do so, you acknowledge with humility the debt you owe to your forebears. You confess that their toil and gains have forged who you are.

Perhaps the most enduring occasion of an *ukuzilanda* was the one I witnessed at Phindangene, the royal residence of Prince Mangosuthu Buthelezi. I had paid him an official visit in 1994 in my capacity as deputy chairperson of the Independent Electoral Commission. This was the body which had been charged with the historic mission of conducting South Africa's first democratic elections ahead of the dawn of our democracy. After brief pleasantries, Prince Buthelezi showed me and my party to the highest point of his traditional but modern homestead. It was perched on high ground overlooking the seemingly endless undulating hills and valleys in the distant blue of the Zulu kingdom. Nearby was a cattle corral. Three of his attendants pulling a black cow on a leather leash came close to where we stood. Before the cow was slaughtered as an offering, the Zulu prince stood full in his stance and looked out across the hills. He recalled, in a spirited rendition, his decorated royal ancestry in the ascending order, starting with himself up to his forebears of the twelfth century.

My paternal forebears appear to have been commoners of Batswana stock. Although they have been close to the traditional rulers of Bakwena ba Pilwe le Mmatau, they have not claimed any royal ancestry. Our verifiable family tree runs into only seven generations of scant detail. Unlike royalty, nobody would have cared to relay or remember their lot with any historical fervour. Unlike the Prince of Phindangene, our family had no ancestral high ground from which we could venerate our extraction. Even so, I have a proud line of ancestry and my own story to tell.

CHAPTER 1

My paternal parentage

My paternal grandfather, Dikgang Samuel Moseneke, was born in 1877. He was the oldest of eight children, four boys and four girls, born of the marriage between Sikwane and Mmakanyane. My great-grandfather, Sikwane, was probably born 30 years before his first child. That would have been about 1847. Sikwane's father, my great-great-grandfather, was a man known as Sephokgele, whose wife is reported to have been Moilwa. He must have been born between 1815 and 1820 and Moilwa would have been maybe ten years younger than him. She gave birth to three sons, Motswadira, Ntwagae and Sikwane.

My grandfather, Samuel, was born in the Waterberg area, his archived obituary informs us. Waterberg is in the vicinity of present-day Modimolle and is a fair distance from our clan's ancestral homes at Pilwe and later at Mmatau in the North West Province. In the cemeteries of these two villages stand many headstones that bear silent testimony to the prolonged habitation of the area by the Moseneke clan.

Not knowing any differently, I imagine that before my grandfather's birth his grandparents or parents may have relocated in order to escape the social upheaval and devastation and plundering brought about by Mfecane wars from about 1815 to 1840. During these wars, Batswana people were pillaged by two large invasion forces. The first were the Kololo, a tribe originating in Lesotho and led by a warrior known as Sebitwane, who reached what is now

Botswana in 1826. The second was the passage of the Zulu general Mzilikazi and his warriors across the territory of Batswana in 1837. Mfecane raids sent many Batswana asunder. And yet neither of the two invasion forces established a state or continued presence within the Batswana territory. Mzilikazi and his warriors settled in the southern parts of Zimbabwe and the Kololo warriors ended up in Botswana.[1]

As we grew up, my father talked of and seemed to have maintained contact with only three from the crop of his eight aunts and uncles. They were his uncles Noah and Obed, and his aunt Baltina. I knew his uncle Obed because he worked at the Iscor steel smelter in Pretoria West. I remember well his frequent visits to our home. In time, he set up his own home on Maunde Street in our township, Atteridgeville, outside Pretoria. Before then, Obed's eldest son, whose names were Rradikgang Ellekanah, stayed with us at our modest urban dwelling in Atteridgeville throughout his studies at a local high school.

Both Uncle Noah and Aunt Baltina passed on before our time. At our dad's insistence, we met the children and grandchildren of Uncle Noah by visiting Melorwe and Mmatau, near Rustenburg. We also met the children of Aunt Baltina. They were my dad's first cousins, with whom he kept up a modicum of connection. Some of our father's cousins visited our home for weeks with no sign that they were about to bid farewell. Our mother, Karabo, just about managed to maintain her composure. She never betrayed any annoyance over the visitors. We, her children in the house, hated these visits. They meant we had less to eat and, by tradition, the younger children always had to give up their beds for visitors. Our mother explained that when our father was young, orphaned and needy, he, too, made extended visits to homes of his uncles and aunts. Just as well – if it weren't for these long visits, we would have lost valuable bonds with our extended family, kinswomen and kinsmen.

Most of my father's nieces and nephews turned out very well. They had the fortune of good education, acquired skills and entered professions. Most were named after our common forebears. We share a common surname and first names drawn from our common ancestry. Unlike their rustic forebears, they need not, and don't, make long urban visits. They command good urban homes of their own. We have come to know each other and we form the core of the present-day progressive Moseneke clan.

Going back to our family tree, this has been reliably constructed by my father's cousin, Rrakgadi Rosina, the daughter of his uncle Noah. She must have been a beneficiary of the family oral history. The two names Sephokgele and Moilwa are perched on its first rung. Thus our father's surviving children, Malatse, Tiego and I, are the fifth generation of Sephokgele, who gave birth to Sikwane, who, in turn, fathered our grandfather Samuel. He sired our father, Samuel Sedise, who, in turn, begot me, Dikgang. I fathered Sedise, whose son is Sedise Jnr. Thus, Sedise Jnr with his sisters Tshiamo and Tiego are of the seventh generation from the patriarch, Sephokgele. These generations have straddled nearly two centuries.

We have come to know more about our paternal grandfather, Samuel, than about his siblings, but, in effect, we know nothing about his childhood and upbringing. Unlike his grandfather, Sephokgele, and father, Sikwane, but like his seven siblings, he was given both an indigenous name, Dikgang, and a biblical name, Samuel. By the time he was born his parents must have been converted to Christianity. That accords well with the recorded pattern of the large-scale conversion of indigenous people of Gauteng (then known as Transvaal) to Christianity from the 1850s onwards. In the Cape the Christianisation of indigenous people had taken root earlier, at the beginning of the 1800s.[2]

It is not far-fetched to imagine that the unremitting plunder of villages and murder caused by Mfecane must have urged on many indigenous people of that time to find succour in religion. New hope was necessary in order to survive a combination of marauding warriors of Mfecane and the incursions of Boer trekkers into the relatively peaceful and prosperous Batswana settlements scattered within what is now the North West Province. Be that as it may, the conversion of Sikwane's family to Christianity was a doorway to our grandfather's primary education. It must be true that Samuel owed much of his early education to the urging of his parents. They must have been good and conscientious parents. And yet his other siblings did not seem to have taken advantage of that nurturing climate within their common home. We do not know or understand why they did not.

Obscure as his childhood may have been, our grandfather seemed to have kept his eyes on acquiring an education and a profession. He went to Kilnerton High School and thereafter to the adjacent teacher training facility known as Normal College, where he qualified as a teacher. The college and the high school were jointly known as the Kilnerton Training Institution. Its alumni fondly called it KTI.

I remain curious about why he made the choices he did. What was the source of his courage to forge ahead with his studies? The labour-intensive and resource-based colonial economy yielded few job options. Young men of his time were constrained to work in mines or on white farms under dire conditions. He escaped what was to be his lot for a more benign route. I wonder how he funded his studies at what was a private missionary school. Did he perhaps reason that teaching and conversion to Christianity were assured paths out of rural ruin and hopelessness?

Kilnerton Training Institution was established in 1886 at the foot of a small, idyllic, rocky hill on the farm Koedoespoort, near Silverton in Tshwane. The hill lent itself to being a natural southern boundary of the farm. At the highest point of the hill stood a chapel with stone walls. The chapel was core to the ethos of the missionary institution. Between the railway line and the western perimeter of the farm ran a clear stream on a stony riverbed. Along the eastern border was the main road between the city centre and Silverton, a white working-class neighbourhood, and further eastwards along the same road lay the African township of Mamelodi.

Kilnerton was founded by the Reverend George Weavind but named after the Reverend John Kilner, secretary of the Wesleyan Methodist Missionary Society of London, who raised the funds for its construction. At that time, all their clergy were drawn from Britain. However, Kilner understood well that the evangelical task at hand could not be accomplished by foreign missionaries only. He supported the recruitment and training of an indigenous clergy. He saw the primary goal of the institution as being to provide high school education for African people and to train educators who would provide a pool for the recruitment and further training of ordained ministers and local preachers.[3]

When Kilnerton was established, indigenous people lived or later settled on nearby land that became known as Kilnerton village. Besides the high school and teacher training college, Kilnerton served the community with two primary schools. This was also where learner teachers did their practical training. Added to that, the church ran a health clinic, special domestic science courses and an agricultural school. In the face of what appeared to be obvious social benefits, many villagers and students converted to Christianity and joined the Methodist Church. The missionary purpose of the church was well served by its captivating spread of social offerings to the villagers and students.

By the turn of the twentieth century, my grandfather had completed his studies at Kilnerton Training Institution. He would have known Reverend George Weavind, the first principal of Kilnerton, who was succeeded by Reverend O Watkins in 1891. But more decidedly, he would have been aware of two very remarkable figures in the life of the newly established training institution and the burgeoning Wesleyan Missionary Church in the Transvaal. They were the Reverend Mangena Mokone and Mr Sefako Mapogo Makgatho.

Mangena Maake Mokone (1851–1936), an ordained minister of the Wesleyan Methodist Church, played a pivotal role in the founding of Kilnerton. Around 1885, he was George Weavind's right-hand man at the construction site of Kilnerton.

His beginnings were humble. He left his home in Sekhukhune, Transvaal, for work on a sugar plantation in Natal. He was converted to Christianity in 1874 and immediately started theological studies in Pietermaritzburg. He worked by day and studied at a Wesleyan night school. At the end of a five-year study period, he was appointed to a preaching circuit of the Methodist

Church in Natal. In 1882 he was ordained and posted to Pretoria to give support to Reverend Weavind and Reverend Watkins at Kilnerton. Having been trained in carpentry, he is said to have built the school's fittings and also the chapel with his own hands. He was rightly one of the founding fathers of the institution. Soon thereafter he was posted to establish Wesleyan missions in the Waterberg and at Makapanstad. My grandfather was posted to minister to these very congregations 25 years later, around 1917.

In early 1892, Reverend Mangena Mokone returned to Pretoria as minister and principal of Kilnerton Training Institution. This was a remarkable feat, given the racial cleavage and profiling within the church of that time. Amongst his students was Sefako Mapogo Makgatho, who was to become a distinguished teacher, writer, leader and freedom fighter, and the second national president of the African National Congress (ANC). However, by October 1892, Reverend Mokone was disillusioned with the Wesleyan Church. He resolved to resign from its ministry and from Kilnerton. He began holding church services in Marabastad, an African urban settlement on the north-western fringes of Pretoria. His letter of resignation listed grievances that displayed a deep distaste for racial discrimination and unequal treatment between European and African clergy. He saw the differentiated employment conditions as a betrayal of the Christian brotherhood, and he was particularly offended that he 'was not esteemed' as principal of Kilnerton and remained without proper authority under the direction of two white superintendents.

He formed a new church – the Ethiopian Church – which was intended to be independent from the mainline Wesleyan missionary hegemony. The Ethiopian Church became the forerunner to a broader religious revolt of African clergies and congregations that craved denominational independence and religious self-government. The name 'Ethiopia', some historians suggest,[4] was inspired by the biblical reference, 'Ethiopia shall soon stretch out her hands unto God' (Psalm 68:31). Others suggest that the name harked back to the fact that Ethiopia was the only independent African state that had survived the European scramble for Africa which started in

1885, and which later successfully repelled the Italian invasion.[5] Be that as it may, in 1885 Reverend Mokone came to know about and understand the workings and ethos of the African Methodist Episcopal (AME) Church of the USA. In 1896 his followers resolved to unite with the AME Church and so, in 1898, the Ethiopian Church became the 14th episcopal district of the AME Church of the USA.

Sefako Mapogo Makgatho (1861–1951) was born sixteen years before my grandfather and outlived him by a good 21 years. His remarkably full life straddled the nineteenth and twentieth centuries in nearly equal halves. He lived through remarkably formative years in our history and was not an idle bystander. He was blessed with leadership qualities, good education and high levels of industry complemented by ample determination. For good measure, he had a trenchant hatred of injustice.

Makgatho, the son of Kgoši Kgorutlhe Makgatho, was born at Ga-Mphahlele in Limpopo. He completed his primary education in Pretoria. In 1880, Makgatho enrolled at Kilnerton for a teacher training course. He was then under the tutelage of Reverend Mangena Mokone, who was the nominal head of Kilnerton. In 1882, Makgatho left South Africa to study education and theology in Middlesex, England. When he returned home in 1886, he joined the staff of Kilnerton as a teacher.

From the relatively youthful age of 25, Makgatho kept his teaching job at Kilnerton for no less than 20 eventful years, until 1906. He must have been an extraordinary inspiration to his young charges. Makgatho would have noticed the changes wrought by the discovery of gold in Johannesburg and would have been angered by the grubby gold rush, as it spawned migrant workers, squalid urbanisation and social decay. He lived through the war waged between the British colonialists and the two Afrikaner republics of the Transvaal and Orange Free State from 1899 to 1902. He must have hoped that the victorious British colonial office would put up an inclusive plan of reconstruction. It was not to be so. They chose to appease the defeated Boer republics. This they did by creating one dominion state out of the four prov-inces under the British Empire. They also agreed to exclude the indigenous

African people from political franchise and to the phasing out of the qualified franchise enjoyed by Africans, Indians and Coloured people in the Cape
and Natal.

These political developments left Makgatho full of fury. He left Kilnerton
in 1906 and went off to form a political resistance movement known as the
African Political Union (APU). He was elected its first president until 1908.
Makgatho went further. In 1907, together with other teachers, he established
the Transvaal African Teachers Association, which became the first union
of teachers in South Africa. In 1908, he became president of another political organisation, the Transvaal Native Organisation (TNO). Makgatho, like
many African people of his time, was outraged by the British parliament
when, in 1909, it enacted the South Africa Act that established the Union
of South Africa. As he feared, the Act expressly provided that no African
person would be represented in parliament save by a white person, and
that those who had acquired the franchise in the Cape and Natal provinces
might remain on the common voters roll until they were disenfranchised
by a statute passed with a two-thirds majority of the two houses of parliament sitting together.[6] It did not take much for the TNO, together with APU,
to merge with South African Native National Congress in Bloemfontein in
1912. Makgatho's highly decorated public life did not stop there, however. He
soldiered on until he succumbed in 1951 at the ripe age of 90 years.

We have had a bird's-eye view of the world in which the youthful Samuel
lived. I often wonder what choices my grandfather made in the face of rising
African resistance to missionary hegemony. What did he think about the
colonial land dispossession and of the political and social exclusion of the
indigenous people? Did he come to know of the charges of racial discrimination made by Reverend Mangena Mokone against the Methodist Church,
and against his alma mater, Kilnerton, before Reverend Mokone left both?
Did he take a view on the later breakaway led by the Reverend Mangena
Mokone? My grandfather must have heard about the Ethiopian Church that
had been set up in Marabastad and later about the new AME Church. Did he
approve of Reverend Mokone's new push for self-determination in matters

of the church?

Did my grandfather give a thought to the causes so vigorously waged by his teacher, Sefako Makgatho, in Kilnerton? Did he join the teachers' union formed by Makgatho? Did he accept the South Africa Act of 1909, passed by the British parliament to establish the Union of South Africa, which, in effect, could properly disenfranchise the indigenous majority? Might he have been at Bloemfontein in 1912 when the Native National Congress was inaugurated? Did the wholesale dispossession of land of the African majority under the legal guise of the Natives Land Act of 1913 raise his ire to boiling point? Once he had been ordained in the church, did his pastoral duties leave him sleepless over the worsening working and living conditions of his flock – the migrant miners and farm workers?

For now, I do not know the answers to these questions. Sefako Makgatho and Mangena Mokone wrote about their lives. They told us what they liked and disliked about their lot. They put their fate and fury to paper. Except for the obituary from missionary archives, the Reverend Samuel Dikgang Moseneke was silent – as quiet as his portrait in which he is wearing a dog collar. We do not know what his answers would have been. Perhaps we may become wiser as this manuscript takes a life of its own.

The one thing we know is that he decided to start a family. After he qualified as a teacher, he married my grandmother, Ephenia Sampisi Masote, who was born around 1887. She was born into the well-regarded Masote and Matseke families that were part of the Bahwaduba people who settled in the village of Kgwadibeng in the vicinity of Waterberg and Bela-Bela. She, too, was a qualified teacher. My grandparents were blessed with no less than eight children, who were born mainly during the first quarter of the 1900s.

My grandfather died young, even for his time, at the age of 53 years. He had a stroke which in time took its toll. My father had only vague memories of him as a tall, very dark and large man with a white dog collar. He was required to accept calls to serve church societies in various townships and villages. His ministerial posting before his death was at the villages around his place of birth, Waterberg and Makapanstad.

The British Methodist Church kept meticulous minutes of their annual conferences. Its minutes of 1930 recite tens of obituaries of ordained ministers throughout the British Empire and beyond who had succumbed in that year. Most of the departed were born in the last quarter of the 1800s. Their recorded places of birth reveal the breadth of the imperial project of the missionary church. The departed ministers were born in places as varied as the island of Ruatan; Delhi in India; Naples in Italy; Freetown in Sierra Leone; and Ch'in Ch'ing Tan in China. Amidst the tributes, under item 14 on page 124 of the minute book, appears the following obituary:

> Samuel Moseneke was born about the year 1877 in the Waterberg, Transvaal. He was trained as a schoolmaster in our Kilnerton Institution, Pretoria and was received into the Ministry in 1917. He maintained a keen interest in the education of his people but gave the first place in his life to the Gospel he preached and his pastoral work. His brief Ministry was marked by his fervent concern for the redemption of his people, strengthened by his loyalty to his Church and inspired by his love for his Lord. Stricken with disease without hope of recovery, he bore his trial with courage and patience and passed on to higher service in the 13th year of his Ministry, on January 8, 1930.

The Reverend Samuel Dikgang Moseneke passed on when my father was only eight years old and his three younger sisters were small girls. His four youngest children, starting with our father, were small and vulnerable when he died. My grandmother, Sampisi, died soon afterwards. Before their demise our grandparents took two life-altering steps. They gave education to their children and acquired a home on a registered freehold title for their family. They must have saved up for this from their combined meagre earnings as two school teachers. For one thing, the demise of their parents did not leave the children homeless. They inherited a common home in which they lived.

The home was No. 259 Fortune Street, Lady Selborne, a township just west of Pretoria. It provided a haven when homelessness and squalor was the lot of people who lived in new urban settlements. From this home, my father and his siblings could venture into the community for education and upbringing. It helped the family find a place within that iconic community.

For my part, our grandparents deserve a special place in our family history. They were transitional figures. They moved our family from the rural ruin and penury of their time to urban hope. Both set a worthy guide on how to adapt to what was achievable within a rapidly changing social and political environment. They were stubborn forerunners of change and hope – personal and social constraints were never insuperable. In their somewhat short lives, they made beneficial choices. They lit up the path without which our family values of cohesion, faith, hard work and education would have become elusive.

CHAPTER 2

My father and his siblings

Ephenia and Samuel's children grew up in Lady Selborne. They lived their early years in a poor urban setting. They shared their needy circumstances with many at home and afield. This was so not only because of racial and social exclusion on the domestic front, but also because of the First World War of 1914 to 1918, which was followed by the Great Depression, which started in 1929, and the Second World War of 1939 to 1945.

By the time the First World War broke out, their children were too young to be recruited into the South African Native Labour Corps (SANLC). This was made up of African troops who were said to have volunteered to serve on the frontline of the war. The troops were sought to provide manual labour needed by the Allied forces in the war effort. Had any of my father's male siblings been recruited into the SANLC, they might have found themselves passengers on the SS *Mendi* troop carrier.

On 21 February 1917, off the Isle of Wight in the English Channel, the SS *Mendi* was struck, in thick fog, by a merchant ship, the SS *Darro*. The *Mendi* sank. Of the 805 SANLC troops on board, over 600 black troops alongside nine of their white countrymen and all 33 crewmen perished. For reasons that are too shameful to repeat now, the crew of the *Darro* made no attempt to rescue survivors.

The African troops on the SS *Mendi* are reputed to have displayed utmost dignity and bravery in the face of impending death by drowning. This was particularly so because they were to meet their death in a war about which they knew little and from which they were not likely to benefit in any way. As the *Mendi* was sinking and the prospect of survival was dwindling, their chaplain, the Reverend Isaac Dyoba, emerged as a remarkable leader in the face of adversity. He called the men together and firmed them up to meet their fate gallantly. His admonishment bears repeating here:

> Be quiet and calm my countrymen, for what is taking place is exactly what you came to do. You are going to die, but that is what you came to do. Brothers, we are drilling the death drill. I, a Xhosa, say you are my brothers. Swazis, Pondos, Basothos and all others, let us die like warriors. We are the sons of Africa. Raise your war cries, brothers, for though they made us leave our assegais in the kraals, our voices are left with our bodies …

The legend goes that the troops still on board took off their boots and stamped 'the death dance on the slanting deck of a sinking ship, far from Africa but united together as brothers and comrades in arms'.[7]

When I was little, the troopship *Mendi* came to mean something to me, too. On a public space known as Mareka Square in Atteridgeville, my home township, stood a tall memorial of coarse, unpolished granite. The memorial had been erected in the memory of the sinking of the *Mendi*. We, as children, never heard who erected the statue or why it stood in our township. I remember us children gathered at the square to watch the yearly army parade by African war veterans. They wore warm, woollen, dark-brown army uniforms that seemed odd in the scorching heat of Africa. They displayed rusted and twisted medals on their chests. The medals bore the likeness of an elephant. The uniforms varied in shades of brown as some had faded over the years. The veterans were old. Their faces had grown gaunt and some were toothless. They marched awkwardly, with narrow limping strides. As they filed past the memorial to the troops on the doomed *Mendi*, they strained their stiffened necks towards it. They seemed to draw strength and pride from the drilling ceremony. The veterans must have known the ache of war much more than we ever could. Even then, young as I was, I quietly wondered why those men had had to go to war. Whose war was it anyway, and what had it done for the troops, and for us in Atteridgeville?

As though this was not tragedy enough, a little over 20 years later the Second World War broke out against the forces of Hitler. Despite much pro-test by a section of the white community, which was sympathetic towards Nazi Germany, General Smuts, who was then the prime minister, joined the war effort in North Africa in support of the British Empire. None of my father's male siblings was drafted. They were spared this ordeal largely because being drafted to war meant being trained and armed as part of the military. The insecure white minority regime could not countenance the voteless and restless African majority bearing weapons of war, let alone being commissioned officers over white soldiers.

As the war raged, the children of Samuel and Sampisi remained home and went to school. All barring two qualified as school teachers or nurses. These were the only accessible professions open to African people in a social order marked by racial and gender exclusion.

Their first son, my uncle Sydney, was born in 1914. He qualified as a teacher and he died, seemingly childless, well before my time. I do not know the cir-cumstances of his demise. The second-born daughter, my aunt Georgina, born in 1916, was also a qualified teacher, and she was married off to the Ngcobo family of KwaZulu, where she was apparently locked into patriar-chal and rural subsistence. I never met her. She died while I was languishing in prison on Robben Island.

The third child was Aunt Gloria, born in 1918. She was a thickset and stoutly self-reliant lady who was known not to suffer fools. She married a man known as Mokgara and had six children. The story is told that dur-ing the course of the marriage, Mokgara fell on hard times. He lost his job. He would wake up early in the morning, take along a lunch-box caringly prepared for him by Aunt Gloria and go to 'market' – to look for a job. He followed this ritual every weekday, but months went by and he could not find a job. One good evening he returned home as usual. However, my aunt had resolved to put him on terms. She told him that his difficulty was that he was choosy and fastidious. He must accept any job offered out there, she warned him, adding sternly: 'If on the third day from now you have not landed a job, don't bother to come back home.' The legend goes that the following day, Mokgara took his lunch-box and never returned home – to this day.

Gloria's younger brother, Uncle Rogers, born in 1920, was a teacher who died an alcoholic before he married, and he had no known children of his own. He bears the dubious reputation of smashing to smithereens the glass-framed photo of his father that hung against the wall in the family's lounge. Our mother tells the story that when she lived with our father and me as a small child in the family residence at Lady Selborne, Uncle Rogers often came back home less than sober, even on school days. One evening he came home quite soaked in alcohol. He slumped into the lounge sofa and looked up at his father's photo on the wall. He could not bear the constant piercing eyes of the man in the collar. He rose in rage, asking why his father was staring at him. A big smash was heard. The rest of the family rushed into the lounge to find the shattered frame and glass of their father's photo lying on the floor.

My mother rather liked Uncle Rogers. They seemed to have bonded when she was a young bride, *makoti*, in Lady Selborne. Many years later, I vaguely remember him lying sick in our family home in Atteridgeville, in a bedroom that was meant for use by me and my brothers. By custom, children had to surrender their bedroom to a visiting elder. This meant that we had to sleep on a mattress placed on the floor in the lounge. Our mother nursed him, with remarkable patience and dedication, until his demise. She often warned that when you nurse a dying patient, '*Mooki o thlokofala pele ga mookiwa*' (You are likely to die before the patient does).

The fifth in line was our father, Sedise Samuel. He was born in 1922 and was followed by three sisters: Rrakgadi Ngeli (Florence); Rrakgadi Masikwane (Susan); and the last-born, Rrakgadi Moipone (Angelina).

Our father, too, grew up in Lady Selborne. This township, which was established in 1905, was unusual. Africans could hold title to land here. But for a few exceptions, Africans in urban areas in South Africa were prevented by law from owning land. Lady Selborne owed its name to the wife of Lord Selborne, who was the British governor of the Transvaal and Orange River colonies until 1910. The township was 292.78 hectares in extent and was situated against the southern slope of Dithaba tsa Mogale (later misnamed Magaliesberg) some ten kilometres north-west of the city centre of Pretoria. Its elevated setting offered a scenic view of the city centre towards the east. A rivulet called Swart Spruit ran in between tall green reeds from west to east along the southern border of the settlement.

Originally, it was a portion of a farm called Zandfontein, which was purchased by a syndicate through their agents, T Le Fleur and CM de Vries. On 26 September 1906 the farm was transferred to De Vries with 440 plots available for purchase to the public. Mainly African people, but also whites, Coloured, Indian and Chinese people, purchased plots there and built homes. Two of the main streets bore the names of Le Fleur and De Vries.

From the outset, Lady Selborne was a mixed-race neighbourhood. Its unique establishment placed it outside the reach of laws that regulated 'native townships'. The area was more akin to a suburb or a peri-urban area of Pretoria. Its landowners paid rates and formed ratepayers' associations. The residents were politically conscious and stood up to the ever-growing state control over their daily lives. After 1910, spatial apartheid started rearing its horrific head in earnest as other racial discrimination laws tightened their grip on the occupation and use of land by African people. The community of Lady Selborne kicked back to retain their rights as landowners, a status which, thanks to the 1913 and 1936 Land Acts, was becoming increasingly hard to come by for African people in their land of birth. The landowners often made the point that they were ratepayers like any others in the city of Pretoria and were as entitled to good governance and municipal services as anyone else in the city.

The community was given to political and social activism. It had an organised political culture that reigned for decades. My grandfather's teacher at

Kilnerton, Sefako Mapogo Makgatho, lived in Lady Selborne. After he ended his teaching career, he started and owned a newspaper and doubled as an estate agent. From 1917 to 1924, Makgatho served as the president of the ANC and led at least two local civil disobedience campaigns. Throughout the 1930s and 1940s, Lady Selborne was the stronghold of the ANC in Pretoria. This explains why, in the 1950s, it had one of the strongest branches of the ANC, and later, in the early 1960s, a prospering branch of the Pan-Africanist Congress (PAC).

In time, landowners in Lady Selborne did well financially. Many homeless people poured into the neighbourhood. Landowners extended their homes and took on tenants, and they were keen to protect the additional income they made from rentals. Financial institutions did just as well, as they expanded their mortgage business. It did not take long before Lady Selborne was densely populated. It offered a rare haven of safety away from laws that regulated other black townships. By 1942 there were about 22 000 residents within a finite residential area with poor infrastructure and low levels of sanitation.

Even so, its residents allowed nothing to keep them down. They worked at and developed a deep sense of community. Remarkable historical accounts shed light on the vibrant community life of Lady Selborne.[8] The community boasted ten primary schools and two high schools where, in the 1950s, 10 000 children attended. Most of the schools and clinics were constructed and run by the residents themselves or by churches. The community raised scholarships to send promising students to further their education at the renowned University of Fort Hare. There was no government to look to for these basic needs and the people knew it.

In that setting of solidarity, enterprising headmasters and good schools flourished. One primary school with a reputation for excellence was the Methodist primary school. Its headmaster, Mr Khuzwayo, took great pride in producing, one year end after another, multiple distinction passes in Standard 6. At that time an excellent pass in Standard 6 signalled more than the end of primary school; it entitled one to proceed to a high school or technical college to learn a trade or technical skill.

Our father attended the Methodist primary school under headmaster Khuzwayo. Soon he was one of the little stars of the school. Around 1936, he passed the Standard 6 examinations with a distinction, something that eased his admission to high school. In 1937, just before the outbreak of the Second World War, he earned himself a bursary to Kilnerton. It could have been to Lady Selborne High School, which, in its own right, enjoyed a reputation as a centre of excellence in secondary education. However, the scholarship was created by the church for children of Wesleyan ministers and was tenable at Kilnerton. Our father promptly qualified himself as a teacher, and in his early 20s he took up his first posting. This was in Marabastad, a growing residential township located on the western fringe of Pretoria. His two youngest sisters, Masikwane and Moipone, later matriculated at the same institution. They, too, were beneficiaries of the church bursary scheme.

In the meantime, dark clouds were gathering over Lady Selborne. A grid of pernicious laws – the 1923 and 1945 Urban Areas Acts and the 1936 Land Act – wiped away rights of African people to acquire or occupy urban land or to move freely in urban areas. The right to reside in an urban area alone or with a family was regulated by a permit and pass system, which was enforced with criminal sanction. These laws compelled every African person to carry, and produce on demand by a police officer, an identity document known as a pass. The pass had to carry an official entry that told whether its bearer was entitled to be in a particular urban area. A black person earned the entry if he or she had been born in the area or had lived in it for an unbroken period of fifteen years. A breach of the pass system allowed a police officer to arrest the offender summarily. As rural poverty deepened, the influx of people into urban areas rose. Hundreds of thousands of African people were stopped and arrested in urban streets and cast in jail. After their rise to power in 1948, the National Party regime added the Group Areas Act to consolidate urban spatial apartheid. This law required that all urban settlements had to be racially segregated; and if they were not, this gave the government the power to forcibly move or relocate settled communities.

Amidst protest and resistance, the minority regime decided to tear Lady

Selborne down. It decided to remove its residents by force. The regime hated the community's ethos of political activism. Its non-racial character made a lie of the claim that segregated neighbourhoods were good. Lady Selborne was at odds with the scheme of residential segregation. Moreover, it was located on a 'white spot' and prevented the westerly growth of the white suburbs of Pretoria. At times, the regime justified the forced removal of Lady Selborne residents by expressing a paternalistic concern about the over-crowding, poor infrastructure and sanitation.

In time, the people succumbed and the regime won. It forcibly expropriated the land from unwilling landowners. As black families were forced out, their residential stands were passed on at nominal prices to white working-class families. The regime smashed that vibrant community at the altar of spatial segregation. Their cherished homes, schools, clinics, churches and history were razed to the ground. The state frogmarched the people of Lady Selborne onto government trucks and had them and their belongings scattered in different, distant and dusty townships and ethnic homelands. The erstwhile landowners of Lady Selborne again lost their dignity. They became landless and impoverished people. They were reduced to tenants of the government under the command of laws controlling occupation in native townships.

One commentator made this insightful observation about Lady Selborne:

> Lady Selborne stands in the same league as other iconic multiracial townships like Sophiatown in Johannesburg, District Six in Cape Town and Cato Manor in Durban ... It was called the township of 'Clevers' (township city slickers) – it was home for trail-blazers like Dr William Frederick Nkomo, Potlako Leballo, Stephen Sondag Tefu and Philip Kgosana (politicians), Can Themba and Arthur Maimane (journalists), Bob Leshoai and SP Kwakwa (educationists), Ernest 'Shololo' Mothle, Joe 'Lopez' Ngoetjana and Betty Mthombeni (musicians), and birthplace of international luminaries like Vusi 'The Balladeer' Mahlasela and poet/ musician/artist Lefifif Tladi.[9]

The list of trailblazers is to be welcomed but it could not possibly be exhaustive. Two other iconic figures come to mind. They were headmasters of the finest and most inspirational two schools of the 1960s: Professor Bob Leshoai, the principal of Lady Selborne High School, and Mr Cuthbert Motsepe, originally from Lady Selborne, the principal of Mamelodi High School. Both ran excellent schools despite the paltry resources under Bantu Education. They found ways to enthuse parents over the education of their children. Learners, too, had responsibilities. They had to make sure their parents came to parents' meetings. Learner academic performance ranked higher than anything else.

Teachers of this pedigree exposed learners to materials well beyond the narrow strictures of official course outlines. Even what appeared to be innocent set-works often opened a vista beyond the liking of the regime's education minders. Teachers of this calibre took care and effort to ensure a sense of self-worth and dignity in their young charges. They found an antidote against the rejection and hatred born of race, class and gender. By the time learners left these inimitable schools, they understood that they were oppressed, but, more importantly, that they were their own liberators. The security branch of the regime feared and, in the early 1960s, hounded headmaster Leshoai and headmaster Motsepe into exile.

I remember Uncle Bob Leshoai with childhood fondness. He and our father kept an enduring friendship. They must have met in their youth while both were students at Mr Khuzwayo's primary school in Lady Selborne. Uncle Bob's wife and my mother would be giggling and chattering for ever during their visits to our home. By then Uncle Bob was the much respected headmaster of Lady Selborne High School. He was a short, stocky man with prematurely receding hair. Over weekends he dressed down. His favourite khaki suit with short sleeves betrayed his broad chest and well-set hairy arms. He spoke loudly and emphatically. Even though I was only ten or so, I remember him often punctuating his conversation with my dad with phrases like: 'Sam, you know, these racists are mad, these Boers are mad in their head.'

Saturday morning was shopping time and all significant shopping happened in the city. Droves of township residents made their way to the city and left much of their earnings there. By law all city traders were white, and yet shoppers of all hues or stations were welcome. No law, amongst the many pernicious ones, precluded black people from buying in white shops. The irony did not escape my father. He often complained to us, his little sons, that township dwellers were fools to leave their hard-earned money with racist traders.

Even so, one Saturday morning he and Uncle Bob decided to find take-away lunch at Spartan's Fish and Chips shop on Prinsloo Street in the city. My dad invited me to come for the ride. The Greek owners of Spartan's did very well and their shop was reputed to sell the best fish and chips in town. The queues were always long. And yet what they made in money, they lacked in manners. When serving their almost exclusively township following, the only African language words they knew and used were swear words. But their version of fish and chips was well liked by their patrons. Its popularity seemingly trumped the bad manners of its retailers.

After standing in the queue for a long time, Uncle Bob and my dad's turn to buy finally came. My dad had on a coat and tie. I don't know why. Maybe he had dressed up to preserve his schoolmaster look even over weekends. More likely, he had hoped to reduce the chances of attracting racial slurs in town. Even the racist types did not lightly mess with a black person wearing a coat and tie. In addition, a pair of reading glasses helped. Or maybe our dad was downright snobbish. Uncle Bob, though, was in his khaki casuals as usual. When their turn came, my father and Uncle Bob placed their order and paid. Now they were waiting. The man behind the counter returned with the wrapped fish-and-chips parcels. He looked at Uncle Bob and shouted, 'Here is your order, boy!'

With that, all hell broke loose. In full voice, Uncle Bob shouted, 'Look in between your legs, you racist! There you will see your boy!' And he threw every one of the wrapped food parcels straight into the face of the owner of the fish-and-chips shop. The owner swore back. Uncle Bob invited him out from behind the counter. My dad joined the fracas, with both men throwing anything in sight at the owner. The man ducked and swore some more but never left his side of the counter. The queue of patrons broke up as they cheered my dad and Uncle Bob on. The owner threatened to call the police and both of them urged him to call the cops as quickly as he could. As the brawl continued, patrons began to walk out. I was no taller than my dad's hip and yet I found myself cheering my two heroes on, too. I remember thinking to myself, Wow! What a damn good fight for a bit of respect.

We returned home without our fish-and-chips lunch and my mother and Uncle Bob's wife were not amused. Ma had to hurry around preparing lunch amidst our giggles and many graphic recountings of the battle.

So as we single out 'trailblazers', we will do well to spare a thought for the unsung residents of Lady Selborne and elsewhere who also put up a good fight against the injustice of forced removals and apartheid. I think of the statue of the Unknown Soldier, which stands in many capitals whose people have fallen to the ravages of war. Often this memorial to the foot soldiers is a lame afterthought long after the generals and politicians have decorated themselves. There were many heroes of the battle of Lady Selborne. The desolate residents who would not move their bodies or belongings until police and soldiers forcibly carried them away in government trucks come to mind.

Our family, too, has a place of pride in the legacy of Lady Selborne. We rightly claim it as our own. Our grandfather was a landowner there, having acquired in the 1920s the house on Fortune Street over which he held registered title. As the church posted him from one circuit to another to do pastoral duty, his children at least had the solace of a stable residence and community life.

It bears repetition that my father was born and raised in Lady Selborne. After he and our mother married in 1947, they lived in the same home. My mother assures me that I was delivered at Little Flower Catholic maternity home in Lady Selborne and lived my first three years with them there. My aunts and their children lived at Ko-Fortune, as the home was fondly known. In time, they also became direct casualties of state coercion. In the 1960s, their home was expropriated and they were forcibly removed to the outlying townships of Mamelodi and Ga-Rankuwa. Before then, the home had served as a crowded but homely nest out of which each sibling flew to set up on his or her own.

CHAPTER 3

On my mother's side

My mother, Karabo Mabel Makhaza, was the eldest daughter of Motho Salome Seatla and Makubande Dickson Makhaza. Her maternal grand-father was known as July Seatla and her grandmother was Kobodimagetleng Seatla. My mother lived with her parents at her grandparents' home at 121 Seventh Avenue in Marabastad. Even in those dire and unsympathetic con-ditions, her grandparents built a sizeable brick house on Seventh.

Her father and mother were working-class people with no or scant formal education. Both were born at the end of the nineteenth century, around 1897 and 1895 respectively. They were given long lives. Grandma Motho lived to 97 years of age and her husband lived to 90 years. Their children and grand-children and great-grandchildren all fondly called them Mma and Papa. Their marriage lasted for a continuous 67 years and was brought to a halt only by Papa's death in 1995.

Papa was a tall and strongly built man with broad shoulders. He spoke a limping isiZulu that was less than mainstream. This perhaps explained why he spoke only when he had to and even that was rare. Papa had not been to a formal school. I remember him telling me that as a small boy he fled his home for Pretoria because of a life-threatening family upheaval in or near Zululand. When he arrived in Pretoria, his initial job was as a night watch-man in a bank. He moved on to work at a hotel. He met my grandmother at Marabastad and they married shortly before my mother was born in 1925.

Mma was born in a rural settlement near Kimberley. She came to live in Marabastad when her parents migrated to Pretoria in search of greener pastures. There she put in years of schooling up to Standard 6. She could read and she managed basic English well. She often charge, somewhat boastfully, that she was a product of the Royal Reader – an early English grammar primer.

She spoke her mother tongue, Serolong, a version of the Setswana language, with poise and pride. She spoke to Papa, and indeed to the whole world, only in Serolong, as if no other language had ever been spoken. Mischievously, but proudly too, she would often hum a little folk song: 'Dumang, dumang, Barolong. Ga lo dume ga lonkgatlhe' (Roar, roar, Barolong people. I become unhappy when you do not roar). Papa would, in turn, reply or initiate conversation only in isiZulu. The language banter seemed to occur with no outward animosity or jingoism. They understood each other's languages perfectly well, but each afforded the other the dignity of using their native tongue. Also, Mma quietly resisted forsaking her mother tongue for her husband's, something that accorded with Mma's remarkable strength of character. And yet she had the gift to soak up emotional hurt and move on. She would say, 'Dikgang, ithute go jara mathata a gago, ngwana waga ngwanake' (Dikgang, learn to bear your burden, grandson). She avoided confrontation and conflict whenever it was possible and would often say, 'A go rene kagiso le lerato ka nako tshohle' (Let peace and love always reign).

Upon marrying Mma, Papa agreed to live with Mma at her parents' home on Seventh Avenue. While this was unusual, it was hardly surprising; nor was it a big ask. Only a few African people were entitled to or had homes in new urban settlements. In any event, Papa did not have the means to set up his own home. At the time he was a young, illiterate worker with a rustic background. In time, he rose from the ranks of a general worker to become a chef at the Union Hotel in Pretoria. Despite his illiteracy, he had garnered enough functional English to hold down his job as a chef, which he did for several decades. His lack of formal schooling gave way to his native intelligence. Perhaps he mastered recipes by careful observation of how experienced chefs went about their business, but the skills he learned and his mastery of the task at hand certainly assured him a small but steady income. It gave him dignity and earned him respect. His world was set to change forever.

Marabastad was an over-populated and culturally diverse urban settlement located west of Pretoria on the banks of the Apies River. Its residents were an amalgam of Africans, Asians and Coloured people. It owed its name to the Maraba village which had been established by the followers of Kgosi Maraba in the 1880s. After the Anglo-Boer War, the government surveyed additional land to the south of the village and established residential stands. This location came to be known as New Marabastad. However, the Transvaal Boer Republic, the government of the day, had not permitted freehold ownership. Residents were not allowed to own stands, but had to rent them from the government for four pounds a year. They were permitted to construct their own homes and to plant crops on empty plots. By 1901, there were nearly 400 occupied stands in New Marabastad and there was no real segregation amongst racial groups other than people classified white.

Marabastad had continued to pose an over-crowding challenge to an ever-increasing number of working people and residents. As numbers swelled, the authorities had little choice but to grant permission for residents to erect brick houses. This gave the new settlement a footing of permanence. Long-term structures like schools, clinics and churches emerged. However, the government did not complement the structures with bulk services. There was no dependable electricity supply. The streets were unkempt and unpaved. Water and sanitary facilities were in short supply as more shacks mushroomed. That was hardly surprising. The city council of Pretoria was resolute not to permit an orderly urbanisation of African people within or near the city. Even so, the inhabitants of Marabastad, culturally diverse as they were, had done much to establish a vibrant community. They built brick homes along its avenues. Schools were built and flourished. Church buildings multiplied. It was there that Sefako Mapogo Makgatho founded the Ethiopian Church, the forerunner of the native AME Church, and ordained its first three ministers, one of whom was the Reverend DZ Tantsi. Commerce thrived and business premises were erected as (mainly Asian) business people made hay. They owned most of the commercial properties and controlled the retail and other business life of Marabastad. Professor Es'kia ('Zeke') Mphahlele memorialised the crippling living conditions as well as the pulsating vibrancy of Marabastad of the 1930s to 1950s in his classic *Down Second Avenue*.[10]

However, as was the case with residents of other racially diverse areas in South Africa, like Cato Manor in Durban, District Six in Cape Town and Fietas and Sophiatown in Johannesburg, the people of Marabastad were relocated to single-race townships further away from the city centre.

The removals, as we know, were inspired by the grand scheme of spatial segregation under apartheid, but two things distinguished the Marabastad forced removals. First, unlike Lady Selborne or District Six or Sophiatown, Marabastad was not razed to the ground. Many of its original buildings were spared and became primarily a business district for Asian shopkeepers. The second was that residents moved to better living conditions. The establishment of Atteridgeville in 1939 was meant to be a step up. The Marabastad community was moved, and compensation was offered to previous owners of property in the form of new houses that they could rent but not own. By 1949 three-quarters of the population of Marabastad had moved to Atteridgeville, and by 1950 the transition was complete. Coloured residents remained longer; they were moved to Eersterust as late as 1963. During 1968 Asian residents were moved, to Laudium.

Marabastad is still there but in a form different from its evocative past. Up to this day, I often drive through Boom Street, past the old Empire, Orient and Royal cinema houses, wondering where the bustling main street of Marabastad, Second Avenue, was located. My mother grew up close by, on Seventh Avenue, and she and my dad were family friends with Uncle Es'kia. They were very much part of his world of anguish and hope all wrapped up tightly together.

In the late 1940s, Papa and Mma's family moved from Marabastad to

Atteridgeville into a five-roomed municipality home. With Papa's job at the hotel, even though his income would have been modest, he was able to afford the monthly rental due to the city council of Pretoria. His new home, No. 1 Mngadi Street, like other homes of the time in Atteridgeville, had running water, water-borne sewage, an indoor bathroom and electricity. The kitchen of every home was fitted with a Welcome Dover coal stove and chimney. At the front of the house there was a small flower garden and, on the two sides, Papa planted two peach and two apricot trees. The yard was marked off with a steel fence and a steel gate leading into the street. The streets were tarred, had flood-water drainage and were lit at night. After the urban squalor of Marabastad, my grandparents' circumstances had certainly changed for the better.

Mma stayed home and took charge of domestic chores and a good few grandchildren. I was one of the children who stayed for a while with my grandparents. Papa made sure that his was a warm and welcoming home with more than enough to eat. The leftover food he brought from the hotel made for ample nourishment. As first grandson, I remember well waiting for him at the gate when he returned from work. I would help carry his work briefcase into the house and be the first to be given a pie or a piece of fried fish or perhaps a slice of pecan nut pie. It did not take long before neighbourhood children caught on that it helped to be near me when my grandfather returned home from work.

On Sunday mornings, Papa was up early to prepare a full Sunday lunch. Men of the time did not cook or prepare food in their homes. It was a social taboo. Real men, it was thought, were entitled to have their wives or female partners cook and serve them. Papa did not care two hoots for the taboo. He put on his white chef top and grey-striped floppy pants and cooked for his family. He gladly laid the table for the Sunday family lunch. He must have thought that as a chef in a hotel, he cooked for strangers of all kinds in any case – why then couldn't he cook for his own?

He would leave the food simmering on the stove while he changed into a white shirt, black coat and tie, and the blood-red waistcoat of *Amadodana ase Wesile.* He would briskly stride all the way to Atteridgeville Methodist Church on Mnzangoma Street, which was about a 20-minute walk, in order to be there well ahead of the morning church service. For over four decades, until he died, Papa rang the church bell every Sunday morning. No one else in the congregation dared touch the chain. The heavy metal bell hung high up in the round red-brick tower above the main foyer of the church. Tolling the bell was no easy matter. The steel chain dropped from high. Papa had to yank it in a way that produced a continuous high-pitched ringing audible near and far in our village. None could match my grandpa in yanking that chain up and down in order to produce that toll. One minister after another came and left the congregation. None interfered with his chosen chore. All of them came to know how long and faithfully he had rung the early morning bell and everyone respected and acknowledged his privilege to summon others to worship, until he was called to meet his Maker.

At the end of the church service, Papa would leave promptly and walk back home in time to serve lunch. As the afternoon drew on, on balmy days he would sit on the front veranda, his wife by his side, with a Sunday newspaper open, as if he were reading it. I knew from my childhood that Papa had quickly learned to find a photo in the newspaper that would tell him which side was up. As tradition dictated, passers-by in the street greeted him – 'Sawubona, Baba Makhaza' – and he would lower the newspaper and greet back. From his placid face and occasional conversation with Mma, one could never miss how self-satisfied he was.

Mma and Papa lived long lives and were both blessed with good health. They brought up their seven children, most of their grandchildren, starting with me, and great-grandchildren. Some of their children, starting with my mother, did well and set up their own homes. With others it did not go so well. A generation later, Mma and Papa were saddled with several grandchildren of daughters who never married or returned to their parental home after a divorce. Two generations later, some of their great-grandchildren were living in their home. For three generations the modest five-roomed home at No. 1 Mngadi Street served as a sanctuary for vulnerable children and adults of their bloodline with nowhere else to go. Mma and Papa shoul-dered the burden with remarkable resilience and care.

In the late 1970s, when I was an adult with a family of my own, on Sunday afternoons Kabo, my wife, and I would visit Mma and Papa after church. By then we had our own home, and we were making our way in our respective professions. We would find Papa and Mma seated on the same old front stoep. As we entered the gate and made our way towards the stoep, Papa, with a proud but subdued smile, would lower the Sunday newspaper and say to Kabo, '*Sawubona, makoti*' (Hello, daughter-in-law). With the same placid look, he would turn to me and say, '*Awu sawubona, Gongi.*' By that time both my grandparents were old and frail and the nest was empty. They spoke little to each other as they sat there side by side, and yet I could sense the quiet love that still flickered after a marriage of nearly 70 years and a little more. They never asked us for anything – not even a brass penny – and yet we owed them so much. They seemed satisfied with what they had or did not have. In fact, they seemed so content with the hand life had dealt them that Papa's refrain often came back to me: '*Kuzolunga Gongi, kuzolunga mntwan' omntwanami*' (It will ultimately be fine, grandson).

Mma and Papa created a warm home. It might have been short of many luxuries but never of good food and love. From his workplace Papa brought enough food for all, and our neighbours were always welcome to share. Apart from the regular Sunday lunch, he cooked and baked often at home, something that continued well after his retirement. For Saturday lunch, he would whip up a meal of fishcakes and chips, followed by jelly and custard. His favourite Sunday two-course servings were a rack of lamb and steamed mixed vegetables, and raisin pudding and warm custard for dessert. Not bad at all for an illiterate rustic who acquired sturdy, hands-on culinary skills over a lifetime of learning and caring.

This ample supply of food attracted many visitors, some of whom timed their arrival well within mealtimes. For me, as a tiny lad, the good food proved a handy buffer against bullying. My little friends around Papa's res-idence were tough as nails and they were bullies. They came from tough homes and so they were tough, too. Many did not know who their fathers were and lived with their grandmothers. My friends had learned to fend for themselves in the township streets. They became street brawlers early on and won their street fights comfortably. They also had the oddest names one could find. My one friend, who swore the most, was named Tsenene. Each time he opened his mouth he spat out something unrepeatable about somebody's mother. Another, Zwenika, had undisguised Indian features – hair and all. He did not know why he looked that way and his grandmother, with whom he lived, never said. Godi was the son of Mr Mboweni, whose family were Papa's neighbours. He had a stable family and did not swear but he certainly packed a punch. He was famous for nearly unhinging another boy's head off the neck with a punch. So Godi was a good antidote against bullies like Zwenika and Tsenene. Another neighbour friend was Amos Sindane. He was as thin as a reed and played excellent street soccer with a tennis ball. He kicked that small ball as if it was a full-sized soccer ball. That did not matter much because his equally thin and tall bus-driver father kept him locked in their yard with instructions never to play in the street.

All my friends fancied themselves winning a fight against me, but they never tried and I was confident that they never would. Common sense prevailed. If any one of them fell out with me during the day, they knew they would be thrown out of the early evening queue of friends at my grandpa's place. The offender would miss out on sandwiches, boiled eggs or fried fish, or perhaps queens cakes or jam tarts.

Papa became old and ill. Towards the end of his life journey, Mma made light of his illness. When Kabo and I visited them, she related how Papa rose promptly from his bed and sat up when he felt sick. He refused to lie down. Instead he dressed up, including putting on a jacket and tie. He would stay up well beyond midnight, walking about the house, seemingly to dodge the call of death. At the end of the little story about Papa, Mma would wear a mischievous smile, gently rock her head from side to side and in Serolong she would say: 'Ga Gabariele a ka mpitsa, are Salome, Motho, o kae? Nna Motho nka se eme ka di nao. Ke tlare: "Ke hano Morena"' (If the angel Gabriel were to call my names, Salome, Motho, asking where I was, I would not rise to my feet; I would promptly say: Here I am, my Lord).

Papa succumbed shortly after his 91st birthday. Given where he'd started, he lived a long and rewarding life. His rustic illiteracy and innumeracy yielded to his raw will to carve out a better life for himself and his family. He and Mma set a remarkable example of marriage longevity and childrearing. On one good morning we received the message that our grandpa was in the last stage of his life and gasping. When Kabo and I arrived Ko-Mngadi, he was in his last mile. Shortly afterwards he took his last breath. Kabo administered the last offices as she was able to do as a young professional nurse.

Mma, as most wives do, outlived Papa and lived as a widow for nearly a decade. She was visibly depressed and lonely. She continued to live at Ko-Mngadi, declining offers to go and live with any of her many grandchildren and great-grandchildren who could have housed her comfortably. We all respected her choice to live in her home of decades rather than anywhere else. Kabo and Koketso, my brother Tiego's wife, and Motlagomang, our aunt's daughter, made sure that Mma was generously and caringly looked after.

Our unspoken consensus was that we would never submit to the growing practice of relegating the aged to a home, even when the care that was afforded there was possibly or often superior. My family often took Mma along when we went on holiday, and my children spent holiday time with their great-grandma. To this day they relate with joy the tales she told them over the holidays. In African communities there is a time-honoured tradition of caring for the aged and vulnerable within our homes or the homes of our children or other family members. When it is possible we should continue to choose the home over care in an old-age home or other institution.

I accept that rapid urbanisation has altered our traditional norms on how to care for the aged. This means families and communities must again think through how we want to care for our aged. I reminded a friend who wanted to put his wife's ailing mother into an old-age home that the way you treat your parents or your parents-in-law in old age is how your children will treat you. You set for them an indelible lesson.

Mma told many a hilarious story about her childhood in Kimberley, her youth, her marriage in Marabastad and her adult life in Atteridgeville. Her emotional reward appeared to come from relating what her children, grandchildren and great-grandchildren used to do or say in their childhood when she brought them up and what they have turned out to be. She remained blessed with a clear mind until she succumbed, by election. She never complained except to her childhood friend, Peggy Modise – Koko Peggy, as we called her – that she was lonely. She had lived so long that she had nobody to reminisce with except Koko Peggy. She often said she was tired of being alive. At times she remarked that the Archangel Gabriel had misplaced her life card; that was why she was not being called to higher service.

Mma ate little – in fact, she nibbled like a bird – throughout her lifetime. In her 97th year she started to skip meals clandestinely until her tall, lean, Khoisan frame shrivelled. Nobody noticed at first because she always ate so little. One fateful morning, Mma went into a coma in her bedroom. We rushed to her, but she went silently in my mother Karabo's arms. Kabo lovingly laid out her corpse, as Mma had directed all in the family that only Kabo would do. We laid Mma to rest in the same grave as her departed husband. This, despite her humorous protestation that she should never be buried under anybody, not even her husband, because when the trumpet sounded on the day of resurrection she wanted to rise, stand tall and say: 'Ke hano, Morena' (Here I am, my Lord). I must say she got her way. She was indeed buried on top of Papa, in the same grave.

Mma and Papa were foundational figures. They lived long, full and fulfilled lives before my eyes, except for a brief absence when I was on Robben Island. I want to believe that both my grandparents had much more to do than my parents with how I was to live my life.

CHAPTER 4

Early childhood

My father qualified as a teacher when he was barely 21 years old. Around 1943, he assumed his first posting and joined the teaching staff of Marabastad Primary School, which was led by the venerated Coloured headmaster fondly known as Meneer Martin. My mother was a college student at St Thomas Catholic Teacher Training College when she met my father, in 1946. She was 21 years old. They married the following year and my birth quickly followed.

When I started law school I was fascinated by the rule of evidence that one's testimony about one's date and place of birth is inadmissible because it is hearsay evidence. I suppose at birth a child is there, but is not a credible observer of its birth. What saves the day is the legal fiction that a birth certificate is deemed to be correct and accurate until shown otherwise. However, if someone were to contest the correctness of a date or place of birth, a mother or another who witnessed the birth, if available, would have to say when and where a child was born.

My mother is still alive and she swears that I was born on 20 December 1947 at nearly midnight, after an interminable spell of labour pains, at a maternity home run by Roman Catholic nuns and known as Little Flower. She became a Catholic when she went to St Thomas Teacher Training College and she valued that she gave birth to her first child under the care of Catholic nuns. The nuns steadfastly provided an oasis of natal care in an area with vast health-care needs. Anyone associated with the community of Lady Selborne remembered Little Flower maternity home as a comforting landmark. It outlived the forced removals, and the nuns continued catching babies well into the 1980s. As fate would have it, 30 years later Kabo gave birth to our second son, Reabetswe Botshelo, at Little Flower. To this day, the tall red-brick walls and the chapel still stand, but the air-gasping screams of newborn babies have gone silent.

Mme left the maternity home to live at my father's parental home on Fortune Street. Tradition required no less. A newly wed bride had to live with her in-laws for a while before she ventured into setting up her own home. She had to get to know them and undertake to love and serve them dutifully as family. The custom flows from the notion that, in an African context, marriage is more than a union between two people. Marriage joins the two families concerned. The groom is deemed to be a son of the bride's family. He may be summoned to perform the chores and responsibilities of a son. In turn, the bride joins the groom's family and so she goes *go kotisa* by living for a while with her in-laws in order to know them better before she sets off to establish her own nuclear family.

That opportunity to set up a nuclear family was not unduly delayed. By then the relocation of residents of Marabastad to Atteridgeville was well under way. Both sets of parents lived in Marabastad, which qualified them to be allocated a home in the new residential area. In 1949, my mother narrates, we became tenants in a new four-roomed home at No. 29 Mbolekwa Street. Both my parents quickly acquired teaching posts at the local schools. My maternal grandparents also left Marabastad and they were allocated a rented five-roomed house at No. 1 Mngadi Street, three blocks away from our home. I spent my early formative years between these two residences. We learned to call my parental home Ko-Mbolekwa and the home of my grandparents Ko-Mngadi.

The first three years of my childhood, which were spent in Lady Selborne and Atteridgeville, were uneventful and I have no real memories of this time. The earliest recollection of my parents was when I was between four and five years old Ko-Mbolekwa. Initially, I saw very little of my mother and father. They kept early mornings in order to start at 7am at school, as all teachers of the time did. I stayed with my grandparents during the week and shared a bed with my Mma and Papa. My mother fetched me from Ko-Mngadi on Fridays and dropped me off on Monday mornings on her way to school. Young female learners were obliged to study domestic science and my mother ran the domestic science classes at Hofmeyr High School, which was just across the road from my grandparents' home. Like her father, my mother knew something about good cooking.

I remember my stay with my grandparents with considerable fondness. Although Papa held the rank of chef at the Union Hotel on Church Street, his duties were more onerous than those of a chef. One of them was to stoke the hotel's coal boiler every morning. Without exception, every weekday morning he would wake up at 2am. And so would I. As he took his morning bath, he would have set the kettle on to boil, and I would join him in the kitchen. I was his first and then only grandchild. Having me wake up with him every morning seemed to please him immensely. 'Here is your morning coffee, Gongi,' he would fondly say in isiZulu. 'Gongi' is what he, and only he, called me from my childhood to his grave. He never called me by my given name, Dikgang. Clearly the name did nothing for him. I do not know why and I never asked who or what Gongi was. I assumed that it might have been the name of a long lost relative in whom he was well pleased but I never really gave it much thought. With the morning ritual over, I would follow Papa to the front door and watch as he walked out into the morning darkness. Then, riding on my toes, I would bolt the door and go back to sleep next to Mma.

One morning I probed his early morning start. I asked him, 'Papa, why do you leave for work so early?' In his ponderous, measured voice he explained: 'You see, Gongi, hotel patrons need hot water for their early morning shower and hot breakfast. So I have to stoke the boiler before preparing breakfast. Steam pots for cooking breakfast work with boiling water. What is more —,' here he paused, 'I must do this every single day.' For as long as I lived with Mma and Papa, I woke up every morning when he woke up, drank my morning coffee, bolted the front door and returned to bed with Mma.

My mother is the heroine and queen of my life. I am my mother's son. Her broad forehead, high cheek-bones, raised nose ridge and tapering chin lend an undying beauty to her face. She has always had a yellow to brown complexion and flawless skin. As the years went by, her skin darkened slightly but she was spared wrinkles. Her dark lips contrast well with her complexion and her sparkling set of teeth enhance her careful smile. Unlike her tall, reed-thin mother, who bore every gene of her Khoisan origin, our mother was shorter, rounder and more jovial. She spoke in soft and measured Serolong, which she suckled from her mother, who came from Greenside, near Kimberley in the Northern Cape.

And yet Mme found a very stern voice when she spelled out home rules to us, her sons. We grew up with no sister. My mother conceived and gave birth to a girl with the graceful name Goitsemang (literally, it means 'who knows the mystery of life'), but the baby fell ill and passed on in her infancy. Even at five years of age, I could see, by looking at her dark eyes, the cutting pain my mother endured as Goitsemang's small white coffin was lowered into her grave. Then we were three boys. The other two were my brothers, Malatse Vincent, who was born in 1952, and Onkgopotse Obed, in 1954. Only the other day I had a flash of childhood memory when I saw a family photo of our mother and father and their three boys, as we were then. I realise now how privileged we were to be nurtured in a family that had the gift of love, care and togetherness.

In the evenings our mother would call us to account. 'Dikgang, have you prepared your school uniform for tomorrow morning?' Or, 'Malatse, have you washed your underwear?' And she was clear about one thing: 'You must pour your own coffee; there is no woman to serve you here. You little fellows must learn to do things for yourselves.'

This last often puzzled me. She was the only woman in the house as against my dad and the boys. We as her boys had no dog's chance to order her around. She made sure that we were at her beck and call. She insisted that we stoke the coal stove as soon as we returned from school in the afternoon. We had to learn to cook and bake and to wash soiled dishes and utensils. She never tolerated any debate on these home chores. Each of us had to accomplish his fair share of domestic duties.

The one chore we detested most was polishing the front veranda floor with red polish in full view of passers-by. Mme would have her veranda floor shine like a mirror and nothing less.

The difficulty about this was the young men and women who walked past in the street, who would break into scornful laughter when they saw us on our hands and knees, yelling that we were not real men because we did chores meant for girls.

The one weekly duty that might have passed for a manly task was joining our mother in the Saturday morning gardening. The patch in front of our house was very small – no more than two to three by six metres – but this was where my mother grew flowers. I remember marigolds, carnations and roses. In the backyard, under her watchful eye, we tended a small vegetable garden.

There was one happy respite from our weekday and weekend tasks. This was Sunday lunch. My mother and father went to teach at school during the week and so the only proper meal we could have together as a family was on Sundays. My mother turned every Sunday lunch into a culinary event. She single-handedly prepared and served a three-course meal at our modest dining room table, which just about managed to seat six.

She had a bubbly sense of humour – and still does – and would often break into hearty laughter well ahead of her audience. We would join in the laughter not because of the punchline of the joke but rather because of her infectious giggle. The older she became, the more she told graphic and hilarious anecdotes drawn from lived-life stories.

Her soft brown eyes were deeply expressive. I think they mirrored her soul – darkening in pain but lighting up and glistening with happiness when something gave her joy. She had the remarkable gift of love and an unfailing trust in the good nature of other humans. She trusted that other people would know and want to do the right thing. Her biggest asset, perhaps, matched only by her sense of humour, was her near-endless capacity to soak up emotional hurt and discomfort without demurring. I remember well her saying to me during her visits on Robben Island: 'Son, you will come out of this, if you learn to soak up the hurt you face.'

Our father was short-statured. He had a broad forehead and a flat round head. His high cheek-bones and modest, well-shaped nose lent his face a handsome symmetry. I inherited his crooked lower teeth that protruded and tended to push the lower jaw and lip open. He was short-sighted and wore reading glasses, which added a slight sparkle to his intense gaze. He did not need his spectacles for fine reading, however. His gentle voice did not match his looks and austere temperament. He always walked at a furious pace, taking long strides; as children, when we went shopping with him in town, I learned to do a little trot with my boyish legs in order to keep abreast of him.

In his younger days, on all accounts, he was a very intense and strict man. He was severe on himself and sought to impose this severity on his children, his wife and everyone around him. He rarely smiled. If he had a sense of humour, he hid it rather well. He was terrified by poverty and want. From our childhood, he told us how much he hated lazy people who were likely to increase rather than diminish poverty, and he constantly heaped praise on Papa, our maternal grandfather. 'There is a man,' he would say, 'who puts in an honest day's work every day. I wish his children had followed his shining example.'

Our mother would not be amused at all by this. Our dad was very critical of her younger sisters. He thought they were not pulling their weight with their studies. He also thought their hectic social lives would end their schooling. He would add that, in time, they were likely to make all of us poorer through their personal failures. I remember clearly that his critical stance towards my mother's family sparked fights between our parents. My mother seemed to think the criticism was as uninformed as it was unfair. He had a lukewarm to utterly cold liaison with her brothers and sisters, who, in his view, were not doing enough to improve on their circumstances. It must be said, though, in all fairness, our father replicated this critical stance towards his own older sisters. The biggest bee in his bonnet was children born out of wedlock with absentee fathers. He made that point over and over again to his own sisters, and to my mother's sisters.

I have to remind myself that our dad was an orphan at the age of eight years and had two younger sisters to look after, and that he grew up poor. My mother had family all around her growing up, but my father did not. He grew up during the Great Depression of 1929 followed by the Second World War, so material want must have been deeply etched in his memory. He taught and practised thrift. Young as I was, he would turn to me and emphatically ask: 'Dikgang, how on earth could anybody use up his or her monthly income or weekly wage without saving a part of it? How would he or she come through in a time of financial difficulty?' He told me that he had saved no less than half of his first pay packet, and every monthly income thereafter. 'Never buy on credit,' he lectured fiercely to me, my mother and his sister Rrakgadi Moipone, when she had returned from Kilnerton during school holidays. His voice grew shrill with the urgency of the message. 'Wait until the day you can afford the item you want to buy.'

He would show us how to peel vegetables so that they were skinned thinly. In this way, he said, you preserved their natural nutrition *and* saved money. He urged us to eat little, to exercise most mornings and to walk briskly.

He worked very hard and demanded the same of us. Besides doing our nightly homework, we had to set aside Saturday and Sunday afternoons for optional reading. He led by example. He read the morning newspaper from front to end. He always retained the word puzzle page for early evening amusement. He then turned to his study guides and textbooks. He was studying towards a Bachelor of Arts degree through the University of South Africa, with history and psychology as his majors. He graduated in 1954. In no time, he was promoted to teach at Hofmeyr High School.

Our family was a little more privileged than many others. We lived in a home with a mother and father. Although their government income from teaching was meagre, it was still sufficient to afford us the bare necessities of family cohesion and care. My mother was the reservoir of all the love we needed. My father chose to disguise his love. He never hugged us; he did not tell us bedtime stories; and he did not tell us that he loved us. He made our upbringing as spartan as possible and yet he never abused us. He seemed to believe that this would be the best gift he could give to his children. His deeds ensured a secure family environment. His mantra of not suffering fools and taking full responsibility for one's actions was soon to become a crutch in my unforeseen incarceration for a lengthy period while I was still a child.

CHAPTER 5

'Eagles, sir!'

I started school in 1954 as a Sub-A pupil, not in my home village but away from my parents in a modest African township known as Bela-Bela – the place of boiling springs. The little town and the white neighbourhood were within walking distance across the railway line. It was named Warmbad – rendered in English as Warmbaths. They were two near, but separate, communities. At that time all local people had free access to the boiling springs after which the town was named. They revered them and believed their steaming hot mud and vapour could heal just about any ailment. In time, the municipality fenced off the natural springs and channelled them into three separate communal baths. The entrances were not to be confused and were signposted: 'Europeans Only' on the one, and on the other 'Non-Europeans' – meaning that Natives go through the one entrance, and Indians and Coloureds through the other.

I had just turned six. My aunt, Masikwane Susan Moseneke, was unmarried and had no children of her own. After her teacher training at Kilnerton, the only post she could secure was as a junior teacher at Mmagabe Primary School, where the headmaster was a veteran teacher named Mr Masemola. At the time Bela-Bela was a small black township with only a few rows of modest homes built by their owners. Unlike at my parents' home, Bela-Bela had no electricity, and fresh water had to be fetched in drums or buckets from communal taps at street corners. I hated the bucket system and, even more, the evening stench when the buckets were emptied from home to home into the municipality sewerage truck. My aunt knew that dinner had to be served well ahead of the stench.

Despite these difficulties my stay and schooling were near-idyllic. My aunt spoiled and loved me. She fed me until I was as round as a balloon. Little girls would burst into laughter and point at my shiny, chubby cheeks. Evening after evening I had to submit to additional tuition by my aunt before dinner, and also by the man who married her, whom I fondly called Daddy Maaka. He taught at Mmagabe Primary School, too. My part was to produce pass grades at the top of my class. Daddy Maaka was a tough rustic, who had grown up on a farm and knew all about self-sufficiency. He procured a vacant residential site and every day after school we made cement block bricks and slowly built our own five-roomed home. He reared cattle in a nearby cattle camp and in the mornings, early, before school, I would go with him to milk the cows. He thought I was a little spoiled and needed to be firmed up with rural living. He would walk me barefooted through the bush and show me by name every living creature, tree and shrub. He once held a snake by its tail and laughed as he got the better of it and then threw it back into the bush. His favourite prank was to take me on a night drive towards Settlers farms. He would stop his rattling old car and ask me to fetch him something out of the boot. Just after I had closed the boot, he would speed off and leave me in total darkness near the dirt road. I would cry and freeze with fear, only for the lights of his car to return a few minutes later beaming in my direction. He warned me never to tell my aunt about trips between men. I obliged.

Before I knew it, I had survived my rural initiation and had passed Standard 2. In January 1958 I returned to my parents' home in Atteridgeville for my senior primary schooling at Banareng Primary School.

Daddy Maaka was a good man. My aunt rose to become principal of Mmagabe Primary School and he served under her without visible rancour. Since they did not have children of their own, all my younger brothers, in turns, lived in his home, attended school at Mmagabe, and had the same

47

rural induction meted out to them. Our aunt succumbed to diabetes while I was on Robben Island. Daddy Maaka followed her several years later and today they lie side by side in the Bela-Bela cemetery.

I was ten years old when I started Standard 3 at Banareng. Bela-Bela had grown me a touch ahead of my urban peers. I earned the highest average passes, close to 100 per cent for all the four quarterly exams of Standard 3. Our principal, Mr Makhudu Ramopo, promoted me past one class, directly to Standard 5. He was most disdainful of the Bantu Education imposed on black learners in the mid-1950s by the apartheid government. He thought its offering was well below the native intelligence of African learners. Every year his school produced several distinction passes. It was liked and properly respected. My parents had no hesitation in sending me to Banareng.

I fondly remember our morning assemblies. They started dead on time – 7am. All the teachers would be in attendance, and all the pupils would be in full school uniform. Class by class, in ascending order, in disciplined silence, we lined up in a semicircle. Mr Ramopo presided over the scripture reading and morning prayer and afterwards, at least once a week, he would tell us a fable attributed to Aggrey of Africa. His booming voice would float over the assembly:

> Once there was a farmer who kept a fowl run. He bred little chickens. One of his chickens was of an eagle whose mother had died and the farmer had saved it from its mother's nest. The eagle chicken grew up like the rest. The farmer wondered whether it would ever fly one day and soar as an eagle did. It never did. It stayed down and fed off the chicken feed. One good morning the farmer stepped into the fowl run and held the eagle chicken high, facing the sun. The farmer burst into a loud voice: 'You are an eagle and not a chicken. You belong to the sky. Look up to the sun and fly!' He threw it up but it dropped down to the ground. He lifted it up again the same way and urged it to fly, as it belonged to the sky. The little eagle stretched its wings and disappeared into the glare of the sun, never to return.

Just before he dismissed the assembly, Mr Ramopo would ask loudly: 'My children – you are . . .?' We would all shout back: 'Eagles, sir!'

In 1957 Ghana became independent and Mr Ramopo would freely rehearse to us the teachings of Kwame Nkrumah, that country's first president. As he dismissed the assembly he would bellow out in his ponderous tone: 'Kwame says Africa cannot be free until every square inch of Africa is free.' Headmaster Ramopo's progressive and prophetic teachings did not stay a secret. He began to be hounded by the security police. In early 1960 he fled into exile and ended up teaching at Surrey College in Nigeria. His family followed. All returned only after 1990 when apartheid was on its deathbed. One of his school staff members, Mr Matemotsa, fled to Tanzania. Later, in 1963, another teacher from Banareng, Jafta Kgalabi (Jeff) Masemola, would be arrested and charged as accused number one alongside me and fourteen other student members of the PAC in the Old Synagogue in Pretoria.

At the beginning of 1960, the regime, with less than pure motives, broke up Banareng and spread its teachers and learners across the schools in Atteridgeville. I ended up in the Standard 6 class of Mboweni Higher Primary School. The school, like others in my home township, bore the name of a community leader and educationist, Mr Godi ka Mboweni. Significant leaders of the people were rarely forgotten. A few blocks away, a prominent primary school was named after Mangena Mokone.

In November that year, I passed Standard 6 with six subject distinctions and an overall distinction aggregate. The school headmaster, Mr Mgulwa, was well pleased, as was my class teacher, Mr Getz Komane. Both men have passed on, and both reached a ripe age after a job truly well done. They and other educators in public schools seemed to have vowed to make their young learners whole beings. Theirs was a passive resistance against the bankrupt Bantu Education. With all its security tentacles, the regime could not police teaching and learning in classrooms. Most teachers were not voluble activists, but they understood the formative attributes of their task. They could alter the course of the lives of their young charges. To that end, most of our teachers exuded self-worth and purpose, which they sought to pass on to their young wards. After all, one cannot discover one's innate dignity and remain worthless. In turn, the learners and the communities they served reciprocated the respect. Teachers were adored. They taught us to think for ourselves, demanded hard work and imposed discipline with all who were open to these things. It must be added that they also resorted, sometimes over-enthusiastically, to the biblical injunction never to spare the rod. Often parents of recalcitrant children at home would bring them to school for corporal correction. It was my inimitable headmaster, Mr Makhudu Ramopo, who bellowed at a morning school assembly: 'You have no business to be lazy when you are poor and oppressed. Your foremost task is to change your condition.'

Those were our teachers. They were educators to the boot. They earned little and yet they gave us their utmost.

By mid-year, our class teacher had us start revision in all examination subjects. He had taught the prescribed material in full by the end of the second semester. In addition each final-year student had to read, bring to class and review a public library book every fortnight. The reading extended to African literature. I digress to acknowledge that despite the morbid designs of apartheid education, the silver lining must have been the space it allowed to indigenous languages. In theory, apartheid taught that people are innately and immutably different. Their apartness is shown by how they look, speak and live. On that view, one must speak, read and cherish a home language. That language had a right to grow and flourish. In an ironic way, African languages and literature flourished. They were taught in schools. Rightly so, an African learner had to pass a home language alongside the only two official languages of the time – English and Afrikaans. Sadly, apartheid abused rather than celebrated our diversity. It deployed outward differences to institutionalise inequality, exclusion and greed.

My home language is Setswana, which was one of my examination subjects in Standard 6. I remember well how I enjoyed reading the meticulously crafted love story *Mokwena* by DP Moloto. I later turned to Sol Plaatje's *Dintshontsho tsa Lorato* – a Setswana translation of Shakespeare's *Romeo and Juliet.* LD Raditladi's Setswana anthology, *Sefalana sa Menate*, boasted a glittering collection of poems and one of the poems, '*Kgomo*', I can recite to this day.

The teacher also insisted that we read a daily newspaper. We set up a kitty of 1 cent per learner for buying the daily. A learner had to read the main news items in the black daily, *The World*, and in the *Pretoria News*, a liberal paper with a readership of mainly urban white residents of Pretoria.

On the morning of 22 March 1960, we arrived at school early. The daily had to be read before school started. We were assured that our future would indeed be bleak if we omitted to know what was happening in the world. But nothing had prepared us for that morning's read. We had been vaguely aware that the leader of the newly formed PAC, Robert Mangaliso Sobukwe, had called for a national protest against pass laws on 21 March. He called on African people, whom the law compelled to carry passes, to leave their passes at home that day. They were urged to march to their nearest police stations to surrender themselves for arrest.

The call by the PAC did not target students, and certainly not at primary school level (you had to be sixteen years of age to carry a pass), so on 21 March we went to school as usual. But nothing could have prepared us for the front-page pictures in the newspapers of the following day. We approached the newspapers truly cold and unsuspecting. These were the days long before South Africa had television, and not only in African townships. The apartheid government actively demonised television and would not have it available or beamed into any home or place. All radio channels were owned, and their broadcasts controlled, by government. I was not likely to switch on the radio in any event. My father had long declared African-language radio stations frivolous and stupid. The English main news broadcasts were just about tolerable, if we were to ward off a near-total news blackout. I should rather read and read, my father insisted. There was no cyberspace yet, and no World Wide Web, let alone anything like social media.

The front page of the morning papers carried pictures of corpses lying in a street. The headlines were panic-stricken: 'A MASSACRE IN SHARPEVILLE';

'PAC PROTESTERS SHOT IN COLD BLOOD'. The two newspapers carried virtually nothing but columns of articles and gruesome images of bloodied corpses and armed policemen. Pages that followed showed pictures of Philip Kgosana, a young student at the University of Cape Town, being carried shoulder-high by his followers. He was said to have led 30 000 protesters in the African township of Langa in Cape Town.

Chilling fear and anxiety gripped our class of twelve- and thirteen-year-olds beyond words. As we took our seats in our classroom a ghostly silence fell over us. The rest of the junior classes were noisy, as they always were before morning assembly. They did not know what we knew. That day the morning assembly did not start on time. It was delayed as our teachers went into a hushed huddle in the staff room. Eventually the assembly bell went and we all filed outside, where the headmaster asked that we all pray for the people of Sharpeville, Langa and Nyanga. He ended the assembly that morning by asking God to bless Africa.

Shortly afterwards, our class read that the PAC, ANC and the South African Communist Party (SACP) had been banned; that their membership had become unlawful; that the government had declared a state of emergency; and that many leaders of these organisations had been arrested and detained by the police.

My parents did not say a word to me, their eldest son, about the Sharpeville massacre, and yet a pall of pain and mourning came over our otherwise lively and jovial home. Both seemed to soak up the grief in silence. They woke up as usual and went to their respective schools to teach, as teachers were required to do. I went to my Standard 6 classes to learn. A few weeks went by and calm seemed to return.

On the last day of school in November, I returned home triumphantly. I gave my mother my statement of symbols. 'A distinction, Dikgang?' she celebrated loudly, and I could see the love and pride in her eyes. Later my reward came in the form of an ample array of cakes and desserts, all of which she had prepared in anticipation. My father looked weary when he came home after the train ride between Atteridgeville and Koedoespoort, the railway station near Kilnerton, where he was teaching. When he was told about my results, he nodded his approval, with no outward excitement, and I received a curt 'Well done, Mokwena'. His posture seemed to say: 'A good start, son, but this is chicken feed. There is a lot more to be done. So get on with it.'

CHAPTER 6

High school days, twice cut short

My schooling fate was pre-ordained. At the beginning of 1961, just after I had turned thirteen, I stepped up to the plate to be the third generation of family devotees at Kilnerton. How could it be otherwise? Going to college at Kilnerton had become an immutable feature of our family heritage. Nearly 60 years earlier, my grandfather was nurtured there. After him, his two sons, Sydney and Rogers, qualified as teachers at Kilnerton. My father and two of his younger sisters, Masikwane and Moipone, matriculated at the same missionary institution – thanks to the church bursary.

When I went to Kilnerton, our father had been appointed to the prestigious multiracial staff of his alma mater. He taught English and history to matriculation classes in senior school, something that was generally reserved for Scottish expatriate missionaries or local white teachers with a Scottish or Wesleyan descent. It was a distinct measure of personal achievement that he was as good as anyone else in his teaching craft. He went about his instructional chores with a swagger that seemed to say 'I was a fresher at this very place, but look at me now'.

With a distinction pass, my admission to Kilnerton was assured. Unlike my father, I did not need a scholarship. He paid the boarding and tuition fees outright. I remember him saying should I fail any one year he would have nothing to do with me. I would have to turn myself over to the labour market. But he knew and I knew that failure was not on the cards. Once the paperwork was done I quickly settled into boarding life. The initiation of *msilas* – freshers – was nothing as harsh as legend had it. Older boys sent you around on stupid errands. I opted to do them promptly and get out of harm's way. Happily, the school had banned all assault and any physical abuse of freshers.

As every dawn broke, like my forebears, I was out of my low dormitory bed well before the boarding house wake-up bell. The communal bathrooms were fitted with cold-water showers only but we did not baulk. Probably we had all worked out that the boarding master and his missionary handlers would not relent on this one. Decade after decade young boarders had to submit to a cold morning shower. My dad did. His father must have. And so, in due course, did I. It was an austere start to the day. Our faithful minders must have believed that our lithe bodies and souls would benefit from a stern morning. There was absolutely no point in pondering over the impending icy splash down your spine. The trick, I found, was to start bright and early and escape the later congestion of shivering naked bodies. I would run mindlessly under the chilly spray, wrap up with a towel and dart back into my dormitory. Then I was set for the day.

My school uniform would be ready because the afternoon before I would have washed and ironed my white shirt and pressed my grey flannel pants in the communal laundry room. On Tuesdays and Thursdays, we wore khaki shirts and pants because we had extramural activities. On Mondays, Wednesdays and Fridays, it was compulsory to wear grey flannel pants and a white shirt, with a school tie and a navy blazer. The left chest pocket of the blazer sported the school's light-blue and gold crest. The top inscription read 'Kilnerton Training Institution' and the bottom of the crest displayed the motto *Per ardua ad astra* (Through hard work to the stars).

As were all junior school boarders, I was on a roster of dining-hall servers. We were split to serve the senior and junior school dining halls. As the first rays of the fickle sun pierced through the clouds, breakfast was served. The resident boarding master was charged with that end of matters. The breakfast stood in sharp contrast to the spartan morning ablution. The menu was basic but nourishing and ample, even for growing lads. By the time the rest of the boys filed into the junior and senior dining halls, the wooden tables had been scrubbed and were fully laden. We, the servers, had to carry the breakfast from the kitchen to the dining halls. The food was the same, but the prestige of being served in the senior dining hall was beyond words for junior school. We carted in tall aluminium jugs of coffee or tea and fresh milk. Generous helpings of oatmeal were served from large, well-used, beaten pots. Four slices of wholewheat bread with a lashing of peanut butter and jam, chased down with coffee, got the day off to a decent start. It was a matter of time, I thought to myself, before I became a senior student, and not a server running here and there with heavy jugs and bread trays ahead of assembly.

The high school assembly bell rang at 7am. The bell was housed in a tall clock tower, the centrepiece of the Victorian architecture of the senior high school building. The building backed onto the foot of a well-treed rocky *kopje*, and the classrooms ran off the tower towards the sides in a rectangular U-shape. They were built of light brown sandstone hewn from the *kopje* and their walls were punctuated by solid wood entrances and windows. The red-brick clay tiles under the tower and veranda were beginning to fade, as well they might after being tramped on by generations of boys. This was where the morning assembly was led. The principal stood beneath the tower and to his sides our teachers lined up. Assembly was a ritual never to be missed, except if one was indisposed. Classes lined up in neat rows, and I would take my place and stand, quietly and obediently, waiting for assembly to start. I could feel and hear my steady heartbeat. I sensed every breath I took. To this day, when I relish a moment of peace and quiet, my heartbeat and breath impose themselves on my consciousness. Also, I was not unaware of my family's connection to that place of learning. My presence there was a privilege and a duty. I was one of only a few African children who could come to Kilnerton.

I did not bring to Kilnerton a virgin mind. I had lost my political innocence at Banareng and later at Mboweni. Our headmaster at Banareng, Mr

Ramopo, had related to us the fables of James Emman Kwegyir Aggrey, a champion of African nationalism, and in 1960 I had been horrified by the Sharpeville corpses I had seen on the pages of the newspapers we read daily. My father kept dated copies of the *New Age*, a mouthpiece of the ANC, and *Fighting Talk*, which was produced by the SACP. He subscribed to the *Africanist*, a newsletter of the ANC Youth League. After 1958, the PAC was formed and it took over the production of the *Africanist*. I read and read. Not all was well with our land, with the lives of African people. During my primary school days I had read *Drum* magazine. I read Can Themba, Lewis Nkosi and Nat Nakasa. The magazine ran features on the potato boycott of 1959, which was sparked by the horrific use of prisoners to work on potato farms in Bethal. The *Rand Daily Mail* wrote on and displayed photos depicting prison conditions of black males.

My own little life before Kilnerton was an eye-opener. My father often took my brother Malatse and me to town on Saturday mornings. There the houses were bigger and smarter than ours; their lawns were greener and their streets were wide and clean. Their school buildings were pristine and the grounds bursting with lush green foliage and well-tended flower beds. By comparison Banareng and Mboweni were much smaller, dusty and pitiable. Once we reached the nice shops in town, we would go about shopping, for clothes, for example, and then our father would walk to the pay-point with our purchases. At the point of sale, with the merchandise on the counter, he would wait to hear how the white salesperson addressed him. If the salesperson ever dared not to address him as 'Mister' or 'Sir', my father would storm furiously out of the shop, loudly making the point that they deserved his hard-earned money only if they showed him respect and deference. There was many a time when Malatse and I had to dart out of a shop to escape the wrath of its white salespeople.

Morning assembly at Kilnerton was different from the routine of primary school. The principal was Mr Nixon and the chaplain was the Reverend Dugmore, who prayed and preached in isiXhosa perhaps better than in his native Scottish, which was difficult to follow. I joined in the rousing singing of the Lord's Prayer. Then the student body was quietly dismissed to start a day of relentless schooling. Only excellence, and nothing else, would do. After all, an admission to this great school was a singular privilege, we were warned. None dared mar its time-honoured reputation of yielding multiple passes with distinctions in the revered Joint Matriculation Board examinations.

Although ours was a co-ed high school as a matter of tradition, the missionaries allowed nothing but strict separation between male and female residential facilities. Girls always had the good sense never to come to boys' hostels, but there was always a daring boy who would breach the perimeter of the girls' hostel, which was a little distance away. He would make an ill-fated dash through the beaming searchlights of the dormitory, hoping to reach his girlfriend's room. When he was caught, which usually happened, he was expelled summarily. That, after all, was the first tutorial to all new boys. Even so, teenage testosterone got the better of some. I was not one of those boys to take the risk. For one thing I had night work – the algebraic formulae and geometry theorems took their toll on me. Having applied myself throughout the day, I went to bed early and slept soundly. For another, I did not have the guts for a night operation, which called for military precision. And besides, I asked myself, how would I ever face my parents over an expulsion so dumb? Moreover, what would I say to my mother? I could imagine her question: what was I looking for at the girls' hostel at night?

As for all public prohibitions everywhere, stories of brave breaches quickly made the rounds. Many heroes of the battle of the girls' hostel – *mzana* – surfaced. Boys who were not known for their bravery would let slip that they had spent an evening in a girl's hostel room. The stories were not verifiable, of course. Nobody was so foolish as to believe them and yet they could not be shown to be untrue. Any possible witness ran the risk of expulsion. So, with no risk of being caught out lying, fanciful claims of romantic nights flourished from *amaromana*, who were known to have girlfriends, and even from *ngobias*, who were high and dry and were yet to go out with a beautiful lady from our campus.

On Sunday evenings I would walk up to the chapel on the hill to hear the Reverend Dugmore deliver his perennial sermons. Like many early missionaries, he was remarkably proficient in the isiXhosa language. At a point during the liturgy, in clear language, he would make known from the pulpit: 'Let us sing Te Deum' – and he would continue in isiXhosa: '*Siyakudumisa Thixo, siyakuvuma ukuba unguJehova, umhlaba wonke ubhedesha wena, oh Thixo ongunaphakade.*' (We worship you God, we accept that you are Jehovah, the whole world praises you, oh eternal God.) The chapel would break into a wondrous song of worship glorified by the best young male and female choir voices that mighty institution could muster.

It was only a matter of time before I submitted to the church confirmation classes. These were run by a young resident teacher, Stanley Mmutlanyane Mogoba, and supported by Reverend Dugmore. In time, and after a memorable stint on Robben Island, the same Stanley Mogoba was called to the ministry. He rose up the ranks of the Wesleyan Methodist Church to become its presiding bishop in Southern Africa. To this day, retired as he should be, he still ministers to the spiritual needs of the villagers in Phokoane, where he was born.

What I did not know then was that my stay at Kilnerton would coincide with its cowardly demise. In our second year, in 1962, the government forcibly shut down that grand institution and expropriated most of the scenic land on which it was located. Their pretext was that it was located on land which they had proclaimed to be for exclusive use or occupation by people classified as white. Like marauding barbarians, the regime snuffed out that proud institution of learning as one would a brave flickering candle. As that timeless Miriam Makeba song about Sophiatown said, Kilnerton was gone. Thanks be to God, in 1994, only 32 years later, after blood and tears and a little talking, we snuffed out the junta which exerted its power so heartlessly.

The closure of Kilnerton meant that in January 1963 I had no school to go to. Many Kilnerton students were admitted to Hebron, a boarding school 40 kilometres north-west of Pretoria. I was on a blacklist of students not to be admitted to Hebron. I came onto the blacklist because I was part of the protest action by students at Kilnerton during September and October of 1962. I was expelled from Kilnerton together with hundreds of other protesting students even before we sat for our Standard 7 examinations. When Kilnerton was shut down, the education department furnished Hebron High School with a blacklist of recalcitrants.

When in trouble, one reverts to one's hometown and that was what I did. I applied to Mr Steve Maboa, the headmaster at Hofmeyr High School. This, I grumbled, was a significant climb-down. Kilnerton had a pedigree of nearly 100 years and now I had to go to the school across the road. But being at boarding school never harmed one's reputation amongst friends who attended a local school. They hated living under the thumb of their parents. Another perk: your prospect of dating a beautiful local girl shot sky-high. But another turn-off was that my new school was located directly opposite my grandparents' home. I had lived there as a child, right under the nose of the school. Familiarity had bred undeserved contempt for a premier institution that had always done well for its young charges. Nevertheless, I had no other choice and I was relieved, at least, that I did not have to drop a class. The school agreed to admit me into Standard 8, even though I had been expelled from Kilnerton before I'd sat for the Standard 7 examinations.

After becoming accustomed to boarding school, I now had to learn to live in a family setting again, with my mother and my four younger brothers, Malatse, Onkgopotse, Kabelo, who was five years old, and the newest addition to our family, Tiego, who was just a baby. When Kilnerton shut down I wasn't the only one to move schools. My father became the headmaster of Wilberforce Training College in Evaton and so he was away during the week. Wilberforce was an outcome of heroic efforts of the African Methodist Episcopal Church to establish an independent training college that would nurture values of self-determination and African Methodism.

Matadingoana Michael Mohohlo (Mike) and I quickly became friends at Hofmeyr High and swopped the first position in virtually every subject in class. Our teachers were dedicated and inspiring educators and their method of instruction was animated and gripping. Mr Moagi who would unfailingly start his mathematics class with his signature pay-line, said in a gruff, smoker's voice: 'Class, in me you have the best mathematics teacher south of the Limpopo.' I liked hearing his claim every morning. Somehow it did something for me. Mr Rikhotso taught us English grammar and literature. He would walk from side to side of the classroom and was prone to bursting into recitals. One of his favourites was from *The Merchant of Venice*: 'Class! The quality of mercy is not strained … It blesseth him that gives and him that takes …' And then, before we knew it, he would be into *Hamlet*: 'To be, or not to be: that is the question: Whether 'tis nobler in the mind to suffer the slings and arrows of outrageous fortune …'

There were less happy moments, however. Mr Molepo, who had a very thin voice for a man, taught zoology in Afrikaans. Mr Kekana had to teach arithmetic in Afrikaans. Both teachers were at pains to explain that they were abiding by a government circular from some big government office. I hated it. Not the language. English was just as foreign to me as Afrikaans. What I hated was the compulsion – the order of the state that we had to be taught in a particular language.

I could not have predicted that my stay at Hofmeyr would last only two months, and my aversion for oppression had not yet risen to a near-choking irritant. You had to be sixteen years of age to be issued a pass, so I had not yet had to queue and be fingerprinted. But the images of those corpses of the people gunned down in Sharpeville had never quite left me. Did they have to be killed for refusing to carry passes? Why did the dependants of the deceased not have recourse? For a long time in my childhood I had hated that African people were an oppressed underclass.

It did not help matters that while I was still at Kilnerton, I had attended a private meeting on the *kopje* behind the college at which Thami Mazwai, a visitor to the college, lectured about the independence of Ghana in 1957 and of Nigeria in 1960. Even the British prime minister, Harold Macmillan, he told us, had openly conceded that there were 'winds of change' blowing over Africa as colony after colony gained freedom and independence. He finished by urging young Africans to rally and unite to unseat colonialism and apartheid – and in our lifetime. Another time I went to a similar lecture by Tommy Mohajane, Jimmy Pambo and Johnson Mlambo. I was enthused by the stress on personal and group agency. I was pressed to free myself in my lifetime: 'Inkululeko ngexesha lethu.'

Within a few weeks of my stay at Hofmeyr, Mike and I met Ike Mafole at his home on Maraba Street. Ike had matriculated at Lady Selborne High School, and he was smart and spoke a lot of sense. In no time he recruited us to join the African Students Union of South Africa (ASUSA). Much later I came to know that ASUSA was an Africanist breakaway from the African Students Association, a student wing of the ANC, then led by Thabo Mbeki.

In effect, the meetings of ASUSA were an entry point for the youth to join the PAC. They were held after school at Ike Mafole's home. Ike, who was both a remarkable teacher and an inspiring orator, asked me and Mike to invite more of our friends and classmates to come along. He warned that we had to be discreet and careful. The system and its security branch would spare no moment to crush us, he said. He taught that we must be our own libera-tors from apartheid oppression. Unlike our forebears, freedom must come in our lifetime. African people, he told us, could not outsource the leadership of their battle for freedom to anybody and certainly not to white liberals or communists. African youth must lead, fight, and liberate themselves. They must want to establish a non-racial democracy inspired by Africanist norms and a socialist economic system.

This meant, he said, that we had to be prepared to serve, suffer and sac-rifice. Robert Sobukwe, who, along with other leaders of the PAC, was by then in prison, also held this line. They had been charged and convicted for leading the anti-pass campaign of 1960. They went through their trials saying, 'No bail, no fine and no defence'. Unlike the activists of the Defiance Campaign of 1952, the PAC leaders did not enter a plea to be released on bail. They chose not to pay fines. They refused legal representation. This, they argued, was a principled stance. Once they had chosen the path of defiance of the pass laws, they expected punishment. They would not take refuge in the niceties of a bankrupt legal system.

Mike and I and others relayed our excitement about Ike Mafole's liberation lectures, and the number of students who came to listen to him increased sharply. Now that the movement had been banned, underground recruitment had to move swiftly. We had to form cells of five to ten people, and the identity of cell members was to be known by cell members only. Sadly, this was not to be. As students, we were ecstatic about the prospect of being part of underground structures of a revolutionary movement. Mike and I thought the faster way of raking in many students was through mass meetings. Those who came could break up into cells of five to ten people once they had been persuaded to join.

Over only a few weeks, Ike had introduced us to a man who lived in Saulsville, John Nkosi, a self-effacing and rather irritatingly quiet man. He seldom made eye contact and he spoke in monosyllables, and yet the word 'revolution' was written all over his forehead. He did not teach Africanist ideology; he talked revolution. He said he was a regional leader of the PAC; he had been to Maseru, where the banned PAC had their headquarters. He had met Potlako Leballo, the interim leader of the underground movement. The next stage of the unfolding programme after the 1960 anti-pass campaign was a popular uprising, which was scheduled to take place on 21 March 1963. Members were commanded to recruit more members. They were to formulate a plan of uprising against state installations and institutions in their neighbourhoods. On the third anniversary of the anti-pass campaign and of the Sharpeville shootings, Potlako Leballo would make the clarion call from Maseru. He would urge all the underground structures and the oppressed African people of South Africa to rise up in revolution.

In my young head the plan sounded credible. I assured John Nkosi that our problem was not numbers. A few hundred students had joined ASUSA and the PAC by then. Mass meetings were held after hours on various school premises. In early March 1963, one other meeting was held at the local rugby field. Student numbers had grown. Also, many more adults were visible within our ranks. Jeff Kgalabi Masemola, who had been one of my primary school teachers, was one of them. He was well known for his unbending political disposition on issues of racism and oppression, and he had now become a prominent leader within the underground structures. Despite his calling as a teacher, he did not address meetings or tutor the youth on Africanist thinking. He headed a highly shielded task team called the 'bomb squad'. Their mission was discreet and dangerous. They stole hand-grenades and bombs stored at an army depot near a shooting range in Phelindaba.

Another in our ranks was my English teacher, Mr Peter Rikhotso. He never talked about the revolution and he never attended mass meetings. Amongst a few young people, particularly to his students, Mike Mohohlo, Mark Shinners and me, he taught the basic teachings of Robert Sobukwe. He urged us to read Sobukwe's inaugural address to the conference of 1959 and the Africanist manifesto. Simon Brander was another adult activist who thrived in public gatherings. He lived his life as if the PAC had never been banned. He shouted 'Izwe Lethu!' whenever he chose. He always addressed a gathering with infectious enthusiasm, and left us confident that we were on an unchallengeable course.

As 21 March 1963 neared, the more the underground structures threw caution to the wind. Our growing numbers compromised secrecy. The regional leadership was unclear, new and experimental. The euphoria of the pending revolution left us wide open and vulnerable. The security branch must have infiltrated the structures without much effort. On 20 March, I went to bed wondering what form the apocalyptic uprising of 21 March would assume. I, for one, had not stumbled into a magical plan that would see any government, let alone apartheid, overthrown in one day.

Around 2am on 21 March 1963, I was woken by loud shouting at the two outer doors of our home and all the windows: 'Police! Open!' Before my mother could reach either the back or the front door, both had been kicked open. A dozen huge policemen were already in the house. A man I later came to know as Warrant Officer Geyser shouted: 'Dikgang Moseneke, your game is up!' He seemed to be in command of the rest and acted very self-assured. They were mainly white men, with a sprinkle of black cops, and they were intent on making a speedy arrest. They conducted a hurried search.

Mercifully, they missed all the banned literature and leaflets that were meant to rouse the populace into a revolt that morning. I froze with fear, but I did not cry. I don't know why. But I was trembling uncontrollably as I set about looking for warm clothing. They cuffed my hands behind my body. They told my crying mother that I was under arrest for terrorism. They were not permitted to tell her where I would be kept. In the street outside a convoy of special-branch vehicles was waiting. In the car, they blindfolded me and we sped off into the darkness.

CHAPTER 7

Arrest, detention and interrogation

The fateful arrest on 21 March was, as the saying goes, a life-changer. It set and dyed my world from then to now. It imposed on me an inexorable path. But for the arrest, my teenage fascination with the revolution may have come and gone as do other youthful fantasies. I would have passed the Joint Matriculation Board examinations ('John Mabulala Bantu', as those who revered the exam called it) with a few distinctions, including in mathematics and science. In these subjects Mike and I outshone our classmates by far. The two of us would have gone to Natal University and studied medicine at Wentworth, the only medical school that admitted black hopefuls. We would have come back home and set up a private practice. After all, only medical doctors had this compelling title. You had to call them Dr Nkomo, Dr Moreosele, Dr Tsele, Dr Mogoba, and nothing less. Doctors saved lives. You never knew when you might have to wake them up late at night – so they were revered. They married the prettiest wives, lived in the best homes, drove the best cars and still they did not have to work for white people. They were gifted the best of all worlds even under racial oppression.

But this was not to be my path after all.

That first night I hardly slept. I stood crying in the dark. I did not want to get under the stinking grey blankets I had been provided with. The dark side walls of the single cell hardly allowed me to stretch my arms fully and there was only room to take a few steps forward before I reached the two cell doors. There were two buckets in a corner. One served as a toilet and the other had drinking water in it. At first light, the two cell doors were flung open. Geyser stood within the frame of the door, his body lit up by the sun's rays. He laughed and shouted loudly: 'Dikgang Moseneke, I said last night – the game is up!' He was accompanied by a huge security policeman named Sergeant Matyeni, Warrant Officer Smit and another security policeman.

They escorted me into a room in the police station. Geyser ordered me to strip down to my underpants. He handcuffed me tightly and tied a belt around the middle section of the cuffs. Each time he pulled the belt, the cuffs cut deeper into my wrist. He pulled the belt several times. One of my wrists started bleeding. Then all four of them started punching and kicking me. Blows rained down mercilessly. My face instantly swelled up under the heavy blows and I screamed and cried loudly. They laughed and screamed back. 'You little rubbish! Whose government do you think you can over-throw?' As I lifted my cuffed hands to parry the blows, blood from my cut wrists ran down my armpits and the sides of my body. I bled from just about everywhere. After about half an hour the beating stopped abruptly. They ordered me to take my clothes along back to the cell. I hankered for the refuge of the cell. Before I went, Matyeni brought a smile to my lips, even swollen and bleeding as they were. In a sneering tone, he said: 'Dikgang, look what a bloody mess you are now, *jou bliksem*, you little shit. You know, white people make aeroplanes. You can't even make a bicycle but you want to rise against their government.' Geyser and Smit smiled approvingly.

The big doors shut behind me. I stood in the cell and wondered what that had been all about. They had not asked me one question about any-thing. They had smashed and belittled me and thrown me back where they found me. My mind whirled with questions. Could I demand a doctor? Was I allowed to lay a complaint of assault? Where were my parents? Was I enti-tled to a change of clothes? Would my tormentors be back tomorrow?

Yes, they were back. They led me to the same room. Again I had to strip. They demanded I run on the spot until I was very tired. While panting heav-ily, I had to sing '*Nkosi Sikelel' iAfrika*'. For good measure that session was topped by another 30-minute session of a flurry of blows from four big security policemen. Again, I was not asked even a single question. By the time I was thrown back into the cell I could barely see out of my eyes. I fell onto the smelly blankets and slept long and strangely peacefully until the following morning.

A few days passed and nobody visited me. Then a tall officious man got me booked out of the cell and took me into an office. He was alone. He spoke politely to me. He served me with a notice stating that I was being held under the 90-day detention law. I would be kept in solitary confinement at Erasmia police station, which was where I was. (Until then I had not even known that much.) I could not receive visitors. I could only be seen by a state doctor. I was not to be seen by or consult with a lawyer. After what appeared to be the end of official business, he said I should work well with my interrogators and answer all their questions truthfully. I showed him my wrists and mentioned the assaults. He assured me that he would look into my complaint. I never saw the man again nor heard about the outcome of my assault complaint.

But as I returned to my cell, I was thankful for little mercies. I was in captivity, but it was finite. I knew when it was going to end. I knew my possible date of release. I etched a calendar of 90 days into the wall of the cell running from 22 March. Every morning I ticked a day off. I had no business expecting a visitor or a change of clothes. Their law said I could not. I had to do with me and myself. I had to give up looking to my parents to save me. They were not allowed to. The message was clear: Dikgang, you must paddle or drown, my boy. Nobody was allowed to or could do it for me. I had to find inner vigour, a big heart, to go through this challenge.

In solitary confinement time moves slowly. The days were long and lazy, but I was in deep despair, pain and anxiety. My youthful zest had soured. I was not allowed reading material. I had no one to talk to. The regular police who brought the meals dropped them inside the door and hurried off. I had to learn to accept my lot. I drank the bucketed water. I cherished the meals which before I would not touch for days. I slept under the grey blankets and their smell had somehow gone. The highlight of my day was the early morning shower outside the single cell. That was the only moment of the day when I saw open sunshine and enjoyed cold water running down my bony body.

I was deeply uncertain about what would happen next. That tensed up every sinew in my body. Was I the only one who had been arrested? Had my comrades succumbed to torture? Had they spilled the beans? When my turn for interrogation came, what should I say? What answers would spare my body from more torture? After 90 days, were they going to charge me or release me? Sometimes, I flirted with the fanciful idea that as a juvenile I might be sentenced to lashes and returned to school. All the answers were with my captors. I had none.

This was not to be for long. One fateful morning, two weeks or so after the detention order was handed to me, I was let out of the cell and escorted into an office. There sat Captain Ferreira, Warrant Officer Stromfa, Geyser, Smit, Vermeulen, and Matyeni. Was this another battery session? I wondered. My teeth went grinding on their own. Ferreira, who appeared to be the leader of the pack, wore a grin akin to a smile. '*Izwe Lethu*, Dikgang,' he greeted me with sarcasm. Afrikaans speakers seemed to find Dikgang easy to pronounce. My interrogators used my first name with frightening frequency. 'We know everything about you, Dikgang. Your comrades have told us all about your little underground structures. We arrested all of them and they are singing like canaries. *Jy is in groot moeilikheid, kleintjie.*' Geyser chipped in with his favourite phrase. 'I told you, Dikgang – the game is up.' He had a smattering of Sesotho and he added: '*Go tonya madi*' (You are going to shit blood). He then made it clear that if I didn't come clean, they would leave, but that they would be back without the lieutenant. That threat was not ambiguous. I instantly said I would cooperate.

The interrogation started.

'Are you a member of the PAC?'

No, I said. I was a member of ASUSA.

'*Kak, man, dit is dieselfde ding,*' one of them chided.

'Kenneth Molatedi says you were the youth leader and addressed meetings of the PAC?' Ferreira asked.

'Yes, I did attend and address meetings of students,' I ventured.

'Dikgang, you are not as smart as you think. You are going to jail for many years, my boy.'

They had done their homework and the session was meant to let me know that. They recited chapter and verse of the ASUSA/PAC activities in Atteridgeville during February and March 1963. I confirmed my participation but denied that the objective was to overthrow the state by violent means. My common sense told me that that would be a fatal admission. The lesser evil, I thought, was to confess my speeches over my hatred for apartheid but deny a plan to overthrow the state. They seemed unperturbed by my foot shuffling. Their overall message was: we have all the evidence we need to put you away. They left without writing out a statement or requiring me to sign one.

I remained in solitary detention. A few weeks later, Stromfa and Vermeulen returned. They asked me whether I would be willing to repeat what I had told them before a magistrate. 'Who knows – he might pardon you and let you go.' The possibility of being freed to return home and to school resurfaced. It was truly seductive. It tied in with my baseless hope that I might be freed because I was so young. Vermeulen said I should tell the magistrate about my participation in the activities of ASUSA/ PAC. That I did not mind. They knew it already and it was true. He went on to repeat other matters he wanted me to mention in a statement before a magistrate.

They were an odd mixture of what I knew in truth, what Vermeulen had gathered from the questioning of other detainees and his own inferences or fabrications. They amounted to this: he wanted me to incriminate my high school English teacher, Mr Rikhotso, as the one who urged his students that apartheid was oppressive and had to be overthrown. He was anxious that I say, too, that Mr Kgalabi Masemola had misled me and other students into political activity and into the plot to overthrow the state. He also wanted evidence against John Nkosi, to say that John had briefed me to advise other students about the instructions from the PAC in Maseru and its planned popular uprising. He stared at me with fixed eyes and with a stern voice said: 'Remember, Dikgang, don't try to be clever with me. That will catch up with you, hey! Whatever statement you make to the magistrate will be given to me. I will know what you said and will deal with you.' Then he paused and pointed at me with his index finger. 'Tell the magistrate nothing about the assault. Pull your jacket sleeves over your cut wrist. And tell him you, not me, asked to make the statement and I did not promise you anything for making it.'

I nodded my agreement.

Vermeulen induced me into making a written statement before the magistrate. As he did, he knew what I did not know then. The admission that I participated in activities of a banned organisation amounted to a punishable offence. So the admission amounted to a confession. Many years later, when studying the law of evidence on Robben Island, I came to know that a confession to an offence before a police officer is inadmissible. I also came to know that a confession made in pursuit of an inducement is inadmissible. I cursed, but rather late. Stromfa and Vermeulen had tricked me and falsely induced me to make a statement of a strange mixture of fabrication and truth before a magistrate. I don't know why, but I did. I was vulnerable and malleable like pot clay in their palms.

Back then, all magistrates were white people. The magistrate I stood before was white. Even so, in a lucid moment, I gathered courage and common sense and I showed him the torture wounds around my wrist. He made a note of the injuries on the face of the statement. When the statement-taking ended, the magistrate invited Vermeulen into the office and gave him the statement. Vermeulen handcuffed me and led me to his car. He eased himself into the driver's seat, where he sat and read the statement. Before long he turned to the back seat and barked loudly: 'Dikgang, why did you talk about the assault, you little rubbish?'

Terrified, I replied, 'The magistrate asked me, he asked me.' I felt I had to say more, so I added: 'Sorry, my jacket sleeves mistakenly moved up and my wounded wrists showed.'

'What saves you, *kleintjie*, is that you said you told the magistrate that you made the statement on your own.'

Without another word, we sped off to the police station and I was back in my single cell. At my trial, the presiding judge admitted the 'confession', warts and all. He held it to be admissible evidence against me.

In the scheme of things, the 'confession' proved redundant. At trial, the state had witnesses against Jeff Masemola, John Nkosi and me coming in a queue from here to Timbuktu. There was no shortage of our own comrades who had become turncoats. They were deserters – able and willing to take the witness stand for the state.

CHAPTER 8

On trial at the Old Synagogue

My mother tongue, Setswana, teaches that *matsha ga ana swele.* For certain, a new dawn will come and displace darkness. And every dawn is a new day. It holds promise of a new beginning. So was it on one good sunny, wintry morning on 20 June 1963. The detention, torture and desolation were to pass. The two massive steel doors of my cell swung open.

'*Dikgang, kom uit!*' Vermeulen yelled.

I wondered what was on my handler's mind and he soon told me.

'You will be appearing before the Supreme Court in Pretoria this morning. *Vandag gaan jy tronk toe vir ewig, kleintjie.*'

As the police car raced to the city, I was quietly joyous. Whatever this meant, it could not be worse than solitude, uncertainty and torture. I might even see my parents and my classmates. I might be entitled to a lawyer. Who knew – perhaps I would be put on a different and better diet. I missed my freedom and friends, but even more I longed for my mother's food.

My daydreaming was spot on. I was right. As we drove into the yard of the courthouse there were many other police cars parked there. Sixteen of us were brought out of solitary confinement in police cells around the city into the same court holding cell. We became a loud group, hugging and ecstatic, relieved and joyous at reuniting. The euphoria was not going to be for long, however. The communal cell door swung open. The sheriff gave each one of us a document called an indictment. It ran to several pages.

We were commanded to be silent and the cell went quiet. Each accused paged nervously through the indictment to work out what charges he had to face. A quick read helped me work out the vital features of the charge sheet. We were six adults and ten students from my high school. I was accused number six, five places away from Jeff Kgalabi Masemola, who was accused number one. The first five accused were adults, and included Klaas Mashishi, Simon Brander and John Nkosi. I sensed that we were ranked according to a descending order of possible guilt. Knowing what I knew, what the police knew and his frequent interaction with senior party members, I expected Mark Shinners to be accused number six or seven, but no – he was placed sixteen. There were also notable absentees on the list of accused. I could not work out where Ike Mafole was. I had been recruited by him into ASUSA. If anybody, I mulled, he should be accused number one. By then, I later realised, Ike Mafole must have been in exile in Botswana.

The quick read showed that we were charged with a statutory crime known as sabotage. It amounted to this. We had conspired amongst ourselves and with other PAC members to overthrow the government by violent means. The alternative and lesser charge was being a member of a banned political organisation. My eyes hurried down the summary of substantial facts. The conspiracy was said to have occurred in Atteridgeville over two months, between January and March 1963. The sting of the charge was that at five or so meetings, we had made common cause with the call of the PAC to overthrow the racist, minority state by violent means in the year 1963. No acts of violence were taken in furtherance of the conspiracy.

Who were their witnesses? I wondered. I did not have to wonder long because an annexure listed them. There were thirteen names, plus Mr X, whose name was shielded from public exposure. We knew all thirteen well. They were our comrades, who served in underground cell structures. They had succumbed and agreed to testify even though they were accomplices. One was an adult member and the rest were students. Mr X was to testify in a closed court, but the rest had to give evidence in an open court. They were

Robert Ramasodi, Kenneth Molatedi, Walter Mashiloane, Ewalt Ramatsui, Phillip Mogaswa, Matthew Seabi, Abesai Dimpi, Nathan Molope, Victor Thulare, Gladwin Khoza, Elias Kekana, Frederick Ramatsui and Lazarus Loate.

The mood in the holding cell dampened, particularly amongst the adult accused. To the rescue came a loud police command that we must file out of the cell into the court dock in the order of our given numbers.

The trial was held, not in the courthouse called the Palace of Justice on Church Square, but in the Old Synagogue on Paul Kruger Street. It was a place of worship which the state had acquired and, after a little modification, turned into an annexe to the main court building. The Old Synagogue became a courthouse drenched in our history of resistance. For nearly five years, from 1956 to 1961, 90-odd activists faced treason trial charges in it. I was not of their age or pedigree in the battle against racial oppression. And yet there I was, a fifteen-year-old boy, thin and nearly mad from solitary detention, about to stand in the wooden dock in which Nelson Mandela, a year later, in 1964, was to make his famous address about his fight against black domination and against white domination – a cause for which, if so it needed to be, he was prepared to die.

As we walked into the courtroom, I could see my mother and father in the upper gallery. They were standing up and waving. So were other relatives. I wondered how they knew what I had not known up until early that morning – the date of our hearing. Nevertheless I was thrilled by their selfless support and the warmth they brought in a grim situation. The upper gallery was packed to capacity and the media were there in full force, with their cameras clicking away and flashes lighting up.

Seated in the court was a veteran attorney, Mokgonane Godfrey Pitje (GM), together with a very young-faced advocate whom we would come to know was Ivor Swartzman. GM rose quickly and came over to the dock to let us know that they were appearing for all of us on instructions of our families.

The court rose as the presiding judge, Judge Peet Cille, entered. Advocate OKE Harwood SC appeared for the state. His investigating officer was

Captain Ferreira. Advocate Ivor Swartzman rose to confirm his appearance. The state said it was ready to proceed with the trial. Swartzman sought time to consider whether to file a motion to quash the indictment and to request further particulars.

I turned my head towards the back of the courthouse again. My mother and father sat close to each other, quietly observing the trial proceedings. I wondered what was going through their inconsolable minds. My maternal grandfather, Makubande Dickson Makhaza, and grandmother, Motho Salome Seatla, were still alive. I wondered whether my mother had possibly managed to calm her parents down over my detention and trial while she herself was so grief-stricken. Both my father's parents had passed on before I was born, but I still wondered what my grandfather and namesake, Samuel Dikgang Moseneke, and his wife, Ephenia Sampisi Masote, would have made of my grim captivity.

Surely, I reassured myself, their lives were not a stroll in the park. They must have lived through searing times themselves. Aside from their personal and family agony, they must have hated the racial humiliation, social exclusion and poverty African people had to endure under colonial minority rule. They would have known that my aversion for unfairness and inequality was inbred, so how could my forebears condemn me for making common cause with the grassroots struggles for equal worth and freedom? They would have accepted that our battle to overthrow unjust rulers was just. I suspect that, even so, they would have thought that the repressive state was too mighty an enemy to be taken on by anyone. They would have feared that I was too young to bear the vengeance of insecure oppressors. In a moment of weakness, they may have wished my piteous lot on the child next door rather than on their very our own standing in the dock.

When I came out of my daydream, the remand hearing was about to end. The judge postponed the case to a new trial date, allowing defence counsel two days to be ready. I heard the words 'Court adjourned!' and saw red robes swiftly vanishing from the bench.

My eyes sought my parents again, and I smiled and waved to them feebly before police hurriedly showed us out of the dock to court cells.

Just after the hearing, we were allowed to see our families and to receive changes of clothing, newspapers and food, glorious food. My mother was well prepared and she had brought lots of food for us, including dessert! My father was visibly moved to see me again. He asked no questions and levelled no accusation. These were desperate times. All the support he could give, he would give me, without judging me. I found this very reassuring, but the family visit seemed to end almost before it had begun.

All sixteen accused were handcuffed and chained – my leg was chained to that of my classmate and friend, Mike – and put into a large yellow police truck. A convoy of police motorbikes and escort vehicles with blue lights accompanied us. Sirens blaring, we took off from the Old Synagogue, up Potgieter Street, to Pretoria Central Prison. Nicknamed New Lock, this was where we would be kept until the end of the trial. None of us had asked for bail.

We welcomed our escape from solitary confinement and to be held together was in itself reassuring. Each one of us had been bruised and demeaned alone in solitude. Our self-esteem had dropped to our ankles. Interrogators sowed deep mistrust amongst us, their captives. They often lied about detainees having spilled the beans about others. They blurred the line between informer and comrade and planted deep doubt about the commitment of others within the movement. The more vulnerable amongst us were young students who were not seasoned in security police machinations. That was now going to stop. That we were charged jointly counted for a lot. It meant that the state adjudged us to be on the same side. The sell-outs were separated from those who must be punished. We were fellow-accused in a political trial and as we closed ranks each of us knew that we had to draw strength from one another.

The reunion offered us the space for needed reparation. We were kept together in a large communal cell in the maximum-security section of New Lock. There we shared the drama and shock of our individual arrests and the ordeal of detention. We compared interrogation experiences. We relived our respective pain. And, perhaps unknowingly, we started the healing process. We also rekindled solidarity by singing freedom songs and praises of the PAC and its leadership. We were revitalised and emboldened after having been cowed and humiliated by solitary interrogation. We needed loads of courage and camaraderie to soak up a pending trial in which our fortunes were bleak.

Two days later, we returned to the Old Synagogue. Ivor Swartzman was led by Sydney Kentridge QC. They had earlier given written notice of a motion to quash the indictment on a number of grounds they said the law allowed. I sat in the dock following only a few of the submissions made by our QC. But I was no less intrigued. Somehow, the judicial process intrigued rather than scared my young mind. Sydney Kentridge had a swagger and fearlessness that thrilled me. His demeanour was an antidote against the special-branch bullies in whose hands I had suffered for three months.

The judge appeared to be listening, but after the hearing, in the late afternoon, he dismissed the motion to quash the indictment and ordered that the trial proceed the following morning at 10am. Mr Kentridge asked for a two-week postponement in which to consult with us on the merits of the charges. He drew attention to our prolonged solitary detention and pointed out that there had been no opportunity to prepare on the merits of the trial. The judge was unmoved. He refused a two-week postponement but did agree to two to three days. It would not have been possible for Ivor and Sydney to hear our sixteen accused people, let alone their witnesses, within that limited time. They were left with no choice but to withdraw as counsel.

The judge set the trial to proceed the following morning. We were facing a capital offence and yet we had no counsel. Our attorney, GM Pitje, briefed Advocate Jack Unterhalter SC to argue a postponement for preparation. The judge heard argument and refused the postponement. Unterhalter SC advised us and the judge that he had no option but to withdraw from the hearing. Unfazed, the judge adjourned the hearing to 10am the following morning. GM briefed Davis SC to appear and seek a postponement in order to consult in preparation for trial. Judge Cille declined the application and ordered that the trial would commence at 12 midday of the same day with or without counsel. Our attorney, too, withdrew.

At 12pm the court resumed. We stood in the dock in the Old Synagogue without legal defence. The judge sat with a panel of two assessors. Harwood SC rose and put the charges to us. Each one in turn, we pleaded not guilty. Just after me, Dakile Madumo, accused number seven, was asked to plead. He pleaded guilty. A chill ran down all our spines. In the few days that we were together, we had debated our stance on how to plead. We would plead not guilty. Guidance had come from Simon Brander, accused number three, a PAC veteran of the 1960 anti-pass campaign. 'We must plead not guilty,' he had emphasised. 'We do not acknowledge the legitimacy of the political crimes they accuse us of nor of their state or courts.' He went on to explain: 'We may have done the things they say we have done, but that does not make us guilty. We have a right to resist our oppression. We have a duty to organise ourselves and seek to overthrow their state. Therefore, it is not for us to help them prove any of the offences.'

After Madumo's guilty plea, the state counsel paused for a few minutes in the hushed courtroom. To our collective relief he then said: 'My Lord, please enter a plea of not guilty. The state is obliged to prove the guilt of the accused despite his plea.' The remaining accused pleaded not guilty. In a moment, the first state witness took the stand. Our trial was under way and each of us had to fend for ourselves.

There was a final line of defence to Judge Peet Cille's hurried disposition. I did not know the defence existed then. As the accused, we thought we had run out of options and were obliged to resort to our own defence. What we should have done, but didn't know we could, was refuse to proceed with the trial without legal defence. We should have declined to cross-examine witnesses or testify in our defence. We should have stayed in attendance but ignored the proceedings. We had legal counsel but were effectively denied their services. Had the judge gone ahead, even under apartheid a mistrial would have ensued.

Fifty years on, as a seasoned judge, I have recently read the record of our trial. Our gratitude is due to the digital Historical Papers archives of the University of the Witwatersrand. Someone made it her business (I have a hunch it was a woman; ordinarily, they tend to be the keepers and primary custodians of human conscience) to preserve a part of the vast account of our prolonged resistance. The collection of political trial records is as impressive as it is instructive. It boasts dozens of digitised records of political trials from the 1960s to 1980s. I recommend them to the young, and old, who want a glimpse of the repressive response of a government that had become unhinged from the people it was meant to serve.

I could almost say the trial was rather boring because the evidence of state witnesses was predictable. The witnesses were many and they had all been well coached. There was not much in their evidence that we could truthfully contest. We directed our untutored cross-examination at over-statements about planned violent conduct. The witnesses' brief was to make the PAC underground cells look bloodthirsty and ready to kill every *impimpi* and every white citizen. Even student gatherings where fiery demands for freedom and equality were made were rendered as high treason. But, to take on the witness and put the record straight was tricky. To do that you had to place yourself at the crime scene. I did that often: 'I put it to you that at the meeting I only said we demand freedom. I never said we are prepared to kill for it.'

Like most political trialists of the time, we were probably guilty as charged. The PAC and ANC had openly espoused the armed struggle after they were banned in 1960. In fact, shortly thereafter, the Azanian People's Liberation Army (APLA) was formed; so, too, Umkhonto weSizwe (MK). None could join or further the activities of either of the two liberation movements and credibly deny its broad design to overthrow the state. That was where the state witness called Mr X came in. He would be a smart, high-ranking former member of the liberation movement who understood and could competently describe its revolutionary or treasonable designs. He attested to the adoption of the armed struggle and how it linked to domestic underground structures. Judges could not take judicial notice of the armed struggle, so Mr X had to tell them. He normally testified from political trial to political trial of a given liberation movement. The PAC trials had one or more Mr X's, and the ANC trials did, too. Perhaps the most celebrated Mr X was the unmasked Bruno Mtolo of Rivonia Trial fame.

The Mr X in our trial took the witness stand to describe the operations of the Pan-Africanist Congress in Lesotho. He unveiled the instructions that Potlako Leballo, the secretary general of the PAC, had given to task force leaders from different regions of South Africa. His evidence connected the underground cell structures to the overall armed struggle plans of the PAC. In this way the state sought to show that we were part of a wider conspiracy. Mr X had met only John Nkosi, accused number two in our trial. Both had attended a briefing session of task force leaders. Our Mr X went on to testify in several PAC trials throughout the country.

On the sidelines of the trial there were many happier diversions. The print media reported on the hearing daily. The newscasts of indigenous language radio stations of the SABC called us terrorists and snakes whose heads deserved to be crushed. Our families saw matters differently. They pledged solidarity by their unfailing presence at the hearing. Mercifully, the trial ran during winter school holidays so my teacher parents were able to attend every day. Most importantly, in my mind anyway, my mother brought plenty of her tastiest food, which I shared with other accused.

But that was not all. In the gallery sat a white lady of my mother's age. I did not know her name and had never met her. She attended the proceedings daily. During lunch breaks she brought me hot soup or hot chocolate in a flask. I shared these treats with my comrades. I came to know that she was Mrs Hain, but I still wondered what her interest was in a trial of this kind. Apparently, she was a member of the Black Sash, and I also learned that she had a son about my age, Peter, who attended Pretoria Boys High School. I was fifteen years old and here I was, on trial. Mrs Hain cried often when she spoke to me. Her disgust for apartheid and racism was obvious. She brought us sustenance every day. She once asked me what I liked eating most. I asked for dessert in the form of chocolate, so every day after that chocolate was what she brought me. The police frequently swore at her in Afrikaans within our earshot. After I was sent to jail I never saw Mrs Hain again. Her son Peter may not have gone to Robben Island as I did, but he became a stirring soul in the anti-apartheid movement of the 1980s in the United Kingdom. He was a big part of the sports boycott against the racist regime.

Later, Peter Hain became a Labour MP and served as a government minister in the Blair cabinet. As these things go, Peter is now Lord Hain and sits in the House of Lords of the United Kingdom for the Labour Party. He hosted me on a recent visit to Lords. He indeed looked the part of a right honourable lord. I could not resist drawing his attention to the irony of a solid lefty turning peer. He shot right back, saying, 'Yes indeed, my Lord, the deputy chief justice of the Republic of South Africa.' The banter ended right there.

In 2015 Peter Hain came to our country to make a documentary on the present state of our democracy and the Marikana shooting. He found time to visit me at the Constitutional Court. I was anxious to know if his mother was well. 'Dikgang, my mother is still alive and well. She sends her fond regards from the United Kingdom. Here is your chocolate from her.'

Even in the worst twist and turns, there are magical moments. Here was one – abundant compassion and solidarity from an unlikely source.

It took no more than ten days to try sixteen undefended accused people. On 2 July 1963, the presiding judge delivered the judgment. He ordered us to stand as he delivered it. Only he spoke. His two white male assessors were quiet. They must have agreed with him. He spoke many words about each of the accused. He convicted fourteen of the sixteen of us and discharged two, about whom the witnesses had said nothing. I heard him say, 'Accused number six, you are found guilty of the main count of sabotage.' Then: 'Do you have anything to say for yourselves in mitigation before sentence?'

The matter had arisen in our cell discussions the evening before. We had agreed that it would be futile to enter a plea in mitigation. By then we knew that the minimum sentence we faced was a five-year jail term without the option of a suspended sentence or a fine. Simply, we were well and truly on our way to prison. And we had come to know what the courts around us had been doing to accused people like us. They had been meting out harsh punishment. The going rate seemed between five years and life imprisonment.

In a parallel PAC political trial, eighteen students from the Hebron College, near Pretoria, stood trial on similar charges. Their hearing was in the Palace of Justice before Judge Hill. They were represented by *pro deo* counsel Advocate Michael Traub. None of that helped. Dimake Malepe, accused number one in that trial, an eighteen-year-old Standard 10 student, was sentenced to life imprisonment. His co-accused and fellow students, Anthony Suze and George Moffat, each earned themselves fifteen years' imprisonment. The rest of the student accuseds' sentences ranged between ten and five years' imprisonment. In the Supreme Court, Pretoria, another trial of young PAC comrades from Mamelodi was swiftly wrapped up just before ours. We read about their sentences in the *Pretoria News*. They were treated most harshly. Judge Ludorf sentenced three of the regional leaders, Ike Mthimunye, Chips Chibane and Philemon Tefo, to life imprisonment. The remaining accused, like Solomon Phetla, Bennie Ntoele, Nick Kekana and Abel Chiloane, were sentenced within a range of ten to 20 years' imprisonment.

So the signs were clear. We knew what to expect and we braced ourselves for the worst. Neither youthfulness nor absence of violent conduct would come to our rescue. It did not escape us that the regime had gone on a warpath to smash the broader liberation movement and the courts obliged. In 1960 Robert Sobukwe had been sentenced to three years' imprisonment for his leadership role in the PAC anti-pass campaign that led to the Sharpeville massacre. His co-leaders had sentences between twelve months and two years. In 1962 Nelson Mandela was charged for his underground activities in the ANC, which ended in his conviction and sentence of five years' imprisonment. These were unusual and harsh sentences for their times. Their crimes were no more than political dissent without any overt acts of violence. None of these sentences forewarned activists, nor the country, of the lurking spate of repression from 1963 onwards. The going currency had changed beyond recognition.

A plea of mitigation would have been inappropriate. None of us wanted to invite an unduly harsh punishment and yet we could not, nor did we want to, display regret and remorse to our oppressors and the broader populace. There was no room for an apology. We could not possibly disclaim our duty and commitment to overthrow the racist oligarchy. 'Our and other political trials,' Simon Brander had lectured us, 'are not legal issues. They are political battles. The regime uses the law to oppress. We must call on mass mobilisation to depose them.' He concluded: 'So we cannot apologise to or ask for mercy from our enemy.' The argument convinced us all and helped shore up our courage, we the fickle and young, who wanted nothing more than to go back home and to school.

'Accused number six, do you have anything to say in mitigation?'

'No, my Lord.'

As I sat back down, I heard a voice from the back of the court. It was my father, up in the public gallery. 'My Lord, I want to testify in mitigation.'

I felt extremely awkward about this. My dad needed a lecture from Comrade Simon Brander. We should not beg for mercy from the enemy. My dad should know this. Thankfully, my father only asked the court to impose the lightest sentence possible. I was a very gifted child, he said, who liked parading his intelligence. He said that he worked away from home during the week, and that if he were at home, he would have made sure that I concentrated on my studies and not political meetings.

No other accused pleaded in mitigation.

Cille directed us all to stand. 'Accused number one, Kgalabi Jafta Masemola, you are sentenced to life imprisonment. Accused number two, Klaas Mashishi – eight years' imprisonment. Accused number three, Simon Brander – five years' imprisonment. Accused number four, John Nkosi, you are sentenced to life imprisonment. And accused number six, Dikgang Moseneke – ten years' imprisonment. The devastation ran down the track as each accused was damned, up to accused number sixteen, Mark Shinners – ten years' 'imprisonment'.

'Court adjourned!' the judge bellowed, and with that his red robes disappeared, followed by his two assessors, who shuffled meekly behind him.

We burst into a loud salute in unison: '*Izwe Lethu – iAfrika*! Long live the spirit of Robert Mangaliso Sobukwe! Long live the revolution!'

Some family members in the full gallery cried hysterically. Others joined in the triumphant salutes and slogans.

CHAPTER 9

Robben Island, here we come …

The euphoria was short-lived. Uniformed policemen with machine-guns surrounded the wooden dock. They ordered us out through the side door. They handcuffed our hands behind our bodies and shackled us in leg-irons. We were forced into a sealed police truck. The convoy, led by motorbikes with flashing blue lights and blaring sirens, was under way. When we reached the prison, a massive wooden door swung open in front of us with no visible human hand. The truck drove in and the door slammed closed behind us.

As we disembarked, a prison warder shouted, 'Welcome to New Lock!' in a distinctly unfriendly and sarcastic voice. We had stayed in the prison during the course of the trial, but this was different. Now we were entering the ultra-maximum-security section, the same place where judicial executions took place. My heart raced, although unduly. None of us had been committed to death. Our judge had not invoked that horrid incantation 'I sentence you to death. You shall hang by your neck until you die.' In one of my many high school readings, I remembered an article in *Drum* magazine on what a judge said when he imposed the death penalty. I wondered why he had to add the morbid bit about hanging by the neck, but the answer to my juvenile pondering had to wait for later. It was only in law school that I learned that judicial punishment must not only fit the crime but it must also be precise. If not, the state may resort to what tickles its fancy in each execution – death in a gas chamber or by a firing squad or poison or torture.

'All line up, face the wall and take off your clothes,' a voice commanded.

On 2 July we were well into winter, and the afternoon was cold and overcast. We all stood naked. I had never seen an adult naked before. The instructions continued. 'Every new prisoner washes and shaves. The showers are on your right and the razors are in a bowl nearby.' In no time our shivering bodies were dripping and our heads were cleanly shaven. Were there towels in prison, I wondered. No. We stood naked and wet.

To our left were piles of items of prison clothing. You had no choice of size. Seemingly a choice was redundant. Their clothing was styled to fit all. The items were massive in size, certainly way too big for a young lad like me, even a growing one. The pants came without belts but there were pieces of long cloth sewn onto the waistline. Mine went twice around my tiny waist. The shirts were collarless and crinkled. I supposed it was prudent to save inmates the bother of keeping a collar sanitised. Similarly, it would have been tricky to iron the shirts. You could add an army brown jersey and open-toed sandals. These appeared to be optional. We chose the sandals and the jersey. It was very cold. The prison did not issue underwear nor socks.

The next order was that we surrender all personal belongings. I had none save for the little pile of clothes I'd left on the floor when I had had to submit to the freezing shower. Those who had them gave in their identity documents, cash, watches and jewellery, pens, books, toiletries and other personal effects. Gone were the external markers of material well-being. From then on the amenities or perhaps the lack of them was even. We all shared the lowest denominators.

We were issued with a prison kit: an aluminium plate with dents everywhere, a cobbled coffee mug, a spoon, a felt mat and three grey-black blankets. But it was what we were not given that struck home. Besides no underwear, the kit had no pyjamas. Did we sleep in the same clothes? We were not issued with a toiletries pack. How were we supposed to wash our faces and brush our teeth?

We looked around at each other in our over-sized prison garb and clean-shaven heads. No one had the courage to say a word. We were in an ominous transition. My will had been supplanted by their will. I was a prisoner and would be for the next ten years. Was this a fair example of an average day in prison? I wondered. Would the prison break up our group and spread us across cells of hardened criminals? That, more than anything else, struck the fear of God into me. What was more, that and all other vital decisions were not mine but theirs.

When the kit process was done, one of the African warders shouted: '*Two, two umthetho wasejele!*' We marched in pairs, each carrying his prison issue, along a long corridor with many gates to pass through. Each gate was manned by a warder. Habitually, the warder who led us would say '*Dankie hek*' to get the gate opened. After many winding corridors and stairs we were all put into an empty communal cell which had apparently been cleared to hold us. Prison doors are never closed gently and quietly. As they banged closed, we were all frozen by the deep discovery that we were indeed convicted captives. And yet we were silently relieved that we had not been strewn across ominous prison cells. We were still together. We might have been stripped bare and cold and then dressed in strange apparel, but at the end of the day, we had each other. When you walk a difficult road, you do well to have a companion at sunset.

One of my naughty erstwhile classmates – it could have been Absalom Nkwe or Mike – came apart laughing and pointing at me. 'Hey, *s'boshwa*, hey, prisoner, your attire is crazy. Look at your wrap-around pants and skinny head.' The jokes rippled across the cell as we laughed out loud at ourselves and at each other in our new, awkward look. The laughter was merciful. My tensed-up jaw eased and the stiffness below my neck let up. The cell was quite big. It was meant to keep a much larger number than ours. We randomly picked sleeping bays the size of a felt mat. You had to place the mat on the floor with one blanket over the mat and two over your body. Before long all of us had taken refuge under the blankets.

The following morning, I rose feeling stronger and certainly less afraid than the previous day. 'Mike,' I said, 'I am no longer a ten-year prisoner. My sentence is one day less. I am left with nine years, 364 days.' After our first prison breakfast we were ordered out to the reception for the admission paperwork. We spent the morning in a queue. They took down personal details. You had to rehearse your family tree. We submitted to fingerprinting and photographs. The process matched slave logbooks. You had to drop your pants and lift your shirt and open your mouth wide because they wanted to record every scar, deformity, unusual feature or teeth pattern. The session of the day ended with a prolonged medical examination. It came across more as a bodily data-gathering than an effort to detect or exclude illness. Then I did not know as fact what they were recording. Now I do, thanks to the National Archive, which recently gave me access to my prison records. The detail of my physical description is truly chilling. It displays a remarkable disregard for personal privacy in favour of a single-minded objective to know your enemy and captive down to the finest detail.

We had no idea how long we would be kept at Pretoria Central Prison. It turned out to be only for a few days. During the second week of July, at the crack of dawn we were woken up, handcuffed hand to hand and chained leg to leg. Like Siamese twins, we were forcibly attached to each other. We quickly learned that for everything you did, you needed your chained colleague to do the same. You had to walk in unison. If one stepped out of sync, both of you fell down. You had to use your cuffed arm in sync. The more you pulled the cuffs away from your partner, the tighter they clamped around both your wrists. We had to consult each other like this: 'Mike, may we stand and stretch our arms?' He had to oblige. 'Dikgang, may we walk to the water bucket? I am thirsty.' And so we did. I even had to go along when Mike wanted to pass water.

Chained in pairs, we had to negotiate the little steel steps up into the back of the yellow closed police truck. It was a very chilly morning. They never formally told us that they were trucking us to Robben Island. We worked this out through an unguarded conversation in Afrikaans, when our captors talked about stopping over in Ficksburg and reaching Cape Town the following afternoon late.

The trip was horrible. The back of the van was porous and the canopy was made of steel mesh. The icy breeze blew right through the steel caging and it froze us to the bone. The warders had tossed a few blankets at us, and placed a drum of drinking water and a bucket for toilet use in the back. With the movement of the vehicle the water drum tipped and water slopped out, soaking most of the blankets. The security convoy never stopped for nearly ten hours as it charged towards Ficksburg in the Orange Free State.

We might have been cold outside but inside we were warm. We were set to serve our long prison terms together on Robben Island. Hopefully, it would be a prison standing on open and generous grounds. That had to be better than a claustrophobic inland maximum-security prison. The maximum-security class of facilities permitted a prisoner a 30-minute walkabout in the courtyard in the morning and another in the afternoon. That was the sum total of natural light we could hope to see in a day in New Lock. There was a more felicitous reason to cheer up, too. We had come to know that there were other political prisoners on Robben Island. At that time, in July 1963, the most significant of those detainees was Robert Sobukwe himself.

The reason for Sobukwe's detention on Robben Island boggled the mind. After the 1960 anti-pass campaign, he served three years' imprisonment with hard labour. While we were in solitary confinement during April 1963, parliament passed the so-called Sobukwe extension clause. This was an extraordinary piece of legislation. It was not a law of general application. It targeted the liberty of one person. The law decreed that Sobukwe must be kept in continued detention, even though his prison term had ended and he had not been tried and convicted of an offence. The Sobukwe extension clause was renewable every year by parliament. The PAC and the ANC had both been declared unlawful organisations and the government was on a path of political repression. To her credit, politician Helen Suzman stood up in parliament and opposed the measure most strenuously. She was the only opposition member in parliament. She bemoaned the fact that a law had imposed an egregious and unlimited breach of a citizen's personal liberty without a fair trial and a finite punishment.

We spent the night at Ficksburg prison. The prison accommodation was comfortable and certainly better than the truck ride. We were also untied from the shackles. The dinner was good – the best we had had, in fact, since our conviction. Next day, again at the crack of dawn, we were placed under restraint once more and loaded back onto the trucks. The convoy set off to Cape Town, into the Cape winter rain and wet wind, which did not let up as we drove into the docks around 5pm.

Robben Island had a quay of its own marked with the prison service crest with green and gold colours. This was my maiden trip to the Cape. Also, I had never seen the sea before. There it was as we got off the truck, chained and manacled together. The sheer size of the Atlantic Ocean terrified me no end. Even to my untutored eye, the sea appeared rough and furious that late afternoon. It looked imperious, in charge. In the distance waves leapt high into the air and came down crashing and roaring. Everything else looked so minute in comparison, even *Dias*, the boat we were about to board. The contingent of warders who were waiting on the docks for us, armed with machine-guns, swiftly surrounded us and shepherded us nearer to the boat. The steel jetty onto the boat was rocking side to side and looked treacherous. Luckily, Mike and I remembered that we had to walk in perfect unison if we were not to end up in the sea even before we got onto the boat.

As we stepped on board the *Dias*, a warder stood on the deck near the narrow steel stairway leading down to the hull. Each chained pair had to make their way down into the hull as he screamed relentlessly: 'Come, come terrorists! You can't defeat our state! We are simply going to dump you in the sea today!' He pushed and held our heads down and hurled us below, causing us to miss the stairs. One after the other we tumbled and crashed below into the hull. The warder laughed as each pair stumbled clumsily and fell.

The ride to the island was very rough and unstable. The boat leapt up and crashed hard onto the waves and the swell moved the vessel violently from side to side. My stomach rose high into my chest and many of my comrades threw up into brown paper packets. I did not. Perhaps fortunately, I had skipped the brown bread lunch so my stomach must have been empty. I feared the boat might sink. We would certainly drown because we were chained. The thought that I would die manacled got my heart throbbing even harder. I hated the thought of dying fettered. Then the warder who had promised us death came down into the hull. He hit those who were throwing up on the floor with his wooden baton. 'You god-forsaken terrorists, you Poqos, you deserve to die!' he shouted as the boat crashed and lurched. His last act of terror was to open a few portholes in the hull, which allowed the seawater to gush in and thoroughly soak us all. This only made him laugh boisterously. 'You are now all going to drown!' We, township urchins who couldn't swim, cried wildly. I remember calling out for my mother to help me. The water helped wash the vomit off the floor of the hull, at least, and although the boat rocked hard, it did not sink.

The turbulence lasted only for 30 minutes or so and then everything turned placid. We could hear the engine running and finally the revving slowed. The *Dias* was docking at Robben Island. We emerged from the hull to find that the rain had stopped, too, and as we stood on the deck we could smell the humid freshness in the air. There was light mist around us, and in the distance objects were invisible. A fog horn went off, making a big booming sound. As it quietened I could hear the varied sounds of seabirds calling and crying – just like you'd hear in movies made on islands. There was something calming and reassuring about these sounds as we disembarked. A man with an officer's baton under his armpit ordered that our shackles be removed immediately. The scoundrel warder on the boat ride stood by, quiet and now well mannered. I hated him but had no courage to finger him to the officer. In time, I came to know him and his twin brother as the Kleinhans brothers.

The shackles were off. Peace had returned to us. We were safe on Robben Island.

CHAPTER 10

Wheelbarrows and handguns: The first six months

Early the next morning, I woke up to the roar of the Atlantic Ocean. The sound of breaking waves overwhelmed the tiny island. The outside air was chilly but crisp. Breakfast was served at 6am outside on a quadrangle near the kitchen. It was as meagre as it was predictable – soft porridge served in a dented aluminium dish, two spoons of brown sugar and brewed black coffee in a mug with the usual dimples. Nearly 475 fellow prisoners filed past the serving window of the kitchen for their helpings. They emerged from sections A, B and C. We came out of section C – Cell C1, in particular, where we had retired the night before. Our landing had been soft and welcoming. The inmates we found in the cell were new themselves. They had arrived over the last month to three months. They gave us a quick rundown before we went to sleep. All the prisoners in the sections had been convicted for activities of the PAC or ANC and had been drafted in from all over the country. Drafts of new inmates came in weekly.

There were a small number of common-law prisoners on the island, but they were housed separately in a temporary jail known as Zinc section – no doubt because it was constructed out of sheets of corrugated iron. Its inmates were meant to tend to the labour and domestic needs of the warder populace on the island. Warders lived with their families in staff quarters and had a semblance of social life beyond their prison duties. The inmates worked in their homes and gardens. Others did public duties like refuse removal, or working on the roads and parks. Another small group served as chefs at the officers' mess. The bulk were deployed in the so-called building group. Under supervision, they built new prison sections D, E, F and a hospital; and they extended the reception offices and constructed more single cells.

The prison observed strict seclusion between us and the other prisoners. They slept and worked separately from us. The briefing from our comrades suggested that the government feared the prospect of politicised hardened offenders. They might be more ready than we were to divert their daring and violent ways towards political objectives. The authorities wanted to forestall politically fuelled prison uprisings across the country or other bold escapades outside prison, so they sought to prevent our revolutionary mission, like cancer, from spreading. They reasoned that every contaminated one of us had to be marooned on a little island. They cared not that political prisoners might further infect one another. Their bother was to prevent the malady from spreading beyond the island. Another concern of the authorities was that as common-law prisoners were entitled to frequent visits from family and friends, these could become couriers of messages to underground structures of the liberation movement.

This fear of the apartheid regime was not entirely irrational. Whatever it was, we were happy and thankful to be kept together and separate from other convicts. The unintended result of the separation was to lend us the room to be cohesive and supportive of one another. We shared ways of overcoming the emotional stress of imprisonment. We took unmitigated advantage of our captivity as we reared faithful followers and leaders of our revolution.

That very first night, we learned that political prisoners, too, had to work. From Monday to Friday, week after week, every inmate had to perform hard labour. No prisoner stayed locked up in a cell. Everyone worked in a group somewhere on the island. This was welcome news. Until this point, we had lived locked up. The outdoor cold or sunshine would be better than vegetating in a sombre lock-up. The briefing gave me a considerable lift, and so I approached my first morning at my new abode for the next decade with a glimmer of hope.

But first we had to submit to admission paperwork. After breakfast, the new arrivals were called by name from the breakfast quadrangle. We were marched in twos (*'Two two mthetho wasejele'*) to the reception. We submitted to a head-to-toe medical examination, which, for me, yielded nothing abnormal. At the time it mattered not one bit to me that I had a clean bill of health, but in retrospect, I realise I needed my young, lithe and healthy body to see me through the most difficult task I had ever undertaken. I had to survive and overcome ten years of captivity. By midday I had my prison card in my hand. It read: Prisoner number: 491/63; Name: Dikgang Ernest Moseneke; Crime: Sabotage; Sentence: 10 years imprisonment – hard labour; Date of sentence: 2 July 1963; Date of release: 1 July 1973; Group classification: D.

Next an officer addressed us briefly. We must obey the command of an officer at all times. The prison card must be kept safely and produced on demand by an officer. The following day we would be allocated a working group. The classification D was the lowest on a scale of A to D of prison privileges. We were entitled to one letter and one visit every six months and had no other privileges. 'On good behaviour,' the officer said, 'you may be promoted up to A group.' He continued, 'Your meal classification is F.' He paused and then explained. The A diet was reserved for white women and B for white males. The C diet was reserved for Coloured and Indian females; and D, males of that race class. African women (he called them 'Bantu', as the government chose to label indigenous African people) were given the C diet, and the males of that race class were given the F diet.

Our induction was done. Now I knew. My hope to write to my parents and report on where I was imprisoned had been dashed. I quickly worked out that I could write to them and possibly receive my first letter and visit only in December 1963.

A new day broke. We were then led out of the communal cell to the kitchen. It stood prominent and removed from the four blocks of communal cells named A, B, C and D. We filed past the serving window to collect the F breakfast. The pitch-black coffee might have been strong and bitter, but it was redeemed by its inviting aroma. Older prisoners nearby softly alerted us newcomers to the ruling etiquette at meals. When you came across a worm in the porridge or other meal, you must swallow and keep quiet. Some quipped that worms were our only and best protein supply. I managed a few scoops, but I have to confess it took a good few days for me to make peace with our forced protein supply.

After breakfast, we were added to the quarry working group. Barring a few, most of the 475 or so political prisoners were placed in the quarry group. We went out to the quarry pit with about 20 armed guards under the command of a tall, well-built man with a boyish red face. This was Warrant Officer Delport. He spoke with a slight lisp and rolled his r's with a Boland accent. He could follow a dash of English but spoke only in Afrikaans. His green cat-like eyes were inexpressive and dull. They betrayed a slow brain. His mainly young armed guards were somewhat nervous. They carried handguns in holsters and automatic rifles around their necks. The guards almost never talked to prisoners except to give terse commands. Delport's first chore of the day was to count over a hundred rows of fours of the prisoners he had to march to the quarry and confirm the number with a recording officer at the exit gate. Presumably, at the end of the working day he had to return the same number of us. Once we had filed up in fours, Delport had to count in fours from front to back. He repeated the counting four to six times most mornings, amidst giggles from the younger prisoners. Adding fours was not the big warrant officer's strength. As I stood in my row, my little brain told me I could be useful to him if he only asked me to add up for him.

The working place was a quarry pit. It was located about four kilometres from the prison. Every working day we had to walk escorted between the prison and the quarry. The rows of four formed a snaking column of human beings moving in the same direction. The warders preferred us keeping a neat, brisk march. We soon learned that senior comrades did not oblige. They walked along in casual fashion and chatted amongst themselves as they went. They did not tell the warders so but their conduct spoke volumes: their demeanour said that they were not going to be regimented by their political foes. The prison had constructed a walking tunnel from the prison to the quarry, which was built with steel poles and reinforced mesh wire. The armed guards walked outside the mesh and so they could not do much to hasten or control affairs inside the tunnel.

For me, the morning walk to the quarry was energising. For one thing, it was scenic. Out of the prison precincts, the island's environment was pristine. It teemed with plant, bird and animal life, and there was always a crisp breeze blowing – unwelcome in winter but a relief in summer. The sea was visible during much of the walk and the steel wire tunnel did not detract from the view. I couldn't help wondering why our captors thought we had to walk caged in that way. Speaking for myself, I was not about to run into the Atlantic Ocean and try to swim to the Bloubergstrand or Table Bay. For one thing you would be shot within a few paces of the dash, and if you did succeed in reaching the sea, the Atlantic would swallow you up within minutes, as it had done to at least two ships that had been wrecked just off the island. If the sea did not take you, the sharks would surely tear you apart.

If you were a new arrival, the morning yielded new acquaintances. We lived in different communal cells, each holding 60 or so people. With care, you could meet other comrades during the walk. Most had fascinating tales to tell about their family circumstances, townships or villages of origin, events surrounding their arrest and detention, their political affiliation and their take on the way forward for the revolution. It mattered little whether the discussion was had with a member of the Unity Movement, the PAC or the ANC. All sides brought to the fore an interesting view of the history of the struggle and its future prospects.

The quarry was located on the north-western edge of the island. Only a road separated it from the ocean. It was a very wide, deep, gaping pit out of which, over the years, tons and tons of blue slate had been extracted. Its closeness to the sea allowed so much underground seepage that it was necessary to pump the water out before the mining operations started. The work was treacherous and not for the faint-hearted. Massive slices of blue slate had to be cut out of the pit. Prisoners were required to drill a line of holes into the edge of the fixed rock and to plug the drilled holes with tempered

97

steel chisels. Another work party would pound the chisels with six-pound hammers until the rock cracked right down and was severable from the fixed rock. After all this there was the risk of the severed slab sliding down and being smashed below and so yet another party had to manage and secure the soft landing of the slate to the bottom.

There were less demanding roles at the quarry. There was a select group who were trained to be masons. With a four-pound hammer and a chisel, they chipped and dressed big slabs into foundation or building stones. Within a week or so of our arrival, more gifted comrades like Jafta Kgalabi (Jeff) Masemola, Anthony Suze and Dimake Malepe were issued with masks and absorbed into the masonry work group. There was a big and busy blacksmith operation to shape, sharpen and temper the chisels. It did not take long before Uncle Jeff became the assistant blacksmith. He had incredible guts and the gift of using his hands creatively.

There were two lowly chores at the quarry. One was pushing a wheelbarrow carting stone from one end of the quarry operations to another. It called for no skill or creativity. Yours was to render a delivery service of medium-sized to small rocks. You had to do as you were told and nothing else. Another chore was crushing smaller stones into concrete or gravel stones. For this job you were issued with a four-pound hammer and a round rubber ring. You had to sit on the ground, place stones within the rubber ring and crush bigger stones into concrete stones or fine gravel stones. I vacillated between pushing the wheelbarrow and crushing stones. The local Afrikaans quip went: '*By die kwarrie maak jy groot klippe klein, klein klippe kleiner en kleiner klippe fyner*' (At the quarry you make big stones small, small stones smaller and smaller stones finer). The quarry was a mad operation to get back at political prisoners, I thought. I suppose the prison had to manufacture hard labour. And that was it.

The treacherous quarry mining and stone crushing was not entirely cynical. Its products were carted away to the building sites of the new prison section, hospital and reception. Bluntly, we were deployed to produce material to build the prison in which we and our compatriots would be locked up. Seen that way, our roles at the quarry made us complicit in our own imprisonment.

The quarry was not always a placid place of work. It was a cauldron of racial and political tension between us and our minders. No black (African, Coloured and Indian) warders were posted on the island. It seemed they were not trusted to mind us with sufficient rigour. The white male warders were hand-picked. They shared antipathy and hatred towards political prisoners and they were aggressive and hostile. They openly called us terrorists, communists and 'the enemy'. For good measure some would hurl the *kaffir* word. Many warders were given to smashing our skulls with their wooden batons. Some demanded to be addressed, not by their official rank, but by the word *baas*. They resorted to stern orders in Afrikaans and demanded that they be replied to only in Afrikaans. They appeared to be buoyed by the arms they carried, and they sought to bully us to make our prison stay hellish and unbearable.

For the first year or so, their favourite torment was to charge you for failing to carry out a lawful instruction or refusing to work. When a warder decided to charge you, he would demand your prison card. You were obliged to surrender it. When the working group returned to prison, he would frogmarch you to the office of the head of prison. The head had the power to try to punish you summarily. The prisoner was always in constant jeopardy because it was the warder's word against the prisoner's. The warder needed to say no more than that he had ordered you to work diligently and that you had not obeyed. The head routinely imposed a punishment called *drie maaltye*. This meant that on a non-working day you were removed from a communal cell and kept in a single cell, where you were not given the three meals of the day. The punishment was an unwelcome mixture of hunger pangs and solitude.

By December 1963, I had been on the island for almost five months and our numbers had swelled to nearly a thousand prisoners. Our stay was brutish but by no means short. The angst and discomfort came from the hard labour. The warders pushed us to work hard and the hours were long. By

4pm you were exhausted. Barring weekends, we had to do hard labour continuously from 7am to 4pm. Another distressing matter was the wanton assaults on prisoners, coupled with swearing and an expression of disdain and hatred. The warders were issued with wooden batons, although some warders preferred a *sjambok*. They viewed and treated us as terrorists and enemies of the state. About the latter they were right; we were enemies of their state. But this did not give them the right to punish us beyond the tough prison sentences we already had to bear.

As others filed for work, some prisoners queued up for medical attention at the prison hospital. This was a way of sparing yourself a day of hard labour. It did not take long before the medical treatment option became unattractive, though. At the hospital, even before you said what your ailment was, you had to take a laxative. This came in the form of the thickest and biggest dose of castor oil you can imagine. It stuck in your gullet as its hideous smell ran up your nostrils. The rumour quickly spread that it was of the variety given to racehorses. Thereafter, many went to work rather than nurse a runny tummy from morning to evening.

We had worked out that formal complaints of assault and ill-treatment during inspection by high-ranking officers did not reduce the attacks nor lead to censure or prosecution. For solace we had to look to our internal camaraderie.

As the first six months came to an end, it was not all misery. I wrote my first letter to my parents. As were others in my draft, I was issued with a single A4 lined sheet of foolscap paper and a finger-long pencil. You had one shot to write the letter. You had to do it without a rubber and within one page. Scarce resources do concentrate the mind. My first letter was without error and ended within the one page. You had to write in English or Afrikaans, the only languages the warders in the censor's office could follow. No indigenous languages were allowed. This was the rule until the prison recruited a warder named Jordaan. He spoke and read isiXhosa in an indigenous accent which he must have learned from farm labourers during his upbringing. His mastery of the language went well beyond the swear words so many white people of the time resorted to and nothing else. Many prisoners jokingly hoped their isiXhosa letters would be censored on a Monday. On Mondays Jordaan's chubby round cheeks seemed to sag and the red bulges under his narrow grey eyes appeared slightly swollen. With this rather ruddy complexion and bloodshot eyes, closer proximity and his stale breath betrayed his indulgent weekends.

The rest of the vernaculars remained out of bounds. The censor's office read every letter from and to a prisoner and blotted out what they did not like. The black marker they used was pretty effective. Not even a keen look at the letter into the sun showed the blacked-out words. Yours was to wonder and wonder what your family or friends wanted to tell you.

My father wrote back saying he and my mother had been given permission to visit me in December. I had much to look forward to – seeing my parents. In the third week of December, my birthday week, I was called out of the cell for a visit. It was a bright, sunny but humid day with a clear blue sky. The sun shone hard on the lime soil with broken shiny pebbles. I was taken in a vehicle to the visit cubicles, which were near the harbour, and as we drove along the light off the chalky road surface stung my eyes. But stinging eyes was the least of my concerns. My heart started throbbing with childlike hope and joy. It must be my mother and father, I thought. As I got to the harbour I was met by Major Visser, the weekend commissioned officer on duty. He was the most benign of them all on Robben Island. He spoke to prisoners in a considerate tone and never swore as most warders did. During his turn of the morning parades, he seemed to listen to the prisoners' complaints attentively and sometimes he would revert with a report on how a complaint had been resolved.

Major Visser led me into a small office within the harbour building. My mother and father rose from their chairs and sized me up from head to toe. Their frames had gone smaller, I thought; they had become much thinner than when I last saw them. My mother was only 37 but she appeared pale and even younger than her age. At 41, my father still looked boyish, with his dark face, high cheek-bones and tapering chin. This was the first time they had seen me in the dirty green prison garb. My shorts were big and loose and the collarless shirt hung from my tiny shoulders below my long neck and shaven head.

The officer said: 'The visit will last 30 minutes only.' He did not say that he was allowing me a face-to-face or contact visit, to which I was not entitled. A normal visit for a group D inmate like me should have been in a cubicle in which the prisoner and the visitor were separated by bullet-proof glass and the conversation was through a speaker-phone. A warder could listen in to the conversation and could record it, if he so chose. The cubicles were known to be wired. No political prisoner ventured an incriminating or reckless exchange in a cubicle.

I looked at my parents and just about managed a smile. I had survived six months on the island. What bemused me was the difference in their responses. My father burst into tears. My mother walked towards me, reciprocated the smile and embraced me tightly. She did not shed a tear. Instead she turned and admonished my father. 'Oupa,' she said (a term of endearment we in our household had heard her use from our childhood), 'your crying does not help at all. We should not weaken him. Dikgang needs strength.' It hurt deeply to see my father being anything but his strong-willed and stern self. I quickly reassured them that I was coping, healthy and benefiting from the protection and solidarity of my fellow political prisoners. I told them I had applied to be allowed to continue my Junior Certificate (Standard 8) studies from January 1964. My dad's eyes started flickering somewhat hopefully.

My mother had something different and urgent on her mind. 'Major, may I please feed my son? This is his birthday month.' Even as she asked, she whipped out of her handbag a bulging silver-foil wrapper. Inside there was a whole brown-fried chicken and fresh bread rolls. The prison regulations were clear. No prisoner was allowed to eat anything but prescribed prison food. Major Visser stood there but said neither yes nor no. His face turned slightly pale. Right then nothing was going to stand in the way of my mother's design. She knew time was of the essence and so she acted with near-defiant speed. If nobody stopped me, I thought, I was not going to let

WHEELBARROWS AND HANDGUNS

the feast go. Mother and son were of one mind. We would bear the censure, if any. My father was a frozen bystander.

On a happier afternoon, many years after my return from Robben Island, we were at a family lunch at my mother's home. She adored family feasts around the table. She lived to feed her children. Her eyes lit up naughtily as her lips parted in a smile. Her prominent cheek-bones lifted as she regaled her other children and their spouses with the story. 'I was never so shocked in my life. He was as tiny as a little bird. I sat and looked at my son, Dikgang, devour a whole chicken, bones and all, in just less than ten minutes. His father and I looked on, hurting. The prison officer seemed stunned as the chicken vanished.' Then she burst into laughter, recalling how she had wrapped up the few bones remaining with the foil paper and thrown them into her handbag.

CHAPTER 11

Taming the wild beast

The repression of political activity of 1963 continued into 1964 and several years thereafter. Prosecutions against members of the PAC, ANC, Unity Movement and other progressive formations were conducted in most of the major urban centres. Draft after draft of new admissions arrived on the island and the numbers grew. They came from all four provinces, with a pre-dominance from the Eastern Cape and Transkei, Natal and Transvaal. We welcomed these new admissions. They were able to furnish us with a general update of the political climate in the country; also, more specifically, brief-ings were held on the underground activity of their liberation movements. Quickly, formal structures of the PAC and ANC sprouted on the island. They were organised prison cell by cell, overseen by a cell committee. Party struc-tures offered new arrivals a soft landing and a safe space to debrief. They helped us cope with the trauma of an arguably smashed liberation move-ment and long jail sentences, ranging from three years to life. The authorities always made it clear that we were enemies of the state and would not benefit from parole or a remission of sentence. And so every one of us had to come to terms with a long stay in prison. As more prisoners came in, the hope that apartheid would be defeated in the short term dimmed.

All the signs affirmed this assessment. News came through about further South African police raids of the PAC headquarters in Lesotho. Some activists were killed, while others were arrested and forcibly returned to South Africa.

Many activists were on the run, fleeing the country into exile. Sobukwe had been moved to the island in solitary confinement, living in a desolate home without his wife and children. In early 1964 reports of the arrest of the ANC high command on Liliesleaf Farm in Rivonia near Johannesburg reached us. Their trial was due to commence in the Old Synagogue. If anything, the liberation movements were on the run, if not tottering. Possibly they were lying prostrate. Apartheid state power seemed impossible to overcome.

We realised that help for us on the island was not going to come from anywhere else. We had to find ways to tame our hostile environment. The first collective resolution was to resist assaults and abuse by prison warders. We resolved not to submit meekly to random assaults, as was the case during the early days. We would address the warders by their titles and never by their preferred racist tag, *baas*. We agreed that a victim of assault or abuse would protest firmly and lay a formal charge with a commissioned officer. One of them made a routine inspection every morning before breakfast, calling for complaints. By the time the officer's retinue entered your cell, which each held 60 prisoners or thereabouts, you would have had to have had your cold morning shower and be dressed; your blankets would be neatly rolled in an army-style bundle. You were required to stand upright near your bundle with your prison ticket held firmly against and across your breast. As you made your complaint the officer could readily see your particulars.

As our defiance campaign set in, I remember with fondness Louis Mtshizana's reaction at the quarry to a warder who threatened to crack his skull with a wooden baton. Louis had been a practising attorney and had appeared for accused people in several political trials in the Eastern Cape. He was detained and convicted on a charge of furthering the aims of a banned organisation. His sentence of two years was mild relative to the going rate. We often teased him as one who had come to dirty the dishes on the island and disappear. He walked tall, with a swagger, even in his prison shorts. He turned to his attacker, stared at him wide-eyed and said: 'You touch me, I will sue your pants off.' That warder, and every other warder never tried to touch him again.

Another memorable incident related to Comrade Fadane from Port Elizabeth. He was a tall man, with dark, strong facial features. He wore black-rimmed spectacles and spoke with a deep voice. When a warder swung a *sjambok* towards him, Fadane turned to him and bellowed: 'I will sue you in your own court and *win* in your own court.' I liked what I heard. Mtshizana's and Fadane's responses reassured me. They reduced my fear of these violent warders. Nevertheless I wondered how this would work. We had all lost in their courts. That was why we were on the island. How could we still win in their own courts? But that did not seem to deter Mtshizana and Fadane from threatening to invoke the apartheid courts.

John Zulu was a task-force leader and revolutionary from Mamelodi in my hometown, Pretoria. He was a quiet, thoughtful person. When he did speak, he was curt and his manner ardent. One day one of the warders at the quarry promised him a hiding. His eyes narrowed into their deep sockets and his lips began quivering. Then Zulu wagged his finger at his would-be attacker, and slowly, in a heavy isiZulu accent, he said: 'This is my body. Did you hear me? This is my body. If you touch my body, I will touch your body.' The warder, although armed, backed off.

Other young activists and I caught onto that line and we all found our moments to say 'This is my body' and watch the warders back off. John Zulu's memorable line became a turning point. The line must have reached many warders and many prisoners. Many other similar skirmishes occurred but we were winning the war. Standing up to bullies does change the world. Doing nothing allows evil people to prosper. For us it was a plain claim that our bodies were inviolable. We were winning the claim to be free from torture, inhuman treatment and abuse. This was not a guarantee the apartheid state promised us but a right we asserted in defiance of them. We did not wait for a formal warranty spelled out in some deed or bill of rights. We had successfully insisted that our bodies and self-worth must be left unmolested.

As wanton assaults were receding, an even more demeaning practice persisted. It was known as *thauza*. The warders also used the word, whose source and origin within indigenous languages remains obscure. Every prisoner who returned to the prison precinct after a day's work at the quarry or other site of work had to be searched at the point of entry. The search was conducted on a large, open, uncovered field located just beyond the gate. Hundreds of us were required to stand in single-file queues of eight to ten lanes. At the head of each queue stood a warder. Each prisoner had to take off all his clothes and hold them in his hands. When your turn came, you had to give one item of clothing at a time to the warder. He would run his palms and fingers through each item and toss them onto the ground behind him. After the last item had been ferreted through, you were required to open your jaws as wide as you would for a dental inspection. Immediately thereafter the warder would shout, '*Thauza!*' This was the command to turn around in a spinning antic while lifting one leg dog-like in order to allow the warder to inspect the middle of your buttocks. You were then expected to walk past the warder's side to collect your clothing from the ground behind him, walk a few metres away and put on your clothes again.

It may be fun and games when, as we often see in the media, hundreds of women and men bare themselves for a group nude photo session. *Thauza* was no such fun. None of us could manage a smile. This was a grave ritual that had the hallmarks of captivity. It had to be observed daily against your will in full view of young and old warders and multiple other prisoners. You had to submit to it on hot and clammy days, on cold wintry afternoons, under a shivering drizzle or in the face of the howling Cape Doctor spitting blinding sea sand.

Thauza was a hideous leveller. Young teenagers, and there were many more besides me, had to face up to the nakedness of men of their fathers' age and older. Leaders in the movement had to bare it alongside us, their foot soldiers. The smarter and the braver amongst us had to stand in naked humiliation, too, as they waited their turn to perform the bow-legged tumble. I often wondered what purpose this heinous search yielded beyond slapping us down. I never heard of any political inmate caught with contraband goods during the search. I suppose the prison authorities' speedy retort might be that everyone was forewarned, but the daily search deterred even the slightest plan to bring in smuggled goods.

Top on the list of contraband was a newspaper or radio. The authorities did much to keep us blank about news from the mainland. They outlawed all access to news. The punishment for possession of a newspaper was harsh. Known as seven days' 'spare diet', this was for the first conviction. You were kept for seven nights in solitary confinement without food except for water and boiled rice water served in the place of meals. For a second conviction the punishment could be fourteen days. I was hungry all the time in prison, and I feared sustained hunger. I thought I would never survive 'spare diet'.

Even so, we had to overcome the news drought. And the news-gathering effort would have to beat the *thauza* system – we could not risk bringing in an item that would fail that search. After several planning sessions in the evenings, a specialised committee of prisoners across political party lines resolved that three young cadres be tasked to gather daily socio-political news. I was one of them. I think I was picked in the hope that my memory would be good and also that my Pretoria smattering of Afrikaans would help with a hurried read of the Afrikaans-language morning newspaper *Die Burger*. The scheme was bound to be risky but hopefully rewarding. The team of three agreed on a daily plan to nick a warder's newspaper, but only after he had read it. One of the team had to create a decoy that separated the warder from his briefcase or bag. A ruse like this would do it: 'Excuse me, sergeant, there is a prisoner behind the shed who is dizzy and about to faint.' I would grab the paper, rush to the toilet and read the main news sections and the daily editorial very quickly. We needed another ruse to return the newspaper into the warder's briefcase or onto his office table. The newspaper had to be returned; otherwise our cover would be blown to smithereens.

The flow of news had to be sustainable. It was not always possible. Some days no subterfuge would get a warder to part ways with his newspaper. But there were also easy pickings. Some good soul would dump the read newspaper in a litter bin. Thank you very much. Most evenings when there was a catch, my duty was to play the role of news broadcaster. 'Good evening, comrades. Here is the news: One! Today in parliament Helen Suzman moved a motion of no confidence in the premier Dr Hendrik Verwoerd. She was loudly booed by members of the ruling party and the motion was defeated by an overwhelming majority with one vote cast in support of the motion.'

One memorable day of my broadcasting role was 7 September 1966. Zola Mjo of the team 'borrowed' *Die Burger* with the professed intent to return it to its owner. He tucked it under his shirt and rushed to me in the smelly toilet where I was ready to speed-read. 'Oh my goodness!' I choked. The front page screamed that the day before Dr Hendrik Verwoerd, the prime minister of the republic, had been assassinated in parliament by an in-house messenger called Dimitri Tsafendas. I needed a witness. Nobody in the cell would believe this news item. Zola squeezed into the toilet with me. '*Mchana,* read the front page,' I said to him. He said he couldn't read much of Afrikaans. 'This Afrikaans you will understand,' I told him. He did. Holed up in there together, our shaking bodies made the little zinc toilet rattle. The evening news broadcast drew doubt and suspicion that Zola and I were being overly creative.

By the next morning all prisoners had heard the news and the national flag on the prison precinct was flying at half-mast. I was mystified that it could be so easy to murder a head of state anywhere, let alone a prime minister in his own legislative chamber. Verwoerd was the architect of apartheid and it was he who led the country away from the British monarchy to a formalised racist republic. Some comrades ventured the speculation that apartheid was on the verge of collapse. I did not know enough to make a meaningful call. The speculation was wrong, however. We were to serve our long sentences in full. Apartheid was to live another virile 30 years after Verwoerd's inexplicable demise. And for that long we had to combat its injustice.

CHAPTER 12

Education project

The lot people are called to endure is never all nasty. Our stay on the island was not all intolerable. One day early in 1964, Mike and I were called to the prison office and told that our applications to study had been approved. Major Visser was responsible for approving applications to study. We were overjoyed. The prison authorities called studying a 'privilege', which they could give or withdraw at will. The study expenses had to be paid by the prisoner concerned. This meant your family or an external sponsor had to fund your studies. I was genuinely thrilled to resume mine. Our parents registered us with a correspondence college and within a month of the approval Mike and I were studying. Study guides for all six Junior Certificate subjects arrived by post. Your family or friends had to buy and send you textbooks and set-works and, the local rule demanded, the books had to be new. I suppose during those days of letter- and parcel-bombs the rule was not unexpected.

The rest of the year sped by. In November, Mike and I sat for the examinations and passed all six subjects with a first-class average. This was no singular feat. By June of the following year we had worked through all the materials and had the rest of the year for several revisions. Of course, we had every midweek evening and every weekend to study. Our curtailed liberty turned into a generous resource.

At the end of 1965, Mike and I sat for the matriculation examination. We needed one and not the traditional two years to complete the prescribed syllabuses in six subjects. There were three languages – Setswana, Afrikaans and English – and three content subjects: mathematics, physical science and history. The memorable thing about our matriculation examination was that we sat in the same examination room with *Ntate* Walter Sisulu, who was then the secretary general of the ANC. The warders warned us sternly not to talk to him in the exam room. He had been brought from the single-cells sections, where leaders were held separately from rest of the prison populace. I was in total awe. Comrade Sisulu had risen to the top leadership of the ANC from an obscure start. He was a revered struggle stalwart. He was reputed to have recruited Nelson Mandela into the movement. He was known to be a self-taught and erudite man who had led the working-class struggles and masses of our people over decades. Here he was, submitting to formal certification which he did not need.

Surprisingly, the authorities did not resist with any seriousness the right of every prisoner to study. Their remaining line was that you might forfeit your right to study if you were convicted of a serious breach of the prison code or if you abused the right to study. Neither we nor they knew how far-reaching the study project would become for prison life and, in time, for our liberation project. The right to study changed our lot more than anything else. It extracted the emotional sting from imprisonment. Only physical restraint and discomfort remained as we took refuge in mental activity. A prisoner who cared to study would, in effect, escape from prison. It was a case of mind over matter. The space to study freed fresh energy and gave us abundant hope.

Formal tuition was offered by a number of long-distance colleges and universities. The popular options were Rapid Results College and Damelin College, both of which offered Junior and Senior Certificate tuition. At tertiary level, the University of South Africa (UNISA) was most used, followed by the London School of Economics. Enrolled students received study guides and were obliged to submit prescribed assignments. We could use the lending facilities of the UNISA library, which posted a vast number of books right into our prison cells. As more of us embarked on formal studies, the volume of the mail parcels that came in and out of prison increased. Another boon was that we had access to stationery. We shared the stationery with all inmates. Suddenly our lives extended beyond one foolscap page and a small lead pencil for the quarterly missive.

Every printed or written word had to be censored before entering the prison. With the increased load, this system became inadequate for the task. New challenges were presented. The censorship system was suited to cope with a few tens of one-page letters a day. The warders charged with censoring knew very little about academic and other reading material sent to us by external libraries. If a book was not banned and available at a public library, the warders had no business to keep it out. In any event, we were entitled to read all of the recommended material. The genie was out of the bottle. The authorities had no means of limiting the number of books nor the quantity of material any one of us might order or keep in the cells.

Formal studying continued and people sat for year-end examinations. This meant that the prison had an additional and new challenge. It had to qualify itself with the national examination bodies and universities as an examination centre. It had to employ officers who were suited to a task which, ordinarily, was well beyond the capabilities of the armed guards at the quarry. So the skills mix of our officers had to and did change for the better. The unforeseen result was that we ended up, by and large, with a civil band of warders and a more humane relationship between the kept and the keepers.

The prison was also obliged to construct book-cases and writing desks. The desks were riveted chest high into the inside wall of the cell. We had no chairs. If we had, they would have had to be tall bar stools. This meant that you had to study or write standing against the desk. The authorities seemed most reluctant to supply us with chairs. They seemed to think no prisoner deserved a chair. Oddly, the standing position imposed on us a level of industry. Our concentration was the better for the standing. Studying tasks tended to be done efficiently and promptly. We looked forward to the evenings.

After dinner at 5pm, you were allowed to study up to 10pm. Well, four to five hours of studying every day would have helped any diligent learner secure a good few distinction passes. After all, we were spared all social diversion.

You were not allowed to read beyond 10pm, but if you wanted to, there was a way to beat the system. We were in an ultra-maximum security prison, so the lights stayed on all day and all night. The guards were meant to be able to see us during their nightly patrols. Every block had four cells, holding about 60 of us in each. The four cells were built into an H-shape. A long passage abutting the four cells allowed the night guard to look into a cell. At 10pm the guard would come into the passage, flick the lights and shout into the cell, '*Slaaptyd*!' At that point you could lie on your belly, screen half of your head with a blanket and continue reading undetected by the night patrols.

Most evenings, I continued reading for two hours after 10pm. I felt a personal thrill to know I was subverting the stupid rule that sought to tell me how long I might read or write. They needed to keep the lights switched on for their own security concerns, but we had many books around us. How could the prison hope to order us not to read after 10pm? They might have wanted us rested and ready for the hard labour of the following day, but I could not have cared less. I knew that my abiding reward lay in the mental nourishment and the escape books afforded me.

Mike and I passed the matriculation examination with a university entrance within one year after the Junior Certificate pass. We both procured decent passes in maths and science after working painstakingly through the prescribed matric textbooks. But we had had to bid farewell to our childhood fantasies of being medical doctors. The island was not exactly a site of the smell of ether or laboratories with burnt sulphur in the air or perhaps of a disgusting sight of human cadavers. I had to settle for a bachelor's degree in the arts. I chose political science and English literature as majors, together with several minor courses like psychology and sociology.

My choice of majors was influenced by Klaas Mashishi. Boet Klaas, as I affectionately called him, had been accused number two in our trial and he was from Atteridgeville. At the time of our trial he was nearly 25 years old, a taciturn and gifted university graduate. He had read English and political science at the University of Fort Hare. He was plainly as well read as he was a passionate Africanist thinker. With remarkable erudition he narrated the lives and thinking of Dr Nnamdi Azikiwe, the first president of independent Nigeria (1963 to 1966), and of Abubakar Tafawa Balewa, independent Nigeria's only prime minister. He drew inspiration from Léopold Senghor, the Senegalese leader, poet, thinker and writer on negritude. He passed on to us his fascination with the pan-Africanist thinking of George Padmore, later amplified by Kwame Nkrumah, the inaugural president of an independent Ghana. He drew attention to valiant fighters against colonial rule during the 1960s, such as Ben Bella of Algeria, Jomo Kenyatta of Kenya, Patrice Lumumba of the Congo, Dr Agostinho Neto of Angola and Milton Obote of Uganda. Closer to home, Boet Klaas would lecture us about the crusade by Kenneth Kaunda (KK) for the independence of Zambia and about the historical but unhelpful rivalry between Robert Mugabe's ZANU and Joshua Nkomo's ZAPU of Zimbabwe. He would tell of Ntsu Mokhehle and his Basutholand Congress Party, pointing to Mokhehle's admirable political intellect in prosecuting a demand for independence within the constraints of a monarchy.

The early to mid-1960s were truly propitious times for the African continent except in Zimbabwe and South Africa. We, Boet Klaas's younger listeners, were spoiled for choice when it came to heroes of wars of African independence. They were leaders whose names were hallowed by historical innocence. They did not yet have the sin of incumbency. They had just been or were about to be vested with public power. They had come to where they were together with their followers fuelled by sheer guts, sacrifice and selflessness. They had nothing to gain except a new beginning for their people. They had earned our ululations. We drew sustaining hope when some continental leaders promised that 'Africa is not free until every square of its land is free'.

But Boet Klaas had an even deeper passion – literature. He held my hand and led me towards discovering and enjoying novels, drama and poetry.

What remained was for me to find the literature and read it. This was my 10pm-to-midnight crusade on the island.

During regular study time I worked my way through reading lists prescribed by the UNISA guides for English literature. They were predictably Eurocentric. I was obliged to work through Jane Austen's *Pride and Prejudice* and *Sense and Sensibility*, Charlotte Brontë's *Wuthering Heights* and George Eliot's *Middlemarch*. Thomas Hardy offered a welcome escape from the prudish English drawing room to the rural countryside with tales like *Tess of the D'Urbervilles*. So did Joseph Conrad's *Heart of Darkness*, *Nostromo* and *Under Western Eyes*, which presented an ominous setting in the cut and thrust of colonial explorations, greed in Africa and Latin America, and revolution in Russia.

One could hardly go through the final year of English literature at UNISA without working through the old dialect of Chaucer. The saving grace for me was that 'The Wife of Bath' was such an engaging and delightful tale once the language became accessible. I also enjoyed DH Lawrence's *Lady Chatterley's Lover*. The course compelled a study of the complete works of Shakespeare, featuring prominently *King Lear*, *Macbeth* and *Hamlet*. The poetry anthologies were dated ones. We had to work from John Donne to Shakespearean sonnets; from William Blake through to William Wordsworth. Some lines in the poetry stuck in my receptive mind only to resurface as an irrepressible ditty in my head. I have a strong memory of pushing a wheelbarrow at the prison quarry and suddenly bursting into the first stanza of Samuel Taylor Coleridge's opium-drenched vision: 'In Xanadu did Kubla Khan / A stately pleasure-dome decree: Where Alph, the sacred river, ran / Through caverns measureless to man / Down to a sunless sea.' On another day it would be the sprightly and melodious lines of Gerald Manley Hopkins humming ceaselessly in my head: 'I caught this morning morning's minion, king / dom of daylight's dauphin, dapple-dawn-drawn Falcon, in his riding ...' Sometimes I would be stricken by the arid and fateful rhyme of the ponderous American poet TS Eliot's 'The Hollow Men'. 'Here we go round the prickly pear ... This is the way the world ends / Not with a bang but a whimper.'

Sometimes the ringing lines went horribly when poorly aligned to the prison filth. I was fascinated by the poet John Keats until one of my fellow literature students, Achmad Cassiem, spoiled my pleasure. Pointing at an uncovered urine bucket full to the brim, he grinned and said to me: 'Dikgang – "With beaded bubbles winking at the brim ..."'

It did not take long before my reading travelled well beyond the orthodoxy of prescribed literature. The ready start was John Steinbeck's *The Grapes of Wrath*. Its theme of pungent social exploitation urged me on to novels that explored personal and social dilemmas. I read Boris Pasternak's First World War and post-October Revolution novel, *Dr Zhivago*, from cover to cover on my belly after 10pm. Emboldened, and much in the same posture, I tackled Leo Tolstoy's unending but philosophical war novel *War and Peace*. Sought-after novels were read in relay, which meant that I had to meet my reading deadline so that I could pass the novel on to the next person in line. In extreme cases, when there was a high demand for a book, we undid the binding at the back of the book. A few of us were responsible for working out a system for delivering revolving batches of 20 to 30 pages a day to people who had enlisted themselves on the reading queue. The enlisted readers had to meet their daily reading targets and pass the pages on the following day. The coterie of readers of the revolving batches had much to talk about. Frantz Fanon's *The Wretched of the Earth*, Karl Marx's *Das Kapital* and even Adam Smith's *The Wealth of Nations* were some of the works that topped the reading charts. Select novels made their way onto the reading list of several comrades. The fiction of Chinua Achebe and Ngugi wa Thiong'o was read side by side with Leo Tolstoy's *Anna Karenina* or Samuel Beckett's existentialist drama *Waiting for Godot*.

Another seminal influence in my studies through UNISA was Dr Mmutlanyane Mogoba, whom I fondly called Uncle Stan. He, too, was a UNISA graduate and teacher before his arrest for advancing the activities of the PAC. He had started studying initial courses in law with a view to swopping teaching for legal practice. That was never to be. He found his God on the island and later moved on to provide pastoral leadership as presiding bishop of the Methodist Church. He had studied Latin earlier, and may, I think, have been studying Hebrew on the island. I became the beneficiary of his flair for classical languages. When I studied Latin he stepped in as a fatherly tutor. At the quarry, we both chose to push wheelbarrows. We walked in tandem as we pushed our wheelbarrows between loading and off-loading points. He would demand that I run through the Latin noun declensions and verb conjugations. I would say, 'Amo, amas, amat, amamus, amatis, amant', and he would call out the correct Latin word when I stuttered and nod approvingly when I got it right. As my mastery of Latin increased he would patiently hear me out translating Cicero. I passed Latin well. Without a pass you could not be admitted to the B Juris or LLB degree.

On one revolutionary principle or another, some comrades eschewed formal certification from apartheid institutions. I never understood the value of that posture. It took little to embrace what was useful tuition and to eschew rubbish. Even so, beyond formal tuition, the start of studying allowed in vigour that enhanced our collective stay on the island and made it truly special. For one thing, we shared the stationery and reading materials with colleagues who had not been granted permission or were not engaged in formal study. They chose to read or write what they liked. Some wrote poetry, others penned short stories and some wrote music scores. Ready examples were Mark Shinners and Achmad Cassiem, both of whom were given to writing evocative poetry. In fact, they put together decent anthologies. Achmad also wrote theological essays on or influenced by Islam. Little wonder then that in his later adult life, Achmad rose to become a decorated scholar of Islam and an imam in the Western Cape.

On the other end of the scale, Harry Gwala developed written modules on Marxist Leninism with a special endorsement of Stalinism. He was an inveterate atheist. He tutored Marxism with remarkable style and conviction to all who cared to sit at his feet. He seemed to place Marxist ideology beyond all blemish. It was from him that I heard for the first time that nationalism was the refuge of a scoundrel. He predicted that the uprising against capitalism would become global and not merely national. This was so because the search for superprofits and accumulation by capitalists went well beyond the confines of domestic borders. The struggle of the working class would liquidate the ruling national bourgeoisie, who, in turn, would give way to a dictatorship of the proletariat. In time the national states would founder and wither away in favour of a classless society. This was astonishing to hear, given that much of pan-Africanism was rooted in nationalism as a rallying and uniting force against colonial division and conquest.

In contrast, John Nyathi Pokela, one of the founding leaders of the PAC, wrote tutoring notes on pan-Africanism starting from Du Bois to Padmore through to Nkrumah and later Sobukwe. He spent considerable time pointing to the wave of independence across the continent. He warned us against swallowing ideologies, such as Marxism, grown on foreign soil. Newly freed Africans, he argued, had to adopt positive neutrality between the ideologies and social arrangements of the East and the West. He urged his young cadres rather to learn about the communitarian values of African socialism – a brand of economic transformation which was embraced by scholars and leaders like Mwalimu Julius Nyerere in the form of *ujamaa*.

On occasion we arranged oral debates on the features of the ideal society we would induct if we were to overcome. These were memorable evenings, ones to cherish. The debates had no timekeeper because none of us prisoners had a watch, but somehow the time allocation was always fair. Thami Mazwai, an Africanist, would often lead the charge in explaining why only pan-Africanism was the appropriate indigenous ideology that should inform our struggle against race-based colonialism. The dispossessed African majority had to organise itself in order to defeat racism and establish a non-racial democracy. The white minority could not be expected to join the struggle for their defeat. Nor would they agree to an equitable distribution of the land disposed or other means of production. African people owed it to themselves to take up the cudgels in order to end their slavery. Harry Gwala would dismiss Thami's eager arguments by pointing out that apartheid was a mere sub-set of colonialism and global capitalism. Working people the world round, irrespective of their race or nationality, had to unite to resist exploitation and to establish a dictatorship of the proletariat. That would be the only way to install an equal society, one that would expect from each according to his means and to each according to his needs.

All of this was fascinating but confusing stuff for my young head. But one thing was certain – the genie had most definitely sprung out of the bottle. In permitting study and reading, unwittingly the prison authorities had opened vast spaces for the prisoners on the island. We could read, write and think. As a result, remarkable creativity and new thinking came forth from these seeds. Our incarceration became bearable. Physical discomfort gave way to the newly found freedom to hope, and to dream of the beginnings of a new society. The mind virtually subdued the matter.

The education on the island went well beyond formal tuition. Access to written materials sparked the quest for constant learning. Several comrades were stalwarts of our resistance movement but had not had the privilege of formal learning. Others cut their political teeth at the workplace within the fledgling labour movement. We set up after-work numeracy and literacy classes in virtually every cell. In some instances, the tuition started with the alphabet. It was common to hear fellow inmates reciting the alphabet as beginner learners did in kindergarten. I had to learn quickly how to read and write isiXhosa and isiZulu if I were to be appointed as a teacher. I had the privilege of teaching my elders by shouting out to my students 'Aaaa! Ebe! Ceee!' and 'One! Two! Three! Four!' and hearing them follow after me. The outcome of the literacy effort was near-miraculous. Comrades who had not been able to before began to read and to pen their own letters. I was as relieved as I was happy. I did not have to continue with the role I had of reading and writing letters for others who could not. From the teaching effort I took away something valuable. Lack of formal tuition does not deprive a person of common sense and native intelligence. A sense of self-worth is not diminished by illiteracy alone. Many in my and in other literacy classes were leaders of the movement in their own right and understood well the repressive exclusion of the political arrangements of colonialism and apartheid.

A chess club was started. It was formed by Jacob Zuma.[11] Initially, the chess-board and pieces were drawn by hand and we learned the game from library books. Enthusiasts were drawn from amongst the prisoners. Some comrades started a choral music society. It held its choir practices on Saturday mornings. So ambitious was this project that the choirmaster procured music scores of famous composers. On one occasion the choir tackled Handel's 'Hallelujah Chorus' from *The Messiah* and JP Mohapeloa's '*Hamba Kahle*'. Some folks, particularly from *eMonti* and *eBaai,* preferred singing jazz. Boet Welcome Duru and Norman Ntshinga wrote and sang Afro-jazz pieces. I remember how well Monde Mkunqwana and Mike Kahla sang in duet. They were inspired by the harmonious a cappella singing of The Blue Notes of the US. At least two such singing quartets were formed and they performed in cell concerts. George Rafuza had another social initiative. He inducted a dance club. Before his arrest he had been a Western Cape champion of sorts in ballroom dancing. It was not popular. The idea of dancing without a female counterpart was just not appealing. Nevertheless George taught the waltz and the foxtrot with arms stretched out onto the shoulders of a partner.

It was Zola Mjo, I think, who started the table tennis association. Table tennis matches could be played in the block passages on Saturday mornings. We collected the money to purchase the table, bats and balls. The prison would not do this for us. I thought I was a reasonable player, and there were many amongst us who played and were good at the game. But none matched Zola. He was left-handed and always smashed the ball to the least expected end of the table. For the years that he was on the island, he won every championship.

Mmutlanyane Mogoba's drama society attracted more fans than the dancing effort. It explored drama writings and performed selected pieces. I joined the society, and we performed Shakespeare's *Merchant of Venice* and later tackled the more opaque and arid Beckett's play *Waiting for Godot.* I got more joy out of the little matter of memorising long lines than performing them. Many lines stayed with me long thereafter.

A few comrades opted for musical instruments. In our cell, Siva Pillay strummed guitar chords in the evening for hours on end. Mercifully, he mastered the scales, at different keys, quite quickly, which made for simple and melodious practices. I studied while he ran up and down his scales and, later, when he learnt new pieces. Achmad Cassiem also owned a guitar, but he never seemed to have the patience of mastering the scales and chords. He would just strum away and sing along; he never played songs off a music sheet like Siva did. Enthralling music also came from the alto saxophone of Hector Ntshanyana. He had played in a jazz band in the Eastern Cape. He played solo pieces three cells away and the music filtered through all four cells of block C.

Another welcome musical sound was from the trumpet of Gabby Magomola, an Africanist activist from Randfontein on the West Rand. He loved to press his trumpet against the prison bars of cell C4 and he would blow a storm into the sunset. He would do a solo of '*Lakutshon' ilanga*' to the pleasure of many of us as we nodded in recognition of the timeless folk song. On another day Gabby would infuse so much passion into his rendition of '*Hamba Kahle*' that our hearts would be full. The trumpet notes filled the quiet sunset air hovering over sections A, B, C and D.

CHAPTER 13

Eighteen-day hunger strike

Everything seemed bearable on the island and yet certain irritants persisted. By the end of my first five years we had by and large tamed the shrew. Studying facilities had lightened our incarceration. Wanton assaults had ended. The hard labour of the early years had receded to an unhurried walkabout with wheelbarrows. The quarry project diminished in importance. The raw materials it had supplied became redundant because the prison had been fully built. More prisoners left than came to our prison and many who had served up to five years' imprisonment since 1963 had been freed. Also the heavy flow of new political prisoners had somewhat subsided. The vicious state repression after 1960 had crushed the internal revolt. Droves of activists had fled the country and gone into exile. As the home front quietened, the PAC set up the Azanian People's Liberation Army (APLA) and the ANC formed Umkhonto weSizwe (MK) in exile. Their respective headquarters were located in Tanzania. Droves of activist left to join these armies.

We with long prison sentences came to accept that our home away from home would continue to be on the island. I had five more years to serve, but many other comrades had to serve much longer – some up to life imprisonment. We required one big push to make our incarceration even more tolerable. This was indeed important and the next terrain of toil.

Although much had improved on the island, much had stayed the same, and much needed to change. Not even the escape brought about by reading, studying and cultural activities kept the physical discomfort of imprisonment fully at bay. Night after night and year after year we slept on felt mats on the bare and somewhat damp cement floor, without beds. The Cape winters were less than kind. We had no underwear – neither vests nor underpants. Indigenous African prisoners, by regulation, wore short pants and collarless short-sleeved shirts. We were issued with open-toed sandals, but not with socks. During the hot summer the attire was tolerable, but in the winter the wet cold froze your very bone marrow and, I am afraid, your balls, too.

Again apartheid reared its unseemly face. Our collective craving was for equal treatment, even in prison, while the authorities were determined to subvert this holy cow. Our Coloured and Indian comrades had to endure favourable treatment. They were issued with long pants, woollen jackets, socks, and boots or shoes. They were served different, better and more food than we were. The racialised food rations were enforced strictly, to the discomfort and hatred of all. The same point could be made in another way. Comrades like Ahmed Kathrada, Neville Alexander, Sedick Isaacs, Mac Maharaj, Achmad Cassiem and James Marsh were offered no choice but to be attired more warmly and to eat better, and more, than Nelson Mandela, Govan Mbeki, Zephania Mothopeng, Jafta Masemola, Nyathi Pokela and Walter Sisulu.

The food was a big source of injury and indignity. It was rationed and there wasn't much of it – just enough to keep your body alive. Regulations specified how many grams of brown sugar you were allowed on your morning porridge. The weight of the porridge and of the sugar was prescribed in so many grams. Also the food was often stale and sometimes rotten. Every one of us, except those who worked in the kitchen, was underfed and thin. We had to survive on nothing but the three meagre daily meals. No snacks or in-between-meals nibbling was possible or allowed. The scant diet must have been researched by some apartheid nutritionist. As a teenager, on the island I was constantly hungry. Other prisoners might have craved for other things, but I craved for food. My stomach always rumbled as it ran empty.

Then I would rush to a water tap. I had learned that water kept hunger pangs quiet for a while. This discovery was valuable. Over weekends supper was served at 2pm, after breakfast at 7am and lunch at 11am. At 7pm, five hours after supper, I would be nursing a rumbling tummy until 7am the following morning.

My comrades and I knew that we had to take discreet steps to supplement our paltry diet. The island was teeming with bird, animal and plant life. As the quarry diminished in importance, the ideal work gang was the bamboo *span*. This was how it came about. The Atlantic Ocean spewed long, black, slimy bamboo weeds onto the rugged, stony island shore. If they were not removed, the weeds became rotten and smelly. In time, the sea reclaimed the rot. Somebody decided that the weeds were valuable and should be removed from the shore. The bamboo *span* performed this chore. Their numbers were much fewer than those who worked in the quarry.

In winter, the bamboo work was cold, miserable and killing. With our bare hands and freezing fingers we had to pull out of the sea and off the shore these heavy, wet, slimy bamboo weeds and pile them up. In summer it went better and we made the work fun. Unknown to the warders, we hunted down and picked up eggs of guinea-fowl and other birds along the shore. One quick shake and a tap on one end of the egg was enough to down its insides into your throat. We called this Operation Protein. Bigger fun was to catch guinea-fowl to supplement lunch. I remember Steve Tshwete explaining with some seriousness our duty to find protein supplements in order to stay alive. We devised a ploy to send the warders in one direction and then a few of us would dash about chasing guinea-fowl in the direction of pre-selected divers. I was one of the latter. As the fowls came scurrying you had to make a low-flying rugby tackle to stop and catch the creature, using your hands and chest. Steve Tshwete would jump about and scream excitedly: '*Ntywilani, makwedini, ntywilani.*' (Dive, young fellows, dive). The division of labour was immaculate. The fire would be lit up quickly and the guinea-fowl cooked to perfection in sea-water – a worthy protein supplement indeed.

Another gnawing grievance was that we had no access to formal recreation. Soccer and rugby were forbidden.

Delegation after delegation delivered a note of grievances to the prison authorities. The prison authorities were dismissive. We formed a joint committee for planning and managing a hunger strike. This required us to act in unison. Dissenters would sow seeds of failure. After all, an injury to one was an injury to all. The joint strike committee announced a starting date for the food strike. We had to refuse the three meals offered by the prison but we were allowed to drink water. For this I was grateful. Drinking water, as I had discovered, can disguise hunger. It manages a purring stomach well. We carved out one exception: if you had a medical condition that required you never to go without a meal – diabetes, for example – you were exempt from the hunger strike. In a few instances old age was also a valid ground for an exemption. Surprisingly, only a few comrades sought refuge in the exemptions. As for the rest of us, we reconciled ourselves to a long period of starving.

On the morning of the first day of the hunger strike, in our hundreds, we were led to the kitchen serving window. Each one of us quietly walked past the serving point but took no food served. Somewhat amazed, the warders looked on but, wrongly, they did not think we would hold out. Just after the breakfast we had not had, we were ordered to line up for work as usual. The penny dropped. They had decided to have us do hard labour on empty stomachs. Could we hold out?

At the end of the first day I lay down on my floor bedding, exhausted and hungry. We had missed our first three meals. The hunger pangs became more pronounced as the evening progressed and the cell grew quiet. Everyone was pondering the road ahead. I resorted to drinking water, but to little avail. The purring stopped but the pangs remained. I dozed off. *Matsha ga ana swele* (dawn will surely break), the idiom of my vernacular consoled. And indeed the morning broke and the daily routine began. They unlocked our cell and we were led past the serving point at the kitchen window. For once the breakfast had an alluring tang but I gave the plate one look and fled past. So did other comrades.

By the third day, my body seemed to have sensed that there would be no food supplies for a while and by late evening my hunger pangs had stopped. My fantasies about food dissipated. In the evenings, I joined in the shouted mantra '*Aluta continua!*' Somehow our bodies had become less restive but, I suspect, more efficient in deploying their fuel. I felt no hunger. I was not tired and suffered no dizziness.

Seven days into the hunger strike, the authorities had made no concessions on our demands. One treacherous thing they did, however, was improve the food considerably. This we saw every morning at the serving point. Comrades who were exempted from the hunger strike confirmed it. This did not help matters.

Our collective leadership core knew that we needed external solidarity to win the battle around the hunger strike. Each comrade who had a visit informed their family that we were on hunger strike. The warders remonstrated harshly but, in effect, they could do nothing about it. It was not an offence for us to report on our state of starvation. The media was prohibited from reporting the goings-on inside a prison. We arranged that word be sent to the International Red Cross and Amnesty International, alerting them to our plight. We came to know that both civil rights entities sought permission to visit the prison. Helen Suzman, who was still the only opposition member in parliament, directed a question to the minister responsible, enquiring whether the prisoners on Robben Island were on a hunger strike. Our communication plan was beginning to inch ahead of that of the government. That was anything but difficult. Strangely, they had hoped to shroud the strike in secrecy until we caved in. We did not cave in.

Even in the grim evenings of gaunt faces, slight frames and light heads, there were hilarious moments. The most poignant was the *Theng' imfene* (Buy a baboon) moment. I named it after the poetic name of its protagonist. After the third day of complete fasting, bowel activity had stopped. As a matter of common sense, there was no cause to visit the latrine. Into the tenth day without food, I walked into the toilet block and there was the unmistakable smell. Somebody was on the toilet seat. He was emitting not hot air but processed food. On the seat was Comrade Thenginfene. I invited two other comrades to the toilet area to savour the floating stench. He was mortified. His courage had failed him and the evidence was beyond all doubt. In a subsequent disciplinary inquiry, he pleaded guilty to breaching the hunger-strike picket line as charged. His mitigating circumstances were compelling. The temptation to breach the picket line and eat was truly high and widely spread. The Thenginfene moment brought home to the leaders of the hunger-strike the gaping risk of dissension within the ranks. Also, it warned possible dissenters that they would be easily caught. The stench was foolproof. Even so, the strike leadership had to find a speedy accommodation with the authorities to end the suicidal foray.

In the third week of the hunger strike we started fearing for our well-being. Nobody had been obese when the strike started, but by then we had become conspicuously skeletal, even ghostly. Several comrades could not rise from their lowly bedding. Their nourishment levels were low. The prison did not insist that we perform hard labour. We opted for a 30-minute walkabout and exercises out of confinement. The food offered at the service window every mealtime had continued to improve markedly, but no concessions on the rest of our demands were forthcoming. The better course was to hold out. The International Red Cross demanded an urgent visit. So did Helen Suzman. The leadership comrades in single cells joined the strike. The prison had as dire a conundrum as we had. We could not persist to our demise. They could not afford mass deaths of prisoners. Even a rogue state has a scrap of self-worth. Also, they needed the continued patronage of the USA and the United Kingdom, who had consistently shielded the apartheid regime from adverse global scrutiny. The two countries vetoed resolutions against the regime in the United Nations and other world formations. A headline that Nelson Mandela and other political prisoners had died in a hunger strike would not have suited them or anyone else.

On the eighteenth day the authorities settled. They conveyed their concessions to our demands to Nelson Mandela and other leaders in the isolation section. This saved face for the authorities and got the leaders to call for an end to the strike. It was a close shave. We might have needed an end to the hunger strike more than the prison officials did. Any respectable avenue to help us end the strike would have been welcome. We had all started looking grimly gaunt and most of us had become light-headed. It was not uncommon for fellow inmates to be heard mumbling incoherently. In our way of surrender was that little mantra of the revolution: 'Forward ever; backwards never.' But the arduous conflict was worth every ounce. It yielded mutual respect and a prolonged truce between the captors and the captives. The second half of my ten-year stretch on the island became something of a frolic.

CHAPTER 14

The Makana Football Association

One of the trophies of the eighteen-day hunger strike was the right, or perhaps the privilege, as the prison would have it, to recreation. We could name no known authority in support of the right of a prisoner to play soccer, rugby or other sport. We argued that the lengths of our stays in prison entitled us to activity that would preserve our sanity. We were entitled to insulate ourselves from the ruin of incarceration. We lived in our bodies and were entitled to preserve them. Perhaps we were invoking a right to bodily integrity or to a whole body and to life. The claim was not different to the one we had made when we earned the right to grow our minds through study. I always held a fuzzy premonition that apartheid would be defeated. What I did not know was when, and so common sense suggested that I had to preserve myself until my release and, in time, the collapse of racial and class oppression.

The prison granted without demur our formal request to play football and rugby. The official response made the point that the government would not pay even a dark farthing to make the sporting codes viable. They would stay out of it. This meant at least two things. One was that, although we were without income, we had to find the money for our merrymaking. The other was that we would be the decision makers in our sporting arrangements. The prison authorities' decision was to let us out of the prison cells on Saturday mornings for an agreed number of hours. Their Calvinist belief system barred sport on Sundays.

Within a week of the formal permission we set up a task force to propose a suitable organisation to run the sport and find ways to fund the operation. Indres Naidoo, an ANC comrade from Johannesburg, and I were unanimously chosen to serve as interim executive of the football association to be formed. At the initial meeting we agreed to form eight football clubs, which would compete in an elite A division and second-rate B division. The league would run over two rounds. This would happen only after Indres and I had presented a draft constitution of the football association for adoption and a plan to fund the association.

Many years later, in 2010, our country would host the FIFA World Cup. Significant to me and many comrades from the island was the premiere of the film made by Anant Singh – *More Than Just a Game*, which FIFA built into its local World Cup festivities. At the occasion Sepp Blatter conferred honorary membership of FIFA on Indres Naidoo and me and other champions of football on the island such as Anthony Suze, Sedick Isaacs, Marcus Solomon and Mark Shinners. The film narrates the palliative character of football on the island. It unfurls the tale of human resolve hidden in a game and the managerial effort of the Makana Football Association, or MFA, as we fondly called our association.

We were not going to name MFA after Robben Island. Who was Robben we wondered. We chose to recall the heroic legacy of Makhanda (also spelled Makana) Nxele ('the left-handed one'). He was a prophet, warrior and military adviser to King Ndlambe. On 22 April 1819, during the frontier wars against land dispossession, Makana led six to ten thousand warriors against the British garrison at Grahamstown. The attack was mounted in broad daylight. Superior British firepower repelled and defeated Makana's warriors and Makana was captured. The British imprisoned him on Robben Island. Several accounts show that they treated him with great respect. They gave him private accommodation, food and furniture. Even so, Nxele continued to be irrepressible. On 25 December 1819, along with 30 other prisoners, mostly amaXhosa and Khoisan insurgents from the Eastern frontier districts, he escaped. Several survived but Makana drowned. Since he had promised his people he would return and never abandon them, they continued to hope for his return for another 50 years before traditional funeral rites associated with closure were observed.

The Makana legend relates how he and his comrades eluded their British captors and swam across the Atlantic to the mainland. He is said to have drowned within the last lap, having reached Table Bay. Every time I looked at the billowing swells of the Atlantic, my admiration for 'the left-handed one' soared. My early schooling had taught me that an island is a piece of land surrounded by water. I knew I could never venture into that cold, rough sea. Even ships went into distress in the nearby Atlantic in our full view. Makana, who had been held on the same island nearly a century and a half before me, had seen matters differently. He had promised his people that one day he would return and so that was what he tried to do. He was a brave and matchless leader, and his was a gripping and uplifting tale. His grit was indestructible. We need heroes. They are a glimpse of what we can be. Our football association was privileged to bear this hero's name.

Indres and I drafted the constitution of the MFA. He had served in non-racial football structures in Johannesburg. I had never managed football before, but my comrades pressed me into it. I was the young lawyer who must know something about writing constitutions. I was none of that – I was still studying for my law degree – but I gave it my best. We wrote the constitution by hand. Delegates from the eight clubs liked it and adopted it unanimously at the inaugural meeting. The delegates voted in office bearers. Indres was elected secretary unopposed and I was elected chairman unanimously. I was the youngest amongst them. How could I deserve to lead the football fraternity? The secretary and I were re-elected unopposed annually for five years. That must count for something.

For the first time since my release in 1973, I saw copies of records of the MFA. Sedick Isaacs had much to do with the rescuing of the records. They include the handwritten copy of the constitution and minutes of the monthly MFA meetings. Also well preserved are minutes of gatherings of the referees' association. The minutes reported on the training of referees based on the FIFA referees' rule book. Perhaps Indres had somehow procured a copy of the refereeing code.

Comrade Harry Gwala was chairperson of the referees' association. He insisted that the refereeing standard would be no lower than FIFA rules demanded. He enjoyed standing between two feuding sides and refereeing himself. The association allocated referees to the weekly league matches. A referee had to lodge a match report with the MFA. We even had a disciplinary committee to mediate protests against the referee's decisions during play or acts of misconduct by players. We had brought into being a democratic and representative governance of our football. Our system of rule was open; we had regular meetings and produced minutes. It was responsive to the wishes and decisions of the club delegates, who, in turn, had to account to ordinary club members.

We needed funds to buy football attire and equipment, and to the surprise and perhaps dismay of the prison officials, we found the money. It was the clubs, not the football association, that needed money and its use had to be in proportion with what each club wanted to buy. The clubs had to raise and use the money. There was no cost at the administrative centre because the best endeavours of Indres and me were free. We used a lot of stationery, which the two of us happily bought as part of our study needs.

The association procured catalogues and price lists for soccer equipment. The clubs made their selections, specifying quantities, colours and sizes. The gross cost was divided amongst club members and supporters. Each club drew a schedule of deductions. Prison officials deducted the specified amounts against the credit of funds held by each listed prisoner. The respective clubs pooled their resources to procure club kits. The amounts contributed were often uneven. Some comrades contributed little or nothing because they had no money to their credit. Others contributed generously to make up the club target. We all accepted that there was no relationship between the contribution of money and the right to belong to and play for a club. In a small way, we did what Karl Marx taught nearly a century earlier:

'From each according to his ability or means and to each according to his need.' Or were we simply observing the sharing and caring values of human solidarity – *ubuntu*?

The formation and naming of our football clubs spawned much joy and excitement. We had cleared one hurdle at the outset. We must play soccer in regular football attire and not in the uniform dirty-green prison apparel. Part of the excitement was mediating club colours and logos. Our roll-out plan was to form clubs, give them names, adopt club colours and then raise money per club to fund the respective playing outfits. The prison officials thought lack of money would bring our irrational fervour to a screeching halt. No, we thought, good plans will exert a pull on the money. An equally important project of the association was to construct a soccer field. Anthony Suze, another football-crazy comrade, volunteered to oversee the identification and conversion of a site within the prison precinct into a soccer field. Instead of regular prison work, a number of us were allocated to perform this self-serving task.

Club formations were intricate. There were no predictable affiliation patterns, but they tended to reflect provinces or towns of origin or political affiliation and, in other instances, football skill. Names ranged from the quaint to the original and sentimental. The KwaZulu-Natal contingent formed Bushbucks FC, named after a renowned club from those shores. Its members included our current president, Jacob Zuma, as well as Matthews Meyiwa, Mfenendala Xaba, Daluxolo Luthuli and Russell Maphanga. Bushbucks FC was a formidable team. Its style of play was steady and centred on competent passes within the midfield play. This was made possible by Matthews Meyiwa. He was short and stocky, and he kept and passed the ball rather well. The team boasted a formidable central defender in Jacob Zuma. This young man stood tall in his soccer boots. His rural background and upbringing must have helped him acquire an athletic frame. He sprinted well and his chest traps were as renowned as his headers. In the end, it was Mfenendala Xaba who procured the goals. His dribbling trickery caught defenders ball watching. The spectators loved him and they would roar their approval: '*Mfene!*' The Bushbucks first team was always in contention for a win in the league and knock-out games.

The Gunners FC drew their inspiration from a club of a similar name from Alexandra township, just north of Johannesburg. Its members were an eclectic lot from Johannesburg and Pretoria. They included Mark Shinners and Moss Masemola. They insisted their team be attired in white shirts with collars and black trunks. They admitted only those who made a credible claim of past football prowess and looked the part. They turned me down.

I made a bid to join Mphatlalatsane FC and I was accepted. It was made up of people who had no delusions of grandeur. It was not inspired by a claim of past football glory. Its name was fresh and original. *Mphatlalatsane* is a morning star that symbolises a new dawn. Our team colours were blue and white. Nobody particularly stood out in our A-division team, nor did we ever threaten the football prowess of the Gunners FC or Bushbucks FC. David Mmutle and Lucas Mahlangu ruled the roost over a rickety team. But we had a vocal support base. Being one of the weakest teams, support was not hard to come by. I was a fervent Mphatlalatsane supporter, even though I could not crack a place in the A division. Occasionally I was called up for a B team match. I must have been a hideous soccer player.

Our immediate competitors were Dynamos FC, named after a famous Russian soccer team. Its members tended to know more about Marxist Leninism than how to play decent football. They opted for the predictable red top. Prominent members included Indres Naidoo, whose secretarial skills were certainly better than his football, Steve Tshwete, Shirish Nanabhai, Sony Singh, Siva Pillay, Reggie Vandeyar and Steve Dlamini. Dynamos vied with Mphatlalatsane FC for the last spot on the annual league log.

Another populist club with an imaginative name was Ditshitshidi FC. *Ditshitshidi* are bedbugs. The club's cheerline or warcry was '*Ditshitshidi ga dina boroko*' (Bedbugs will not let you sleep – they are a bother you can't wish away). They were a motley collection of comrades from Pretoria and Johannesburg. They trotted onto the field in maroon and white shirts and white trunks led by island personalities like Gabby Magomola, Bennie

Ntoele and Abel 'China' Chiloane. Their pre-match confidence of a triumphant outcome was unmatched. When they lost a match, which happened
more often than not, their banter was matchless. Sadly, like Dynamos FC
and my team, Mphatlalatsane FC, they never lifted the league or the knock-
out trophy. They were guys of good cheer but scant talent, except for one of
them. They knew their limitations and endured them merrily. The exception
was Solly 'Dr Rubbish' Phetla. He nicknamed himself Dr Rubbish for he did
not suffer inept defenders who could not cope with his dribbling wizardry.
He made true fun of his front striker role and managed to score goals for
Ditshitshidi FC despite the dismal play of his untalented teammates.

Another class act in our prison football was Manong FC. *Manong* are
vultures. Its captain was the inimitable Dimake 'Pro' Malepe. As an eighteen-
year-old student from Hebron High School, Dimake had been sentenced to
life imprisonment for proscribed PAC activities. In those dark days a sentence of life imprisonment condemned you for your natural life except if you
were rescued by a parole release. This meant only the state could let you out.
Your incarceration was at the absolute discretion of your keepers. But your
keepers were your adversaries. No political prisoners ever benefited from
the parole system of the time.

As we often said with heavy hearts: lifers had to wait for the revolution to succeed. History vindicated our fears. Lifers like Jafta Kgalabi
Masemola, John Nkosi, Philemon Tefo, Samuel 'Chips' Chibane and Isaac
'Ike' Mthimunye were all convicted for PAC acts of resistance. They served
27 years, from 1963 to 1990. This was, of course, also true of Nelson Mandela
and the Rivonia Trial combatants.

When Dimake arrived on Robben Island he turned deeply ponderous and
he was quiet as a grave. He felt every ounce of his captivity. Keeping hope
alive was barely possible. I had a finite term and could look forward to its
end on 1 July 1973 at 10am, but Dimake had nothing to cherish but the fuzzy
biblical promise that 'this, too, shall pass'. My gusto to study and gather academic qualifications, was kept afloat by my far-off but certain release. He had
no such date to look forward to.

At high school Dimake had earned first-team football colours. Tony (Anthony) Suze had played under his captaincy. When the island football project started, Dimake gained a flicker in his eyes. His near-hidden dimples began to show up again. He agreed to form and lead a soccer club and the result was Manong FC. Tony Suze became chairman of the club and 'Pro', as Dimake was fondly cheered by his supporters, assumed the role of captain. Another colourful figure of that successful island club was Jacob Nkatlo from the Vaal region. Manong FC played excellent soccer. Their most able competitors were Bushbucks FC. Dimake lifted trophy after trophy as Manong FC won from season to season.

For all the wonderful things island soccer did for us, I choose one thing to cherish – that football rekindled Dimake's fire. It supplied him the fuel for the stretch. After 27 years on Robben Island, he came back home – as a somewhat unsung hero of our struggle. Nobody seemed to remember or care. Not long after his release Dimake succumbed. We buried him in torrential rain, scooping out bucketful after bucketful of water from his empty grave in order to bury him.

Indeed, football on the island was much more than a game.

CHAPTER 15

Prison letters, visits and unfailing support

Once I had crossed the halfway mark of my term of imprisonment, the remaining stretch was manageable. My football managerial role nearly consumed me, but I was astute enough to make sure it took modest time in comparison with my ongoing study project. My leadership role of MFA served as a well-earned break from my constant study. I must, though, confess to moments of loneliness and homesickness, especially when some of my fellow accused and other compatriots left the island for home. Mike Mohohlo, Philbert Mohlaka, Absalom Nkwe and Ndaki Madumo returned to Atteridgeville. My family must have relived the pain when they saw them return home without me. Uncle Stan Mogoba and Thami Mazwai had left for home two years earlier than them. Other colleagues, like Monty Seremane, Baker Mogale and Gabby Magomola, were also released. But then many other compatriots remained on the island and had much longer to serve than I did.

From 1968 onwards the prison population was thinning down and there were fewer arrivals. Our numbers on the island were dwindling to hundreds rather than the initial few thousands. It seemed that the state tyranny within the country had secured a lull. Leaders and prominent followers of the PAC and ANC were either in prison or had fled into exile. For the moment it appeared that the internal revolt had been snuffed out and the apartheid diktat and repression had gained a hold. Nothing on the horizon seemed to threaten the apartheid security state under the helm of Prime Minister Balthazar Johannes Vorster.

Even so, I had reason to be satisfied with the trajectory of my studies. In 1969 I had reached my final year of the BA degree. My majors in English and political science afforded me a moving feast of engaging literature and political philosophy. My intellectual faculties were tested to the hilt as I marvelled at new knowledge that demanded my critical assessment. For once, I needed more time to study than the ample time prison afforded me. Klaas Mashishi was my ever-dependable sounding-board and mentor throughout my studies. I secured additional time to work on my studies when I was roped in to help start a library for inmates. I was spared the hard labour at the quarry or bamboo work sites.

The library was a welcome project. Up to then, we had to order every book we needed from a distance lending library at considerable postage costs. We never came to know who donated a few hundred books to the prison. My new role required that I start the accession and cataloguing system for the library. The collection was dominated by dated English novels and short stories. The books seemed to have gathered dust somewhere in a bunker over many years. I selected approximately 10 per cent of the books for the start of a library for the isolation prisoners. My librarian counterpart in the single cells was Comrade Ahmed Kathrada. He would send written messages through the prison warder requesting books or enquiring after a specific read. The notes were always checked carefully. We could not pass on messages that had not been approved by the warders. It was a source of satisfaction that my librarian counterpart in the isolation section was a revolutionary of Kathy's pedigree.

Once I had the books sorted and up on the newly built shelves, the prison fixed Saturday morning as the lending time. Only a few of our colleagues skipped the Saturday morning soccer in favour of browsing in the library, but those who did found little that was of genuine interest to revolutionaries who were bent on replacing the devastation of apartheid with a just society.

I completed the BA degree and my father was beside himself. Many of his learners at Dr WF Nkomo Secondary School tell that daily, for a week, he told his learners at the morning assembly that his son on Robben Island had passed the BA degree. He could take that liberty at the school assembly because he was the headmaster. He joined the audience at the April 1970 UNISA graduation ceremony, if only to derive solace from the chancellor conferring the degree on his son *in absentia*.

In 1971 I applied to study the LLB degree. The prison turned down my application on the bizarre ground that their rules did not permit me to study for a post-graduate qualification. In plain Afrikaans one of the warders said to me: '*Kleintjie, jy het 'n graad, man. Dit is genoeg*' (Little one, you now have a degree. That is enough). Comrades before me had sought to do post-graduate studies and they had also been turned down. They were allowed to study further provided it did not entail post-graduate work. Sedick Isaacs, who had arrived on the island as an applied mathematics graduate from the University of Cape Town, could not get leave to do post-graduate work, so he made a hobby of collecting a string of bachelor's degrees. Neville Alexander came to the island already holding a doctorate from a German university. He was not permitted to pursue post-doctoral or any post-graduate studies. He, too, had to resort to a string of bachelor's degrees. So the die was cast for me. I changed course and registered for another bachelor's degree, this one in law, known as the B Juris, which I completed in 1972, just before my release. It was an expedient halfway route to completing the LLB degree.

In 1972 I was within a year of going home. The time had passed quickly, I thought. Had I finished nine years on the island? I was heading for my 24th birthday, feeling a little older and steadier than I had at the start. I was truly grateful for many things. I had overcome the ordeal of long-term imprisonment, thanks to many mercies. Foremost was the dubious, if not ironic, blessing of youth. I was spared the chronic conditions associated with advanced age. Many elderly fellow prisoners were unwell. They had to battle hypertension or diabetes, sometimes both. For reasons that were not obvious, several were afflicted by asthma and tuberculosis. Several elderly people had to endure piles, which was believed to be caused by the cold working its way up your rear. The chill came from sitting on cold ground or stone at the quarry. A few comrades died of illnesses on the island; they paid an untimely, supreme price for an unaccomplished struggle for freedom.

Barring acute sinusitis, associated with the cold and wet conditions, I was spared ill-health. My age was in my favour. I may have been underfed but I had a thin, lanky but lithe and healthy body. I was well. I had not left a wife or partner behind. I had no child when I left home. I had none of the emotional family burdens many of my older comrades had to endure. A good few were served with divorce summonses while they were on the island – events that unleashed a deep grief of rejection. In some instances, news would arrive that a child had been excluded from school on financial grounds or that a daughter had fallen pregnant. News of that kind hurt more than the scorn of captivity.

During his six-monthly visits, I told my father about my chronic sinusitis. As he left, each time, he wrote a letter to the minister of justice demanding that he be permitted to send me sinus medication. For good measure, he also asked if he could add vitamin tablets and a bottle of malt. The answer was a curt 'No – the prison has adequate medical facilities'. He never told me about these requests and the rebuffs. Many years after my release, when I gained access to my official prison and Department of Justice files from the National Archive, I discovered what he had done. It hurt to read his pleas to the minister each of my ten years in prison. He also asked, if not demanded, that I be released on early parole. Had he told me this while I was on the island, I would have said he should not bother. No political prisoner had been freed on remission of sentence or parole. It was astonishing that the minister courteously replied to every petition my dad wrote, only to say 'No'.

Another affirming feature was family support. I had young parents who vowed to stand steadfastly behind me. They never judged my conduct that attracted the conviction. They could not. They knew of and hated the brutality of apartheid well beyond my distaste. My incarceration must have hurt and inconvenienced them terribly, and yet they stayed the course. Every six months, for ten years, my parents undertook the trip to Cape Town together.

At first they came by train; in later years by car. They stayed over in the Methodist Church hall or the manse in Langa township. With their combined teacher stipends, they could probably have afforded to stay a night or two in a boarding or hotel facility, but that was not to be. The apartheid law did not permit African people to stay in a boarding or hotel facility. The prison visits lasted for 30 minutes and were conducted across a narrow cubicle window. Except for that first visit from my parents, when my mother had watched me devour her brown-cooked chicken, we had to give each other turns to speak into the one-way speaker-phone. The conversation was taped and a warder listened in. He was entitled to stop the visit summarily should the conversation, in his view, career towards politics or current national news. Over the years, I had learned not to endanger the visit. The conversation stayed within our family. I chose to save time by listening to my mom and dad talk about the well-being of my brothers and our extended family. My mother was always the stronger of my two parents. She would ask me to step back to the entrance of the cubicle and turn around – presumably to assess my state of health. Towards the end of the 30 minutes she never omitted to say: 'Son, this, too, shall pass. We love you, Dikgang.' She used the 'royal we' because my father never dabbled in unmanly stuff like 'I love you'. He tended to be matter-of-fact. He would probe the progress in my studies, and ask whether he needed to send me any prescribed books or money, and whether I had grievances he should know about.

Most visits were short, pleasant and reassuring – except for two. The one related to my father's youngest sister, Moipone Lethale (born Moseneke). She braved her deepest hurt and fear and decided to come along with my mom and dad to Cape Town. Her first ride on a boat across the Atlantic was turbulent and threatening, and when she walked into the visitor's cubicle, she was out of breath and visibly upset. My parents had given up their visit in her favour and so she was alone. She took one look at me in my prison clothes and let out an uncontrollable scream. I tried to calm her down, but to no avail. I said, 'Rrakgadi, thank you for coming. I am fine and the worst is behind me. I will be out soon. Look at me, I am fine.' She looked, but she continued to cry hysterically and the visit was aborted. The warder led her away and I was returned to prison. It hurt me to see my aunt in such anguish.

A few occasions later, both parents were teary and kept poor eye contact with me as they greeted me. I feared for one of my siblings. But their sad news was that my most loved paternal aunt, Susan Masikwane, with whom I had lived as a little lad in my early primary school years, had died of diabetes and had been buried a few weeks earlier. They had not written to me about her death, not daring to disclose it in a letter. In our way, the death of a loved one is never relayed in a letter. The recipient of the awful news must be spared sorrowful burden without consolation. My parents had to relive their own anguish as they struggled to let me know in a poky cubicle about the demise of my father's sister, Rrakgadi Ntshiko. It hurt deeply. *Robala ka Kagiso Mokwena*! (Rest in peace Mokwena).

By my ninth year on the island, I was entitled to one letter every two months. My invariable correspondents over the years were my mother and father, my brother Malatse, and my maternal uncle, Malome Patrick Makhaza. Writing a letter to a political prisoner could be freedom- or career- and sometimes life-threatening. The security police followed up correspondents outside one's family circle. Whoever wrote to a political prisoner had to explain what their interest in that prisoner was. Their letters attracted security police surveillance and sometimes police detention without trial. We never expected anybody other than members of our families to expose themselves to that risk.

The Marshes were a family who took that risk. Who were they? Mr and Mrs Marsh were a working-class couple and they had eight children. Two were boys and the rest were beautiful girls. They were a highly politicised family with considerable antipathy towards apartheid and its resultant racial bigotry. I gathered that Mrs Marsh's family were victims of the race classification laws. Some of her siblings were classified white and others Coloured. This tore their family apart and politicised the children. When her husband died Mrs Marsh moved to 12 Poleman Road in Salt River.

Their second son, James Marsh, arrived on the island one evening in 1964 together with Sedick Isaacs, Abdurahman Williams and Achmad Cassiem. They had been convicted of anti-apartheid activities and their sentences ranged from five to twelve years' imprisonment. James was to serve five years, imprisonment and Sedick, their maths and science teacher at Trafalgar High School, Cape Town, was lumbered with a twelve-year sentence.

Sedick taught me mathematics in matric. Achmad and I had endless debates about the place of religion in the workings of a just society. He argued that Islam ought to be the basis of an ideal just order. I thought a secular state would best advance a modern and socially inclusive democracy. James believed in the Maoist doctrine of the people's revolution.

Beyond all the serious political debates, I asked James about his family. I enquired whether he had any sisters and when he said he did, I immediately decided to call him *swaer* (brother-in-law). I sought to persuade him that I might correspond with one of his sisters. Without much demur, he said, '*Swaer*, you may write to one of my sisters, Elsie.' I did. She never replied. James sought to make amends by saying, 'Okay, *swaer*, write a letter to my youngest sister, Aletta.' He warned me that she was only fifteen years old and in Standard 8. Armed with the family address in Elsie's River, I wrote to Aletta. She wrote back. I was thrilled to the core. Her letter was not much more than: 'I am 15 years old; I stand 5 feet and 8 inches. I wear long raven black hair. I am the youngest daughter of my parents, the Marshes, and James is one of my brothers. I hope you will like my enclosed photo. Please send me yours.' There was no photo, of course, in the censored letter; the prison had confiscated it. ('You are not entitled to any photographs,' the censor's office warder retorted to my grievance.) When Aletta learned from my next letter that they had confiscated her photo, she wrote to the prison authorities and demanded it back. They returned it to her. It thrilled me no end. I had a friend in a gutsy fifteen-year-old young woman. I knew something about facing up to a brutal regime at just about the same age and her courage struck many melodious chords. As for me sending her my photo, she did not press the matter. The penny must have dropped. Besides other impediments, a photo in prison garb could hardly be an object of endearment.

Before long, Aletta applied to the prison authority to visit me. They turned her down. She had to turn sixteen years of age first, they said. Within a month of her sixteenth birthday, Aletta secured a visit permit. She walked into the prison visitor's booth on elevated cork heels and a knee-length cream-mustard dress. She was tall, slim and stunning. She had brown eyes and very fair skin, and her long black hair hung down her back. When she smiled she had dimples in both pink cheeks. Giving me a soft, tentative smile, she waved her slim fingers. 'Hey, you must be Dikgang Ernest Moseneke? I am Aletta Marsh.' I was smitten and speechless. It fell on her to make the small-talk as I stood tongue-tied. 'They sent me from pillar to post before they granted me a visitor's permit,' she said.

Within a month of the first visit, Aletta wrote to my mother and father and invited them to stay with the Marshes when they visited me on the island. Aletta came across by boat at least once a quarter to visit. In the last few years of my stay, my parents lived with the Marshes, who laid out Cape cuisine and much other hospitality for them. The two families exchanged gifts and visits. Those family bonds lived on for a long time, well beyond my stay on the island, and when Mrs Marsh passed on, my parents and I went down to Cape Town to pay our last respects.

Aletta and I had a beautiful and special relationship, bordering on the romantic, but undeniably, if not forcibly, platonic. She was arguably my first love. She saw me through the terrible patch of captivity on the island. She was generous and selfless. She was trenchantly non-racial in a place where most saw the world through the lens of race. She had no business squandering her weekends and pocket-money to care for an unknown prisoner. Her childlike innocence and twinkling fearlessness made her even more desirable. While I was on the island, outside of my mother and Helen Suzman (and the difficult visit from my aunt), she was the only woman I set eyes on and I loved her purely. Aletta still lives to this day. She never married and has no children of her own. Each time I see her or think of her I develop a knob of guilt in my throat.

CHAPTER 16

Homecoming

Se se sa feleng sea tlhola (every hardship comes to an end), so our fore-bears reassure us in times of adversity. In mid-March 1973, the reception office monitor called my name loudly in the breakfast hall. It was normal that when the authorities had business to transact with a prisoner, his name would be called at breakfast. It could be horrendous news, like a divorce summons, or an indictment for a further or new charge, or the death of a loved one. It could be good news, like a successful appeal freeing one or reducing one's sentence, or perhaps a money order in one's favour to be signed, or a modest inheritance from a deceased relative.

The monitor shouted: '*Sabela wena*, Dikgang Moseneke, *uya bizwa! Sabela S'boshwa!*' (Answer, Dikgang Moseneke, you are being called. Answer, you prisoner). It had been ten years since I had been spirited away on 21 March 1963 from my parents' home. I had been on the island for nine years and nine months. As the monitor called my name, my gut took over. It felt hollow and my stomach churned. I yawned widely and swallowed hard. A few pebbles of warm sweat formed on my forehead. Had my moment come? Did I have to pinch myself out of disbelief? Soon thereafter a childlike thrill ran through my sinews. I rose to my feet. Could this be the last breakfast I would eat on Makana Island? The prospect was in itself as unthinkable as it was terrifying. This place had become home away from home, as the cliché goes. On balance, though, I was overjoyed and filled with excitement.

My expectation was legitimate. When I arrived at the office my prison files were on the officer's desk. The officer produced a ledger detailing the balance of money in my account. I signed off a number of documents that seemed to indemnify the prison from any liability. I was escorted to my cell to collect my books and personal belongings. The warder explained that I was on a 'home-go draft', as he called it. I was to be taken to a prison near my place of release.

The road trip to Leeuwkop Prison, near Johannesburg, was uneventful. I was dressed in semi-civilian clothes and I was not handcuffed. I may have sat on the back seat of a sedan vehicle, but I don't even remember. It would have been moronic to have thought about escaping when I had only three months' imprisonment left. On arrival at Leeuwkop, I was placed in the ultra-maximum-security single-cells section. That suited me just fine. I needed the space to catch my breath and think of the possible way ahead. I could not but contrast my first and last quarters of my captivity. In the 90-day solitary confinement I had been a tiny child, terrified, crushed and defeated. Now I was a young man in my mid-20s. I felt salted, wiser to the ways of the world, fearless and triumphant. I had not bent. If anything, I was perhaps a touch unbended and arrogant. Nothing could be bigger and heavier than a ten-year stint on the rock.

Whatever they were told, the prison warders left me to my own devices in my Leeuwkop isolation cell. I was fed well and had all the time of day and night to foreshadow my looming new world. My stay at that prison triggered one childhood memory, the recollection of which lingers to this day. This is so particularly when I preside over graduation ceremonies in the Great Hall as chancellor of the University of the Witwatersrand. In my maddest dreams, I would never have guessed that one day I would return to the Great Hall as chancellor or to Leeuwkop as prisoner. This was an uncanny crossing of the past and the present.

When I was a little over ten years of age my father and mother took me along to watch a musical drama – *King Kong* – which was staged in the Great Hall at Wits. This was one of the very few public amenities where audiences were racially mixed. We took our seats and the maroon curtain rolled up on its own as the stage lights came on. Wow! I thought. Then the beautiful Miriam Makeba appeared. She sparkled on the stage, with her white, toothy smile, gentle dimples and stunning voice. Beneath the spotlights, I watched entranced as she moved gracefully across the wooden stage. My dad leant over and whispered to me: 'Son, the pianist is Todd Matshikiza.' Matshikiza pounded the keys, his head bobbing from side to side. 'The guitarist is Len Pillay,' my dad added. What stayed with me especially was Miriam Makeba's rendition of 'Back of the Moon' – a song that paid tribute to a famous she-been in Alexandra township. Nathan Mdledle and his Manhattan Brothers stepped in with their melodious harmony. The cast sang, danced and tap-danced with abundant zest in an African township setting. The township storyline was strong. King Kong was the name of the main character, who was a budding boxer. In time he gained fame, but also arrogance, as he knocked out every opponent. About this, Muhammad Ali, the boxing leg-end, famously warned a few decades later: 'It is hard to be humble when you are great.' At the high point of the musical, the cast burst into the theme song: 'King Kong was stronger than a lion. King Kong, king kong'ed them all.' King Kong turned his wrath on his girlfriend. He murdered her out of a jealous heart. The court sentenced him to many years in jail – in Leeuwkop. During his long term of imprisonment there, he committed suicide by drowning in a prison dam. The musical ended with an eerie and plaintive song – 'King Kong Is Dead'.

When my daydreaming about King Kong ended, I wondered how far away the dam was. It would be good to see it, I thought. But then a prison is not a tourist venture, certainly not for an inmate. What mattered was the ticking clock. From day to day, I waited lazily for my time, counted in days, to run out. I had a few nightmarish dreams about a world that might have changed in my absence from when I'd left it ten years earlier. Of less concern to me was the ten years of social lag. I hoped to acquire survival skills fairly read-ily. I was 25 years old but had no home of my own. My parents were unlikely to lock me out of their home and they would certainly feed me. I realised I had no personal possessions of any description, that I would have to acquire basic clothing, and perhaps a watch. I would probably need money. I wondered how I would earn it. Who would employ me at an income? Was my dream of becoming a lawyer attainable? I had the right law degrees, but I could only practise law after a compulsory three-year term of apprenticeship in a firm of attorneys. Would any law firm let me in? I had only one friend I could count on and certainly no girlfriend. In this slim sense, prison had left me socially poor, and yet it presented me with a clean slate to start afresh – perhaps without any social baggage.

The other thought that randomly bubbled in my mind was whether, on my release, I should stay in the country or flee into exile. Many of our PAC and ANC comrades left the country upon their release. They chose to combat apartheid from beyond the easy reach of the domestic security apparatus. It wasn't long after my extended incarceration that I made this choice: I chose to postpone, if not suppress, the thought of going into exile. I chose home. I don't know why. My gut told me it was the right decision.

On 1 July 1973 I was back in Pretoria Central Prison, having been brought there from Leeuwkop overnight. When the warders brought me breakfast that morning, I kicked the plate and mug to the farthest corner of the tiny isolation cell. The soft porridge flew out of the aluminium plate to the one end and the coffee to the other. I did not have even a trace of fear. I had started my stint in prison in this place. Now I had returned – not broken, but whole. I had overcome the little ordeal and I was not going to leave this place carrying prison food in my belly. This dawn was a new day. It promised a true fresh start. I needed the swagger of a winner, the disposition of a champion, when I walked out of there.

A little before 9am, one of the warders led me out of the cell to the reception. My heart started galloping. 'Here is your release attire,' he said in a stern, Afrikaans-accented voice. The penny dropped. I owned nothing, not even a set of civilian clothing. I had hoped that my parents would bring me civilian clothing, but they were nowhere in sight. I settled for the prison shoes, a crinkled white shirt and a grey flannel suit. It hung awkwardly on my tall, lanky frame, accentuated by my almost gaunt, long face. The chief of the prison went through some routine paperwork and asked me to sign a form, which I did not even bother to read. All I wanted to see was that massive wooden door swinging open so that I could walk out of prison. Within a few moments, in stepped three security policemen. I recognised one of them. His name was Smit. Ten years before, he had been part of the team of men who had detained and later tortured me during detention. He looked much older, as one would after losing most of one's teeth. His cheek-bones looked swollen. He was with Khoza and Mokgabudi, who were sergeants, the highest rank black policemen could reach. They referred to Smit as 'Lieutenant'. I quickly worked out that in ten years Smit had moved up the ranks only two spots. He must be dull as hell, I thought. I wondered what the three cops were doing there.

The relationship between us had altered irreversibly.

'*Goeie môre, Dikgang,*' Smit said wryly.

'*Goeie môre, Smit,*' I fired back. I did not think he deserved any title or any respect from me.

'We are here to take you home,' he said.

As I was led out through a side door of the prison I kept wondering where my parents were. I got into the back of Smit's sedan and we sped off westwards towards my home village, Atteridgeville. He tried to make small-talk. I did not reply. He and I had nothing in common. We had nothing to talk about. Khoza and Mokgabudi, the two other security policemen, followed in another car close behind us. Smit pulled up at the gate of my parents' home. My mother was standing in the frame of the front door. She broke into a high-pitched ululation. With great joy and excitement, she screamed: '*Goroga ngwanake, Goroga Mokwena!*' (Arrive my child, arrive Mokwena!). In no time, the front stoep was filled with my extended family. Many broke into song to welcome me. Neighbours and friends also joined the excited welcome.

Smit approached the door amidst this excitement, as did his two colleagues. He was obviously edgy and uncomfortable. He asked my mother to be allowed into the house. It was just about that moment that I realised I had not seen my father or my brother Malatse (who now enjoyed the nickname Mighty) amongst the welcoming people. Smit's presence remained a mystery. He had a brown paper file in his hand and asked whether he could sit down. Out of the file he produced a document. He read it painstakingly, stumbling over the obscure legal terms, and then asked me to sign and acknowledge its receipt. It was a banning order, and it included house arrest.

Its essence was that from the moment he gave it to me, for five years, I was not to leave my parents' residence between the hours of 6pm and 6am every weekday, and over weekends I had to remain indoors for 24 hours each day except if I chose to attend a church service, and then only between 9am and 11am on a Sunday.

A couple of minutes later, my dad burst into the living room where Smit was seated. I have never, before or since, seen my dad in a rage like the rage I saw that day.

'You evil little man!' he shouted. 'You keep us waiting at the main door of the prison for nothing, only for you to dodge us through a side door. Who the hell do you think you are? Why do you think you, Smit, have the right to impose so much pain on other people? I wonder what you are doing in my house? Stand up and get out!'

Smit looked perplexed, then faked a smile, a barely concealed grin. 'Mr Moseneke,' he said, 'I have just come to do my duty. I have been sent to serve a banning order on your son.'

My dad exploded even harder. Like a dragon spewing flame, he emptied ten years of wrath all over Smit. He told him how much he hated him and what a callous, selfish racist he was. All the anger my father could muster about his past racist humiliation and my imprisonment he poured right over the captive Smit in our lounge. And when he was finished, he shouted, at the top of his voice: 'Get out of my house! Did you hear me? Get out of my house!'

The ladies who had gathered on the stoep and in the lounge started crying. The initial moment of joy as I arrived home had become one of anger and many, many tears. Two people there did not cry – my mother and me. I suppose my mother's tears had long since dried up. She must have learned how to cope with difficult moments over the ten years of my absence. Perhaps more accurately, she must have shared every ounce of my father's anguish. His pain, as we say in our language, was her pain. For my part, crying was the remotest of all responses. I stood there with my chest high and my heels firmly rooted to the floor. I smiled at my father and then burst into applause. 'Well done, Dad, great stuff!' I was profoundly proud of my dad's strength to stand up to a little racist bully and to claim his right to be master of his own home. He was entitled to show Smit the door and he did. Smit's two sidekicks ran after him like wet puppies.

That epic exchange between my father and Smit meant this: the banning order did not permit me to attend any gathering at home or anywhere else. It specified that a gathering was the presence of two or more people at the same time and place, except in the presence of my named family members. In effect, I was banned from being part of the big family party that had been arranged to welcome me home. Nevertheless I insisted that the party go ahead. I would confine myself to the bedroom. It seemed to me that Smit and his government had no power or right to regulate the merrymaking of my family and their guests. One family member after another entered my secluded bedroom to greet and welcome me home. In this way we observed the law but defeated its purpose.

Two visitors on my first evening at home deserve a special mention. The one was expected, the other not. While I could not join the welcome party, I was entitled to receive not more than two visitors at a time in my bedroom or any other room in the house. One of these was Mike Mohohlo, my childhood friend and schoolmate who had left me on Robben Island after serving his prison term of five years. Then, at around 9pm, my brother Mighty announced that there was a lady to see me. Her name was Naomi Kabonina and she was asking if she could pay me a brief welcome-home visit.

I did not remember ever having met Kabonina before, but when she was led into the bedroom and I looked at her face intently, the penny dropped.

Nearly two years before my release, I took out a subscription to *Drum* magazine. The cover girl on the front page of the first issue of *Drum* that I received was a young woman from my hometown, Atteridgeville. The write-up explained that she was a student nurse at Baragwanath Hospital. Besides her stunning looks, she was in the media because of a drama piece she had written and produced called *The Pride of the Family*. The piece lauded the life of a young student nurse who avoided the indiscretions of youth in favour of her training and future career as a health caregiver.

I wrote letters to Gabby Magomola and Mike Mohohlo, who had both left Robben Island by then, asking them to find the postal address of the cover girl. Gabby obliged. It later turned out that it did not take much detective work for him to get the information I sorely needed. His girlfriend then and now wife, Nana, was a student nurse at Baragwanath. I wrote three carefully worded letters to the cover girl, Kabonina, and sent them off – a bit like hurling a stone into a deep pond. I received no reply to any of them. I gave up my amateur fishing session and forgot about the target of my attention.

As Kabonina entered the room, I looked again, but I still could not remember who she was. I wondered how she knew about the date of my release. There she was – neither one day earlier, nor one day later. She came despite the scary news of my banning order which, I was told, spread quickly across our township. The story went something like this: 'Dikgang is out, but not quite out. He is still locked up in his home.' Once I had made the connection, I also wondered why she would care to visit now, when she had not bothered to reply to any of my letters.

'I was so interested to write and yet so scared,' she explained in a soft, husky voice. 'I received all three of your letters, but they had big red prison stamps all over the brown envelopes. I was truly afraid to write a letter to someone in prison.'

We exchanged some further pleasantries and Kabonina's visit ended.

Sometime before midnight I dozed off. I must have been run down by an emotion-sapping day. More so, it was the first time that I slept in a bed in ten years. The welcome party went on without me until the wee hours of the morning.

CHAPTER 17

Coping with the new world

The prison clock kicked in. On my first morning at home I was wide awake at 5.30am. Hopefully, my body clock would adapt. In the calmness of dawn I read the terms of the banning order and house arrest. They were horrendous. For one thing, the order stated that the house arrest was to last for five years beyond the ten years' imprisonment I had already endured and which had ended the day before. In pompous legalese, the house-arrest order ran something like this:

> By virtue of the powers vested in me as Minister of Justice, by the Suppression of Communism Act, 1951, I order you Dikgang Ernest Moseneke not to absent yourself without the prior and written consent of the Chief Magistrate of Pretoria from the house, 29 Mbolekwa Street, Atteridgeville, Pretoria on every Monday to Friday between the hours 6pm to 6am and during the whole day of every Saturday and Sunday, except between the hours of 9am and 11am on a Sunday for the sole purpose of attending a bona fide Christian church service at the Methodist Church situated at Mnzangoma Street, Atteridgeville. Also, you shall not absent yourself from the magisterial district of Pretoria without the prior written permission of the Chief Magistrate of Pretoria.

The order ran into several pages and imposed telling restrictions and commands. For the next five years, every Monday between 6am and 6pm, I would have to report in person to the local police station. Over the same period, I was not to leave the magisterial district of Pretoria without prior written permission. I was banned from attending or addressing any gathering of any nature whatsoever. A gathering was said to be a presence of two or more people. I was not permitted to attend any place of learning, including a school, college, technicon or university, without prior permission. I was not allowed to publish or distribute to the public any material I had written.

PC Pelser, the minister of justice, never sought my views before he made the order, nor did he say why he thought I was a threat to the security of the state after a long absence from society. I had completed the punishment imposed by a court of law and had not again been found guilty of any offence whatsoever. In any event, I could not have made myself guilty of any offence as I had come out of prison less than 24 hours before the order was served on me. Pelser, in his absolute discretion, had effectively extended my incarceration, the only difference being that I would be restrained within the comfort of my parental home. This was punishment without trial not by a court of law but by an executive who had breached every tenet of administrative or criminal justice. What was more, the statute Pelser relied on shielded his order from judicial review. It placed the order beyond the reach of the law. It stated that no court of law might pronounce on the validity of a banning order issued by the minister. I read and reread this draconian order with near-disbelief. It was not yet *uhuru* (freedom). I had to find a silver lining at the edge of thick, dark clouds.

There were many things to be jubilant about, however. My family was well and intact. My parents were still together and both continued their roles as parents and teachers. My father was headmaster at Dr WF Nkomo High School and my mother taught at Kgabo Primary School. On a school-day morning our home became a hive of activity as parents and siblings got into a mad rush to beat the 7am starting time at school. My parents had also expanded the modest family residence in the expectation of my return. They had built and furnished what passed for a granny flat with adequate ablution facilities and a desk at which I could read and write.

My brother Malatse was 20 years old and had grown to be a big man with wide shoulders and the massive arms and hands he needed as an A-team football goalkeeper. I could see how he had earned himself the nickname 'Mighty'. He was studying at a post-matric teacher training college.

Onkgopotse Obed came just after Malatse. He was born in 1954. From childhood he was afflicted by epilepsy. He succumbed to epilepsy while I was on the island. It was hard to overcome the horror of losing a brother whose funeral I had not been permitted to attend. But what was more, I learned about his demise from my parents during a prison visit a good few months after Onkgopotse's death. A letter bearing such devastating news would have been inappropriate. Onkgopotse's death hurt deeply.

Kabelo, another brother, born in 1958, was a chubby, enterprising and fearless fifteen-year-old, who attended a local secondary school. No household or outdoor chore was too big or daring for him, although his industry did not advance his cause. If anything, he ended up slogging alone. He became like the proverbial industrious donkey about which the isiZulu idiom says: '*Idonki sishaya le idontsayo*' (We whip the donkey that pulls the most). In time he became very close to Kabo and came to live with us in our new home on Gwangwa Street.

Tiego was the last of the boys, born in 1962. He had been a mere four months old when I left; now he was a rather chubby, talkative ten-year-old in primary school. He asked of and about everything. He related to me many of his school escapades, somehow skilfully managing to evade the household chores like washing dishes, gardening or even washing the old man's car. One story he told me, with obvious glee, was about how he had solved the problem of bullying at school – at least when it came to him. He had befriended a couple of the most feared boys in the school, he told me, and so nobody dared to bully him.

My mother continued to cook up a storm. Her Sunday lunches got all six of us around the table after the morning church service. To me the joy of reconnecting with the family was priceless. I was grateful that our family had not disintegrated when many African families succumbed to the ravages of an unkind and uncaring social repression. Also, our extended paternal and maternal families were reasonably cohesive. I was blessed and privileged to have a solid family plank on which I could stand from the first day of my release.

Within days of my release, I was out there to see whether my childhood village had changed for the better. In fact, I found that little had changed. The red-brick homes looked older and their inhabitants more gaunt, and the children still ran around with swollen pot-bellies and flies under their nostrils. Those streets that were tarred were full of potholes, and the others were as stony and dusty as they'd always been. The schools looked shabby and under-resourced. The shops were still housed in narrow brick cubicles and carried sparse stock. Nobody seemed to be thriving.

As I walked in the street past their homes I was aware of people peeping at me through their curtains. They seemed terrified to be seen talking to me. Word had gone round that I was back home, but under a severe banning order. The people of Atteridgeville knew who I was, but they also knew there was a price to pay for being connected to an ex-political prisoner, particularly one who continued to labour under severe restrictions. Common sense told them that I was no doubt being watched by the security police. In short, the apartheid security apparatus was well and truly in place and most residents lived in fear of its reprisals.

My walkabout in the township did not show only gloom, however. Along the main roads, like Seeiso and Mareka streets, young women dressed up and they looked truly gorgeous. They seemed to have chosen glitz above or despite the dimness of social repression. They wore skirts that ended much higher than their knees, and on the high cork-platformed shoes that seemed to be the fashion that year, their legs appeared extraordinarily long. They sported handsomely curly and rounded Afro hairstyles. Some young ladies wore tight-waisted bell-bottom trousers with their high-heeled shoes. I knew none of the beautiful ladies and none acknowledged me. I probably looked like a stranger to them, one with a horrible dress sense. The loss was mine, as I walked back home to beat the 6pm curfew. Soon, it became plain that the only place I could possibly meet a lady friend would be in the sanctuary of my parental home. My edge would be with a lady who visited the house knowing who I was. Mercifully, it did not take long before the word went round that I was a lonely but eligible bachelor who was home-bound, but allowed to receive one guest at a time.

Our family consensus was that I needed at least six months of indolence and learning how to live outside a prison. My mother thought I should be fed properly and my dad was convinced that I needed time to think my way forward. None of us had any illusions about the challenge of advancing a career or securing a profession after a long stint on Robben Island, coupled with an extended house arrest. So, as everybody in my family rushed off to school each morning, I remained at home. My lazing around was not for long, however.

Apartheid oppression seemed to have broken the resistance of many black communities, but this was not true of young activists, particularly at centres of learning. The South African Students Organisation (SASO) had been formed in 1968 at the University of Natal's black campus when black student activists broke away from the National Union of South African Students (NUSAS), a liberal student organisation pioneered and led mainly by white liberal students. The student movement was led by Bantu Steve Biko, ably supported by near-fearless young activists like Saths Cooper, Onkgopotse Tiro, Strini Moodley, Barney Pityana, Bokwe Mafuna and Harry Nengwekhulu.

By 1973, when I was released, SASO had come to articulate more clearly its article of faith – Black Consciousness. While we had heard of the rise of Black Consciousness during my island days, the newspaper reports on the political activity of the movement were scant and infrequent. This was so particularly because the *Cape Times* and *Die Burger* paid little if any attention to the activities of SASO.

The starting point of Black Consciousness was that in their fight for freedom, oppressed people had to free their minds first. They had to acquire a consciousness that filled them with pride about their identity and that was determined to break the chains of oppression. The duty to liberate black people rested, in the first instance, upon themselves. They had to articulate their own understanding of the struggle against racism and economic exclusion. This meant that they were not to collaborate in their own oppression. That understanding could not and might not be articulated through the lenses of others, like white liberals. In this sense blackness is less about skin colour and everything about a state of mind ready to defeat racial supremacy. SASO had grown in confidence as its student support increased and was on a course to assert an independent organisation.

By July 1972, SASO leaders and representatives from some 27 black organisations had established an adult wing of their student organisation. This was the Black People's Convention and their first president was Winnie Kgware. So at the time of my release, and unbeknown to me, leaders of the Black Consciousness Movement had come under increased police surveillance and state repression. Most predictably, by February 1973, the minister of justice, Pelser, had issued banning orders against eight of the SASO leaders, arguing in parliament that SASO had to be stopped from spreading its message of what he called 'the black revolution'. Shortly thereafter, SASO was banned and, in 1974, it was listed as an 'affected' organisation under a law targeting organisations of its kind. That law prohibited organisations like SASO from receiving any foreign support or funding. The intention was to cripple them and thereby prevent them from pursuing their objectives. Not long afterwards, Onkgopotse Tiro was killed and most of the other SASO leaders were prevented from providing effective leadership to the organisation.

One evening in September I was alerted that I had a clandestine visitor from Alexandra – Bokwe Mafuna. I went up to the gate for a quick meeting. 'We welcome you from Robben Island, comrade,' he said. 'I have been sent from the Black People's Convention underground structures to enquire whether you would want to "skip". If you were inclined to leave the country, there is a batch of comrades leaving through Zeerust to Botswana.'

Time was of the essence. We both understood that we had to communicate quickly as both he and I were under constant security police surveillance.

'Comrade Bokwe, I want to think about this,' I replied. 'I will send you a message should I decide to go into exile.'

He understood, I thought, that I meant that I preferred to remain inside the country. I had expected an approach of this kind, but by then I was of a fairly firm mind that my continued role of combating racism and repression had to be advanced within the country. I had not formulated any rational reason for my preference. It was a matter of gut rather than brain. Moreover, I was significantly emboldened by another wave of resistance amongst young people, spearheaded principally by SASO and the Black People's Convention. But for now, I would stay in the country. It was here, I believed, that my contribution to the liberation effort was likely to yield value.

CHAPTER 18

The start of a career

My first festive season since Robben Island came and went off enjoyably but rather quickly. My New Year's resolution was not obscure. I had had a full six months since my release to catch my breath, but I could not loiter forever. I had to start a career or find a job. I had worked many years but never before for a salary. I simply did not know where to start. I had a matric certificate and two university degrees, and still had the third and fourth years of my LLB studies to complete. I was eligible to be appointed an apprentice in a law firm for three years – if anybody were to have me. I knew nobody who would want to. I trawled the job pages of newspapers and applied to a few insurance companies that had posted vacancies requiring legal skills. Most applications led to interviews, which ended when I disclosed, as I had to, that I had been on Robben Island and that I was under house arrest. Nothing came of those blindly hopeful, if not naive, efforts. In that climate, no right-thinking employer would have wanted a 'terrorist' in its backyard.

Next was to set my sights on law firms in Pretoria. After all, I had always wanted to be a practising attorney. Thanks to the Yellow Pages listing of law firms, I wrote to between ten and fifteen of these in Pretoria enquiring if they had a vacancy for an articled clerk. Five or so responded and called me in for an interview. I thought I interviewed rather well. I always went armed with my matric certificate, BA and B Juris certificates, and a transcript of my third-year LLB results. All seemed to go well until the moment of truth. I knew I had to spit it out at some point. I was not ashamed of having been on Robben Island, but I knew that this disclosure would be a death knell.

One of those five abortive interviews lingers in my mind. I walked into the office of the senior partner of Rooth and Wessels Attorneys in Pretoria. My interview was with a Mr Bam. He was a rotund man and of not much height and he filled his chair. He had glasses with thick lenses and round rims that sat at the lower end of his nose. I couldn't help noticing his black waistcoat, which sported a fob-watch chain that ended in the little front pocket. He had an enormous desk. To the right end of it was an old-fashioned telephone, the kind you really only see in dated movies. The rims of the mouth-piece and the ear-piece of the handset appeared gilded, although this may very well have been brass. From the time I sat down in front of him for the interview to the time the interview actually started, Mr Bam answered several telephone calls while I waited. Each time he took a call, he tilted backwards and swivelled his chair in a distinctly self-satisfied manner.

In time, the interview got under way. He seemed suitably impressed. He turned his podgy-cheeked face in my direction. 'Young man, I think you have earned yourself articles at this great law firm.' I could hear my heart throbbing. I knew that his verdict was premature. I still had to tell him about my sojourn on Robben Island. I knew this would have an effect but not the effect it did. As I mentioned the words 'Robben Island', Mr Bam tilted his chair so violently backwards that he almost toppled over. Breathing heavily and half-suspended in the air, he called out loudly for his personal assistant. She charged into the room and helped tilt the chair into an upright position once more. When he was settled, Mr Bam fixed his eyes on me and raised his voice almost to a shout. 'No, you do NOT have a job, young man. And you must leave – immediately!'

I hastened out of his office, devastated. I had come so close to getting a job. Thinking about it, I probably wouldn't have fitted in there anyway.

During the third quarter of 1974, and as my anxiety of staying at home began to rise, one morning my father came to me and said: 'I know an attorney named Piet Hartman. He did odd legal work for me. He has promised me that he will introduce you to Dan Neser. His wife is Jenny Neser. Dan is a partner at a law firm called Dyason, Douglas, Muller and Meyer.'

Dan Neser was a tall, big, jovial man. He chuckled, and sometimes laughed, when few people would. He seemed to take life in his stride. His father had been a judge and his wife's brother was a judge. Dan was attached to a securely Afrikaans-speaking firm, whose senior partner at the time was a charismatic man named Mike Meyer. Hilgard Muller, whose name appeared on the firm's letterhead as a consultant, was a cabinet minister in charge of foreign affairs at the time.

Dan Neser agreed to meet with me. He suggested that we meet at his home, which was located on Lawley Street in Waterkloof Ridge. I was awestruck by the leafy suburb with its many trees and beautiful homes. Dan's wife, Jenny, was friendly and chatty and welcomed me inside. They were liberal people who were determined to do good, even in the face of racial fissure. It did not take long before Jenny told me that she had been at school with Fikile Bam (no relation to the chair-swivelling attorney). Boet Fiks, as I affectionately called him, spent twelve years on Robben Island, just about the same time I was there. Jenny was way more leftist and opposed to racial segregation than her husband, who was a member of the United Party. Jenny was a Black Sash kind of activist and she talked about Sheena Duncan with open admiration. She was a charming, vivacious and caring human being. Later, Jenny and I, together with Johann Kriegler and other generous trustees, would work together for many years in Project Literacy. It was Jenny who started this project, in order to provide adult education to domestic workers and gardeners who were employed in the leafy eastern neighbourhoods of Pretoria. She badgered the governing bodies of whites-only primary-schools to allow her and the worker-learners to use their children's classrooms in the evenings. In no time, Jenny learned Sepedi and she spoke it fluently to her charges as they sat low down on the small primary school chairs during evening lessons. She sneered at apartheid boundaries. To restore the self-worth of outcasts was much more important to her.

That evening I told Dan and Jenny my story, and that I wanted to become a practising lawyer. Dan expected resistance at his firm. Most of the partners at Dyason were middle-of-the-road ruling-party supporters, and the firm, being the largest Afrikaans law firm in Pretoria, sourced most of its work from the state, which they lauded and supported. Nevertheless, Dan said, he would raise the matter with the most senior partner, Mike Meyer.

A few days later, clad in a dark suit, a fresh white shirt and a tie, I was heading for Mike Meyer's office on Pretorius Street. I had cracked an interview with him. At the end of the interview, his flashing green eyes pierced straight into mine. He pulled in the edges of his mouth as if he was about to smile. 'You have a job, as a law librarian and researcher,' he said. 'We employ only LLBs. As soon as you complete your LLB, you will have a job as an articled clerk.'

I was stunned. I had made a full revelation to him about my past and he still gave me the job! Dan must have paved the way. Where was the catch, I wondered. Might he change his mind once he had received a call from the security branch? They must have easy access to him. Maybe, I thought, he had told them beforehand and they thought it would make it easier for them to monitor me if I worked at a leading Afrikaans-speaking law firm. Whatever the truth was, at that moment it didn't matter a jot – I had a job.

My first job was special in many ways. I was allocated an office with my own telephone extension just near the entrance of the library and opposite the office of another senior partner, Marius de Klerk. Of course, back then I could not have known that Marius and I would end up as fellow advocates at the Pretoria Bar and that, later, a part of our terms as judges of the High Court in Pretoria would coincide. At Dyason, I had to make sure that I was a worthy appointee. I had to manage the library exceptionally. But even more importantly, I vowed to produce the best-quality legal research work, if I were asked. Mike Meyer insisted that I be paid as an articled clerk, a package that included a clothing allowance every three months so that I looked the professional part. He sent out a circular directing all non-lawyers in the firm, and secretaries in particular, to address me in writing and orally as they addressed all other professional lawyers. The form of address was *Meneer*. That was a small progressive step if one remembered that all the other black people who worked in the law firm were either cleaners or messengers.

There were eight new articled clerks, all drawn from Potchefstroom and Pretoria universities. All of them were Afrikaans speaking. Even so, we soon made friends. It was remarkable how young people with backgrounds such as they must have had leapt at the opportunity to cross artificial boundaries. Mutual respect amongst us developed very quickly. Each of my young colleagues, who included Zak Ferreira, Willie Nortje and Anamarie Venter, had to apply to the Department of Justice for permits to come and visit me in the township. They were all genuinely keen and eager to turn their backs on their prejudiced upbringing.

At a career level, however, I was less than happy. Despite the fact that I was entitled to enter into articles of clerkship by virtue of my B Juris degree, the internal rule at Dyason was that I had to actually hold an LLB degree. Before long I started looking around the Pretoria area for a law firm that would take me on to start articles immediately. I landed an interview with Mr Ned Klagsbrun, a senior partner at Klagsbrun, Schewitz and Partners. The interview was conducted by his son, Steven Klagsbrun. With him, I chose to make the Robben Island disclosure up front. If that broke the back of the camel, so be it. I had resolved that I wouldn't have another consultation that might at the end blow up in my face. Remarkably, Steven Klagsbrun was quite relaxed about my political conviction. Within 30 minutes of the interview, he said to me: 'You have got the job' – provided that the Law Society agreed to register my articles of clerkship.

The law of the time required that the agreement between the principal and a trainee law clerk had to be registered with the Law Society, which was obliged to satisfy itself that the law clerk was a fit and proper person to be admitted as an attorney. I had to submit to two interviews with a panel of senior members of the council of the Law Society. My position was uncomplicated. I made the point to them that I had not been convicted of any offence that went to my honesty, integrity or competence. The panel members may have held different political views from mine, but that was no reason to bar me from training and later practising as an attorney. I pointed out that attorneys held divergent views about the merits of the political system of the country. That divergence of opinion could not possibly undermine their ability to serve their clients faithfully and competently.

Within days, the Law Society supported the registration of my articles of clerkship for a period of three years. If I were to complete the LLB degree earlier, the term would run for two years only.

By the end of 1977 my articles were fully served and I had indeed completed the LLB degree – at the end of 1976. What was more, I had passed my attorneys' admission examinations after obtaining the highest pass mark ahead of all the candidates who sat for the examinations that year.

Steven Klagsbrun was extremely supportive. I owed my excellent pass rates to the immaculate and thorough practical training I received under his tutelage. I prepared my admission papers and served them as required by the Law Society rules.

Then, to my total surprise, the Law Society filed a notice of intention to oppose the application for my admission as an attorney. They advanced only one reason: this was that only a South African citizen or permanent resident might be admitted as an attorney. I was no longer a citizen of the republic and therefore I no longer qualified to be admitted as an attorney. Their reasoning was pegged on a quaint statute: the Status of Bophuthatswana Act. This was the law that was passed by the South African parliament with a view to breaking up our country into little homeland states where black South Africans had to find homes, citizenship and democracy. The law sought to confer some level of self-government on homeland governments. Bophuthatswana was one of these. At the time, the apartheid government was rather intent on rendering every black South African a stranger in their land of birth. The object was to terminate their South African citizenship and to ascribe a new citizenship to each black South African.

· The Status Act provided that a person who was Motswana by birth or descent or whose vernacular was the Setswana language ceased to be a South

African citizen and had compulsorily become a citizen of Bophuthatswana. It is so that my forebears had their roots in what is now known as the North West Province and, up to this day, many of my kith and kin are to be found in the villages of Tlhabane, Pilwe, Melorwe, Bierkraal, Modimosana and Mmatau. A sprinkling of the Moseneke clan can also be found in the village of Ledig. They are closely allied and connected to Bakwena ba Modimosana. All of this worked against me in my application for admission as an attorney. I was indeed a Motswana by birth or descent. And my home language was Setswana.

Here was the rub. I had never been to any of those places where my roots were supposed to be. As I have related earlier, I was a third-generation resident of Pretoria and a South African citizen. What was more, the law that rendered me stateless was passed *after* I had commenced my apprenticeship as an attorney and yet the Law Society argued, with unexpected vigour, before court that I was not a citizen of South Africa and ought to be barred from being admitted as an attorney of the Supreme Court of South Africa. But the argument the Law Society did *not* make was that I was not a fit and proper person to be an attorney because I was an ex-convict or had served time on Robben Island. At the commencement of the period of my apprenticeship, they had enquired into that matter to no end. They had concluded that I was good enough to become an attorney, and so their stance in relation to my formal admission was a surprising *volte-face*.

Steven Klagsbrun and I agreed that we would brief not a regular senior counsel at the Bar, but a professor of constitutional law at the University of South Africa – Professor Marinus Wiechers. The rumour was that he had had a lot to do with the drafting of the mini constitutions that conferred independence on Bantu homeland governments. The Law Society briefed Frank Kirk-Cohen SC, with Meyer Joffe as his junior. Acting Judge President Boshoff chose to preside in the matter together with Justice Henry Moll, a senior judge of the division, who later became the judge president.

At the end of the argument, which lasted only one day, Boshoff made a pronouncement that was totally life-changing for me:

May the applicant rise and step forward. Mr Moseneke, having heard submissions made before us today, this Court is unanimous that you should be admitted as an attorney of this Court and it is so ordered. Reasons for this decision will be furnished in due course. Mr Moseneke, would you step forward to take the prescribed oath.

The inside of my mouth dried up. I could feel my heart pounding as if it would pierce through my rib-cage and I would have to pick it up from the floor. My knees felt wobbly. I had to firm them up. My eyes dilated and immediately became moist. My nostrils took in huge gulps of air as I strained to master this incredible moment in my life. The judge's clerk rose and asked me to raise my right hand. All I remember of the oath was the last sentence: 'And I shall be faithful to the Republic of South Africa. So help me God.' Even before the two judges rose and disappeared, loud applause broke out in the courthouse. My family and friends would have been the culprits. Steven Klagsbrun, my principal and mentor, gave me a warm hug. Kabo, who was my new bride, had come to court with my father, and Willie Seriti (who is now a judge of the Supreme Court of Appeal) and his wife, Yvonne, were also in attendance. Many in the media and other South Africans seemed to join in this triumphant moment. They understood what the journey from an ex-convict to an attorney of the Supreme Court of South Africa meant. The reserved reasons for the judgment were delivered more than a year later and are memorialised in *Ex parte Moseneke* 1979 (4) SA 885 (T).

When I peered into the reasons, I was quite amazed, if not flattered, that in admitting me, the Court relied on the celebrated case of *Incorporated Law Society, Transvaal v Mandela* 1954 (3) SA 102 (T). In the aftermath of the Defiance Campaign of 1952, mounted by the ANC, Mr Mandela was convicted of an offence associated with resisting and defying racist laws. As he was an admitted attorney, the Law Society approached the court seeking his removal from the roll of attorneys for the reason that he had a previous conviction. The court per Ramsbottom J refused to strike Mr Mandela from the roll of attorneys because the offence he was convicted of did not show a lack of integrity that signified a lack of fitness to act as an attorney.

Whatever the legal niceties may have been, I was on the verge of a career which was to consume almost all of me for the next 40 years.

CHAPTER 19

Husband and father

I have narrated the pit-stop visit Kabo made to my home on the day of my release from prison. To this day she has not explained what prompted her to make that bold but risky stopover. Then she was only 23 years of age, a petite and stunningly beautiful woman. Kabo spoke softly, releasing her words in a measured, careful manner. Her lips were dark and full, and she had large brown eyes and a steady gaze. On that first visit Kabo had briefly mentioned that she was a nursing sister at Kalafong Hospital and that she still lived with her parents in Maunde Street in Atteridgeville. And, of course, she had explained the reason she had not replied to the letters I had written to her from Robben Island.

It was such a fleeting visit. She left after only a few minutes. Like a phantom in a fairy tale, she was there and then instantly nowhere. But she left behind a lingering impression.

About two weeks later, I asked my brother Mighty to call Kabo and ask her to visit on a Sunday afternoon. She did. Before her visit, though, some family friends came to my parents' home to welcome me back. They brought their 20-something daughters along, evening after evening. The word may have gone round, my mother smugly remarked, that I was an available bachelor, and not the worst-looking guy on the block either. The young ladies bedazzled me. When they visited they were dressed to the nines: high-heels and tight bell-bottom pants that fitted snugly around their tiny waists, or skirts with hems well above the knees. They were charming and entertaining, but they looked at me intensely as though they were wondering what could be going through the mind of a 25-year-old newly released long-term prisoner. Frankly, I was consumed by desire.

Kabo came to visit on a Sunday afternoon. She had to come to my parents' home because I could not go to her under the terms of my house arrest. On the strength of that visit we began to build a friendship, and soon we were dating. But it would be dating with a severe twist. Kabo worked at the hospital and could visit only after work or over weekends, so we had no option but to be home-bound. The house arrest kicked in from 6pm to 6am during the week and covered full days over weekends. Occasionally, when Kabo was off duty, we would rush off to a matinee movie in Marabastad, but we had to speed back to my home before my 6pm evening curfew. I had no choice. I had to observe it on the pain of criminal sanction.

And so for just under two years Kabo and I dated indoors. Then, on 3 May 1975, we celebrated our wedding. My father thought the marriage was ill-advised. I had no business marrying at 27 years of age, he said. I was robbing myself of the opportunity to see the world. In contrast, my mother thought I had made an excellent choice and that I should go straight on to marry Kabonina. On this one I trusted my mother's instinct.

As our wedding festivities constituted 'a gathering of more than two people', I had to apply for permission at the security police headquarters to be part of my own wedding. The chief magistrate had to grant me leave to do so. We had been here before. Kabo had put together an engagement party of friends for us, but for that event the police had refused to relax my banning order. This meant I could not attend my own engagement occasion. Tiego, my youngest brother, had to fill the gap. He was my duly appointed proxy to convey my promise to marry. At the party, I am told, he made a moving and passionate engagement commitment – and it was widely reported in the public media.

I applied again, but this time to attend my wedding and also to go to Durban on honeymoon for a week. Probably the cops did not want to invite another media fall-out showing them as petty and heartless bullies and so they granted the relaxation.

Kabo and I had become good friends with Zak Ferreira, Willie Nortje and Anamarie Venter, all of whom had been my fellow articled clerks at Dyason Attorneys. They and their partners attended our wedding in the township. This was not a done thing under apartheid. In effect, they were contravening the law which required them to seek a permit to enter a black residential area. I admired their guts. Young Afrikaners were raising their heads above the apartheid parapet. The security cops hovered around the wedding ceremony but stopped short of arresting my guests. To be honest, I was disappointed. If six young white people had been arrested, it would have made even better copy.

After a joyous community wedding Kabo and I drew the last penny from our bank accounts, shut down our bank-books and left for honeymoon in Durban. I alerted Boet Griffiths Mxenge of our impending visit. Jacob Zuma, with whom, you will remember, I had spent ten years on the island, met us at the airport to much excitement because he kept on calling me *Sboshwa* – fellow prisoner. So-called white hotels, by law, did not take in black people. Zuma took us to the Himalaya Hotel, and this was where Kabo I stayed. Griffiths and Victoria Mxenge looked after us with much love and care. They took us to nightclubs in and around Durban, and through them we met Thembile and Sayo Skweyiya, who extended the hospitality. I admired Thembile hugely. He was a young successful African advocate. His kind were few and exceptional. He helped me make up my mind to become a practising advocate. Just about the same time, Kabo and I met Zac Yacoob, another black advocate. He and Thembile were practising in a building away from white advocates. The law of the time did not permit them to occupy the same chambers as their white counterparts. Zac cheekily assured me that he and Thembile were quite happy to be set apart. The problem of racism was not theirs but that of racists.

Our week in Durban went quickly and soon it was time to go back to work. And to think about raising a family.

Kabo and I lived with my parents until 1977, when we were allocated our own municipal four-roomed home at 35 Gwangwa Street. The ordinary rule was that no African person could own land in an urban area. All township homes were owned by the municipality. In turn, all African people were tenants of the municipality at a decreed rental and service costs. Kabo and I had to wait our turn on the municipal waiting list. Even so we rebuilt the house substantially in anticipation of the coming babies.

Our daughter Duduzile was the first to stay with us. Shortly thereafter Sedise Gabaiphiwe, our son, was born, in June 1976, amidst the student riots which started in Soweto but quickly spread to other townships, including ours. On the evening of his birth, a wing of the hospital where he was about to be born caught fire after being petrol-bombed by rioting youth. Thankfully the maternity wards were safe and well secured.

Within two years of Sedise, in November 1978, our second son, Reabetswe Botshelo ('Bo'), was born.

Kabo and I were fortunate. It wasn't long before our home was bustling with three joyful children. We brought them up at a time when both of us were on career trails. Kabo started studying full-time again, in a bid to further her qualifications. Armed with a diploma in nursing education from the Medical University of South Africa, she left bed-side nursing for an academic career. She began teaching at Lebone Nursing College. Not long afterwards she had her Bachelor of Nursing Science degree and an honours degree from Wits University. I watched with admiration as she moved up her professional ladder.

In turn, I charted my own professional path. Even with our remarkable and compatible drives to achieve, Kabo and I kept together a wonderful family of two parents and three children. My mother-in-law and father-in-law gave us invaluable support in caring for these wonderful children as we ventured into the world to achieve and make a difference.

But for Botshelo, who would succumb early in his life to complications of diabetes, our family nest has been blessed with care, compassion and stability. Kabo provided our children and me with unstinting support throughout a full and sometimes frenzied career and life. The children have done well in their own right. They all married and amongst them yielded six incredible little souls. The grandchildren – Lindokuhle, Tshiamo, Zintl'intombi, Sedise, Lwandle and Niara – fill up our home and set it alight with laughter, quarrels, screams, romping, eating, and above all manipulating Kabo and me – to our joy and the total disgust of their parents. It is perhaps for that reason that Kabo remains my mother's favourite to this day. Forty years later, I can still say I was right to trust my mother's instinct that I marry Kabo.

CHAPTER 20

Maluleke, Seriti and Moseneke

The distant rugged hilltops were snow laden – I could see them from my hotel room on Rue de Lausanne – but the walk along Lac de Genève was irresistible, even on a freezing, drizzling December afternoon like this one. I was wrapped up warmly in a neck scarf, gloves and a full-length black overcoat. To the locals I must have looked ridiculous. Joggers moved past me wearing only black thermal suits. A few ran in shorts. Others were content with a brisk walk. I did not feel one bit ashamed. I am from balmy Africa. In South Africa it was mid-summer. The Swiss must have been bred, like seals, in the cold, I thought. My long walk ended at Pont du Mont-Blanc. By then it was getting darker and colder. Once I had inhaled enough of the cold and feasted my eyes on the watery beauty along the Quai, I made my way to one of the main streets to board the tram back towards the Palais des Nations. I alighted just opposite the World Trade Organization headquarters.

In the Palais, a day earlier, the United Nations High Commissioner for Human Rights, together with the Centre for Human Rights of the University of Pretoria, had hosted the 6th Nelson Mandela World Human Rights Moot Court Competition for university law students from around the world. I was the High Commissioner's guest, together with four other judges. It was 2014, just over a year since former president Mandela had passed on. The moot court competition was not only named after him but was also held in memory and honour of his life. I was invited as deputy chief justice of our republic but also as an executor in the estate of the late president Nelson Mandela. From the bench where I presided with four other distinguished judges and law scholars, the competitors looked so young and fresh-faced. They seemed much brighter than I had been when I was a budding lawyer. They displayed a remarkable grasp of global norms of human decency wrapped up in international humanitarian law. They seemed to understand well that fundamental rights and freedoms are interrelated, indivisible, universal and inviolable. Their constant breach, and sometimes with impunity, does not disprove but rather reminds us of their worth.

In my long cold walk along Lake Geneva, I cast my mind back to the start of my practice as an attorney. It was a modest start, offering little to rejoice about. There was no partnership on offer at Klagsbrun, Schewitz and Partners. I was grateful that they had inducted me to completion, but our common understanding was that I would move on to nurture my own career.

I had built a close friendship with Willie Legoabe Seriti. We were reasonably confident that we could start a sizeable law firm in Pretoria to tend to the obvious needs of many clients sidelined by the racialised law practice of the time.

Seriti had completed a law degree at the University of Fort Hare. About the same time I was at Klagsbrun's, he was serving articles of clerkship at another local firm, Angelopoulo and Co. We studied Latin I together and Seriti passed it with an A symbol while I managed only a B. He had a gift of cramming Latin conjugations and declensions. It was a moment of joy and singular achievement when Willie was admitted as an attorney a few months ahead of me. He was from an underprivileged family. I admired his vow that he would never again become poor. Seriti introduced me to a man who had been admitted as an attorney earlier and who had a noticeable set of names: George Sammy (but never Samuel) Shane Maluleke. His friends resorted to GSS, and he seemed to revel in the initials. It took only a few meetings before we became friends and the three of us had a draft partnership agreement to settle. We were to be equal partners, each holding a third of the equity in the law practice. We named the law firm in the order of our dates of admission as attorneys: Maluleke, Seriti and Moseneke. We had great intentions, a binding partnership and a name – but nothing else.

First we scanned the law practice landscape. White law firms were out of reckoning because they hardly bothered to attract black clients. At that time there were three practices of black lawyers in the vicinity. All three were a one-lawyer practice and they were worthy pathfinders in providing legal services to black people in Pretoria. The first to set up shop was Attorney Dabulamanzi Zachariah (DZ) Tantsi, who lived in Atteridgeville. He was particularly well qualified for his time. He was revered for holding a BA degree from Fort Hare and an LLB degree from the University of the Witwatersrand. The aura around his Wits qualification was well founded. DZ had made it where angels feared to tread. The legend was known to young law students of the time that Nelson Mandela had abandoned his LLB studies at Wits because he had been assured by one of the law professors (possibly Ellison Kahn) that no black person had enough intellect to pass an LLB degree. So to us, who heard the legend of the law professor, DZ was living repudiation of this racist claim.

I visited DZ's busy law offices in Marabastad, to which location apartheid geography had consigned his practice. It was well patronised. He spoke with a slight stutter, but one could not miss his erudition and deep sense of self-pride. In time, his popularity proved to be his nemesis. He had far more work than any one attorney could perform well. He was a founding member of the Black Lawyers Association, which was to become a vanguard formation for activist lawyers and the social issues that hurt their clients.

Another early pioneer was attorney Sam Shilubane Makhambeni. Boet Sam, as we younger lawyers fondly called him, was a self-made professional. His is a story of personal heroism little sung. He, too, emerged from a humble home. After matriculating, he found a post as a clerk at the Bantu Affairs commissioner's office. African people aptly called that office *Ndabazabantu*. I pause to remember that it was meant to be the alpha and omega of the lives of black people. A commissioner's office was located in every town, big or small, and was the only point at which black people could be served. There and there only a black person had to register births, marriages, deaths and deceased estates. There they had to procure an identity document, a residential permit, a work permit, a travel document or passport, a gun licence or even a dog licence. There people collected unemployment benefits, workmen's compensation, disability grants and work pensions. Every black male person paid a coercive general tax known as poll tax, and the commissioner's office was where the tax had to be paid. Those who were self-employed also paid their income taxes there. The precincts were always filthy, poorly lit, smelly and crowded. The daily human queues were many, varied and long. The machinery of apartheid slavery turned ever so slowly.

One section of the office housed a court presided over by a commissioner. The prosecution was run by police who had lock-up cells at the venue. In big urban locations hundreds of people were detained there and charged for not having one or other permit or pass required by apartheid law. Some would be sent to jail and others deported to their 'homelands' away from urban areas. Many were held for being unemployed and tried summarily without legal or other representation. The charge was known as vagrancy, or *louferskap*. The vagrancy law was designed to create a cheap labour pipeline for industry. The only defence that was available to an accused person was to show that he had been looking for employment continuously but had not been hired. The proof required was a stamp by whichever would-be employer from whom the person had sought employment.

This gigantic machinery of indignity and repression must have driven Boet Sam nuts. He must have worked grudgingly by day and studied feverishly by night for over seven years until he completed the BA and LLB degrees through UNISA. After a stint doing articles in Johannesburg, he set up practice in Khamisa Building in Marabastad. One visit to his law offices on a Saturday morning left me in awe. As one would expect, those clients who were working during the week could only manage to visit a law office on a Saturday. The queue was longer than a queue at a busy bus-stop. It wound round the tiny double-storey building a few times. Bra Sam arrived around 10am and walked up the steel staircase. He excitedly assured me that, on occasion, his staff issued to every waiting client a numbered coupon that would help to keep one's precedence in the snaking queue. He shared with me his long drives to far-flung courts to do the bidding of his clients. His calling, he explained, was to minister to the grievances of rural people, who were often hapless. Bra Sam seemed to have a clientele at least twice the size DZ had. I could not work out how he managed. Even so, Bra Sam was much loved, patronised and lionised by his many followers.

The third law firm that preceded ours in Pretoria was that of Attorney Tholi Felix Vilakazi. Tholi was younger than DZ and Bra Sam. After obtaining his law degree at Fort Hare, he received practical training under DZ, but in the end he chose to go on his own. He was a taciturn but careful and thoughtful lawyer. He rarely spoke out of turn. He was a stickler for legal norms regulating both the process and substance of his clients' disputes. He kept a successful but moderate practice. In fact, Willie and I had approached Tholi for a possible partnership, but he had politely declined, making the point that he preferred a solo practice in which he could regulate his life free from collective restraints. Tholi practised in a newer and modern building in Marabastad side by side with two respected veteran attorneys from Laudium – Mr VJ Kathri and Mr AS Cassiem.

Sadly, it fell on me to read the eulogy at DZ's funeral some years later. Boet Sam followed, and shortly thereafter Tholi, too, passed on at a rather young age. These three pioneering attorneys lit our pathway and for that we admire them.

Maluleke, Seriti and Moseneke was founded in 1978. The three of us were inspired by shared ideals. Foremost was the emerging trend amongst black lawyers of plying legal skills in a collective setting. There was no shortage of thriving examples. The two most immediate and prominent models were Ngoepe, Machaka and Nkadimeng, a newly formed partnership in Polokwane, and Kunene, Moshidi and Makume, a law firm in Johannesburg. George, Seriti and I visited both practices. They were thriving in inner-city locations supposedly reserved for occupation by white businesses or professionals. The black populace supported the new law firms by giving them plenty of work. Like the new practices, we sought efficiency, decent surroundings and legal services that restored human dignity to our clients. We needed to reinstate our own self-worth by putting up a respectable and competent professional practice in the eyes of our clients and of our white counterparts. We had stereotypes to slay and prejudices to vanquish. We dared not fail. As Donny Hathaway had us believe, we were 'young, gifted and black'.

It must also be said that beyond our public-spiritedness, we needed to generate an income for ourselves. Seriti and I had just survived the meagre earnings of an apprentice, so we were as poor as church mice. Both of us were newly wed and had small children to feed. My son Sedise was about to turn two, and Kabo and I were expecting Reabetswe, our second son. Willie and his new bride, Yvonne, had a little girl, Pontsho. George had family obligations as well, but he was decidedly better placed financially. He had qualified as an attorney earlier than we had and had always backed up his earnings from the law practice with returns from an agile family retail business.

We set up our practice on the first floor of Omar Building at the corner of Strubens and Prinsloo streets. We repainted the interior and furnished the place to a professional standard, thanks to Grant Andrews Furnishers, who accepted steady instalments. We laid carpets for our needy working-class clients. We bought crockery and cutlery and served them tea or cold-drinks and biscuits as they walked into the reception area. All staff had a dismissible order to address every person who walked in by his or her surnames prefixed by *Mme, Ntate,* Mr or Mrs. Seriti was the first to notice that the refreshments bill was rising sharply, and somewhat faster than client briefs and earnings. After a brief debate we agreed that, in fact, it was just fine. Those who consumed our beverages and biscuits in vain would still pass on our virtues by word of mouth. This they surely did, and by the second month the reception area was busy due to passing trade or personal referrals. We no longer had to wait anxiously in our spanking new but empty offices, wondering when someone would step inside.

Our landlord warned that we would have to apply for a Group Areas permit because our practice was located in a part of the city reserved for occupation by white people. We did not apply. We hoped to be charged in a court for transgressing. We dared the apartheid system in the hope that they would haul us before a court and give us the opportunity to resist loudly and vigorously up to the highest court in apartheid land. By then, we expected, our law firm would have been etched in the hearts and minds of all who hated racial profiling. The Group Areas enforcement officers chose to ignore us, but we were not in total loss. Our clients, present and future, caught onto the rumour that our law firm was so powerful that even the apartheid stalwarts had backed off. That helped. Our clients admired anyone who had the courage to stand up to the racial bullies. We had shown we had courage aplenty, they thought.

Our law firm grew fast and beyond our expectations. Our net earnings rose steadily well beyond the break-even point. Willie and I started refurbishing our modest homes in Atteridgeville and we bought new cars. Before long our flow of work justified recruiting a new partner. Moses ('Moss') Mavundla, who had previously clerked under DZ, joined us as our fourth partner. He was a meticulous and thorough trial lawyer bent on a positive outcome for his clients. Moss had the remarkable gift of staying calm even in the most trying of conditions. He taught us that in a shared workplace we needed three essential things – patience, understanding and mutual respect.

Our support staff, like our professional staff, also grew as we took on young law graduates as law clerks. Billy Motlhe and Lazarus Mahlangu joined us as clerks in our Pretoria office, and two more clerks joined our branch office located nearly 30 kilometres north-west of Pretoria in Ga-Rankuwa and run by George. Later, a petite young lady from Port Elizabeth, Ms Nonkosi Mhlantla, joined the professional team. In time Ms Mhlantla worked her way up the judicial ladder. She served as a judge of the High Court and of the Supreme Court of Appeal and during 2016 she was appointed a justice of the Constitutional Court, where she served alongside me, her former principal.

We quickly caught on that we could not write up our own accounting books as we had done in the early stages. We appointed a bright young accountant and auditor from Laudium – Akhter Moosa CA. He was delighted to come on board. Akhter and I had become friends when we had met at UNISA in 1976. He was studying the post-graduate certificate in the theory of accounting, then a precursor to the accounting board exam and admission as an auditor. I was studying final year LLB. We were, in effect, neighbours. He lived in Laudium, which was reserved for 'Indians', and I lived in the adjacent township of Atteridgeville. The two townships were set apart by a little mountain. Small-talk between us was easy and abundant. We were the only two people in a queue reserved for 'non-whites'. The 'whites only' queue was long and winding. We were all there to fetch study material, but no one in the 'white' queue would abandon it and join ours, not even to take advantage of the prompt service on account of the 'non-white' queue being a whole lot shorter. Akhter and I laughed loudly and provocatively at these pathetic victims of their self-made racism.

Akhter built an impressive auditing career. In time he became the deputy chairperson of Price Waterhouse Coopers. To this day, when he is happy after a good round of golf (which he invariably loses) he confesses that we were his biggest client at that stage of his career. If truth be told, we needed him more than he needed us. He inculcated tight record-keeping and financial probity within the law firm. He kept a watchful eye over our trust accounts. After all, we kept funds of clients in trust accounts and these were used only for an authorised purpose. AH Moosa and Co saw us through the annual audit certificates required by the Law Society. We were delighted to have him in our corner. It freed us to keep our eyes on the practice while the accountants took care of financial accounting. Most black attorneys of the time, and sadly even now, who were removed from the roll of practising attorneys owed their misery to inept book-keeping and questionable management of trust funds. We swore that we would never go down on that flimsy and disgraceful ground. Our mission was too precious to be stained by financial indiscretion. The Law Society of the time would have loved to have taken our wicket for that shameful reason. We were not going to let that happen.

Our practice was lucrative and varied, and it had a strong struggle bias. In the beginning our case profile was predominantly run-of-the-mill concerns of working people and their attendant social malaise. Family law disputes presented in divorces, and child maintenance disputes flowed strongly. The criminal law practice grew fast. Moss Mavundla looked after this end of things most ably. The fees were modest, but the volume of instructions made up for this. It was not long before Moss was known as the divorce king of Pretoria. He easily moved between ten and fifteen unopposed divorces in one morning in the northern divorce court, the court that was set apart for divorces between black people.

This court was another enigma of apartheid: an epitome of racial profiling gone bananas. It had jurisdiction only over 'Bantu' people. The first thing a party seeking a divorce had to prove was that she (or he) was a Bantu and that their spouse was one too. A Bantu was defined as 'a member of an aboriginal tribe of Africa'. If the one spouse was of mixed origin, or of 'Indian' or 'European' descent, as defined, that court could not hear the case. Similarly, it could not make custody or maintenance orders about children who were not of the suitable descent. So Moss's initial task in a divorce case consultation was to play the race-profiling gatekeeper. He must have done it well because his divorce practice flourished.

George (GSS) developed a robust civil debt recovery practice, which he ran with remarkable volume, speed and efficiency. His clients were large corporations chasing debtors residing in the newly carved out Bophuthatswana. Side by side with the collection practice, GSS cultivated a personal injury motor vehicle collision claims practice. These claims, once opposed, morphed into a robust superior-court civil practice. He was a competent civil litigation lawyer within lower and superior courts.

Willie did not vacillate when it came to his practice preference. Like George, he set up a robust personal injury practice. Their preferences must have been formed by the practices in Johannesburg which had afforded them training under articles of clerkship. It was an area of practice suited to serve indigent clients. Willie and George took on cases without prior funds from clients at any stage of the claim. This meant that the law firm had to bear the disbursements associated with medico-legal expert reports, road accident reconstruction witnesses, counsel fees and other trial costs. The high and unsecured risk of litigation costs focused the minds of the claimants' attorneys' and George and Willie became adept in assessing early the merits of success in a personal injury claim early in order to ensure a high rate of success and minimal loss. It would be less than candid to suggest that our law firm took up personal injury claims only out of philanthropic sympathy towards needy victims. The many victims of road violence amongst the poor and working-class people provided a secure pipeline of new claims. Many people were maimed or died as pedestrians or as passengers in public transport. As a result this line of practice was dependable and lucrative. In a successful motor accident claim, the judgment debt was never bad. The state was the ultimate debtor. It would always be good to settle the capital sum and costs in full. In fact, the debt was sovereign.

CHAPTER 21

The business of business and football

During the early phase of our practice every partner did a bit of every type of case. Beyond it, I started attracting a reasonable crop of commercial clients, thanks to the emerging but small black merchant class. The 'independence' of Bophuthatswana did not have only adverse consequences like creating a class of stateless people within South Africa, something I came to know about when I lost my citizenship – the bother that had threatened my admission as an attorney. The one useful consequence was that it created space, which was singularly absent in urban apartheid, for black enterprises. African people were not meant to be producers and purveyors of goods and services beyond and outside of their labouring lot. A plethora of race laws aimed at keeping them well and truly workers, devoid of productive capital or other means of production.

During the mid-1970s, *Ntate* Solly Lesolang moved his retail enterprises from Soweto to Ga-Rankuwa. There he set up and ran an impressive collection of Nissan new car dealerships and fuel filling-stations. He chose a brand name – Rantol. He briefed me to review advice on and sometimes to draft multiple fuel-supply agreements. He was as polite and soft-spoken as he was resolute in pursuing his business ambition. He was a founding member and loyal supporter, and one of the financial benefactors, of the National African Federated Chamber of Commerce (NAFCOC) led by Dr Sam Motsuenyane. When it came to the origins of business by African people despite segregation, he was a remarkable storyteller. The one bee he had in his bonnet was undue interference of government in his business activities, which brought jobs and development to the people, but came with considerable taxes.

Ntate Mothusi was another of our clients. He had developed impressive farming and trading assets in Ganyesa, near Vryburg. He briefed us to hold his hand through the procurement of a variety of liquor and trading licences. Virtually all applications at the time had to be lodged through the local magistrate's court offices. The head of the office doubled as its executive and judicial arms. One moment he made decisions about executive matters, including business licences, and the next he presided over alleged breaches of business control laws. Mr Mothusi's prolific interests in a rural setting and small town ran him into charges related to his operations as well as frequent squabbles with the Bophuthatswana government authorities. I spent a great deal of time travelling between Ganyesa, where most of his operations were located, and Mmabatho, the seat of government of Bophuthatswana.

Ntate Mphafudi, of Temba, Hammanskraal, was arguably our most financially successful client. He owned large tracts of land, farmed extensively and bred a variety of high-end livestock, a skill which for many wrong reasons had become exclusive to white farmers. Beyond his love for the land, he owned multiple trading outlets in the Moretele environs and beyond. He had an ongoing need to expand his operations. To that end he concluded many partnerships or joint venture agreements. Mr Mphafudi soon caught on to doing business through trading companies. Our job was to minister to his needs for deal-making, drafting contracts and registering new companies, in Pretoria and Mafeking.

In one of the business acquisitions, the sellers of a hardware store located in Temba insisted that Mr Mphafudi furnish a bank guarantee for R1 million ahead of the fulfilment of certain conditions precedent. In 1979, R1 million was a lot of money for any entrepreneur, let alone an African township dealmaker. The sellers were white businessmen who had procured the trading rights for a hardware business in Temba (barely 30 kilometres north of Pretoria) because it was part of Bophuthatswana, a state in which white business people could acquire trading rights despite the racist business practices of the neighbouring South Africa. I thought that the guarantee demand was exorbitant and unreasonable and not much more than a ploy to make the most out of our client. Mr Mphafudi did not demur, however. Within a day or so he came to my office. He placed a bank fixed-deposit receipt for R1 million on my table. I nearly fell off my chair. In truth, I should not have been that surprised. No oppression is absolute. Even in rabid exclusion, an honest million was made by many black entrepreneurs. From my neck of the woods, I think of the Motlhes of Lady Selborne, the Shibambos of Wallmansthal, Walter Dube of Mabopane, and the Ndlazis and Pitjes of Mamelodi. In this vein, the Sowetans would want to mention the Maponya and Shabalala business efforts. People from Limpopo might want to raise the hand of Habakuk Shikwane, that prolific cane-furniture industrialist despite the odds. Many others would want to mention Herman Mashaba, then a young entrepreneur, who set up a production line of ethnic cosmetic products, Black Like Me, to great return.

Oom Si Mogotsi was a businessman of considerable skill. His roots were in Klerksdorp, where he retained some of his business interests. He extended his operations to Temba, and that was when we were privileged to look after his business affairs. Besides helping Oom Si with legal challenges around his bottle-store business, I travelled with him to Klerksdorp for support around his agrarian business.

From my home village, Atteridgeville, we gave support and advice to *Ntate* Kgomo KT Masemola and *Ntate* Schulz. We also did considerable commercial work for a self-tutored entrepreneur, Mr Ngoasheng, in Tembisa. Mr Ngoasheng's original home was in Limpopo. After we helped him procure a series of business approvals, he constructed the biggest and well-appointed shopping facility Tembisa had ever seen. In it he operated a collection of retail outlets, including a restaurant, bar lounge and the nightclub Easy by Night. We, as his attorneys, had to hold his hand through a labyrinth of mortgage bonds, pledges, suretyships and loan agreements required by banks from a township business person before they would part with even the most modest of loans. Mr Ngoasheng had a considerable appetite for commercial risk and his rewards were plentiful. It was a privilege to earn his trust as we enjoyed the front-row view of his steely business efforts.

I also served smaller business entities, such as the shebeen on Serote Street in Saulsville. It was run by a massive man who had earned himself the nickname 'Man Down' because he enjoyed the reputation of knocking over errant customers in his pub. He had many clashes with the law.

I dutifully served *Ntate* Moshidi, who converted his little tailor shop on Mareka Square to a grocery store. I had to resolve his woes of converting his trading licences, something that was not easy. The past regime did not look kindly on African people who had the gumption to conduct any trade. Mr KT Masemola ran one of the oldest grocery stores on Mareka Square. At one time he drove the biggest and best 'fishtail' Ford or Chevrolet in town, a mark of his success. He also had beautiful daughters. When he fell ill, the children were less than diligent with the affairs of the shop and I had to do much for *Ntate* Masemola in his legal wrangle with the children and impatient creditors until he passed on.

For my part, I thought I was a useful servant of the nascent business class of the time.

Even in the turbulent 1970s, football had a special place in the hearts of marginalised communities. It was a sport that seemed accessible to every boy and girl and there were no social barriers. Every open field, and there were many, could be enhanced with two goal posts and imaginary touch-lines. Referees were easy to come by as they needed nothing more than a smattering of football rules and a whistle. Beyond playing, there was even more delight in watching senior football. Back then no club was truly professional because many players had to work and so they played their football over weekends to make ends meet. The spirit of their supporters never flagged and the crowds at weekend matches were large and enthusiastic. They adored their sporting heroes, who provided regular weekend escapes from the rough end of listless living. There was something therapeutic in the ritualistic swaying and singing by supporters at soccer matches, with everyone decked out in the clubs' colours and holding banners.

Pretoria Callies FC was one such home-grown footballing outfit. The people of Atteridgeville worshipped the blue-and-white attired club; they claimed it as a community asset owned by no one but themselves collectively. By the early 1980s, Callies had become a footballing force. It was the only Premier League professional side from Pretoria and, not infrequently, it got the better of the Soweto giants Kaizer Chiefs and Orlando Pirates, particularly at Super Stadium. It boasted prolific soccer talent, starting with Mecro 'Masterpieces' Moripe. The locals reverently called him *Modimo wa bolo* (the god of football). Another notable was that prolific dribbler Potsho 'Let Them Dance' Molala. The club's fame, and its revenues, shot up and the inevitable ownership dispute arose.

To our delight, the community approached our law firm with the instruction to seek declaratory relief from the High Court, in the name of the club, that it was owned by the collective and not by Mr Bernard Motlhamme, its sole manager, who acted and dealt with its assets as its exclusive owner. Sadly, the people lost and Mr Motlhamme won. In a reported judgment,[12] the High Court held that the constitution of Pretoria Callies did not create it as a *universitas*, a voluntary association that has a life beyond its members and may sue or be sued in its own name. If you asked *Ma-Roma* (the Romans), as staunch Callies people styled themselves, that loss was the beginning of the end. Gored by the loss, the community went its separate way. Spurred by the victory, the sole manager must have dispensed with governance and public accountability. It was not long before the club lost Premier League status and was demoted through the lower divisions to oblivion. '*Ma-Roma weee!*' the people of Atteridgeville often wailed.

Perhaps the calamity that befell Pretoria Callies prepared our law firm for our next football-related assignment. Around 1980 we were approached by two medical practitioners, Dr Sebotsane and Dr Itsweng of Mamelodi, to help them purchase the professional status of a football club known as Sundowns from a businessman, Ingle Singh. The terms were crisp and uncluttered. Our clients acquired the professional status, name, assets and exclusive management control of the club for a fixed purchase amount. They were entitled to, and did, change the name to Mamelodi Sundowns and the club colours to Brazilian navy blue, green and gold. They took on only a few handpicked players from the previous club – the rest they would find and hire themselves. The home ground of the club would be at HM Pitje Stadium in Mamelodi. We closed the transaction to the satisfaction of all concerned. The community of Mamelodi, and indeed of most of Pretoria, embraced the new club as a worthy bearer of the footballing aspirations of Pretorians who had always felt that, barring the bluster, they were a more refined footballing breed. No one in the community sought or expected control of the affairs of the club by dint of being a supporter.

Within a few years of the debut of Mamelodi Sundowns, its joint owners approached the law firm with a request to draw another purchase and sale agreement. They had received an offer they could not resist. The new suitor was Zola Mahobe. He came to our office in the company of Stanley 'Screamer' Tshabalala to settle the terms of the offer. He was a good listener. He spoke quietly and seemingly thoughtfully. He offered a price nearly ten times the price our clients had paid for the club only a few years earlier. He would pay the purchase consideration in full and in cash. He would not change the name, colours or headquarters of the club. He would keep the players and management team, but reserved the right to ring in changes to players and staff. He was happy that we draft the acquisition agreement. At the point of closure of the agreement, Zola asked our law firm to remain the lawyers of Mamelodi Sundowns.

The transition to the Mahobe regime was smooth and the club moved into its golden years. The players had mixed feelings towards Screamer, who was both manager and coach. They feared him and yet they played for him. The club fared well in league and cup competitions. Zola afforded the financial injection the club conceivably needed. He had the money and was not shy to use it on the club. He attracted the best players in our and other towns. Sundowns had the reputation for paying the best salary packages to players and staff. From time to time Zola splashed out on food and beverages for ardent supporters, particularly those who followed the team to away fixtures. Money and loyalty bought him love. One year he took his entire team of players and their partners to the FA Cup Final in Wembley, London, on an all-expenses-paid basis. I must add that he always paid our fee notes promptly and without demurring.

Zola's source of income was not obvious, but one thing was certain: his millions were not about to run out. He talked about having bought racehorses as an investment. He drove an exclusive imported Mercedes S500 coupé and he certainly had the best girl in town. This was Ms Snowy Moshoeshoe. She was smart, well-spoken, beautiful and vivacious. When Zola was present she took the back seat and chose to be somewhat on the taciturn side. Snowy was known to be computer literate and worked for Standard Bank, where she managed the cheque clearance centre at its head office. She was reputed to perform her banking chores on line. She hardly ever took leave given the heavy reliance the bank placed on her skills. She was one to be proud of when so few black people had gained access to computer-based skills at that time.

Zola often invited Willie and me to Sundowns soccer games both at home and away. He provided the business class tickets and hotel accommodation. He would say: 'I am a man of many challenges. I like to travel with my lawyers and my gunman next to me.' He should have added that he was always pleased to have Snowy nearby, too, when he travelled. He funded drinks for his guests but he himself never drank in public, nor when he was amongst his friends. He never talked about his upbringing in Soweto, his business path or how he had risen to the fantastic level of affluence he enjoyed in the 1980s. The bit that equated lawyers with gunmen had a Mafia ring to it and was a source of some concern. In 1983 I chose to further my law career as an advocate arguing cases in the superior courts and so I bade Zola an appropriate farewell. He remained a client of Maluleke, Seriti and Moseneke. My contact with our most astute and loaded client ended there, only to resurface in later years and in trying circumstances for Zola and Snowy. Zola's other commercial briefs helped pay the rent handsomely, and to firm our hand to do public interest litigation.

CHAPTER 22

Activists in revolt

In 1978, we launched our law firm against a backdrop of widespread youth revolt across the country. Well beyond the now celebrated Soweto uprising on 16 June 1976, many townships were on fire.

I had my own particularly frightening memory of that month. Our eldest son, Sedise, was born on 22 June 1976 at Kalafong Hospital near Atteridgeville. I chose not to go to theatre to support Kabo and witness my son's birth. I was too ignorant and afraid to be useful in that situation, but I was consumed by the anxiety of a novice father. As I was pacing up and down the hospital corridor, a security alarm came through the back end of the maternity section – rioters had set the hospital alight. My whole abdomen went hollow and I began shaking like a leaf. Will mother and child be well? I wondered. After much agonised waiting, the report came through that the fires had been doused and mother and child were indeed well.

Apartheid's enforced use of Afrikaans at schools was not much more than a short fuse to the widespread domestic explosion against racial repression and economic exclusion. Young people did not share the patience and forbearance of their parents and elders. Youth leaders sprang up everywhere, and their followers in primary and high schools, and in the streets, were many. They were nearly fearless. Many young people across the country were shot and killed by the security forces, but the protest did not stop. It spilled into the streets and continued to spread. Every death engendered more revolt. Activists younger than my fifteen years when I went to Robben Island took to the streets, demanding freedom and the end of Afrikaans.

I remember accompanying the Ditshego family to Komane Street to gather the remains of Boitumelo Ditshego, their son, from the surface of the road. His skull had been shattered by a bullet from an R1 rifle during a student protest in Atteridgeville. At Tumi's funeral, protests continued as young people sang freedom songs and vowed to achieve freedom in their lifetime. A few more were shot dead and many more were taken into police custody.

Schools were disrupted routinely. Young, hardened activists moved into classrooms and drove learners out into the streets to join protests and clamour for demands, which varied from place to place. Teachers and parents took refuge in the mantra that education of children must come ahead of everything else. In a normal society that was, of course, true. But did it hold in a society in turmoil and revolt?

Our law firm took the view that we would seek out and represent child detainees of this class. Neither they nor their parents could fund their legal representation. And yet every court appearance, particularly with representation, said the youth were worthy of our care and admiration. The charges were often couched as unlawful gatherings or riotous assembly or public violence. The young activists were rarely found guilty and sentenced. This was because it was notoriously difficult to prove the charges beyond the police claim that they had arrested the accused at or near the vicinity of a gathering or rioting. Witnesses regarding what each accused person was supposed to have done were hard to come by. No one – neither the accused nor innocent bystanders – dared testify against activists in an open court. Even if someone did testify, it was simply too difficult for any witness to reconstruct a fast-moving scene in a riot and attribute roles to the accused youth.

Once we had perfected the art of getting young accused activists let off, they went straight back and fanned the uprising over and over again. Given our law firm's location, we covered most of the riot cases in African residential areas in and around Pretoria. Most mornings the partners went in different directions to cover preliminary or trial appearances in courts in

Atteridgeville, Mamelodi, Tembisa, Mabopane, Ga-Rankuwa and Temba. In comparison with the uprising of the 1960s, in which only a few youth had been involved, the uprising in the 70s saw thousands of young people joining in the protests and participating fearlessly. They had little or no fear for state reprisal. They had seen other young activists die at the hands of the police. Also, they knew that incarceration, even of children, could be overcome. As their fear of retribution receded, the system of state repression started to falter.

Although it was to last for a further terminal fifteen years, the 1976 uprising marked the beginning of the end of apartheid colonialism. In that time, the securocrats thought it would still be possible to upset the balance of power between the racist and moneyed ruling elite and the masses in revolt, but they misread the depth and resilience of the social and political dissent. The young activists who barricaded township roads, set homes of black police officers alight and necklaced people they thought were *impimpis* (sellouts) were not doctrinal. Their conduct was not animated by the Africanist Manifesto of the PAC or the Freedom Charter of the ANC. They had not heard of, let alone read, the works of Marx or Lenin. If anyone, the name they would have heard was that of Bantu Steve Biko, given his ultimate death in detention and the predominance of the structures and activities of the Black People's Convention founded on principles of Black Consciousness. The thousands of juvenile activists our law firm appeared in court to defend might not have displayed obvious political depth, but they certainly knew what they were fighting for. They did not want to be taught in Afrikaans. They detested poverty and racial exclusion and they wanted freedom in their lifetime. In time, they would mature, make political elections and do something about their choices.

Several youth leaders were hounded enough by the security cops to want to leave the country for military training. Those who chose to or had to leave for exile often came to our offices to ask for material support to travel to Botswana, Lesotho or Swaziland. One such example was Ngoako Ramatlhodi, the former premier of Limpopo and now a cabinet minister.

Back then, however, he was a student leader at the University of the North and on the run from the security police. He rushed into my office one day and shouted urgently: 'Comrade Dikgang, I need money to go into exile!' I did not reply. Instead I rose swiftly from my chair and put my open palm over his lips to prevent him from saying a word further. We operated on the basis that our law offices had been bugged by the security cops. I forgave the over-zealous but well-meaning young activist. He did not seem to know that an attempt to leave the country in order to join a banned organisation was an offence punishable with an imprisonment sentence of up to 25 years. In turn, abetting and supporting anyone who sought to leave to join Umkhonto weSizwe (MK) or the Azanian People's Liberation Army (APLA) was punishable by imprisonment, also for a term up to 25 years. I led Ngoako out of our offices into the street. After a hasty scan of the surroundings, I produced my wallet, gave him R500 in cash and said: 'Good luck, Comrade Ngoako.' The next time I saw him was nearly twelve years later, in 1990, when he returned to the country triumphantly as the chief of staff in the office of the president of the ANC, Comrade Oliver Tambo.

A less happy ending related to Dr Fabian Ribeiro. He was a well-liked medical practitioner who lived and ran a general practice in Mamelodi. He was known to be a compassionate, caring and generous man. He saw patients who could never afford to pay for his services. He and his partner, Mrs Florence Ribeiro, were staunch Catholics. Dr Ribeiro did not wear his political conviction on his sleeve. The giveaway was when he allowed young comrades to hold evening meetings in an unused garage at his residence. Word went round that he treated injured young activists for police-inflicted bullet-wounds and for removal of shrapnel. An injured activist would not have to go to a public clinic or hospital, where they would be arrested by security cops on arrival. Bullet-wounds, cops thought, would be cogent proof that the victim had been at a crime scene. But then, to that point, the good doctor had committed no offence. If anything, he was well within the bounds of the Hippocratic oath to treat anyone in need of medical care.

One morning in 1980, my home phone rang. It was Mrs Ribeiro and she was in tears. She told me that her husband had been arrested in a dawn raid. She asked me to enquire into his circumstances and let her know what I could find out. The security police headquarters in Compol Building confirmed his detention under the 90-days terrorism legislation. They refused me access to him. I pulled out the well-tested trick by asking if he might be visited by a priest, Father Smangaliso Mkhatshwa, or a medical practitioner, Dr Abe Nkomo. The cops said no. 'We have a doctor or a priest, should he need one,' they said. They boasted that he would be brought to court on trial for aiding and supporting an act of terrorism. Our law firm had to be content with taking fresh clothing to Dr Ribeiro, but for 90 days we were not permitted to see him.

The day the solitary confinement ended, Ribeiro was served with an indictment in his detention cell. On the same day, I went to visit him in Pretoria Central Police Station. My choice, they said, was to have a customary 30-minute visit or to spend the better part of the day with him – in his police cell. I chose the latter. His lock-up was spacious and certainly bigger and better lit than my 90-day detention cell in Erasmia. I had been in this space before, but now the circumstances for me were different. There I was in my business suit in the cell, hugging the sobbing Dr Ribeiro – but only for a short while. He soon wiped away his tears and straightened himself up. He was a tall man who stood well above six feet. During the time he'd been in detention his body had shed weight and he was slim and muscular. His light brown skin was paler than usual but his eyes were steady and piercing. He still had his booming baritone voice.

'Dikgang, thanks for coming. These Boers are mad!' he said.

That gave me courage. They had not broken his spirit.

'Did they torture you, Doc?' I asked outright.

'No, they interrogated me endlessly, but they never touched me. I would have fought back.'

His words instantly made me recall how I had been beaten to a pulp and how I had cowed down. The thought of fighting back had never occurred to me. Dr Ribeiro came out of detention, strong and unbroken. His Catholic faith seemed all the stronger and he detested apartheid repression even more. All this meant that he was ready for a gruelling terrorism trial and possible imprisonment. He enquired after his wife, Mama Florence, and the children, and I was able to arrange a visit for them.

Dr Ribeiro was charged under the Terrorism Act for aiding and supporting terrorism. He had a defence and informed the police so in a written statement. A young student activist from Mamelodi, in the same way that Ngoako came to me for assistance, had also approached Dr Ribeiro at his residence and asked him for money. On the activist's version, he told Dr Ribeiro that the money was meant to help him to 'skip the country', as the jargon went. Dr Ribeiro gave the young man a cheque, which he cashed the same evening at a local chemist. The lad, with a few others, was arrested the following day in a minibus en route to Swaziland. On arrest he confessed to trying to skip the country for military training and added that the trip was made possible by our client's financial generosity. The security police rushed to the bank to ferret out the cashed cheque and they traced it back to the chemist. Armed with the cashed cheque as an exhibit, the next step was to convert the young activist into an accomplice state witness against Dr Ribeiro. The obvious carrot to him was the promise that if he were to tell the truth in the witness box, he would escape prosecution on the charges of terrorism that carried a minimum jail sentence of five years, but had a going rate of ten to fifteen years' imprisonment.

Dr Ribeiro cut to the chase. He had a defence and he was going to stand or fall by it. He told his defence team, Advocate George Bizos and me, that the witness had come to his home one evening by appointment. He had showed the state witness some plumbing work he required him to do at the house. The state witness had asked for a deposit of an amount of R500. He made out a cash cheque for him. It seemed that the state witness had converted the cheque to cash the same evening at the chemist. He saw the cheque again when it was brandished by his interrogators during his detention. They assured him that the cheque was proof of his support for terrorism. Dr Ribeiro denied that he ever had a discussion about the witness skipping the country in order to undergo military training.

The trial came soon. The cross-examination of the star state witness by George Bizos was terse but wounding to the state's version. It went something like this:

Q: Is your father a plumber?

A: Yes, my Lord.

Q: Do you do plumbing work with him and sometimes on your own?

A: Yes, my Lord.

Q: When you assume a new assignment do you visit your client at the home where the work has to be done?

A: Yes, my Lord.

Q: Do you ordinarily demand a deposit amount before you start the work?

A: Yes, my Lord. I have to take a deposit amount because I have to buy materials needed for the repair work.

Q: When you are paid a deposit with a cheque what would you do?

A: I cash the cheque at a local retail facility. I have to, my Lord, because I don't have a banking account of my own.

At the end of the trial, Dr Fabian Ribeiro's version was upheld and he was found not guilty as charged and freed. The jubilation in the courthouse and at home is best left to the imagination. The Justice and Peace Commission of the Southern African Catholic Bishops' Conference and its executive secretary, Father Smangaliso Mkhatshwa, were most supportive throughout his detention and trial. So, too, was Monsignor Daniels, who arranged the funding of the legal costs of the trial, a support he had extended to many people in political detentions or trials even before the Ribeiro trial. Kabo and I, and our law firm partners, were invited to several thanksgiving occasions. A significant one was the celebratory mass at the Mamelodi Catholic Church.

But what the apartheid securocrats could not achieve in court they did by other means. In 1986, Dr Fabian Ribeiro and Florence Ribeiro were shot dead in the courtyard of their residence by unknown gunmen, who sped off in a motor vehicle. We all knew their murderers were state agents. The state denied this vehemently. At the Truth and Reconciliation Commission (TRC), the death squad of the state made a clean breast of their murderous deeds. They confessed to murdering the Ribeiros.

On Wednesday, 7 April 1999, the former commander of the South African Defence Force's Special Forces Unit, Charl Naude, told the TRC that he took 'full responsibility' for the murders of Dr Fabian Ribeiro and his wife, Florence. Naude said he did not know who had ordered the couple's execution. He said they were killed because they transported activists to Swaziland for military training, allowed military training to take place in their house and gave financial assistance to activists in Mamelodi township near Pretoria.

Even if each of these allegations against the Ribeiros was true, neither the state (particularly one whose governance had become a crime against humanity) nor any of its agents had the right to execute them. The TRC granted the murderers of Florence and Fabian Ribeiro amnesty from prosecution. They were held to have made a full and frank disclosure of the murders and their political motive. The threshold for forgiveness was astonishingly low. All the killers had to do was admit to the murders and say they had killed to defend apartheid. That was enough to absolve them from criminal responsibility for their dastardly and unjust deeds, which were unlawful and punishable even under that hideous racist rule. The confession of the state death squad was deemed adequate to oust retribution. Instead, impunity reigned. The 'truth' was thought to be sufficiently therapeutic to trump justice – even transitional justice.

The state repression of political activity in the aftermath of the 1976 uprisings displaced many of the country's youth and encouraged them to resort to exile. By 1980, many had given up protest activism, believing the way forward was to undergo military training beyond the borders of the country. Around this time a collection of activists in Atteridgeville decided to go into exile. Many young people made the choice whether to join the ANC or PAC only once they were in exile. Not so for this lot of young activists. They included Dickson Mathe, Ronnie Mamoepa and Arthur Mkhwanazi.

They had chosen to join the military wing of the ANC even before they had left the country. Thamsanqa Gerald Mkhwanazi, a senior journalist at the *Sunday Post*, a newly founded weekly published in Johannesburg, came to know about the imminent departure. He wrote the story. Zwelakhe Sisulu, who was the news editor, ran it on the front page.

Need I say that, at the time, a media blast of young comrades about to skip the country to join the armed struggle was simply unheard of. Young activists left the country often, but in hushed tones. It was an offence to try to or leave the country by jumping the fence, so to speak, without a travel document. It was an even bigger crime to leave in order to undergo military training and join armed warfare against the state.

But here was the rub. The very morning of the front-page sensation, the would be MK members were accosted and arrested by the police on their dash to the border. Police also arrested Thamsanqa Mkhwanazi and charged him, together with the rest, as the first accused.

The Monday following the headline article, Zwelakhe Sisulu phoned me: '*Mfokabawo*, I have been served with a section 205 subpoena. The security police are here in my office. They insist that I come along with them to the regional court in Pretoria to answer questions under oath before a regional magistrate. They want me to disclose my source as a journalist. I may not and will not.'

I replied: '*Mfokabawo*, I am rushing to court. I will meet you there. Please insist that they do not proceed without me, your attorney.'

Zwelakhe was a seasoned writer and activist. His struggle pedigree was without parallel. He was, after all, the son of Albertina and Walter Sisulu, that inimitable struggle couple. I had left his father on Robben Island, where he still was. His mother was a banned person and under house arrest. Virtually all his siblings had fled the country into exile. Just about everybody in his family was part of the enterprise to bring freedom and democratic rule to our land.

So Zwelakhe, the journalist, knew just about all there was to be known about the coercive questioning of journalists under section 205 of the

Criminal Procedure Act. He had worked as a career journalist from around 1975 to 1978 at the *Rand Daily Mail*. His roles as a journalist and as a freedom fighter often converged when he reported on the youth uprisings and other mass struggles. In 1978 he became president of the Writers Association of South Africa. He led his fellow black journalists in a variety of marches to protest workplace injustice and to claim freedom of expression and of assembly.

In the maze of the magistrate's court building, I found the court in which Zwelakhe was to appear. I sought time out to consult with him. The issue was narrow: was he prepared to divulge his source or not? If not, he would be liable to a summary conviction and imprisonment for up to five years. I explained that the prosecutor would have the court swear him in as a compellable witness. The terrorism laws compelled anyone who came to know of an impending act of terrorism to report it. The source of the information on the impending departure would be punishable as severely as the young activists who were bent on joining Umkhonto.

Zwelakhe looked at me, wagged his finger and drew a line in the sand: '*Mfokabawo*, I cannot do that. I will never disclose my source – not even on my life. I will tell them so.'

By the time Zwelakhe and I walked into the courtroom, it had filled up. The gallery was taken. The news hounds had caught onto their leader's and fellow journalist's plight. More so, the issue at stake was an article of faith for progressive journalists. The case was called and Zwelakhe stepped into the witness box. He affirmed the first few questions on his identity, that he was the news editor and that the story had been run in the *Sunday Post* under his direction. The core question soon followed: 'Mr Sisulu, who or what was the source of the alleged facts in the news article?'

The silent court went frigid. Zwelakhe took a deep breath, looked in the direction of the magistrate and said he would not answer the question. Raising his voice, the magistrate told Zwelakhe that the law said he must answer the question. Zwelakhe shook his head from side to side and said he would not. The magistrate summarily sentenced Zwelakhe to three years' imprisonment without an option of a fine. He did not observe even a smattering of the set sentencing procedure. The proceedings were conducted in unseemly haste. They were done in minutes.

I did the thing lawyers do to a court when they are indignant and defiant over a ruling they deem patently unjust. I rose to let the magistrate know that my instructions were to appeal the conviction and sentence forthwith and to seek that my client be released on bail pending the appeal. It was a little like spitting in the face of the magistrate. In effect, I was saying: you are wrong as a matter of law and on all other counts. The magistrate fired back: 'The court rules require a written notice of appeal. Where is it? Constable, take the convicted accused to the cells. Court adjourned!'

I rushed off to a public phone and dictated a notice of appeal to Willie Seriti, who was at our law offices. Willie wasted no time in hurrying to court with it, where he found Zwelakhe and me in the court cells. I moved for bail and Zwelakhe was freed that afternoon pending appeal to the Supreme Court.

Our law firm briefed Ismail Mahomed SC (who in time would become the chief justice of our land) and Advocate Jean Birrell to argue the appeal. Ismail faced a hostile all-white, all-male full bench in the Palace of Justice. He survived the initial antagonism well as he had an astute and compelling argument that the prerequisites of a conviction under section 205 had not been met. He argued that the provision was harsh and coercive. It placed a risk on people who themselves had not committed an offence. For that reason case law required the magistrate to follow a number of cautionary steps in favour of the potential witness before, so to speak, she or he banged the witness over the head. Here the magistrate did not care to alert Zwelakhe to the risk he faced. The omission was a grave irregularity and sufficient to vitiate the conviction and sentence. The beauty of Ismail's forensic stratagem was that the appeal court did not have to ask whether, if he had been properly warned, Zwelakhe would have answered the questions posed. There was no proper section 205 enquiry and, in the absence of one, the appellant's answers were irrelevant.

We won the appeal and Zwelakhe was spared, despite his recalcitrance.

He went on to cause even bigger political mischief. In 1980, shortly after the appeal, Zwelakhe was banned for three years. This did not prevent him from founding the *New Nation* in January 1986. His concerted activism earned him repeated long spells of detention without trial, the longest being for 721 days to December 2008. Much of that detention he shared with my fiery youth-leader brother, Tiego Moseneke, at Johannesburg Prison. Then Tiego was studying law at Wits University. He was the leader of the student movement on campus and of the broader students' movement then known as the Azanian Students Organisation, which later mutated into the United Democratic Front and the Mass Democratic Movement. For that he earned himself very prolonged detention without trial under emergency regulations.

Weekend after weekend, my mother, Karabo and I met up with Mama Albertina Sisulu at the prison's visitors' facility. My mother and Mama Albertina exchanged pleasantries as though all was well, even though both had sons in detention for well over a year with no end in sight. While waiting to be called into the visitors' cubicles, they would ask me how Zwelakhe and Tiego could be freed. The detention was by diktat. It was as long as the security apparatus of the state chose. It could be for good, bad or no reason at all. Its validity was immune to a legal challenge. To my total shame, anger and considerable pain, I had no answer for these proud mothers who bore multiple scars of apartheid repression.

Tiego was my mother's fourth son to be incarcerated. After my release, all seemed well with my mother's soul, but much more pain of a similar kind awaited her. After completing a teacher training diploma, my brother Mighty chose to go to Fort Hare University to study for a BA degree in languages and drama. His choice was on target because he had won several high school and college awards for acting and drama. Mighty was and still is very well spoken. In the early 1980s, Fort Hare erupted into a prolonged strike and student protests. Many students, Mighty amongst them, were expelled. He returned home but to townships that were in revolt and under the grip of a prolonged state of emergency. In a winter dawn raid, the cops knocked on all the doors and windows of my parents' home. Again my mother had to open for them and again they turned the entire house upside down in a search and sped off into the night in a convoy, this time with Mighty locked inside one of the vehicles.

My mother turned to me, then a practising attorney, to find Mighty. I had become an expert in tracking down detained people. This was something our law firm did routinely to protect detained activists. If a detained activist was known to be alive, it was difficult for the security cops to make him or her disappear. Within the day, the cops confirmed that my brother was being held without trial at Modderbee Prison under state of emergency regulations. That simply meant he would be kept in prison for as long as the security cops and their minister of state chose. At Modderbee, Mighty was in high spirits. This was because he was locked up with scores of other opponents of the state – including Zoli Kunene, Moss Chikane, Dr Yosuf 'Joe' Veriava and Titus Mafolo. I took Mighty a heavy army overcoat, a change of clothing and lots of food from his mother. I also drove my mother and father to Modderbee to visit him. That occurred many times because the detention lasted for many, many months.

Kabelo, my third brother, went to study at Ngoye – University of Zululand. In the mid-1980s the university predictably burst into violent protests. Of course, universities were fertile grounds for revolt because youth, the world over, don't tolerate repression. They are more prone to rise against power than their elders. University unrests were sparked by domestic discontent such as financial exclusion or poor living conditions on campus. In truth, the protests were a proxy for the larger uprising against the exclusion and unfairness of apartheid and colonialism. During the riots, on one occasion Kabelo had to jump out of a window from the second or third floor of a students' residence building to escape police. He nearly drowned in a nearby river trying to flee from them. He ended up being caught and detained by the police for long periods. The family was thrown into the same state of misery as we repeated the ritual of prison visits, changes of clothing and food parcels.

But Mama Sisulu was worse off. Her husband was on Robben Island. A few of her children had fled into exile and Zwelakhe languished in indeterminate detention from time to time. There were many other mothers like these in our land.

Detention without trial was beyond judicial review. As an activist lawyer I felt a little paralysed. I had not found a legal stratagem to pierce the soft belly of that beast – state coercion. I knew it was not a matter the law could resolve. Only a successful revolution could do that.

The Bethal trial was a seminal one. In its essence, it was a treason trial against the president of the PAC, Zephania Lekoane Mothopeng, and seventeen other PAC activists. The criminal prosecution gained its name from its location in the small, desolate town of Bethal, which is now in the province of Mpumalanga. Then major political trials were banished out of the sight of the public in order to avoid popular contagion. As though that were not enough, the presiding judge, Curlewis, ordered a secret trial in order not to 'imperil' the 165 state witnesses who were due to take the stand. Only a few journalists accredited by the commissioner of police were permitted in the court during selected parts of the proceedings, and, in fact, few journalists cared to cover this momentous trial. They seemed to join the conspiracy of silence against a major marker of national resistance.

The trial started in December 1977 and lasted for over eighteen months after more than 100 court sittings. The transcripts of the court records ran into more than 7 000 pages, excluding exhibit documents. The indictment documented the internal revival and covert activities of the PAC from 1963 to 1976. It charged that internal operatives of the PAC entered into alliance with youth and student movements that culminated in the 1976 uprising. All this, the indictment charged, was aimed at the violent overthrow of the state. Seemingly no less than four detainees related to the Bethal trial died in pre-trial detention. As was expected, the trial ended with long-term prison sentences imposed on PAC functionaries.

Griffiths Mxenge was the instructing attorney for the accused persons. Thembile Skweyiya and Andrew Wilson SC were counsel. At the time I was banned and under house arrest and unable to leave the magisterial district of Pretoria until July 1978. This meant I had no active part in supporting victims of state repression, but as soon as I could travel out of Pretoria I went to visit the accused compatriots. I did correspondence work in the Transvaal province for Mxenge. On some occasions, our law firm briefed counsel to appear on behalf of recalcitrant witnesses who faced jail terms for refusing to testify against the accused.

The Bethal trial touched harshly compatriots who were very close to me at a number of levels. And yet circumstances beyond me held me back. The residual legal and comradely support I provided towards the end of the trial was less than I could have given. It was deeply sad to see salted freedom fighters like *Ntate* Zeph Mothopeng, Mike Matsobane and Mark Shinners going back to the island under the weight of even more prolonged prison sentences. The story of the full pain of our past repression is yet to be told. Despite the heavy Bethal casualties, the efforts to unseat the vile colonial regime had to go on.

CHAPTER 23

The Black Lawyers Association

One paradox of the 1970s was a sturdy trickle of black legal practitioners despite apartheid odds. They were not the first amongst indigenous legal practitioners. From the turn of the twentieth century, a few exceptional black people were enrolled as attorneys and advocates. For reasons that are not immediately evident, the laws regulating the admission of legal practitioners had no race bar. I suppose there were other high hurdles. One had to acquire a university law qualification, which included a mandatory pass in English I, Afrikaans Nederlands I and Latin I. Thereafter, one had to serve a three- to five-year period of apprenticeship or clerkship under a practising attorney in good standing. Clerkship in a law office was hard to come by in a profession that was no less than an adjunct of racial power. Law firms of the time enforced an unwritten race bar. Even if you were employed as a law graduate, you earned no more than a modest stipend. Few could survive on this for between three and five years, let alone feed their families – a class barrier. My own experience of seeking a place for articles of clerkship in Pretoria in the 1970s is testament to this. No black person before me had been enrolled as an articled clerk in a white law firm in Pretoria. Even so, against these odds a few and exceptional people of colour made the roll of attorneys or advocates.

The first of noteworthy mention would be Mahatma Gandhi. He arrived in South Africa in 1893 after studying law in London and being admitted to the Bar there and in India. His law practice both in India, to which he returned after his admission in the United Kingdom, and in South Africa was short-lived. Once he had arrived in this country, Gandhi had to make a court appearance in Pretoria. He bought a first-class train ticket to travel from Pietermaritzburg to Pretoria. A conductor walked up to him and ordered him to leave the first-class for a third-class compartment because he was Indian. Gandhi stridently refused on the ground that he had a valid first-class ticket. His rational response did not come to his rescue, however. The conductor, presumably with the aid of his colleagues, forcibly ejected him from the train. Gandhi is reputed to have spent the wintry night in a desolate Pietermaritzburg station, which now bears a plaque in his honour.

Immediately thereafter, Gandhi turned his attention away from law practice in favour of fighting racial oppression against inhabitants of Indian extraction. He did this until 1914, when he returned to India. Gandhi insisted that the struggle for equal treatment of South Africans of Indian origin had to be seen as and kept separate and distinct from that of indigenous African masses. About this, history proved him wrong. The class and race oppression of people of Indian ancestry had much in common with that of African working-class and poor people. In time, they correctly made common cause with the broader liberation movement as they joined up with the PAC, Black Consciousness Movement, Unity Movement, ANC and worker formations.

Perhaps the most visible entry of black practitioners into the legal profession occurred in 1952 in Johannesburg. The practitioners were no less than Nelson Rolihlahla Mandela and Oliver Reginald Tambo. They set up shop in Chancellor House on Commissioner Street, in downtown Johannesburg. Inside the entrance of Chancellor House there was a brass plaque that read 'Mandela and Tambo Attorneys'. I was only nine years old when I saw this plaque but it left an indelible impression on me. I had accompanied my father into the city, where he had come to consult Mr Mandela over a compensation claim for his family's forced removal from their Lady Selborne home. I remained in the rather congested but quiet waiting room as my father was called into an office. That fleeting visit must have left something in me. Nearly 40 years later, Mr Mandela could remember who my dad was but not the visit to his law offices. I was a little saddened as my vanity was dashed, but I could hardly have expected him to remember just one of the thousands of consultations he must have had four decades earlier and during over more than four years of practice in Chancellor House.

Mandela and Tambo Attorneys was the first African law firm, certainly in what was then known as the province of the Transvaal. It endured from 1952 to 1956, when both its partners were arraigned for treason.[13] The state claimed that the two of them, with 89 other members of the Congress Alliance, had conspired to overthrow the state by violent means. The Treason Trial lasted for five years and ruined many families, careers and livelihoods of, and the effective political activism by, the Treason trialists. It also disrupted the activist programme of the ANC Youth League. The state had to prove the allegations of treason. At the close of the state's case two-thirds of the 91 accused persons were discharged. In 1961, the remaining accused people were also acquitted at the end of the trial. Perhaps one of the intended objects of the Treason Trial was to put asunder what Mandela and Tambo had put together.

Recently, I have read a fascinating account of the law practice of Mandela and Tambo Attorneys. Its hallmark appears to have been compassion for and service to those who lived on the margins of racial privilege. The firm must have stood out like the beckoning flicker of a steadfast flame. Practising African lawyers were unheard of at the time. Younger admirers came to know that it could be done. The partners of the law firm were overwhelming personalities and no useful purpose would be served by narrating their remarkable and well-lauded lives here. They were outstanding members of the ANC and leaders of its Youth League. They chose to harness the law of the time to expose its wickedness and injustice. They brought short-term relief to their vulnerable clients by mounting challenges against the laws they had to live under. And yet both understood that law practice under oppression was palliative. It was not meant to nor did it alter power relations in society. The usefulness of law practice by an activist was at least threefold.

It afforded the activist lawyer the space to show all – clients and the public – that apartheid law was no law but a codified repression. Court cases became sites not only of mass mobilisation and resistance, but also of political or ideological contests. The accused, and so too, their counsel, claimed the space to display their superior notions of a just society. At a personal level, activist lawyers worked for themselves. This placed them beyond the controlling reach of the government or powerful business interests. What was more, activist practitioners were free to choose the correct split, if any, between their day job and struggle formations.

Tambo and Mandela did not need much encouragement before they both jettisoned their law practice for the start of a full-blown revolution signified by the formation of MK in 1961, and later the Azanian People's Liberation Army (APLA). Oliver Tambo was to be exiled for three decades, and it was from exile that he led the liberation struggle. Mandela was to spend nearly all of the same three decades imprisoned.

I take a moment to observe the irony of the political imprisonment of many great leaders of our people: Robert Mangaliso Sobukwe, Jafta Kgalabi Masemola, John Nyathi Pokela, Bantu Biko, Saths Cooper, Zephania Mothopeng, Walter Sisulu, Ahmed Kathrada, Johnson Mlambo, Bram Fischer, Mark Shinners, Winnie Mandela, Raymond Mhlaba, Bongi Mkhabela, Mosibudi Mangena, Barbara Hogan, Neville Alexander, James Marsh, Nchaupe Mokoape, Harry Gwala, Govan Mbeki, Raymond Suttner, Matthews Meyiwa, Stephen Dlamini, John Nkosi, Wilton Mkwayi, Sedick Isaacs, Dimake Malepe, Joe Gqabi, George Moffat, Ben Ntonga, Elias Motsoaledi, Marcus Solomon, Mac Maharaj, Andrew Masondo, Thandi Modise, Terror Lekota, Njongonkulu Ndungane, Isaac Mafatshe, Deborah Matshoba, Vusi Nkumane, Steve Tshwete, Bennie Ntoele, Reggie Vandeyar, Achmad Cassiem, Denis Goldberg, Mlamli Makwethu, Indres Naidoo, Jacob Zuma, Dennis Brutus, George Naicker, Ngila Muendane, Joe Khoza, Anthony Suze, Isaac Mthimunye, Peter Magano, Philemon Tefo, Gabby Magomola, Jeff Radebe, Thami Mazwai, Napoleon Letsoko, Mike Matsobane, Tokyo Sexwale and Jan Shoba. Their incarceration served as a silent but potent inspiration for many to battle their oppression.

Godfrey Mokgonane Pitje[14] took up law after an illustrious career as an academic at the University of Fort Hare, where he taught anthropology. Once his term ended as president of the ANC Youth League, he signed up for articles of clerkship at Mandela and Tambo Attorneys and qualified as an attorney in 1959. He set up a law practice in Macosa House on Commissioner Street – not far from Chancellor House. Not long thereafter, Ms Desiree Finca, a former domestic worker from the Transkei, became the first African woman to be admitted as an attorney. She joined GM Pitje's practice as a partner.

During the 1960s through to the mid-1970s, there was a relative flurry as a number of African practitioners were admitted within the old Transvaal. These included JN Madikizela, JM Semenya, J Netshifhefe, T Dlamini, Collins Ramusi and TT Mokone. Like black practitioners in Pretoria, these Johannesburg attorneys resorted to one-person practices. While this accomplished much for their marginalised clients, many could have done with the better and pooled resources that a partnership would have provided.

As the political repression of the 1960s started to fade, in the mid-1970s university colleges set apart for black students only produced a decent trickle of law graduates. They were younger, more idealistic and assertive. They were buoyed by the resurgent defiance spawned by the Black Consciousness Movement, which was fearlessly led by a cadre of other university students – notably Onkgopotse Tiro, Bantu Biko, Barney Pityana, Mamphela Ramphele, Nchaupe Mokoape, Strini Moodley, Harry Nengwekhulu and Saths Cooper. The new entrants claimed the right to practice law for both personal gain and public service. They opted for viable formats of practise that went beyond the subsistence patterns of black practices of the 1950s and 1960s.

Partnerships with significant professional clout sprang up. By 1978, we saw new entrants like Kunene, Moshidi and Makume in Johannesburg. To this recollection I must add activist law firms like Shun Chetty and Co, which was based in Fordsburg. Shun Chetty's good work was later continued by

Priscilla Jana and Co after Shun Chetty was hounded by the security police until he fled the country into exile. Krish Naidoo and Ismail Ayob also ran valuable Johannesburg law practices that exuded a useful activist flavour.

As we have noticed, in other parts of the province law practices flourished from the mid-1970s. Ngoepe, Nkadimeng and Machaka set up shop in Pietersburg, and, of course, there was Maluleke, Seriti and Moseneke in Pretoria. Not long thereafter, Phoswa, Mojapelo and Makgoba took root in Nelspruit. Prominent in the Free State province was the law firm Moloi and Fantisi.

It must be added that even earlier, law practices were established by African and Indian practitioners in Durban and Pietermaritzburg. These included attorneys like Justice N Poswa, KK Mthiyane, Griffiths and Victoria Mxenge, Navi and Gaby Pillay, AB Ngcobo, Archie Gumede and Justice Moloto. In addition to attorneys, there was a steady increase in the admission of advocates, and Durban led the pack. Amongst those practising at the Bar were Thembile Louis Skweyiya, Marumo Moerane, Zac Yacoob, Pops Abubaker, Pius Langa and Nathan Ponnan. In the Cape, perhaps the most prominent of the progressive practitioners were attorneys Dullah Omar, Siraj Desai, Ahmed Allie, Percy Sonn, Essa Moosa and Advocate Benny Kies. In the Eastern Cape, including Transkei, several African graduates were admitted to practise law. Many were located in the metropoles of Port Elizabeth, East London, Mthatha and Bisho. These towns were natural sites of law practice given their dense populations and the location of a High Court and magistrate's courts within its margins.

There were some outstanding attorneys in Port Elizabeth. Two who come to my mind are Silas Nkanunu (Oom Si) and Herbert Fischart. Both were well embedded in their communities, which were in revolt. They served on the frontline when it came to intervening in the detention and trials of political 'offenders'. In time, when I became an advocate, I accepted briefs from them on the unwritten understanding that I would be paid only if they actually procured funding for the political trials in which they instructed me. The silent arrangement did not pass the Bar Council rules which obliged advocates to blacklist attorneys who failed to pay within a set timeframe of three months.

In East London, black attorneys practised in Mdantsane, a residential compound set apart for habitation by African people. This diverged from the strident stance of attorneys in other parts of the country that they would ignore spatial segregation and practise in towns and cities reserved for white occupation. However, their location took nothing away from the legal services they offered their clients. In my estimation, the law offices of Ben Ntonga and Hintsa Siwisa stood out in their intervention in a myriad of repression-related litigation, inquests, labour disputes and political prosecutions. Their clients, particularly in the Eastern Cape, were impoverished. Making money was simply out of the equation. They served and briefed several progressive advocates on the understanding that they might not be paid. From time to time they would receive financial support from the Defence and Aid Fund based in London and the Lawyers' Committee for Civil Rights, run by Gay McDougall from Washington DC.

From the mid-1970s to 1990, Mthatha and Butterworth, too, boasted a collection of fine attorneys, which included Dumisa Ntsebeza, now a distinguished senior counsel. Perhaps their most prominent advocates were Tholi Madala SC (Bhut Tholi), who was appointed by President Mandela to serve on the inaugural bench of the Constitutional Court from 1994, and Fikile Bam (Bhut Fiks), who became a judge and the first president of the Land Claims Court from 1994 until his untimely death in 2013. May both find eternal rest. To the list, I must add Advocate Nona Goso. As a female advocate, she was a rare species in those dark and truly patriarchal days. I must also add Themba Sangoni and Templeton Ntsaluba, who set up in Butterworth and conducted an agile practice within local courts and the High Court in Mthatha. I recall also the commendable law practice Tabatha, Smith and Van der Heerden in Bisho and King William's Town. I, like a few other black counsel, earned their briefing nod often. I appeared in their clients' cases heard in the Bisho High Court.

The point to this little excursion is this: the legal practitioners of the time had a raft of challenges that thrust them into each other to form a non-statutory progressive association of lawyers. First, many occupied offices unlawfully and were often issued with race-based eviction notices. Their practices were located in so-called white areas and apartheid law did not permit them to conduct practices in an area other than a so-called black area. But there were no office blocks in residential townships set apart for African people. Clients who sought the services of a lawyer were ordinarily employed in the city, and only returned home at the end of a working day.

The statutory Law Society was perceived to be much more stringent with black practitioners and often unfairly sought their removal from the roll of attorneys. Established white law firms, barring a few, did not employ young black people as interns, a prerequisite to admission as an attorney. It did not help matters at all when the news spread amongst black practitioners that the Law Society opposed my admission as an attorney. Its stance was hard to follow. The Law Society had debated at length whether I could enter articles of clerkship. In the end, it gave the nod. The reasons for the opposition incensed many practitioners. The Law Society was arguing, as the apartheid government did, that I was no longer a South African citizen. They argued that I had lost my citizenship just before my admission as an attorney, when Bophuthatswana became excised from South Africa as an 'independent' state. Not so unwittingly, the Law Society took sides with the apartheid project to take away the citizenship of many indigenous South Africans.

Aside from the little grievances black lawyers might have had, all of our professional challenges occurred within ever-increasing state repression and racial injustice. We were oppressed because of our race, class and gender. That meant we, too, bore the responsibility to close ranks with other progressive forces and liberate ourselves.

Godfrey Pitje was the near-natural leader of the project. During June 1977, he phoned around and sent a few faxes inviting black practitioners to an informal discussion at his offices in Johannesburg. The turnout was surprisingly high. In fact, his modest premises overflowed with young and seasoned practitioners alike. Their collective grievances were too plain to bear repetition here. A number of colleagues reported on the challenges of finding practice accommodation within the city or on threats of eviction. They decried the numerous race-related obstacles. I was asked to inform the meeting of the looming legal battle between me and the Transvaal Law Society. The meeting resolved to form the Black Lawyers Association (BLA). Godfrey Pitje was nominated its interim leader and president, and Seun Moshidi (who is now a judge in the High Court) and I were tasked with preparing a draft constitution to be considered for adoption at an inaugural meeting set for October 1977.

This was a significant event in the consciousness of black legal practitioners. For one thing they recognised the inherent contradiction of practising law within an unjust society. Their predicament was not new. In essence, they were glorified slaves trapped within the same oppression of the vast masses of our people. They sat and operated near, but in fact on the periphery of, the ruling elite and financial privilege. This meant that they had to fall back on the tried-and-tested strategy of the broad liberation movement. They had to identify the source of their social disability. They had to organise themselves and openly revolt against statutory regulation. This awakening made easy work of the objectives of an organised activist group which made common cause with the plight of the broader struggle. The core group reached out to all practitioners discriminated against. The BLA espoused a non-racial stance while it made its primary concern quite plain – the vital interest of black practitioners and the people they were intent on serving.

The inaugural conference of the BLA in Johannesburg attracted just over 30 practitioners. We received messages of support from a number of activist and progressive professional bodies which were beginning to rear their heads at that time. These included the Black Management Forum (BMF), the South African Black Social Workers Association (SABSWA), the National Council of Women, the Black Theology Caucus, and several trade union formations. This favourable nod assured us that we had chosen the correct side. Our lawyering had to be contextual and spanned in to swell the revolt against racial and economic exclusion.

A few white progressive lawyers attended the inaugural conference, albeit with a measure of discomfort. Their discomfort was misplaced. The BLA, like many activists' formations of the time, welcomed the support from the ranks, by definition, of the minority ruling elite. And yet BLA members grasped firmly that they existed as a collective to destroy race-based social arrangements in favour of a non-racial just society. Their political inclinations varied, but common to all were non-racialism, non-sexism and the equal worth of all in an inclusive, open and accountable democracy. Apartheid colonialism was the antithesis of all that. The natural and sound starting point for the BLA and others similarly placed was to organise and unite people who suffered, in the main, common political and social disabilities. It was important to place the full agency of destroying oppression in the hands of the oppressed people themselves. It was not open to oppressed lawyers to outsource their push for dignity, equality and freedom. They had to step up to the plate and become their own liberators. They had to agonise and wrestle with their miserable lot in a way only they could understand. They knew that activist lawyers could rightly earn the respect and support of white fellow-travellers only when they themselves took up cudgels against their wretched condition.

From its inception onward, the BLA grew steadily. Nearly every admitted black attorney or advocate joined the association. We had to find practical programmes to retain organisational cohesion and social relevance. The first was to establish the BLA Legal Education Centre as a public interest entity. Its formation was in part spurred on by the beneficial activities of the Legal Resources Centre (LRC) founded by Arthur Chaskalson and Geoff Budlender. Conference took a resolution that required Phineas Mojapelo and I to formulate a funding proposal to submit to the Rockefeller and Ford foundations.

Both these US funders were already providing support for the LRC. We did not want the funders to ask: 'Why don't you join the LRC, which we are already funding?' Our funding proposals were intent on distinguishing ourselves from the LRC. Our focus was aligned with what black lawyers needed most. This was continuing legal education. We needed to strengthen our lawyering skills. We saw an obvious need to transform our side of the legal profession. For one thing, we wanted sharply to increase new admissions to the profession. For another, we wanted to provide continuing legal education in areas which, because of social exclusions, were obscure to black practitioners. We none-the-less wrote into the trust deed of the Education Centre a power to litigate in the public interest on exceptional occasions we may choose.

Phineas and I secured appointments with each of the programme officers sent out to South Africa by the two foundations. After refining the proposal a few times, the Rockefeller Foundation sent its first cheque to the BLA Education Centre. The grant was of great help but it was modest and only valid for a renewable two-year term. The Ford Foundation was likely to make bigger grants, but it also had many more bureaucratic hoops to be jumped through before a grant was approved. At the urging of GM Pitje, I flew to New York, armed with our funding proposal. GM had heard that Franklin Thomas had been appointed president of the Ford Foundation and he thought a face-to-face presentation of our proposal to the new president was more likely to yield fruit. Thomas was a distinguished lawyer and later a respected senior executive in grant-making circles. He had also been a significant figure in the US movement against racial segregation and for social change.

I secured an appointment with a junior programme officer at the Ford Foundation headquarters in New York. Instead I gate-crashed into the grand office of Mr Franklin Thomas himself. Fortunately, he did not call security. Perhaps my opening lines spared me: 'President Thomas, I am from South Africa. Please hear me out.' He listened while I made an impassioned presentation explaining why the BLA was so vital to the fight against apartheid. I left a copy of the proposal I had presented to the foundation's point person in our country. Within weeks, their cheque reached the centre. And for many years afterwards the Ford Foundation supported the centre and assisted us in the vital and progressive work at the BLA.

Our president, GM Pitje, left his practice to become the centre's first executive director with the support of two programme officers and secretarial staff. The centre ran many excellent programmes. Foremost of these was the placement programme. We recruited young law graduates from black universities and found for them apprenticeship posts under practising attorneys. BLA paid their stipend. In essence, the programme funded scholarships for trainee lawyers over the three-year period of internship. In this way, a practising attorney, who otherwise could not afford the stipend, was encouraged to employ young graduates and benefited from the increased capacity they brought to the law office. BLA placed graduates even in law firms that did not need the financial grant. The ethos of training our young law graduates ourselves soon took root. They did not have to go begging for placement in large white law firms. We had assumed near-full agency in producing young legal minds for a yet uncertain future.

Justice Moloto succeeded GM Pitje as director. Perhaps his term of office at the centre will be remembered mainly for the trial advocacy training programme. Its core mission was to impart forensic craft to legal practitioners. The centre imported trial experts from the USA to train local trainers. Significant personalities in the team were James E 'Fergie' Ferguson II, a veteran attorney from North Carolina, who was a founding partner of the African American law firm Chambers, Ferguson and Adam Stein, renowned for mounting civil rights litigation. Another was Kenneth S Broun, also an attorney from Chapel Hill, North Carolina, who later ran for and became mayor of that city and a law professor at North Carolina University. Ms Geraldine Sumter, an African American attorney also drawn from North Carolina, was a remarkable trial advocacy practitioner and trainer. She did much to keep in check our male inbred smatterings of gender and race stereotypes. As it turned out, she inspired all of us and even more so the female aspirants amongst us.

Trial advocacy training flourished as it attracted scores of practising advocates and attorneys, so much so that the programme had to be extended beyond Johannesburg to far-flung cities like Cape Town, Durban and Port

Elizabeth as demand grew. Again, BLA members assumed responsibility for improving their forensic tools outside the statutory offerings that they saw as tainted. It was quite a feat for the BLA to persuade an outstanding collection of advocacy coaches, and indeed civil rights lawyers of note, to dare domestic segregation. This was possible because of another earlier achievement. In 1982, the BLA persuaded the Rockefeller Foundation to fund the travel and visit of four African American lawyers who were champions of civil rights. Two were federal judges, Julius Higginbotham Jnr, a judge of the United States Court of Appeals for the third circuit from Philadelphia, and Thomas Hendersen, a federal trial court judge from San Francisco. The other two were veteran attorneys Julius LeVonne Chambers, who practised in North Carolina, and Ms Sarah Mitchell, a practising attorney from Philadelphia. Then, Julius was the director-counsel of the NAACP Legal and Defence Fund.

The visit was remarkable on several levels. There had never been people of colour who were judges in this land. No law expressly forbade it and yet the silent norm of that society made it nearly unthinkable that a black person could be elevated to that public office. The all-white male judiciary was an annexe of the racialised and gendered social arrangements. We at the BLA wanted to show that these exclusionary arrangements were false and bankrupt.

We paraded our guests for all to see. We took them to progressive lawyer gatherings, law schools, townships and villages. They did not visit state institutions. We declined an under-the-table invitation that the judges only visit the High Court in Johannesburg and the Appellate Division in Bloemfontein. If they had done that, they would have become glorified white males. We at the BLA were, in effect, thumbing our noses at the glass barrier of apartheid. We were showing the system our two middle fingers. Our guests were a collection of fine and well-decorated jurists, writers and social activists. Judge Higginbotham, who wrote the epic narrative on slavery, race and the legal process in *In the Matter of Color*,[15] reminded us that we owed it to ourselves to liberate ourselves. In time, he predicted, African people would grace the benches of this land. And, indeed one of his law clerks from South Africa, Sandile Ngcobo, rose through the judicial ranks to become our chief justice.

Julius LeVonne Chambers[16] talked passionately about the intersection between legal practice and social justice. He traced civil rights struggles in the United States and the supportive role of the NAACP Legal Defence Fund. He urged us to embark on public interest litigation even within the narrow confines of apartheid arrangements. He warned again and again that public interest lawyers had to be careful not to disempower aggrieved communities or social movements. Their role was to support and not to take over grassroots voices.

Sarah Mitchell was a black woman. She knew much about the triple and mutually reinforcing burden of class, race and gender even as she went along with her duties as an attorney. She spoke to young female and male law students about what was within their professional reach, and to all of us about how central gender parity and freedom were to the betterment of society as a whole.

Another ambitious project of the BLA was to start a law journal. The first issue of the *African Law Review* produced by the BLA Education Centre saw the light of day during 1983. Mojapelo and I served on the editorial board and produced the initial articles, which were to be followed by several others from the members of the BLA. We opted, so to speak, for alternative media, with shorter articles cast in simple accessible language with little or no pretension of academic research. We wrote and chose matters for their practical value to non-established practising lawyers. The *Review* could have passed for a slightly smug newsletter, and yet it brought tremendous pride to us. In those days of few written words amongst the deprived, we had space for conversations that were important to us, even if not to others.

The mission of the centre inspired admirable commitment to serve selflessly. Many members of the BLA were quite ready to forego the financial comfort private practice could offer for the developmental work of the centre. It was not long before Advocate Mojanku Gumbi agreed to assume the role as director of the centre when Justice Moloto retired. With the arrival of democracy fifteen years later, Mojanku Gumbi was to become the legal adviser to the deputy president and later president of the republic, Thabo Mbeki. Ms Dolly Mokgatle agreed to serve as a full-time litigation officer and resident attorney of the centre. Dolly, too, in time moved on to become a powerful executive director at our national electricity supplier. Advocates Ishmail Semenya and Vincent Maleka, who are now eminent senior counsel at the Johannesburg Bar, left their practices at the Bar to set up a fully fledged litigation unit within the Centre.

It may now be said, with considerable pride, that the BLA turned out to be a crucible of progressive legal practice in our country. BLA initially served as a dyke against colonialism and racial exclusion. Few could have predicted its future usefulness. With democratic rule, virtually every member of the BLA of my generation has risen to become a judge of our superior courts at all three levels – the High Court, the Supreme Court of Appeal and the Constitutional Court. Offering to serve in the public space must have come readily. But for them, the bench would have taken much longer to transform. Former BLA members, in the main, made racial and gender equity within the bench possible.

Other BLA members have assumed senior law practice within the Bar and Side Bar. A few others have found roles in business. The BLA's contributions ought to give us, its founder members, reason to have a quiet swagger. For its current members, there is all the more reason to interrogate its current relevance, and identify the overhaul it needs in order to advance its mission of professional excellence in the service of a free, inclusive and just society.

CHAPTER 24

The Bar

One of our colonial legacies is a divided Bar. Attorneys, also called solici-tors in other parts of the former British colonies, practised alone or in partnership in a general practice. They saw clients first, collected fees, kept trust accounts and had a right of appearance only in lower courts. They were obliged to brief or refer to an advocate or barrister work that required appearance in the superior courts. Advocates were not allowed to see clients directly and without a referral from an attorney. This meant the referring attorney had to collect from the client and pay the advocate and the client had to pay both. In time, experienced advocates took silk. That entitled them to be issued with letters patent by the head of state. Simply, they became senior counsel. They were expected to enjoy some precedence over their jun-ior colleagues, do more complex legal work, and be paid more money for their services. And they could expect to be elevated to the bench towards the end of their careers. Judges were appointed only from the ranks of senior counsel.

At the unkind end, one may say the divided Bar tradition had a whiff of a self-serving feudal hierarchy. Perhaps a kinder assessment is that a divided Bar has fostered high levels of specialisation and teams within the attor-neys' profession. Attorneys are the consummate specialists in all fields of law except perhaps in forensic work or court appearances. Lately, the dual Bar system has been, rightly, whittled down. Although in practice the historical dividing features remain stubborn, appearances in the superior courts and appointments to the bench have become open to attorneys and advocates alike.

I always saw my attorney's practice as a stepping stone to practising as an advocate at the Bar. This desire may well have been embedded in the early recesses of my consciousness. When I was a little lad, I grew up under the watchful but caring eye of my father's sister, Masikwane Moseneke, who became the headmistress of the small primary school in Bela-Bela where I started my schooling. She once asked me, 'Dikgang, what do you want to be when you grow up?' I looked up at my aunt towering over me, then looked down as I pondered the question. What did I want to be when I grew up? Into my mind came the picture of the high-and-mighty traffic cop who controlled the only intersection – it was a busy one – in that small town. I remembered admiring his long, white leather gloves, polished knee-high boots, bulging knickerbockers and dark glasses as he rode off on his shiny motorbike. I looked up again and said: 'Aunt, I want to be a speed cop.' 'No, no, Dikgang,' my aunt retorted angrily. 'You are not going to be a speed cop! You are going to be an advocate.'

My dear aunt passed on while I was on Robben Island. She must have had much to do with all the furious studying I did while I was there. Within three years of my return, in 1977, I had completed the LLB degree and articles and, not without considerable legal obstacles, I was admitted as an attorney.[17]

I had a most rewarding stay at the Side Bar. From 1978 through to 1982, I was a partner at Maluleke, Seriti and Moseneke, the first significant black law firm to set up practice in the city centre of Pretoria. Including Moses Mavundla, we were four young partners who sought to create a niche and make a difference despite numerous social and political constraints.

In 1982, at the end of five years as an attorney, the moment had come for me to move on to the Bar. To the surprise of my excellent partners, all of whom now grace our bench as judges, I gave formal notice of my desire and ambition to join the Pretoria Bar. George Maluleke and Moss Mavundla were less surprised and more accepting of the pending move to the Bar than

Willie Seriti. He was not as forgiving and he questioned the wisdom of my decision. How could I leave behind the steady and handsome income of the partnership for the uncharted path of the first black advocate at a potentially hostile Bar? How many black people litigated in the Supreme Court? Who would brief me when there were so few black law firms? How would I survive the initial pupillage period of six months without income? Seriti's doubts were well merited, but they were not enough to deter me. I wanted to be a practising advocate within a Bar setting. That no black person had practised as an advocate in Pretoria spurred me on rather than frightened me.

The Pretoria Bar was an obvious choice. In my very essence, I was a child of *Tshwane ya ga Mamelodi a Maraba*. My beautiful young wife, Kabonina, our daughter, Dudu, and our sons, Sedise and Reabetswe, lived at our home there. Everyone in my village of Pheli knew me and I knew most of them. So did my extended family and clan. Hopefully, I thought, over my five years as a practising attorney, I had built a reputation in Pretoria and might attract custom from clients and practising attorneys alike. There was no African advocate in Pretoria. I thought the time had come for one of us to raise his hand. I raised mine.

The Bar Council was chaired by William de Villiers SC. Its members were all white males and almost exclusively Afrikaans speaking. They were prime candidates to be elevated to the bench of those dark times. They included Louis Harms SC, Marius de Klerk SC, Chris Botha SC, Willem van der Merwe SC and Fanie Mynhardt SC. Virtually all of them became judges of the High Court. As a judge, Louis Harms chaired the infamous Harms Commission which probed certain alleged improprieties of the apartheid state security apparatus. During democracy he rose to become the deputy president of the Supreme Court of Appeal. After his stint on the High Court bench, Marius de Klerk retired in the Cape. Botha became a fine judge and, under the new democratic constitution, he wrote the impressive judgment in the Treatment Action Campaign claim for access to antiretroviral treatment. Willem van der Merwe's distinguishing moment as a judge under democracy might have been when he presided over the rape charge against

Mr Jacob Zuma. He found him not guilty. After that trial, he was elevated to the role of the deputy judge president of the Gauteng North High Court.

As was required of me, I set up an appointment with the honorary secretary, Phillip Ginsberg, with a view to obtaining the prescribed application form for an aspirant member. During my visit to his chambers, Ginsberg was courteous and betrayed no apprehension that I might very well be walking into a hornet's nest. On the other hand, I was well aware of the troubled history of the Pretoria Bar on race and gender issues. But it had become well known that after a few abortive attempts, the requisite majority of members of the Bar had secured the deletion of the provision in the constitution that restricted its membership to 'white people'. At a formal level there should be no problem, I thought.

The honorary secretary invited me to an interview before the full Bar Council. Its chairperson, William de Villiers, was flanked by Louis Harms and Marius de Klerk SC, Phillip Ginsberg and a few other members. I had met Marius when he was a senior partner at the law firm Dyason, Douglas, Muller and Meyer, where I was employed at the start of my law career. Louis Harms and the rest of the all-white male panel I had never met before.

The chairperson fired away with an unsympathetic and inquisitorial questioning. He sought to know why I wanted to join the Bar knowing full well that it was made up of white advocates only. He reminded me that I was free to set up and join a Bar of black people only – a sentiment reminiscent of separate but equal opportunity. He also insinuated that I might very well not be fit and proper to be an advocate or a member of that particular Bar because of my past political conviction. He virtually suggested that I withdraw my application for membership and walk away. At a certain point, De Villiers added that it was open to me to set up a society of advocates that would cater for black people only.

Before I made any substantive response, an unexpected hero of my interview emerged. Louis Harms sat up straight in his chair, tilted slightly forward and turned to his left towards William de Villiers. The irritation and impatience on his face was unmistakable. To my surprise, his statement was firm and clear. The constitution of the Bar, he reminded De Villiers, had been duly amended. Any South African properly admitted as an advocate was entitled to apply. As Moseneke had been admitted as an advocate by the Supreme Court, he added, whatever his political background might be, it was not the place of the Bar Council to seek to keep Moseneke out only for the reason of his race or his political history.

The room went silent, but only for a moment. Marius de Klerk joined the fray and expressed his unqualified support for the stance taken by Louis Harms. In no time the majority of the committee members had filed up behind Louis's position. De Villiers was alone and defeated. But for the courage of principle displayed by Louis Harms when it mattered most, I might never have been a member of the Bar. What he did was not an easy thing to do during an era of racial orthodoxy. Louis stood up against this bigotry when expedience could have better served his career and social cause. I became the first black member of the Pretoria Bar.

Shortly after his courageous intervention, Louis Harms was elevated to the bench, as was Marius de Klerk. In time, William de Villiers, too, was appointed to the bench. By that time, I was a senior member of the Bar with a considerable practice. I attended De Villiers's farewell function in the common room. At the end of his farewell speech, he paused for a minute, turned his eyes in my direction and said that as he left the Bar he had one regret – and that was his opposition to my membership. He publicly apologised to me and wished me well in my further career. That was big of him. Several years later, when I was elevated to the Pretoria High Court, I found William there. I happily and respectfully served side by side with him under our new constitutional democracy.

My further stay at the Bar meant that my path would again cross with that of Justice Harms. I remember too well how he ran a busy motion court roll with remarkable efficiency. If your papers were in order, you could extract an unopposed order within half a minute. But if they weren't, you would also be out of court within half a minute.

While the racial spat of my admission to the Society of Advocates in

Pretoria carried on, I applied for pupil membership at the Johannesburg Bar. Thankfully, there I expected no drama – and nor was there any. A few people of colour and women had been members of the Johannesburg Bar from the early 1960s. Ismail Mahomed was one, and Philemon Pearce Dumasile 'Duma' Nokwe was another. Although both were members and qualified advocates, they could not take up chambers in the communal space reserved for practising advocates because the chambers were located in so-called whites-only areas. Both occasionally squatted in the chambers of sympathetic white colleagues such as George Bizos. Both were men with ample talent and character and, over time, they were to become household names.

Advocate Duma Nokwe, proudly from Evaton, did not practise at the Bar long. He was hounded by the security cops because of his political activism until he fled the country in 1960 for exiled life within the ANC hierarchy. He became its secretary general over the decade of 1958 to 1969. After a gigantic contribution to our struggle for liberation, he died in exile in 1978.[18] Ismail Mahomed continued practising law at the Bar until he soared to the height of senior counsel. His enormous intellect stood him in good stead in a number of intricate political prosecutions and civil claims. After the dawn of democracy, in 1995 President Mandela appointed him the deputy president of the Constitutional Court, and later he became the chief justice and head of the Supreme Court of Appeal.

In 1982, when I arrived at the Johannesburg Bar, Ismail Mahomed was still there and he was a well-respected senior counsel. And yet the number of other black and women practitioners had not swelled. The Bar was a little more racially tolerable and yet at its core it was an old boys' club. The cream of the crop was white, male and well pedigreed. They knew somebody or somebody who knew somebody in big corporations or government litigation departments. They were well heeled financially, they owned their world and they were, by and large, arrogant.

Legoai Pitje had just started a junior practice. He was my contemporary and friend. But also, he was the son of GM Pitje, the veteran attorney and the president of the BLA. Legoai did much to ease my passage at the Bar, as he would later do for Vincent Maleka, Ish Semenya and Kgomotso Moroka. I was allocated Advocate Guy Hoffman as my pupil master in Group 7 located in Innes Chambers. The group had an interesting assortment of advocates. One who stood out for me was senior counsel Ernie Wentzel. He was a large, portly man, endowed with considerable intellect with which he managed a large commercial practice. His generous laughter would roar down the passage, matched only by his great (and saucy) sense of humour.

My master, Guy Hoffman, enjoyed one of the largest motion court commercial practices in town. I lived with him in the opposed and unopposed motion court hearings, nearly from Monday to Friday. What he did not do, Ernie Wentzel did. Ernie gave me an excellent opportunity to wrestle with complex legal questions and to write down what I thought the correct answer was. The deal I had with him was uncomplicated. He had in his chambers many opinion briefs which had been gathering dust over the months. The arrangement was that for every draft opinion I wrote, I would be entitled to a lunch with him and Guy. I drafted many opinions for him. The lunches were as many, and mostly very long, boozy and raucous.

The Bar Council had put together excellent pupillage classes. I took them seriously and worked hard. One lesson that comes readily to mind was the motion court class, which was taught with remarkable gusto by Val Fevrrier. Towards the end of the pupillage stint of six months, he revised with all the candidates, using the examination papers of previous years.

The examinations came and went. Each candidate had to submit to an oral examination. My panel comprised judges Booysen and Kees van Dijkhorst, with senior counsel Arthur Chaskalson.

'Moseneke,' Judge van Dijkhorst said jovially as I entered the room, 'you don't have to submit to an oral. You have had one of the highest overall marks to be earned by a pupil in these examinations. Good luck with your career at the Bar.'

I ran out, completely insane with excitement. I called Kabo, my parents, all my brothers, and every acquaintance who was an attorney. Within a day,

attorneys Mathews Phosa and Phineas Mojapelo drove over 300 kilometres from Nelspruit to Innes Chambers in Johannesburg. They arrived at
my new, and as yet unfurnished, chambers. Phineas was pushing a wheelbarrow. The barrow was heaped to the hilt with light blue briefs neatly held
in green ribbons. They gave my practice at the Bar an unforgettable lift-off.
Not to be outdone, the next day Attorney George Maluleke, my former
partner, caused to be delivered a few tens of briefs he had delayed until my
membership at the Bar. In the one week I had more briefs than many senior juniors at the Bar. Mainly black attorneys in Pretoria and Johannesburg
had seemingly conspired to use my services aggressively. My briefs were
mainly in the High Court. I was spared a junior practice of petty crime,
matrimonial disputes and magistrate's court civil hearings. This was welcome because, as an attorney, I had well and truly graduated from these
areas of practice. I had left the attorney's profession for a rigorous forensic
experience in superior courts. That was what I was blessed with from the
first day at the Bar. Many more gave me unstinting support. I was grateful
to attorneys too many to mention here, including Hosi Cedric Shilubane
Mhinga, MN Bogoshi, Richard Ramodipa, Godfrey Hetisane, Muzi
Msimang, Sakkie Maboa, Don Nkadimeng, Jerry Shongwe, Krish Naidoo,
NM Mavundla, WL Seriti, Sisi Khampepe, VJ Kathri, Felix Vilakazi, Allan
Wilson, Priscilla Jana and Kathy Satchwell. The briefing support ran well
beyond my home province. I received briefs from Griffiths and Victoria
Mxenge from Natal; from Jake Moloi in the Free State; Ben Ntonga,
Hintsa Siwisa and Silas Nkanunu in the Eastern Cape; Dumisa Ntsebeza,
Humphrey Luso, Themba Sangoni JP and Templeton Ntsaluba in the
Transkei; Dumisani Tabatha from the Ciskei; and Abdullah Omar, Yusuf
Ali and Percy Sonn from the Western Cape.

I was indeed fortunate and well supported by attorneys. My earnings
quickly became steady and way beyond my wildest expectation. The generous time I used to spend with my daughter and two sons had to yield to
the explosion of a new challenge. Very swiftly I became the anointed one
amongst predominantly black attorneys. I had no expectations of briefs from

the apartheid government or from big business. In any event, I appeared so frequently on the side of the vulnerable and powerless that I was unlikely to earn the favour of the mighty and powerful. An activist practice was my predestined path of advocacy. That worked just fine for me. I played on the side I cherished most.

CHAPTER 25

Some notable cases

When I assumed my role as an advocate at the Bar, our nation had been in revolt for a while and the minority state was beleaguered. It was in more trouble than all of us, its opponents, realised. As a sequel to the 1976 uprisings and the Frelimo Rally prompted by the independence of Mozambique, the SASO Nine were charged and tried. SASO members organised the so-called Frelimo Rally to mark the independence of Mozambique. At the rally they advocated for the overthrow of the apartheid regime, and for that, they were charged.

On 21 December 1976 they were sentenced to five- and six-year jail terms on Robben Island. Just about the same time, Winifred Nomzamo Mandela was released from detention and, early in 1977, she was banished to Brandfort in the Free State. In the year before February 1977, eighteen political activists had died in police detention. They included, notably, Mapetla Mohapi. Seen in this way, Steve Biko's detention held an ominous, if not fatal, prospect. He died on 12 September 1977 in police detention at the untimely age of 30. His funeral was held on 25 September in King William's Town and attended by an estimated crowd of 15 000 mourners. It hurt that I could not attend his funeral. It was bound to be this epoch-making event that energised our struggle beyond words. But in 1977 I was still banned, restricted to the magisterial district of Pretoria and under house arrest. I had not met Bantu Biko personally, but he had sent me personal greetings through Bokwe Mafuna when I returned from Robben Island, where I had spent several years together with Bomvana Biko, who had been convicted for PAC activities.

And yet here was the irony. If one had asked the enraged 15 000 mourners at Biko's graveside in Ginsberg township whether the apartheid state would collapse within eighteen years of his death, they would have roared back with clenched fists: 'No, comrade! We have a long struggle ahead: *Aluta continua!*'

True to form, and terrified by the increasing boldness and defiance of organised activists, the apartheid state responded with the most comprehensive measure of repression until then. The date 19 October 1977 came to be known as Black Wednesday. Under the Internal Security Act, the regime declared over eighteen movements affiliated with the Black Consciousness Movement (BCM) unlawful. They included SASO, the Black People's Convention (BPC), the Black Parents Association, the Black Women's Federation, the Border Youth Organisation, the Christian Institute of Southern Africa (a non-racial organisation of anti-apartheid churchmen), the Eastern Province Youth Organisation, the Medupe Writers' Association, the Natal Youth Organisation, the Transvaal Youth Organisation, the Union of Black Journalists, and the Western Cape Youth Organisation. The actions provoked worldwide shock and protest. The police arrested and detained over 70 leading activists and restricted or banned scores of others. One of those detained was Dr Nthato Motlana and seven other members of the Soweto Committee of Ten, a community social movement opposed to apartheid. The proclamation shut down the daily newspaper *The World* and its editor, Percy Qoboza, was detained. The ban also closed the related weekly *Weekend World*. The state imposed banning orders on white activists such as Beyers Naudé and Donald Woods, who had openly supported Steve Biko and the BCM.[19]

After the carnage of the 1970s, fatalities, detentions, banning orders and banishments, all seemed lost. The political landscape looked like a war zone with smouldering smoke and lifeless corpses. Many young activists fled the country to join the military wings of our exiled liberation movements.

However, this setback proved to be only a false lull before the big push to come. The 1980s were to become years of worker unionisation and mass solidarity expressed in widespread strike action and internal revolt against the apartheid state. It saw the formation, in 1983, of the United Democratic Front (UDF), a coalition of over 400 civic organisations, churches, and student, worker and other formations. It boasted a stellar leadership.[20] Early in its life, the UDF adopted non-racialism and the Freedom Charter, a stance which set it apart from the dominant political genre of the Black Consciousness Movement (BCM), on the one end, and of the Inkatha Freedom Party (IFP), on the other. At the initial stages, some measure of collaboration was maintained between the BCM and the UDF but, sadly, the camaraderie was short-lived. As the UDF gained ground and the influence of the BCM receded, turf wars ensued. Again, to the dismay of many, the contest was not always peaceful. Many people on both sides died.

Hot on the heels of the formation of the UDF, the labour movement found its voice. It united organised workers in their hundreds of thousands through the Congress of South African Trade Unions (COSATU) in 1985 [21] and the National Council of Trade Unions (NACTU) in 1986.[22] The two distinct labour federations were, in the main, ideological clones of the Charterist tradition and the BCM or Azanian school. This meant that their respective demands ran beyond workplace grievances. They were, in effect, directed at state power and monopoly capital.

In the 1980s, the youth uprising of the mid-1970s assumed an even more militant form both at sites of learning and on social issues. The youth disrupted schooling, enforced work boycotts and attacked symbols of state power. Township councillors, police officers and other 'impimpis' bore the brunt of youth anger. The victims of youth wrath ran the risk of being killed by the notorious 'necklacing' method. The attackers would douse the victim with petrol, forcibly fit a motor vehicle tyre around the person's neck and set him or her alight. This horrendous form of killing drew quick and harsh criticism from the leaders of all the resistance movements. This inhumane vigilantism suited the propaganda of the state securocrats. Shots of death by necklacing were shown repeatedly on television at home and abroad in order to diminish the superior moral claim of our freedom struggle. Rightly so, Bishop Desmond Mpilo Tutu and the South African Council of Churches (SACC) publicly and roundly condemned necklacing as barbaric and unacceptable. Aside from the necklacing distraction, virtually every township was a site of struggle and was policed daily by the army, which was becoming stretched and weary.

In the 1980s, global solidarity against apartheid had risen to loud and high decibels. The minority government was presiding over a pariah of the world. The United Nations (UN) had toughened its stance well beyond the initial 1962 General Assembly Resolution which had followed on the heady post-Sharpeville shooting days. That ground-breaking resolution marked the beginning of a little less than three decades of global solidarity against apartheid. The UN established the Special Committee on Apartheid and condemned apartheid as a violation of South African obligations under the UN Charter. It called for a voluntary boycott. After more than two decades of resolutions against the South African government, in 1986 the Security Council unanimously adopted Resolution 591. The vote included that of the USA and the United Kingdom, who over the years had vetoed or abstained from voting for resolutions against South Africa. The council recognised the struggle of the South African people, who demanded the establishment of a democratic state with full civil and political rights. The resolution condemned South Africa for its repression against opponents of apartheid, the killing of demonstrators, the holding of political prisoners, and its defiance of Security Council and General Assembly resolutions.[23] The resolution imposed mandatory economic and military sanctions. By then, the UN had declared apartheid a crime against humanity. But for a few, most nations had voluntarily imposed an arms embargo and economic sanctions, as well as cultural and sports boycotts against South Africa. South Africa was expelled from just about every multilateral or international body. Most of those countries that had traded with or were invested in South Africa started a process of disinvestment. We were expelled from virtually every international sporting code. Our country had become the skunk of the world.

That was the leitmotif of my practice at the Bar. As will become plain later, my chores as a practising lawyer were intertwined with the grassroots and global battles against the apartheid state. Like many activist lawyers before me, I elected to manage the schizophrenia of being at once an officer of the court and also a freedom fighter bent on destroying the illegitimate state to which the courts owed their allegiance. Here is the point. When the regime did not maim or kill its opponents or make them disappear, it played *lawfare*. It blasted them with the laws it made. Apartheid stood on the stilts of laws. Through laws it denied most of its citizens freedom, peace, human dignity, equality and economic equity. The law disguised the barbaric coercion of that system. The corollary of this proposition was that courts were necessary and expedient sites of contestation for the victims of exclusion. The weak, vulnerable and perhaps apolitical could gain short-term relief. On the other hand, the active opponents of the repressive regime had the facility to press their case not to the presiding judge but to the world as the Treason trialists of 1956 had done. As Robert Mangaliso Sobukwe did on trial in 1960 after he led the anti-pass campaign. As Nelson Rolihlahla Mandela did at the end of the Rivonia Trial. And as the SASO Nine did on their conviction in 1976. The trials presented a once-off but memorable platform to broadcast one's claims. I regret to this day that in 1963, at our trial in the Old Synagogue, I was too terrified to lay bare to Judge Cille my article of faith – my own and my people's right to freedom, equality, human dignity and social equity.

Despite the inevitable political overlay, the causes that came my way as an activist advocate at the Bar were many and thrilling. I was blessed with a generous range of work that included extensive drafting of pleadings, furnishing of opinions and court appearances. When one starts a practice at the Bar, attorneys tend to send one to the magistrate's courts and to matrimonial and maintenance courts. I was spared that entry-level agony. From the outset, but for a few exceptions, mine was a highly pressured High Court practice. I had to manage and survive the hurried hustle of the motion court in the High Court, Johannesburg, before the daunting Judge Gert 'Snor' Coetzee,

LEFT: Revd Samuel Moseneke.
Personal collection

BELOW: Dikgang's mother, father and two siblings, Malatse and Onkgopotse, in 1958.
Personal collection

(14) SAMUEL MOSENEKE : born about the year 1877 in the Waterberg, Transvaal. He was trained as a schoolmaster in our Kilnerton Institution, Pretoria, and was received into the Ministry in 1917. He maintained a keen interest in the education of his people, but gave the first place in his life to the Gospel he preached and to his pastoral work. His brief ministry was marked by his fervent concern for the redemption of his people, strengthened by his loyalty to his Church, and inspired by his love for his Lord. Stricken with disease without hope of recovery, he bore his trial with courage and patience and passed to higher service in the thirteenth year of his ministry, on January 8, 1930.

The obituary of Revd Samuel Moseneke, secured from the official archives of the Methodist Church. Personal collection

The soccer pitch on Robben Island. Photo by Anthony Wilson-Prangley

LEFT: Dikgang's cell on Robben Island.
Photo by Anthony Wilson-Prangley

Dikgang's view from his Robben Island cell. Photo by Anthony Wilson-Prangley

LEFT: Kabo and Dikgang during the courting stage of their relationship in 1973.
Personal collection

BOTTOM LEFT: Kabo and Dikgang exchanging their marriage vows in May 1975.
Personal collection

BOTTOM RIGHT: With newly born son, Sedise, in 1976.
Personal collection

Dikgang is admitted as an attorney in April 1978. Photo by Gallo Images/Avusa

Partners in Maluleke, Seriti and Moseneke. From left: Dikgang, Willie Seriti, Moses Mavundla and George Maluleke. Personal collection

Dikgang is admitted as an advocate in July 1983.
Photo by Gallo Images/Avusa

Official portrait when appointed as a High
Court judge in 2011. Personal collection

Deep in conversation with Nelson Mandela. Personal collection

TOP: With Mpho Tutu and Desmond Tutu.
Personal collection

LEFT: With Peter Hain.
Personal collection

BELOW: With Mangosuthu Buthelezi.
Photo by Gallo Images/Avusa

With Helen Suzman at the Wits Founders tea in 2012. Personal collection

Karabo Mabel Moseneke, Dikgang's mother. Personal collection

Sedise Gabaiphiwe Moseneke, Dikgang and Kabo's first-born son. Personal collection

Duduzile Moseneke, Dikgang and Kabo's daughter, with brothers Sedise (left) and Bo (right) on her wedding day. Personal collection

Kabonina Naomi Moseneke, Dikgang's wife.
Personal collection

Reabetswe Botshelo, known as Bo, Dikgang and Kabo's second-born son. Photo by SuperSport

The graduation of Boipelo Moseneke, Dikgang's niece. Personal collection

LEFT: Tshiamo and Sedise Jnr with Niara, the youngest grandchild of Dikgang and Kabo. Personal collection

RIGHT: Kabo and Dikgang with their grandchildren, Lindokuhle, Tshiamo, Zintl'intombi, Sedise Jnr and Lwandle. Personal collection

Shortly before the start of Dikgang's final sitting at the Constitutional Court.
Photo by Oupa Nkosi/*Mail & Guardian*

and in the Pretoria High Court presided over by the cutting and dismissive Judge Louis Harms.

Within a year, most of the pleadings I had settled converted into trials. I relished preparing advices on evidence for my instructing attorneys. I carefully identified the minimum elements of my client's claim and visualised the evidence I needed in order to establish each element. I insisted that I consult with witnesses well ahead of the date of hearing. I enjoyed cross-examination, which I prepared days before and revised my line of questioning the night before the hearing. Whenever she heard me loudly firing questions at imaginary witnesses, Kabo would burst into loving laughter and say, '*Ke eng monna: wa gafa na?*' (What is all this, husband: have you gone mad?) I enjoyed closing arguments. I learned quickly that judges welcomed written heads of argument. They serve judges well. A judge can read and reread heads during later reflection. No competent advocate wants his or her best argument to miss the target of persuasion – namely, the presiding judge. In any event, counsel who lightens a judge's burden is likely to earn a receptive hearing.

I quickly learned that ethical conduct was central to the success of my task as counsel. A judge must always trust what counsel conveys in court. I took seriously the cardinal rule that I should never knowingly convey an untruth to a court. My duty was to convey my client's version of events to the best of my ability. But once I came to know that my client's version was false, I would not perpetuate or repeat the lie to court. While I was not required to judge my client's truthfulness, I never knowingly became a conduit of an accused person's lies. I would never help my client fabricate a version or convey to court what I knew to be false. At that point my duty was to withdraw from representing a mendacious client without pronouncing him or her a liar from the rooftops. This was because the communication between a client and a lawyer is privileged and may not be disclosed without the client's permission. In addition, should a withdrawing counsel spread the erstwhile client's untruthfulness, the disclosure is likely to imperil the fairness of the pending court hearing.

In consultation, I always urged clients to be truthful. Once a client confessed to guilt, I urged the client to plead guilty. My energies would then be directed at mitigation of sentence or of the extent of civil damages. However, where a client had a probable defence resting on possibly credible facts, I would invest all my intellectual vigour in advancing his or her course. Not all cases were as clear-cut as the ethical rule of advocacy required. The most agonising for me as counsel were political trials in which the accused faced charges of crimes against the state. These included treason, terrorism, sedition, sabotage, public violence, and membership of a banned political organisation. Then the ANC, PAC, the SA Communist Party (SACP) and, later, organisations under the BCM were all prohibited organisations. Being a member of or participating in their activities was a punishable offence. It followed that being part of MK or APLA or the Azanian National Liberation Army (AZANLA) was forbidden and punishable under terrorism laws.

The first class of accused people was usually young activists or students who were in domestic revolt against the state. They routinely faced charges of public violence arising from a protest march, rioting and damage to public property. They would have been arrested on the scene of the alleged crime. The other category of clients was trained and armed combatants who had been infiltrated into the country under the command of exiled liberation movements. Both classes of accused people were moved by what they saw as a higher principle. They rejected the moral legitimacy of the state and many thought it their duty to render the state ungovernable or to destroy it. Without exception, the accused would refuse to plead guilty even if their deeds technically amounted to punishable conduct. In many instances, they refused to plead to the charges on the ground that they were not answerable to a government whose founding apartheid policy had been declared a crime against humanity under international law.

To each, I would repeat the lawyering mantra that, even under apartheid law, they had a right to remain silent. They had no duty to say anything and, even less so, to incriminate themselves. They were within their rights to demand that the state prove their guilt. The state carried the onus to prove their guilt beyond a reasonable ground. This posture worked well with young activists who were part of the internal uprising. Not one of the few thousands accused of public violence or sedition whom I defended over the years was ever convicted. This is why: the state's evidence went no further than that the accused had been arrested on at a rioting scene. The state's problem was the dictates of individualised responsibility. Vicarious liability was not sufficient to prove the crime charged. An accused person could not be guilty only because people who were near him or her were breaking the law. The evidence had to show the discrete act or conduct of each accused that led to or contributed to the public violence. The plain irony of the time was that even the illegitimate courts of apartheid were bound by and upheld this tenet of criminal justice. Happily for the accused, helmeted riot police in armoured cars, once in court, could never remember the faces and deeds of every young person in the accused box who had been arrested at the scene of a riot. They were usually called to testify in court a few months after the incident, which did not help matters. Or was it a case of all young black rioters looking the same to young white riot policemen in armoured vehicles? Their evidence on identity, and indeed that of black riot policemen, was always open to severe doubt. The accused were the beneficiaries of the uncertainty.

The rioting youths I defended were always found not guilty. This fuelled impunity. They joined one protest march after another, and they were arrested and charged as many times. At the end of a trial Magistrate Johnson, who sat in the Atteridgeville court, and Magistrate De Waal, in the Mamelodi court, speaking in Afrikaans, would often say: *'Beskuldigdes staan op! Ek dink julle is inderdaad skuldig. Van julle was hier te vore. Ek glo dat julle was die klipgooiers. Maar die staat kan dit nie bewys nie. Julle is vrygespreek.'* (The accused, stand up! I think you are certainly guilty. Some of you were here before. I am convinced that you were the stone-throwers. But the state cannot prove it. You are found not guilty.)

The young rioters must have thought I was a magician. They were arrested at the crime scene. They did not have to say a word in court, and yet they were found not guilty. They gave me grateful hugs, saying, 'Thank you, comrade advocate' as they left the courthouse singing freedom songs and dancing. Many would go straight back to another protest site in the knowledge that the state would struggle to make them account for their seditious deeds. This parlous conviction rate on the part of the state may, in part, explain why the public riot unit of the time often resorted to shooting and killing or maiming young activists in the streets rather than turning them over to prosecution. It was deadlier to kill than prosecute.

The criminal trials of militarily trained combatants presented a different forensic challenge. These men and women were infiltrated into the country mainly through Botswana or Mozambique. On their arrest, they were detained in indefinite solitary confinement under 'terrorism' laws. Intense interrogation of the detainee would follow and would always include torture. Very few held out with their denial. They saw no reason to endure torture when they were not ashamed to admit to their military training under the exiled liberation movement. They were proud freedom fighters under capture. Sadly, the quick admission did not end the torture. They were required to point out the internal activists who had 'assisted or concealed terrorists'. Here came the rub. One who helped hide or otherwise assisted a 'terrorist' was guilty of an offence and liable to the same punishment as a 'terrorist'. Internal operatives would be arrested. Either they would be put on trial with the trained cadres or turned into state witnesses. They faced an agonising choice when they thought they wanted to assist the trained combatants who had 'outed' them, so to speak. In other trials, one or two of the arrested combatants would be groomed to become state witnesses against their erstwhile comrades.

The one miracle about the solitary detentions was that a word of the arrests always leaked. Often, black security police breached their duty of confidentiality. A discrete number of lawyers would come to know of the detentions. Underground structures of the liberation movements had cultivated and kept liaison with activist lawyers at home to support the detained cadres. They also tipped off activist attorneys on how to source overseas funds to defend political trials. The consequence would be that inevitable telephone call to me from activist attorneys, instructing me to request access to a detainee. A formal request of that kind from an advocate, sent to the security police headquarters, was an important device to save the life of a detained APLA or MK combatant. It served as notice to the security police and the state that we were aware of the detention of a particular person and that we would continue to demand access to the detainee. Activist practitioners had come to know that, after their detention, guerrillas disappeared without a trace. Some were shot and killed allegedly in combat against the police or army; others were last seen in detention and never emerged from it. In other instances, an attorney would phone me to appear for the accused on the first day of appearance in a pending terrorism trial.

The relief on the faces of our comrades when they saw me enter the holding cells in the courthouse was huge. Other than their captors, I would be the first person they met. As I walked into the cell, I would warn the accused, using sign language, that the holding cell might be bugged. I would keep the exchange formal and stick to facts such as confirming their agreement that I appear for them and, importantly, procuring their family links so that my attorneys might inform the family members of their detention and pending trial. This last was absolutely essential. Many trained combatants had left home in the 1960s and 1970s. In many instances, by the 1980s, unknown to exiled combatants, the composition and location of their families had changed.

I appeared in the regional court and High Court, in all four provinces of the time, in scores of trials for fighters of the ANC and PAC, and in one trial of AZANLA combatants. It was indeed a privilege to support young patriots who, having left home and submitted to military training, had it within themselves to dare a return into a militarised state. The hazards were enormous and life-threatening. They entailed capture, torture or possible death in combat or detention. The jeopardy called for courage beyond words.

The life of counsel in political cases was not easy. The security cops saw little difference between the accused and their counsel. Attorneys and advocates were, in their eyes, cover-ups for 'terrorists'.

One morning in 1984, I arrived at my chambers in Nedbank Building in Pretoria to discover that it had been blown up by during the night by an explosive device. The ceiling and roof had caved in, windowpanes were shattered, and my law books, briefs and other belongings were scattered in all directions. Fortunately, the timer of the device seemed to have malfunctioned. There was no point blowing up an office without human contents. The security cops came round, gave me a blank stare, took pictures and sped off. I salvaged my practice belongings and asked the Pretoria Bar Council to allocate me another chamber in Standard Bank Building on Church Square.

One time, in 1986, I was away from home for three weeks conducting an ANC terrorism trial that was being heard in the picturesque town Kenton-on-Sea. Advocate Denzil Potgieter and I stayed in a motel in Jeffreys Bay for the duration. We had been briefed by attorney Silas Nkanunu. During my absence, one evening after midnight, Kabonina heard several male voices around our bedroom windows. The perimeter wall of our modest residence in Mazakhele, Atteridgeville, had obviously been breached. Someone knocked violently on the front door, shouting: 'This is the police! Open!' Kabo put her hands in the pockets of her dressing gown as she neared the front door. Duduzile, Sedise and Botshelo accompanied their mother. They put on the indoor and stoep lights. Outside they saw a collection of security cops, black and white. Their three cars were parked near our front gate. One of them, Kabo swore, looked like Joe Mamasela, that notorious *askari* who led the state's death squad of the 1980s. One of the white officers asked where I was. Mamasela, who stood within the door, blocked the way with his rotund frame and played interpreter. Kabo sensed enormous danger. She thought it safer to say I was resting in the bedroom. They backed off, jumped over our perimeter wall, got into their cars and sped off without putting on their headlamps. To this day, Kabo proudly relates how she scared the hell out of that many security cops. They were terrified by her bold stance and hands in her pockets. In a sense Kabo was right. The *askaris* would have had to wipe out my wife and three children before they could get at me, ostensibly in our bedroom. That would have been a price too heavy for the state to pay. During that time *askaris* routinely murdered opponents of apartheid – the Ribeiros, for example, who were shot dead in their courtyard by gunmen who sped off in a motor vehicle. The assassinations were confirmed during the Truth and Reconciliation Commission.

After South Africa had attained democracy, I set my sights away from the ravages of our past. In 1999, however, I received a subpoena from the secretariat of the TRC to attend an amnesty application hearing. Commissioned officers of the security police had applied for amnesty from prosecution for having attempted to murder me at least twice. I requested Advocate Vincent Maleka to appear on my behalf. Lo and behold, the presiding judge of the amnesty process, in a panel of three, was Judge Sisi Khampepe. How quickly had our world changed! Activist lawyers had become judges. And state securocrats, the predators, had become the hunted. Like rats out of a sinking ship, killer cops were running for cover to escape criminal liability for their dastardly deeds.

State repression yielded fascinating victims and an opportunity to fight their wars in the courtroom. I did not mean to thrive on the misery of my clients any more than a surgeon who looks forward to operating on a patient who presents a condition that requires intricate surgery.

Ingoapele Madingoane was a poet. He wrote many lines, but perhaps his most known epic poem is 'Africa My Beginning'. The rousing poem was widely read and recited by students and young activists alike. It was not long before the state banned the possession, reproduction or distribution of his anthology. In 1984, the police raided his home, arrested him and charged him with being in possession of banned literature. Security police, without a warrant, routinely searched the homes of activists for banned literature. That was the easiest ruse to keep activists locked up and out of political commission. A conviction on the charge attracted a jail term of up to five years.

Nobel laureate Nadine Gordimer headed a progressive writers' ensemble. She asked George Bizos SC and me to appear in court for Ingoapele. The proscribed literature found in his possession was written and caused to be published by him. During the search of his home, the over-zealous policemen had a long catalogue of banned publications, but did not bother to verify the names of the authors. Even if they had, they would have probably arrested Ingoapele regardless.

The narrow question in the case was whether the ban on possession of literature extended to the author of a publication. The statute was couched in customary language: 'no person may possess banned literature'. The court rightly held that the ban did not extend to the author. If it were so, it would mean that for an author to escape criminal liability, he or she must disavow and destroy their own creativity, which preceded the statutory ban. That would not be a plausible meaning of the prohibition. Ingoapele walked out free. Nadine was well pleased with George Bizos and me.

Mathatha Tsedu is now the executive director of the South African National Editors Forum (SANEF). In his younger days, in the 1980s, his public posture was more radical. He filed for *The Sowetan* newspaper as its bureau chief in Polokwane. Otherwise, he was a leftist trade unionist. He led the Black Agricultural and Allied Workers Union. The rump of its members worked as citrus fruit pickers at Zebediela Citrus Farms, which were wholly owned by state trust. The citrus produce was exported to Europe under the brand name 'Outspan'. The working conditions on the citrus farms were horrendous and the wages were a pittance. The workers balloted for a strike and downed tools. Management, shocked by their impertinence and ingratitude, fired several hundred workers summarily. The workers would have none of that. Mathatha assured them that their dismissals were so egregious that even an apartheid court would set them aside as unlawful.

Mojanku Gumbi and Dolly Mokgatle of the BLA Legal Education Centre briefed me with advocates Francis and McCaps Motimele to procure an urgent order from the High Court for the reinstatement of the workers. With Mathatha and other shop stewards in attendance, we prepared papers overnight in Mokopane. In their hurried arrogance to dismiss the workers, management had committed gross procedural lapses. The following morning we drove to the seat of the High Court in Pretoria to move the application. In a surprise turn, counsel for management asked the court to stand the matter down because they wanted to make the workers an offer of settlement. Armed with a deed of settlement, Mathatha, other shop stewards and the legal team drove to Mokopane to seek the workers' ratification of the deed of settlement. We relayed the terms of the bosses' offer in a mass meeting. All workers on strike were to be reinstated forthwith. Their wages were to be increased by a whopping percentage. Their accommodation and other working conditions were to be changed for the better – also forthwith.

The outcome was beyond all belief. The workers broke into ecstatic song and dance. They were rural people who tended fruit trees and picked the yield. They were poor and underpaid, but they had learned to accept their lot. They had never dared to defy their employer before, let alone embark on a strike. Even so, they had mustered a flicker of collective courage and it had paid off. Although those were dark days of collective bargaining and unfair labour practice, in this instance worker solidarity had overcome. Grassroots working people's sense of fairness in the workplace had been awakened once and for all time. Equally important was that bosses had learned that their lucrative export of Outspan citrus produce could come to nought without consenting workers. I drove from Mokopane to Tshwane wearing a slight smile as I recalled the excited workers of Zebediela, their faces bursting with triumph.

Away from the testing issue of struggle was the trial of the *State vs Zola Mahobe*.[24] I had said my goodbyes to Zola Mahobe when I opted for the Bar in 1983. His football club, Mamelodi Sundowns, which, you will recall, I had helped him acquire, was well resourced and flourishing. It had soared up the league log and had taken its deserved place alongside premier football clubs such as Kaizer Chiefs and Orlando Pirates. In the mid-1980s Zola had enough money to splurge on his players and he did so, often lavishly.

All picnics come to an end sometime. In 1987 Zola got into trouble with the law. His girlfriend, the beautiful and vivacious Ms Snowy Moshoeshoe, was arrested. Snowy was always by Zola's side at soccer matches and social occasions. She smiled only occasionally, and her quiet demeanour concealed her enormous intellect. She faked subservience to Zola and yet she often summoned him to her side. He never demurred. Their exchanges were quiet and difficult to follow.

Snowy was charged with defrauding Standard Bank of R11.4 million. As head of the computerised ledger account at the bank's head office, everyone thought she had an awesome job. She was well ahead of her time. She was a woman and a black person in a world where the artificial ceiling of race and patriarchy held sway, and yet she was computer literate and managed hundreds of millions of rand in the bank's suspense account of uncleared cheques and other promissory notes.

On hearing the news of Snowy's arrest, Zola escaped to Gaborone in Botswana, leaving behind his wife and children, a few mansions, a professional football club, racehorses, a couple of German luxury sedan cars and a good few other valuable items. Zola called me from Botswana and Seriti, my erstwhile partner, went there to see him. He wasn't happy there, he told us. Gaborone was too much of a sleepy hollow for him. He would rather come home and face trial. The police had already procured a warrant for Zola's arrest and so Seriti and I arranged with the investigating officer for his return. The deal was plain. On his return to South Africa, Zola would surrender himself to the police in the presence of his lawyers. In turn, the police promised to take him immediately to court for a formal remand and the fixing of bail. On our part, the plan was meant to avoid him sleeping even one night in police detention.

On arrival, Zola was whisked off to court. The charge was knowingly receiving stolen money totalling R11.4 million, the property of Standard Bank. The court pegged the bail at R1 million. I felt triumphant that our scheme to keep Zola out of prison had worked, but our client wasn't happy. As the court adjourned, Zola, still in the dock, turned to me and Seriti and pleaded that we pay the bail money out of our pockets. He had no money to do so. I looked at him, amazed. I was a struggle lawyer. I had no million to lend him. He had seen the charge sheet. I thought he should have spared at least a million to buy off his liberty in time of need.

Sadly, Zola stayed in detention awaiting trial. In the meantime, Snowy's trial progressed. She faced multiple charges of theft of all those many amounts from Standard Bank. In a summary trial, she pleaded guilty and admitted to making a raft of electronic transfers from the suspense account she managed into Zola Mahobe's Standard Bank current account to the extent of R11.4 million. She was sentenced to twelve years, imprisonment. She steadfastly refused to testify against her lover.

On 8 July 1988, Zola was sentenced to fifteen years, imprisonment after a long gruelling trial in which I was his counsel. It was a case Zola could never win. The bank paper-trail in the state's dossier was plain and damning. He admitted to receiving the money in his current account from Snowy. His defence was that he believed that Snowy was a princess and daughter of King Moshoeshoe of Lesotho. He said he thought she donated the money from the royal largesse of the kingdom. The court dismissed his version without more ado and sent him to jail forthwith. I advised him to forget about an appeal as there were no prospects of success.

In another channel of litigation, Standard Bank secured a sequestration order against Zola's estate. The curator mopped up Zola's conspicuous assets – racehorses, luxury cars and holiday apartments and, of course, Mamelodi Sundowns FC. The bank's teaser was that the club was successful and enjoyed vast popular support. In discussion with the bank executives, I stumbled into their near-irrational fear. They did not want to be seen as destroyers of a successful black enterprise. Without Zola's pipeline to it, the club would have collapsed in a week. Through the curator of the insolvent estate, Standard Bank was forced to throw Mamelodi Sundowns FC a lifeline. In an ironic twist, the bank continued to pay the bills of the club as it had done during Zola's reign. It had to hold the baby in its hands until it could unashamedly give it away. That happened many months later, when it disposed of the club for a pittance – and after it had funded the club by a few multiples of R11.4 million.

During the political crises of the 1980s, attorney Richard Ramodipa had his practice in the town of Potgietersrust, as Mokopane was then known. He handled high volumes of trials involving young activists charged with arson, public violence and sedition. The security police saw him as a vital resource for the domestic uprising and wanted to snuff him out. They procured a warrant for his indeterminate detention without trial under the state security legislation of the time. His wife turned to me and rightly so. I did considerable work as counsel for Attorney Ramodipa's clients.

The security laws under which Richard was detained ousted the jurisdiction of the courts in plain and certain language. The statute stated that no court might pronounce on the validity of any security detention for any reason whatsoever. And as a matter of practice, detention warrants of this ilk were never challenged, because it seemed futile to do so.

During the consultation, Mrs Ramodipa mentioned that her husband was detained in a police lock-up. The warrant of his detention detailed that he be detained in a prison. I promised that I would apply my mind to her husband's situation and revert to her. During my morning shower a day later, a flash of excitement streamed through my body. 'Yes, yes!' I screamed. I had it! There and then I rehearsed my plan. 'I will not be challenging the validity of the warrant of detention, which their law says I may not. I will be challenging the implementation of the warrant. A warrant of detention is an instrument that takes away one's liberty. He who executes it must do so in a manner faithful to its contents. He cannot keep a detainee where he chooses; like in his fowl-run or farm or nightclub, or similarly in a police lock-up when the warrant directs differently. *Hurrah!*' I raised my voice as I left the shower.

The minute I got to chambers, I drafted court papers, called in Mrs Ramodipa and asked her to sign them as I shared my fanciful brain rush with her. The following morning, I came before the urgent motion court wondering which judge I was likely to draw. My colleagues in the court foyer informed me in lowered voices that Harms J was in the urgent motion court. I wondered whether he was the right judge for my case. My apprehension was fuelled by the prevalent superstition of barristers that there are judges for causes. The mantra goes that success at the Bar is predicated on drawing the right judge for each brief.

As I rose to my feet to call my urgent motion, my heart started racing.

Harms J looked up: 'Yes, Mr Moseneke, what matter do you wish to mention this afternoon?'

'My Lord, this is an urgent application in which the applicant, an attorney of this honourable court, Mr Richard Ramodipa, seeks his release from continued political detention under section 29 of the Terrorism Act. My Lord, the matter is self-evidently urgent because it relates to the liberty of a person. Whereas under that provision it is not open to my client to attack the lawfulness of the warrant issued by a designated officer under section 29 of the Act, he does impugn the lawfulness of his continued detention. The warrant under which he is held specifies that attorney Ramodipa must be detained in a specified prison. However, my Lord, he is being kept in a police lock-up. A warrant that takes away a person's liberty must be executed in a manner absolutely faithful to its terms. I respectfully submit that his continued detention is unlawful, my Lord.'

Harms J required me to sit down immediately. Turning to counsel for the state, he sternly enquired whether it was true that attorney Ramodipa was being kept at a place other than the one specified on the warrant. Counsel stuttered, but confirmed this fact. Harms J followed up, enquiring why his continued detention was lawful. Counsel for the state managed only a few minutes of submissions before Harms J delivered an *ex tempore* judgment. He granted the application right away; he declared the continued detention of attorney Ramodipa unlawful and directed that the warrant for his release be issued instantly. What was more, the state was directed to bear the costs.

Well, well, well. As the court adjourned, the high-ranking security police in the courtroom were not amused. I was amused, however. I ran out of that court in a dizzy spell of excitement. Attorney Ramodipa, whose known fault was to take instructions from too many political activists in the area of Mokopane, was released from police detention within an hour or two of the order. Again, even in those dark days the presiding judge had what it took to call it right when it mattered most.

During the mid to late 1980s, the infiltration of armed combatants increased sizeably, with the principal routes back into the country still being through

Botswana and Mozambique. Arrests of trained cadres also increased. One such prominent arrest was that of Jan Shoba, a member of the military high command and of APLA. His original home, like mine, was in Atteridgeville. He went into exile in the early 1980s and was returned in command of several APLA operatives. I was called upon to appear with Ronnie Selvan SC in the trial of *State vs Jan Shoba* and other accused. The trial, which was held in Potchefstroom, went on for weeks on end. The accused faced multiple charges related to external military training and the possession of arms and ammunition, and they were said to have committed other acts of 'terrorism'. The outcome of the trial, like many others, was predictable. The accused of their kind never pleaded guilty to charges by an 'illegitimate regime'. And yet they were quite ready to confess to the military training and a determination to unseat the minority government. Jan Shoba was remarkably fearless and unwavering. He continued to play the commander towards the other accused even on trial. He chose to make his affiliations and commitment to the ideals of the revolution plain. Ronnie and I took all the legal points open to the accused. Nevertheless they were convicted of the charges and whisked off to Robben Island.

Jan Shoba was released shortly after the 1990 unbanning of liberation movements. He deeply doubted the viability of the negotiations between the ANC and the government and he immediately resumed APLA activities. By day he served as the bodyguard of Mr Mlamli Makwethu, then the president of the PAC internally. In 1992, he died under a hail of bullets one night in the backyard of his home in Saulsville. His killers were never found. They were believed to have been *askaris*, that assassination collective of the regime.

On another occasion attorney Phineas Mojapelo called me to Nelspruit (now Mbombela). My brief was to defend the accused in *State vs Kotse Maserumule and Others*. The trial lasted weeks. It offered me the opportunity to witness closely the principled response of compatriots in distress. This was an intriguing trial of MK cadres who had been infiltrated through Mozambique into the north-eastern part of Limpopo. They had set up an impressive communication system across Mpumalanga through dead-letter boxes (also known as DLBs). The hide-out boxes were usually located in remote bushes, and they were used to relay written commands, messages, maps, target descriptions and related messages. In bigger DLBs, arms and ammunition were sometimes passed on within the deployed unit. After the arrest of one of the unit members linked to the DLBs, several other arrests followed as the police set up traps and relayed false messages in the DLBs. Again the accused anticipated their fate. They never disavowed their affiliation. They seemed to carry proudly the badge of their military training on their sleeves. This alone was an offence that attracted a minimum sentence of five years' imprisonment. Maserumule and his comrades were sentenced to long jail terms and they, too, were bundled off to Robben Island.

Nkosinathi Nhleko was indicted for murder before the High Court of the Eastern Cape sitting in Queenstown. Attorney Hintsa Siwisa instructed me to assume his defence. This was not a run-of-the-mill killing. On an afternoon, in a tiny township adjacent to a small town in the Eastern Cape, young activists decided to necklace a 78-year-old resident, who was also a traditional healer. Nkosinathi was the leader of the young comrades. Their difficulty was somewhat obscure. In truth, they wanted to necklace a local policeman who was believed to be allied to the security police and had joined in the torture of young detainees. The story went that twice Nkosinathi and his colleagues entered the precincts of the policeman's home, but had to run off quickly. This was because their hair straightened in a way which suggested that his residential premises were jinxed. The young enthusiasts came to know that the policeman procured his protective charm, or *umuthi*, from the local traditional healer. The solution, the activists thought, was not far to find. If they made the traditional medicine man disappear, the policeman would forfeit his mystical cover.

On a rather warm mid-afternoon, Nkosinathi and a few other activists forcibly entered the modest residence of the aged healer, who, it seemed, lived alone. The youth were armed with a can of petrol and matches. The medicine man escaped through a low window and ran down the tarred main street of the township. To the astonishment of bystanders, the old muti-man outran his young pursuers by some way, until someone in the path of his running tripped him. He went down, panting furiously. Then, in full view of many, Nkosinathi poured the petrol over the man's prostrate body and set it alight. The police took many pictures of the burnt corpse partly hardened into a spasm with his abdomen burst open.

In our pre-trial consultation, Nkosinathi himself rehearsed these facts to me as his counsel. On his version, he was guilty of intentionally killing another human being. The motive for his conduct was plainly political. He would not plead guilty because he had killed in order to advance the struggle for freedom and democracy. He was entitled, Nkosinathi reasoned, to eliminate agents of the system as well as their allies. I explained that, in law, the motive for an intentional killing is irrelevant to the enquiry of whether or not he was guilty of murder. Motive was, however, highly relevant when a judge considered an appropriate sentence. This meant that, even then, courts convicting on murder were obliged to hear and consider evidence and submissions on the moral blameworthiness of the conduct of the accused. A judge had to conduct a full extenuation-of-sentence inquiry. I also made it plain to Nkosinathi that he was entitled to ask that the state prove the charge against him beyond a reasonable doubt. He had no duty to help the state procure a conviction against himself. This was particularly true when the motive for the crime was to resist an oppressive state.

Nkosinathi's murder trial was conducted in the Supreme Court sitting in Queenstown before Deputy Judge President Zietsman. In its opening address, the prosecution made its position clear that it would, on conviction, ask for the death penalty. But for that, the trial was uneventful. The facts were uncontested. The prosecution started with handing in a photo album of gruesome pictures of the burnt and stiffened corpse with its spilled intestines. The necklacing had happened under the glare of the mid-afternoon sun and in full view of many township residents. The eye-witnesses were plenty, but somewhat reluctant. My cross-examination could only be tentative and limited to testing the accuracy or truthfulness of the accounts of the state's witnesses. We had no alternative version to put to the witnesses. More so, the few co-conspirators turned state witness against Nkosinathi. All guns were turned on Nkosinathi and him alone.

By the end of the week, a little before the lunch adjournment, Nkosinathi was found guilty of murder with aggravating circumstances. The presiding judge gave notice that he wanted to proceed with extenuation, if any, and sentencing after lunch. Court was adjourned.

My stomach started feeling hollow as if all of it had been excavated out of me. I developed a slight cold shiver. I had to take deep gulps of air to maintain a semblance of calmness. I turned to Nkosinathi, who still stood in the accused stand. His body was trembling uncontrollably, and he had broken into a heavy sweat that ran profusely from his head, down his forehead and his rather chubby face. As our eyes met he knew, and I knew, that he might be sentenced to death to hang by his neck until he died. That was the formulation of the death sentence judges of the time had to use. They were obliged to specify the means by which a convicted person had to be killed. The death warrants read that the convicted person had to hang by the neck until he or she died.

Like an ominous sea of blue, the number of armed police in the courthouse increased suddenly.

I had to see Nkosinathi and myself through this daunting lunch break. I preferred talking to him in the courthouse rather than in the court cells. I knew everything about his personal circumstances necessary for extenuation, so I did not need a formal consultation for extenuation. The real teaser was to find factors that would reduce, in the eyes of the judge, the moral blameworthiness of Nkosinathi's conduct. No, put more directly, I had to think as hard and smartly as I could about how I could save Nkosinathi from going to the gallows. Neither of us thought about lunch. My young client's sweat ran down and formed a wet circle around his feet on the wooden base of the dock. I asked him if we should seek postponement to the following day before pleading in mitigation. He shook his head feebly from side to side. He was visibly terrified, but he seemed to prefer facing the bad or good news right away. I shared his stance. I did not think either of us would survive the night waiting in uncertainty. Nkosinathi dripped even more sweat. In front of my very eyes, he shrank from a robust, round and boisterous lad into a thin, bony, almost ghost-like figure. I have never seen anyone shed so much body weight instantly. It hurt deeply.

I sent a message to the presiding judge that I would be ready to address him not at 2pm but only at 3pm that afternoon. I needed to make common cause with Nkosinathi that, in these dire circumstances, we had to locate the crime charged firmly within the historical and current repression of the majority in their land of birth. His was not a regular criminal or dastardly deed, but one animated by his deep quest for equality, freedom and human dignity. He had acted in pursuit of high ideals, which must have informed and altered his level of judgement.

At 3pm, I rose to my feet. All I remember was my initial statement: 'My Lord, the accused is not a common murderer, but a man moved by high ideals no less glorious than those embraced by the French Revolution – *liberté, égalité, fraternité*. My Lord, one need not embrace his ideals to appreciate the intensity of his pursuit of them.'

It took me two hours to make my impassioned plea in mitigation. Nkosinathi escaped the gallows.

I had heard much about the APLA commander Clement Zulu. In underground structures, he was reputed to come into the country from Tanzania at will. Apparently he had infiltrated several armed combatants ahead and set up an operating headquarters in Ngwavuma, which was located in the remote northern parts of KwaZulu. He was known to be stern, disciplined and virtually fearless. He spoke in monosyllabic isiZulu and isiXhosa useful for issuing commands. He followed English, but never spoke it. He was a man of considerable height. He had broad shoulders and a bush of thick black hair greying slightly at the temples. Although the police had his identikit, for several years he succeeded in staying out of their clutches. His public disguises were legendary. He travelled to the environs of Ethekwini and made contact with several activists. On the one occasion, he paid an unexpected visit to Stanley Mogoba, the presiding bishop of the Methodist Church, whose official church residence was in Pietermaritzburg. Zulu moved on to Cape Town to re-energise APLA combatants. He also made contact with Sedick Isaacs and Achmad Cassiem of the Islamist revolutionary formation Qibla. He had a few harsh things to say about leaders of the guerrilla army who chose to remain in exile rather than lead from the frontline.

Ultimately, the security police caught up with Zulu. He was tried together with Qibla activists from Cape Town led by Imam Achmad Cassiem. Attorney Allie of Cape Town instructed Advocate Abdullah Omar, who in time would become our first minister of justice under democracy, to appear for the Qibla accused. Allie briefed me to appear for Clement Zulu. The trial was held in the regional court, Pretoria. I was meeting Zulu then for the first time. With Achmad, it was different.

Achmad arrived on Robben Island in 1964 with James Marsh and Abdurahman ('Manie') Williams, his fellow matric students from Trafalgar High School, and their mathematics and science teacher, Sedick Isaacs. They were convicted in the Cape High Court for revolutionary activity. James and Manie had a five-year term and Achmad an eight-year term of imprisonment. Their former teacher, Sedick, had been sentenced to twelve years imprisonment. Achmad spent at least eight meaningful years on Robben Island. He studied as I did. He wrote poetry, which we shared, and he composed music for guitar. Unlike the poetry, I did not think much of his music, but to his credit he sang his compositions well. He was not shy to spark doctrinal debates and he spent considerable time trying to persuade me that Islam was superior to all other faiths, and to Christianity in particular. I held no brief for any faith. I read both the Holy Qur'an and the Holy Bible. Their genesis and historical narratives were both foreign to me. They did not resonate with my African ancestral roots. One fact stood out, however. I was brought up in a Christian home and that stayed with me. I went to a

Christian school out of no choice of mine. Nearly always, children become what their parents want them to be. I was no different. In my later years, I veered away from institutional religiosity or religious dogma. I accepted that there is a befitting place for deep and personal spirituality. It is not always present in temples, mosques, churches and synagogues.

But the task Dullah and I had was to provide the best defence that both these distinguished activists deserved. The Muslim community in Laudium came behind the trialists with considerable support. That made the task lighter. The accused were well clad, fed and given support with a high attendance of the hearing from local communities.

Clement Zulu, who I defended, never denied his role as a commander of APLA. He admitted he had re-entered the country from Tanzania several times and that he had caused APLA combatants to enter the country on military missions. He was predictably sentenced to a long term of imprisonment on Robben Island. A harrowing documentary, *The Long Journey of Clement Zulu*, records that after his release from Robben Island, he had no home. He ended up in a shack in an informal settlement in Newcastle and died, destitute, in a motor vehicle accident. The punch line of the documentary is: 'Not everyone walked off Robben Island and became a president.'[25]

CHAPTER 26

The end of exile – and of apartheid

For many years after 1990, people continued to ask each other: 'Where were you when De Klerk made the announcement?' Mr De Klerk was president of the apartheid state. Everyone seemed to know which announcement. They heard it live on radio or soon thereafter at dinner tables, in the workplace, in taxis, at shebeens, pubs and everywhere else. It signalled a life-altering moment – that was, if you believed him. What he announced was not to be believed. Not only was it unexpected, it was completely out of sync with what was happening on the ground. The feeling was that his political party and securocrats would never let him do what he was promising. Still, beyond words, the announcement held up the fantasy of a fresh beginning.

It was a sunny Friday mid-morning, 2 February 1990. I had just left the offices of the township superintendent in Atteridgeville, where I had been briefed to make representations to him on the allocation of a home to a widow in a deceased estate. The municipal housing regulations of the time excluded women from being registered tenants of city council homes, except with the permission of the superintendent. The adult son of a widow qualified to be a registered tenant, but not his mother. I felt good as I drove away. I had succeeded in my mission of fighting the twin scourge of patriarchy and racism even within a blighted state.

'I have decided to unban the African National Congress, the Pan-Africanist Congress and the Communist Party of South Africa ...' The voice filled the cabin of my car. I was driving back to my advocates' chambers. When De Klerk said, 'I repeat', I pulled my car off the road and brought it to a stop. My breathing quickened, although more from disbelief, I think, than excitement. Amidst '*Hoor! Hoor!*' from party backbenchers and a few boos, De Klerk pulled through the address in parliament. It included a pledge to release all political prisoners, including Nelson Mandela, and the return of political exiles. I was thoroughly startled, if not shocked. This was not the kind of news one should receive alone. In our custom, no one ought to take delivery of devastating news, like the death of a loved one, alone. I needed to hug somebody in jubilation or to share the disbelief.

I had always fancied myself as having good political antennae, but I did not see this one coming. Up to that moment, the regime blew hot and cold. The announcement was at odds with the objective conditions on the ground. There was a country-wide grassroots revolt. Political detentions and prosecutions were widespread. State operatives continued to maim and murder opponents of the regime. Racist right-wing dissent was also on the rise and had become a threat of sorts. Mr De Klerk was making these extravagant undertakings in the face of significant headwind. Where was the trick? Like many freedom fighters, I had readied myself for a nearly lifelong insurgence. Now freedom appeared to be tendered on a silver platter by the enemy. Was the offer real? Where was the catch? Was this a Trojan Horse deception?

In the mid-1980s, Seriti and I had travelled to Botswana, where we had met with Comrade Johnson Mlambo, the head of the PAC high command. We also visited with Kgosi Molotlegi, the father to Kgosi Leruo wa Bakwena ba Phokeng, who was exiled in Botswana at that time. None we talked to foresaw an early exit from the struggle. They were unbending and resolute that the struggle must and would go on. Around 1987, I met the commander of AZANLA and chairman of the Black Consciousness Movement, Mosibudi Mangena, and his central committee in Harare. My consultation was meant to be professional. I needed a background briefing related to AZANLA combatants who were standing trial on charges of terrorism. I was their defence counsel. The central committee spat fire and brimstone and promised more guerrilla incursions. None of its members suggested an impending break-through or change of tack in the pattern of the insurrection.

On a different occasion, in 1988, also in Harare, I met with Zola Skweyiya and Penuell Maduna at a Southern African Development Community (SADC) law conference, together with Johann van der Westhuizen, a young and brave Afrikaner activist law professor from the University of Pretoria, and Advocate Abdullah Omar. In time, Johann was appointed by President Mbeki to serve with me on the Constitutional Court for just over a decade. Dullah became our first minister of justice in the Mandela cabinet of 1994. Again, there wasn't even a whiff of change in the air. Around 1989, I also met several exiled lawyer-activists at a conference in Geneva on fundamental rights and freedoms. The attendees from the diaspora were drawn from the liberation movements and were apparently sponsored by the Anti-Apartheid Committee of the UN and the World Council of Churches Programme to Combat Racism. It was then ably, if not vigorously, led by a South African, Barney Pityana. I remember brief but animated discussions with the exiled Kader Asmal. I also talked with Brigitte Mabandla and Zola Skweyiya. Both were more contained and less effervescent than Kader. It was also instructive exchanging ideas with Richard Sizani, a PAC lawyer-activist then located in Australia. The point is this: none of the exiled senior members of the liberation movement claimed to know of the impending new road. It must be added, though, that the rump of the conference discussion was about a bill of rights that might come into being in a new democratic South Africa.

But then, hindsight is 20/20 vision. A good few pundits within the liberation movement knew it all. The announcement, they say, was no surprise but rather a product of their wise anticipation and planning. Of course, a constellation of global and domestic conditions helped foretell the untimely demise of the regime. The Cold War was ending and the USSR was unravelling. Confederate states of the USSR were seceding from Russia and opting for independent, democratic republics. The Berlin Wall had come down in 1989 amidst victory celebrations. We read how people plucked out pieces of the wall as souvenirs. The global solidarity against the apartheid state had reached fever pitch. Our minders had been expelled from virtually every international body. Although busted by some in many clandestine and lucrative ways, over time economic sanctions had taken their toll. The domestic economy continued to shrink as inflation shot through the roof. So did unemployment. In turn, state indebtedness soared. Fewer and fewer foreign lenders and bankers were willing to roll over the sovereign debt as the apartheid state wobbled on the brink of bankruptcy. There was no peace on the home front either. Even in the precursor years before the announcement, the PW Botha regime trusted repression – *kragdadigheid* – more than anything else. A show of weakness, they seemed to think, might court more revolt. Even so, the security apparatus of the state could not quell the domestic popular revolt. It had assumed threatening proportions.

In February 1988, we saw the regime ban, again by executive decree, seventeen community and political organisations, including AZAPO, COSATU and student formations. In addition, it restricted eighteen of their leaders and, in June, renewed the state of emergency. It permitted police to detain activists indefinitely without the bother of a formal trial. The restrictions and the state of emergency prompted the most towering show of worker and popular resistance yet. More than one million workers, at the call by South Africa's two biggest trade unions, COSATU and NACTU, held a nationwide stay-away from 6 through 8 June 1988 to protest apartheid, the restrictions, detentions and the state of emergency. Working people, united in action, came to marvel at their power and the state became the weaker for it by the day.

Wave after wave of activists vowed to render the state ungovernable. On 20 August 1989 scores of anti-apartheid organisations, mainly members of the Mass Democratic Movement (MDM), declared themselves henceforth 'unrestricted' and free to join the defiance campaign. As fast as the police forcibly broke up demonstrations, fresh ones emerged. Defiance marches took place in most cities. Notably, during August 1989 people marched to the British Embassy in Cape Town protesting its veiled support for the apartheid regime and the conditions of political detainees. Later in the same month, students held a large rally at the University of the Witwatersrand in Johannesburg, at which they unbanned themselves and vowed to revive 'restricted' student groups. On that occasion they had a running battle with police, who broke up the meeting. Battles of much the same kind flared up in most townships.

The prime armoury of the state – death and imprisonment – had lost its bite. Unionised workers increased in number as organised labour gained purchase and assumed a pro-resistance stance. The army barracks were empty as soldiers patrolled country borders and townships alike. More and more soldiers were recruited from the black populace. The new recruits took refuge from endemic unemployment by joining the army. The defence force took them on because the number of white male soldiers was dwindling. Young white people had other ideas about their future and careers. The strategic implication of an increasing number of black soldiers did not escape most opponents of the tottering state. It was only a matter of time before the armed women and men would turn their guns on their commanders. And yet in all this, the schizophrenia of PW Botha, the president at the time, persisted as events moved irreversibly to his personal and political demise.

Perhaps the early sign of the change of tack of the ANC in exile was the Dakar meeting. Amidst speculation, in July 1987, as many as 61 South Africans of mainly Afrikaner extraction met with the ANC in Dakar. The ANC delegation was led by Thabo Mbeki. Soon thereafter, both the ANC and the apartheid state denied that they had been in contact with each other. Tentative as the meeting seemed from afar, on 5 November 1987 the government released Govan Mbeki, one of the foremost leaders of the ANC, with a terse statement that pointed to his ill health as a probable reason for the release. I wondered, as many activists did, whether there was any line to be drawn between the two events. I thought not. Oom Gov's distaste for secret talks with the regime was no less vociferous than that of Harry Gwala.

But on the opposite end, a myriad of security and military operations of the apartheid state sent severe messages of attrition. In January 1988, fierce fighting erupted between Angolan and South African forces for control of the strategic town of Cuito Cuanavale in Angola. Happily, by June of the same year, Angolan, Cuban and apartheid state representatives hammered out an accord (which was signed in December) that saw a withdrawal of Cuban troops from Angola and an agreed roadmap towards independence for Namibia. In February 1989, the UN Security Council unanimously endorsed the settlement and plan to have Namibia become an independent state from 21 March 1990. To us who battled settler colonialism, the success of the liberation forces in Namibia held great promise. It spurred us on to put our oppressors to the sword.

The loss in the Battle of Cuito Cuanavale did not, however, deter the state's further external military incursions. In February 1988, its commandos raided the capital of Botswana, Gaborone, in search of ANC members. A few months later, in April, Albie Sachs was seriously wounded and lost a limb in a car-bomb explotion in Maputo. South Africa denied responsibility for the attack, but every activist worth his or her salt could see the hallmarks of the security forces all over it. During the TRC process the state killer commandos confessed to having staged the attack and they sought amnesty.

The report on Albie's attack struck a chord of deep sorrow in me. This is why. In the mid to late 1980s, I met a young university professor, Albie Sachs, in the Edison Hotel, a modest London place. He was a South African advocate like me but lived in exile. He may have been attending the same or a related law conference. He taught at a law school in Maputo, Mozambique. He was able-bodied and had two normal upper limbs. He was a soft-spoken man who chose his words carefully. He looked around often and furtively. He asked about the struggle at home and spoke briefly about the liberation struggle abroad. There was no inkling of a breakthrough, we both thought. Like me, he was set for a long haul of resistance. Neither of us had any idea that we would serve for nearly a decade as colleagues at our highest court. We did not have even the foggiest hint that we would be called upon to help lay the foundations of the jurisprudence of our land, or that together we would wrestle intensely with what it was to be a just, inclusive and caring democracy.

The commando raids persisted. Zimbabwe was next in line. That country had the reputation of being the most vigilant and militarily competent Frontline State. In June 1988, Zimbabwean security forces thwarted a commando attempt to rescue five agents awaiting trial for bomb attacks against South African exiles in Zimbabwe.

The strategy of the Botha regime was not 'shock and awe' only. It dangled a few carrots. It made symbolic gestures of *toenadering* (rapprochement). It began to release political prisoners. This was unheard of. The state president always had the power to grant pardon or amnesty to any convicted prisoners. Also, prison laws had a parole regimen. However, it was an inflexible state policy that political offenders must serve their sentences 'to the last dish', as the phrase went. No opponent of the regime left prison even a day earlier than full term. Medical parole was simply unheard of. On a few occasions, high-ranking political prisoners were offered an early release, provided they publicly renounced the armed struggle or objectives of the liberation movement. No political prisoner I know ever accepted the condition.

On 26 November 1988, nearly a year after the release of Govan Mbeki, the regime freed, unconditionally, two leaders of considerable stature: Zephania Mothopeng, the president of the PAC, and Harry Gwala, a trade unionist, socialist, ideologist and an ANC member. They were allegedly released on medical and humanitarian grounds. I had had the privilege of being under the tutelage of both freedom fighters. Comrade Mothopeng had taught me the history and tenets of Africanism. Comrade Gwala taught me all the theory of socialism I knew when I left Robben Island. It was true that both men were elderly and ailing, but neither was about to throw in the towel in the battle against inequality, dispossession and exclusion. And yet they received the regime's nod to go home while their organisations were still banned – a confusing message indeed.

The regime's split personality persisted into 1989, only a year before FW de Klerk's major announcement. On 15 October that year, the regime released, without any conditions, the Rivonia trialists – Walter Sisulu, Raymond Mhlaba, Ahmed Kathrada, Elias Motsoaledi, Andrew Mlangeni and Wilton

Mkwayi. On the same day, my former teacher and fellow accused, Jafta Kgalabi Masemola of the PAC, was freed after serving the longest prison term of just over 26 years on Robben Island. Within three weeks, on 23 November 1989, PW Botha granted reprieves to the Sharpeville Six, who were six people condemned to death for being part of a gathering that killed the deputy mayor of Sharpeville in September 1984. In December 1989, the regime freed, from Robben Island, the five Delmas trialists and anti-apartheid leaders, imprisoned in 1988 for political activities. They included the general secretary of the United Democratic Front, Popo Molefe, and its publicity secretary, Patrick 'Terror' Lekota.

At face value, I thought, these occurrences were pregnant with hope. But this benign take was dashed emphatically by state-sponsored violence against its home opponents. Activists continued to disappear or be killed. For instance, in June 1988, a 27-year-old MDM activist from Mamelodi, Stanza Bopape, was detained and then murdered in detention. The security police dumped his body into the crocodile-infested Komati River near Mozambique.[26] Less than a year later, in May 1989, David Webster, a Wits social anthropologist and prominent anti-apartheid activist, was murdered in Johannesburg outside his home by security forces.[27] In August 1989, Khotso House, the main office of the SACC, was destroyed by a bomb blast. Six weeks later, in October, Khanya House, the main offices of the South African Catholic Bishops Conference (SACBC), was gutted by fire. Both religious groupings charged that apartheid was heresy and an affront to God's will and people. They openly supported and funded popular protests against apartheid. The Catholic Bishop Daniels and Father Smangaliso Mkhatshwa, who became the secretary general of the SACBC, both come to mind. From the ranks of the SACC one recalls the support, and indeed bravery, of the Reverend Beyers Naudé, Bishop Desmond Mpilo Tutu and the Reverend Frank Chikane. As time would let us know, the attacks on their head offices and the murder of activists were sponsored by the state security apparatus.

Two other strains in the leitmotif of the impending change were the power-play going on inside the ruling party of the time, the National Party, and the rumours of secret talks between that party and the ANC.

Then President PW Botha was felled by a stroke. The *Groot Krokodil* limped. He had a slur in his speech and his face was skew, with one eye looking bigger than the other. One wondered whether he could still point his threatening finger at enemies of his state. And yet he wanted to remain the state president. After an unsightly internal spat, he succumbed, but only in part. In early February 1989, he agreed to resign as leader of the ruling party, but would not vacate the top office of head of state. FW de Klerk, then one of his cabinet ministers, became the party leader.

Seemingly undeterred by the turmoil, De Klerk's ruling party called an all-white general election and won it resoundingly, despite the white *broedertwis*. The electoral victory, albeit of a tiny white electorate, must have reassured De Klerk that his people were ready to embrace a managed change. He was sworn in as state president on 20 September 1989. For me, and certainly for the majority of the opponents of apartheid, the turmoil within the ruling elite was an undue irritation. Whites-only elections were old hat. The regime appeared to be flying several kites, but in truth it remained stubborn and it still had to be defeated. The beckoning prize was its demise and the induction of our reimagined society. Even so, if the truth be told, the ascendancy of De Klerk was not unimportant. It set the stage for a new drama that would lead inexorably towards a negotiated denouement.

Much towards the same finale, rumours were rife about secret talks between 'the Boers', as the phrase went, and Nelson Mandela. Many thought Mandela had been moved, in December 1988, from Robben Island to a house on the grounds of a prison farm outside the Western Cape town of Paarl to make him accessible for secret talks with high-ranking state functionaries. But was Nelson Mandela not a prisoner? I asked myself. How was he in a position to negotiate meaningfully our freedom with his captors? The swirling rumours were swiftly confirmed. In a press release, justice minister Kobie Coetsee confirmed a meeting between Nelson Mandela and PW at his office in Cape Town on 5 July. Coetsee was at pains to explain that the two had not engaged in negotiations – they had only confirmed 'their support for peaceful development in South Africa'.

The news evoked widespread shock and discontent amongst the highly mobilised MDM and other resistance formations. The notion of closed talks with a repressive regime repulsed many, who thought it was premature. It was just at that time that the MDM had declared itself 'unrestricted' and was set to take up a defiance campaign and to render the state ungovernable. The police were responding with further repression.

On 12 July 1989, Nelson Mandela released a statement through the prison authorities admitting to the meeting, but explaining that dialogue with the liberation movement, in particular the ANC, was the only way to achieve peace.

During the last quarter of 1989, the ANC in exile took a firm and clear stance towards a negotiated settlement. It took or facilitated a number of vital steps that made negotiations with the apartheid regime inevitable. Most of the steps took the form of garnering international support, and particularly from the Organisation of African Unity (OAU), the Non-Aligned Movement and the United Nations. All three bodies were fervent supporters of the struggle against apartheid. They recognised the ANC and PAC as liberation movements and legitimate representatives of the oppressed people of our country. Both movements had non-voting but deliberative roles on matters that affected our country and they could and did lobby friendly countries to sponsor or support desired resolutions. The OAU had an even closer and more committed role. Its Liberation Committee funded APLA's and MK's 'peaceful' operations. Some of its members housed operatives and provided military and other training. The Frontline States that shared borders with South Africa provided financial support, free passage and refugee status for APLA and MK cadres. For this they often had to bear the brunt of commando raids sponsored by the South African securocrats. It was also true that most of the Frontline States depended on a modicum of trade with South Africa. All of this meant that the OAU Committee on Southern Africa was likely to support an initiative directed at ending the military conflict between the liberation movement and the minority state.

In August 1989, the Assembly of Heads of State of the OAU met in Harare and adopted a declaration on South Africa as suggested by the ANC. The Harare Declaration recognised that possibilities existed for a resolution of South Africa's problems by negotiation. It authorised and encouraged liberation movements to explore a negotiated resolution of the stand-off. Within a week of the Harare Declaration, President Kenneth Kaunda held a meeting in Livingstone, Zambia, with Acting President FW de Klerk and declared that he supported South Africa's moves to reform apartheid. Not long afterwards, in November 1989, President De Klerk announced that he would disband the National Security Management System, whose prime purpose was to identify and defuse security threats to the country.

The Harare Declaration was later endorsed by a summit meeting of non-aligned countries. On 14 December the UN General Assembly, at its 16th Special Session, adopted by consensus the Declaration on Apartheid and its Destructive Consequences in Southern Africa, calling for negotiations to end apartheid and establish a non-racial democracy. The declaration laid down steps needed to create a climate conducive to negotiations, modalities of negotiations and principles for a new constitution.

The road to negotiation found important domestic endorsement in December 1989, when the MDM adopted the Harare Declaration, which set out preconditions for negotiations and a new constitutional future. The MDM, the domestic alter ego of the ANC, had earlier adopted the Freedom Charter. They appeared at ease with the notion of engaging in preliminary discussions with the government. While they espoused the idea of a patriotic front, they did not see it as a precondition to meeting with the regime for talks. Some of its senior leaders, and notably Jacob Zuma and Penuell Maduna, were secretly brought into the country to clear the way with the government before the so-called talks about talks. Amidst much suspicion, it was unknown to the other liberation movements and the vast population just how much clandestine contact the ANC leadership had with the minority regime. All indications, however, were that the ANC was committed to suspending the armed struggle, and to negotiating with the apartheid state.

Perhaps the clearest sign was Nelson Mandela's prison visitors. Mandela started a process of 'consultations' with stakeholders in society. The nature and extent of the prior talks he had held with the state officials was not known to most stakeholders he consulted. The Black Lawyers Association received a letter from Mr Mandela while he was at Victor Verster Prison. The letter invited our then president, Keith Sandile Kunene, and I to visit him. It was widely known that he had been inviting a spread of political and other social formations to his prison home.

Keith and I had lunch with Mr Mandela in a modest but well-furnished and comfortable home on the prison grounds. He was wearing civilian clothes. There were no bars on the windows nor even burglar-proofing. There were no visible prison wardens, barring the one who laid the lunch table and left. At a point, Mr Mandela walked off to his little wine cellar and offered us a sumptuous Cape red. Of course he, and I knew each other from Robben Island, but I'd last seen him seventeen years before and his face had aged since then. He had done his homework on the BLA. He knew who Keith Kunene was. He talked with and embraced Keith with the same outward affection he showed me. Beyond the pleasantries, he had to broach the purpose of the invite. First, he commended the BLA for the work it had done to mobilise black lawyers and to resist apartheid. He was well informed about the historical profile and projects of the BLA. He recalled his own life as a practising attorney. Then, as if with the turn of a switch, his mood changed. Looking sombre, he told us he would be released from prison shortly. He was asking for support from Keith, me and the BLA when he started the task of leading the people towards the end of apartheid through a negotiated settlement. Keith and I were suitably flattered that we and the BLA were on the radar screen of the celebrated leader and freedom fighter. We explained that the BLA was a politically non-aligned body. Its individual members made their own unique party political choices. But the BLA would support the broader push for freedom, we said, and he could trust that it would support him in that regard.

Nelson Mandela was released from prison in gripping television coverage.

Our nation, as did the whole world, waited nearly two hours before he stepped out of the precinct of prison side by side with his wife, Nomzamo Winifred Madikizela-Mandela. I knew both protagonists closely. And yet I had no cause to expect that, from that historic moment, our lives would converge so irreversibly. For a good few years after the release, I would act as Nomzamo's legal counsel at the express request of Mr Mandela. Nomzamo would later enjoy telling me about the two-hour delay before Mr Mandela's release. With a mischievous smile. The gentle dimple on her right cheek flickering, she started relaying what she considered one of her finest moments in the course of the struggle. That morning she walked into Mr Mandela's Victor Verster home. Her arrival was beamed into every home on television, but what was happening inside, behind the closed doors, the public could not see. Nomzamo was anxious that Madiba's first speech should strike an appropriately militant chord. After a few pleasantries, she demanded to see the prepared text. Madiba hesitatingly gave it to her. She ran her eyes through the speech. When she looked up, her frown said it all. She was less than happy. Without more ado, she tore the text to smithereens in full view of a few high-ranking prison minders. The room went icy and silent. The next two hours, while the world waited in a high state of anticipation, were used to cobble together a new speech – and this was the speech the world heard Nelson Mandela deliver that day at the Grand Parade in Cape Town.

Mandela was amongst the last of the political prisoners to be released. By far the majority had been released ahead of him. The legend had it that he chose to lead from behind by being amongst the last to be released. Also, by then, exiled activists had started making their way home. They included many senior combatants within the liberation armies. I remember well Seriti and I being asked to procure written assurances from the security police of free passage for returnees. Most returnees carried passports other than South African ones and had to be cleared with the security police and passport control. None was arrested on his or her return. The government was seen to be 'walking the walk' as more and more activists came back home from prison and exile. Party banners fluttered everywhere. Supporters were free to claim their allegiance publicly and the numbers at rally after rally swelled. One such rally welcomed Jafta Kgalabi Masemola, and an even bigger one was the one that welcomed the Rivonia trialists, barring Mr Mandela. These were obvious confidence-building measures and yet they made the path to negotiations irreversible.

There was a spring-like anticipation of rebirth and mirth in the air. Many dreamt of and hoped for a final putsch for freedom in their lifetime. In sum, the apartheid state could win only a few battles, but not the war. The war they were certain to lose and they knew it. Our sheer numbers and the moral force of our struggle assured us victory against the minority regime in the end. Also, the economy was very sick. It would remain critically unwell for as long as apartheid lived. In those circumstances, big business must have clamoured for an early and possibly favourable political settlement rather than a long, drawn-out, winner-takes-all scenario. Mr De Klerk and his securocrats chose the path of a negotiated settlement. They appeared to have made peace with the minimum demand of 'one person, one vote' – a historical red rag to white supremacist bulls. Given the demographics, this meant they would have to surrender political power and hope to salvage historical privilege and wealth. They would also want to escape personal retribution for past atrocities that amounted to triable crimes. The securocrats were expected not to support the transition, if they were to end up criminally liable while the ruling elite went scot-free for their misrule. So beyond the exchange of political power for proprietary safeguards, amnesty from prosecution was to become a central plank of Mr De Klerk's transition stratagem.

CHAPTER 27

The PAC and the indecision

O ne of the helpful responses of the PAC to the newly found political space
was to sponsor the formation of the Pan-Africanist Movement (PAM),
which was to act as a front for the banned liberation movement. PAM was
launched in Johannesburg in November 1989 amidst much political fervour.
The excitement was well founded. It was the 30th anniversary of the founding of the PAC and it had been nearly 29 years since it was banned and exiled.
The launch of PAM was not only an act of defiance but also one of affirmation
that the struggle continued to live. More crucially, the internal adherents of
Africanism had lagged behind the MDM, which by then had developed a
national footprint. The MDM had been astute at organising mass protests on
bread-and-butter issues of unhappy communities and learners under catchy
slogans like 'rolling mass action' and 'rendering the state ungovernable'. In
time, the MDM nailed its colours to the mast by adopting the Freedom
Charter. It was no longer a non-aligned mass movement. It chose sides. This
meant that Africanists needed to cultivate a grassroots following across the
country or they would vanish from the national psyche. The PAC's affinity
to the union federation NACTU, tirelessly led by Cunningham Ngcukana,
provided a priceless presence, but it was not nearly enough.

PAM adopted all the basic documents of the PAC, and assumed its salute,
colours and insignia. It was a replica of the banned PAC, but different in
name. Clarence Mlami Makwethu and Benny Alexander (who later famously

renamed himself Khoisan X) were elected interim president and secretary general respectively. Unlike the MDM, PAM did not take a definite stance on the possibility of negotiations with the minority regime. Its near-natural posture was to be highly suspicious of the motives of the minority state. The scepticism was captured by Khoisan X's revolutionary mantra, possibly borrowed in part from Malcolm X. At PAM rallies Khoisan X would shout:

> Comrades, comrades! When the enemy says 'Sit!' you must stand up, comrades! And when the enemy says 'Stand up!' you must sit down, comrades! You have no identity of interest with the enemy. What the enemy wants you must not and cannot want!

The early response of the PAC in Dar es Salaam to the Harare Declaration and the complementary Non-Aligned Movement (NAM) and UN resolutions was to reject the open invitation to suspend the armed struggle and enter into negotiations. They argued that the balance of forces did not support the start of negotiations. The regime had to be weakened further in order to exact an outcome more advantageous to the people. They added that if there were to be 'talks about talks', they had to be at a neutral venue outside the country. A domestic venue would unduly favour the incumbent government. The PAC favoured the formation of a patriotic front with the ANC and the Black Consciousness Movement (BCM) ahead of even 'talks about talks'. United, oppressed people would hold more sway and ensure a credible transition to democracy. The BCM, too, rejected outright the proposed negotiations; it wanted first to explore the prospects of a united front of liberation movements.

In February 1990, De Klerk made his announcement. This spelled the end of PAM. Correctly so, PAM immediately converted itself into a body seized with the preparation of the second national conference of the PAC since its inaugural conference of April 1959.

I digress to remember that, in April 1959, I was in primary school. When I started my childhood activism, the PAC had already been banned, since

March 1960. In other words, the movement had lived freely for no more than one year from its birth. In the wake of the 1960 anti-pass campaign and the Sharpeville massacre, its leaders were first jailed and thereafter viciously hounded. Its president, Mangaliso Sobukwe, was banished to Robben Island for years without a court conviction or defined sentence. Its secretary general, Potlako Leballo, and national executive committee member, AP Mda, took refuge in neighbouring Lesotho. Other National Executive Committee (NEC) members, like Nana Mahomo, ZB Molete and Elias Ntloedibe, fled further afield into exile. Those NEC members who remained in the country, like Zephania Mothopeng, Selby Ngendane and Nyathi Pokela, were rearrested, charged and jailed on Robben Island.

Even with my childhood limitations, I felt there was something enigmatic about this Congress. I looked for the basic documents of the PAC and read them. I was struck by their clarity. Mangaliso Sobukwe's inaugural address should be prescribed reading for every young person in our land. He made an unanswerable case against the bankruptcy of racism, and for non-racialism as well as for African humanism, better than any other Africanist thinker. The Africanist Manifesto traced the genesis of our oppression at home and in the diaspora, and graphically described the true character of our oppression as colonialism marked by land dispossession, racial oppression, economic exploitation and social degradation.

The aims and objects of the Congress were, to borrow from Sobukwe, 'a clarion call away from protest and petition politics towards the start of a liberation struggle'. They were an undisguised invitation to revolution. They were cast in clear and accessible language. I came to know them by heart: (a) to rally and unite African people under the banner of African nationalism; (b) to overthrow white domination in all its forms; (c) to establish an Africanist, socialist democracy; (d) to project the African personality; and (e) to strive for the establishment of the United States of Africa.

The plan for revolution was entirely on point. The primal starting point was to unite the oppressed people in full recognition of their African identity and duty to liberate themselves. The first task was to overthrow racist oppression and economic exclusion. That task could not be outsourced or achieved by proxies. The oppressed people themselves had to be the protagonists of their freedom struggle. In the end, the triumphant people had to induct a sharing and inclusive democracy guided, not by Eurocentric or other foreign values, but by values of African humanism.

The notion of 'African personality', as part of the aims and objects, was crucial. The founding mothers and fathers were concerned that colonialism and apartheid had dehumanised and mutilated the self-worth or consciousness of oppressed people. They had first to recognise their battered self-esteem and then take steps to heal themselves. In time, Bantu Biko and the BCM made the consciousness or the self-identity of oppressed black people the central plank of our understanding of our political redemption.

I found the objective of establishing the United States of Africa heady stuff. Up to then, domestic political targets tended to be couched in national and not continental terms. Sobukwe and his comrades were drawing from the finest pan-Africanist thinking on the continent. The quest for a free, independent, non-aligned and united Africa echoed the pan-Africanist sentiments of leading lights of the 1960s – notably Kwame Nkrumah of Ghana,[28] Julius Kambarage Nyerere of Tanzania,[29] Léopold Sédar Senghor of the Senegal,[30] Abubakar Tafawa Balewa of Nigeria[31] and Patrice Emery Lumumba[32] of the Congo. Here was a new breed of liberation movement with a remarkable ideological thrust for its time.

I return to the end of the year 1990, when the second congress of the PAC on home soil was held at Nasrec, a vast public showground facility near Soweto. Thousands of excited delegates arrived from across all provinces of the country, flying banners and flags. The two-day affair turned out to be celebratory reunion of song and dance. It was certainly not to be a policy conference. The delegates were intent on electing a domestic national executive and going back home. They did not spare time to think through how the newly elected domestic national executive would relate to the central committee led by Chairman Johnson Mlambo in Dar es Salaam. Nor did the delegates spare a thought on what would be the new reporting lines, if any, of the APLA military command.

However, nearly 30 years after the inaugural conference, much had changed. For one thing, the regime had adjusted its stance and removed all restrictions on the activities of the movement. Secondly, while the PAC was no longer banned, for over 30 years it had recruited and trained a guerrilla army. What should its fate be? In the third instance, there was an invitation to the party to explore the prospects of a peaceful resolution of the long, drawn-out liberation war. The substance of the oppression may not have changed, but new and different means to disestablish white domination and usher in an 'Africanist socialist democracy' might now be necessary.

I was nominated from the floor to preside over the electoral process. Mlamli Makwethu and Khoisan X were returned unopposed as president and secretary general respectively. The position of deputy president was split into the first and second deputy presidents. Johnson Mlambo was unani- mously elected first deputy president, but in his absence. This was achieved by nifty footwork on the part of Khoisan X, who was trying to manage the possible rift between the domestic and exiled party members.

When the post of second deputy president was to be filled, a loud and uncontrollable chant rose from the floor.

'Moseneke for deputy president!'

Thrice I was nominated and thrice I declined. In the end I relented. I was not unaware of the difficult conversations to be had within the PAC in light of the threats posed by the beckoning transition. There were the unresolved and difficult questions of the armed struggle and the ultimate command of the army. I was equally concerned that the elective conference did not confront any of these difficult questions. Instead, delegates veered from slo- gan to slogan, which were devoid of a deeper grasp of the complexity of the altered objective conditions. For instance, 'One settler, one bullet!' might have passed for a wartime chant, but in truth the slogan was simplistic. It promised combat and nothing else. It insinuated a relentless war with no peace or freedom in sight. It confused the party followers on the direction of the PAC and its vision on how to bring democracy to the people. In short, the slogan complicated the strategic weight lifting that lay ahead for the PAC.

I made peace with my reluctant assumption of office. I decided that during my tenure I would concentrate on four principal things. First, I would use every opportunity to lecture on the basic tenets of pan-Africanism as an antidote against crude sloganeering. Second, I would travel across the region and continent in order to understand the position of government leaders on the Harare Declaration and efforts at a negotiated transition to democracy. Third, I would do as much as I could to forge a patriotic front with the ANC and BCM. And fourth, I would help find funds to set up a head office and regional offices, and expand the party's national footprint. Several NEC members such as Barney Desai, Patricia de Lille, Moses Mavundla, Willie Seriti and Ace Mgxashe supported this four-pronged action plan. The secretary general, Khoisan X, was a useful ally, but he clandestinely imagined himself to be an APLA combatant by night and a political leader by day.

We raised decent funds from a diverse range of businesses and branch membership subscriptions. The party also received numerous anonymous monetary gifts. On one occasion, we hosted a successful fund-raising gala dinner in Sandton. The PAC opened a head office on Anderson Street in Johannesburg and regional offices across the provinces. We employed full-time staff, starting with Khoisan X, the secretary general, and paid salaries regularly. I did not receive a stipend. I chose to retain my practice as an advocate at the Pretoria Bar. The show appeared to be on track and it was well resourced.

On the patriotic front, on 15 and 16 April 1991, the PAC met with the ANC in Harare. The meeting was brokered by President Robert Mugabe. It was consistent with the Harare Declaration's call for a patriotic front of representatives of the oppressed people for the purpose of securing the end of apartheid. The ANC delegation was led by Nelson Mandela, who was then the deputy president of the ANC. I led the PAC's domestic delegation. I make the distinction because most of the leaders of the central committee of the PAC and of APLA had not returned home. An external venue was meant to secure the attendance of the commanders of APLA and, in particular, its number one, Sabelo Phama, and chairman, Johnson Mlambo. Neither had returned home; they remained in Dar es Salaam. Up to that point, their attitude towards the turning tide of dialogue was opaque. Barring Gora Ebrahim, none attended the Harare meeting.

Again the encounter with the ANC was as historic as it was congenial. The PAC and ANC had never met since the breakaway in 1958. Then the ideological differences were palpable. Thirty years later, the differences were mainly historical and institutional. Both movements had embraced varying doses of socialist thought. The ANC was funded and supported by Russia, while the PAC enjoyed the patronage of Communist China. The ANC was blessed with a steady hand of the same veteran leaders, whether in prison or out in exile, over three decades. In all that, OR Tambo played a remarkable role and emerged an astute and steadfast servant-leader.

In contrast, virtually all of the inaugural leaders of the PAC, starting with Mangaliso Sobukwe, died over the three decades. This opened the way for an overly high turnover of leaders. None of those who remained in exile rose to a striking stature or had the requisite gifts of leadership. The tenure of Potlako Leballo as chairman was marked by considerable internal strife and dictatorial tendencies that led to his expulsion. The exception was John Nyathi Pokela. He was a dedicated leader with a tireless quest for internal unity and cohesion. He became chairman of the central committee from 1981, after his release from Robben Island. He assumed the role after Vusimuzi Make, who had voluntarily resigned in deference to Pokela, who did much to quell the internecine strife and leadership battles within the party. In 1982, under his watch, he persuaded the Azanian People's Revolutionary Party (APRP), a group that had broken away from the PAC during the disruptive leadership of Potlako Leballo to return to the fold of the PAC. He restored internal stability and this helped to reclaim the regard the PAC had enjoyed within the global community and, in particular, within the UN, NAM and the Organisation of African Unity (OAU).

But again death rudely intruded. Nyathi Pokela died in a hospital in

Zimbabwe in 1985. President Mugabe gave him a state funeral in honour of his contribution to the liberation struggle.[33] Presiding Bishop Stanley Mogoba travelled to Zimbabwe to perform the funeral rites. Johnson Mlambo became Pokela's successor. He presided over the events that posed difficult questions about the appropriateness of engaging in dialogue with the ruling regime.

Not much came out of the rather costly Harare meeting with the ANC. Both parties agreed on the usefulness of a patriotic front, but there was no clear consensus on its purpose. Nelson Mandela and the ANC had long committed to negotiate with 'the Boers' on home ground. The PAC had not. The one important resolution of the meeting was to continue with the united front efforts domestically, and these included the BCM.

The home-based united front effort would be coordinated by a three-person committee drawn from each of the movements. The ANC seconded Jacob Zuma, the BCM deployed Father Joe Seoka (he is now the Anglican Bishop of Pretoria), and I was the third member. We worked hard and efficiently to advance the patriotic front project. The crowning moment was when, on 25 October 1991, the ANC and PAC, together with the BCM, convened a patriotic-front conference in Durban. It attracted nearly 70 organisations. I co-chaired the meeting with Tata Walter Sisulu. This was because, at the ANC's first national conference after 30 years, he had been elected deputy president. The gathering turned out to be too big and it also lacked cohesion. The voices were many and lacked a common purpose. For instance, there was no cohesion on whether to dismantle apartheid through negotiations. The only agreement appeared to be around the position that a constituent assembly of elected delegates (not a few, unrepresentative people) had to draft the constitution. No real patriotic front emerged at a practical level. There was no minimum programme sufficient to glue the parties together.

The ANC had already concluded the Groote Schuur Minute of 4 May 1990 and the Pretoria Minute of 6 August 1990 in which it undertook a peaceful negotiation of a new dispensation. It formed and participated in joint working groups with the regime on the release of political prisoners and the return of exiles. In the latter Minute, it suspended all armed action with immediate effect and undertook to persuade other groups to forswear the use of violence. Within days, MK issued a statement calling for a ceasefire in the country.

If the truth be told, the patriotic-front effort was a low-value item in the plans of the ANC. The path it had chosen was not open to change at the behest of patriotic partners. In fact, the Durban patriotic-front conference occurred amidst active preparations between the ANC and the government for a fresh Convention for a Democratic South Africa (CODESA) session. This took place on 19 and 20 December 1991. The BCM and the PAC wavered between the bearings that they would talk only at a neutral venue and that they would never negotiate their freedom, or that the constitution must be crafted by elected delegates.

During the course of 1991 and 1992, I packed my travelling bags and headed off to a number of African capitals. President Joaquim Chissano received me and Patricia de Lille at the State House in Maputo. He was courteous and expressed support for the liberation struggle, but he did not offer the financial support we had been hoping for. Thinking again, our hope was misplaced. In May 1988, his predecessor, President Samora Machel, had re-committed to the Nkomati Accord with the apartheid state. Its effect was to deny liberation movements bases in or free passage through Mozambique. Tens of MK combatants were hurriedly displaced from Mozambique into Mpumalanga. The security police arrested many as they crossed the border. The law firm Phosa, Mojapelo and Makgoba of Mbombela and I ran an 'ambulance service' to rescue or tend to the social and legal needs of the displaced cadres under arrest. President Chissano found a moment in the conversation to say that the two recognised liberation movements must form a united front and engage in talks with De Klerk's government to end apartheid.

Soon thereafter, Seriti and I visited Zimbabwe. President Robert Mugabe gave us ready audience at the State House. Historically, unlike Joshua Nkomo and his Zimbabwe African People's Union (ZAPU), Mugabe and his party, the Zimbabwe African National Union (ZANU), were closely allied to the PAC's Africanist posture. His country provided refuge and material support to many PAC refugees and APLA combatants. After pledging his country's support for our revolution, President Mugabe pointed out that Frontline States like Zimbabwe were bound by the Harare Declaration. He urged the PAC to engage with 'the enemy' and explore a peaceful settlement, but with caution. His practical suggestion was that the PAC should not repatriate combatants until a democratic transition had been secured. His advice boiled down to this: 'Talk to the regime, but stay ready to mount an armed assault again – if needs be.' In other words: 'Have one foot in the bush and another in the negotiating room.'

Frederick Chiluba was elected president of Zambia in 1991. He unseated Kenneth Kaunda (or 'KK' as he was fondly known), who had ruled the country for 27 years since its independence. The president readily agreed to receive a delegation from the PAC. This was welcomed because his predecessor had had all the time for the ANC but little or none for the PAC. I was struck by how diminutive President Chiluba was at just over 1.5 metres. What he lacked in height he more than made up for with a deep powerful voice, boisterous laugh and a very firm handshake. He was still basking in the electoral victory against KK, who for nearly three decades had appeared invincible. As for most post-colonial leaders, in time KK's liberation struggle dividend ran out. A coalition of trade unions, Zambia Congress of Trade Unions (ZCTU), led by Chiluba, secured his electoral demise. After all, one can milk a historical benefit for only so long. In time, the voting citizenry becomes more discerning.

President Chiluba was first out of the blocks. He explained that Zambia was in transition and that he had to do much to get the economy going again. Our request for financial support was ill-fated. He admitted to being new to Frontline State and OAU politics, and proffered the advice that the PAC must consider taking its place around the dialogue table.

On another occasion, in mid-1992, I led the PAC delegation at the Frontline

States heads of state summit in Harare. Mr Walter Sisulu, accompanied by Dr Frene Ginwala, represented the ANC at the summit. It had been convened against the backdrop of the resumption of negotiations in CODESA II in November 1991 and the whites-only referendum of March 1992, in which De Klerk sought a mandate to negotiate the dismantling of apartheid. Also, the PAC had stayed away from the planning session of the multi-party negotiating forum because its demands for a neutral venue and constituent assembly had not been accepted by the other parties in the forum.

Mr Sisulu reassured the gathering that the ANC had resumed an inclusive dialogue with the apartheid regime for a peaceful ending of the conflict. He regretted the PAC's reluctance to join CODESA II, but said the ANC would continue. My task was a little more complicated. Despite the passage of two years from its unbanning, the PAC had not assumed a firm or agreed position on what the Harare Declaration and UN declarations required of it. This meant I was not free to promise the PAC's preparedness to enter discussions on home ground or elsewhere. My rhetoric was predictable. I pledged that the PAC was ready to prosecute the liberation struggle until democratic rule was installed. Adroitly, I said nothing about the armed struggle or negotiations.

The chairperson asked Mr Sisulu and me about the importance of the whites-only referendum of March 1992 and the overwhelming 'Yes' vote for a negotiated democratic transition. I was dismissive of its importance. Mr Sisulu decried the fact that it was a racist referendum, but welcomed the positive outcome as a valuable step towards a peaceful transition to a full-blown democracy.

The response of the heads of states was to be expected. Through its chairperson, President Mugabe, they reiterated their position as formulated in the Harare Declaration that conditions existed for a peaceful resolution of the conflict in South Africa. They added that the two accredited liberation movements were expected to take active steps to explore that prospect. They urged the PAC to join the negotiation platform forthwith.

At our subsequent NEC meeting, I sensitised President Makwethu and all members to the mounting continental, if not global, pressure for the PAC to form a patriotic alliance with the ANC, to suspend the armed struggle and to commit to negotiations that would lead to non-racial democratic rule. Somewhat impatiently, I drew attention to the urgent need for the PAC to adopt clear and consistent strategic positions on each of the issues.

At the time, the chairpersonship of the OAU was vested in Nigeria. President Ibrahim Babangida offered to mediate between the PAC and the South African government. His office sent formal invitations to both parties to an exploratory round of talks. The meeting was held in Abuja in April 1992. The PAC delegation of six was led by Mlamli Makwethu. Foreign minister Pik Botha led the government delegation. The meeting was chaired and facilitated by the Nigerian foreign minister. The PAC felt vindicated that its demand for a foreign venue had been met. Its sense of importance was considerably enlarged by the preparedness of the OAU and the repentant minority government to engage it and plead for its inclusion. Comrades like Gora Ebrahim, who was the PAC's secretary for international affairs, and a few other members of the NEC seemed to believe that the PAC held all the political trump cards in the transition game. Gora even came close to insinuating that the negotiations for the demise of apartheid could never go on without the PAC. To me this was a self-deluding over-statement. Sadly, this sense of self-importance and complacency did not augur well for the muscular strategic thinking that was necessary to transfer socio-political power from the racist minority regime to an inclusive and non-racial majority.

The Abuja meeting was cordial but frank. Pik Botha sought a threefold commitment from the PAC. It had to abandon or suspend the armed struggle; abandon the demand for a neutral negotiating venue; and agree to join the pending three-cornered talks including the ANC and the National Party. The PAC had not resolved firmly on any of the three matters. This meant the delegation could not make the undertakings sought. Makwethu promised to revert on each of the issues. Save for dispelling crude prejudices of each other, little came out of the 'neutral venue' encounter in Abuja. The joint press release was bland. It described the discussions as fruitful and cordial, and the parties agreed to meet again. However, the Nigerian president and foreign minister got their pound of flesh. First, they hosted FW de Klerk in an unprecedented state visit to Nigeria in April 1992. And next, Nigeria facilitated the PAC meeting. Nigerians must have been very pleased with their role as important peace-brokers in the long and intractable conflict of the south. And their big-brother-of-the-continent stature must have been the better for it.

After Abuja, I travelled to Gaborone, Botswana, where I met with President Quett Ketumile Masire. His country's economy was reliant on ours. Thousands of Batswana worked in South Africa. His country bore the frequent brunt of raids by South African commandos in search of exiled insurgents. For that reason, he located refugee camps in the far north, in Francistown. Also, many trained guerrillas were infiltrated into South Africa through the Botswana border. President Masire was soft-spoken and hospitable but direct. He made the point that the region would thrive in all senses only when the colonial rule in South Africa had ended. The PAC must submit to the peace process. He acknowledged the force of the argument that credible talks had to be held at a neutral venue. He offered his country as a neutral venue for further talks with De Klerk's government. He would ask his minister of foreign affairs to serve as a convener of another exploratory session. The meeting was arranged promptly and chaired by the foreign minister of Botswana. Pik Botha repeated the demands he had made in Abuja. Of course, if the PAC had agreed to suspend, but not abandon, the armed struggle and to enter negotiations on home ground, the path of its history would have been markedly different.

On 16 December 1992, I resigned my position as second deputy president of the PAC and as a member of the party. My resignation occurred within a few days after my return from Abuja. Seriti and I travelled to Abuja to seek funds for the upkeep of the PAC's internal activities. I was received by General Ibrahim Badamasi Babangida. He was affable and professed to be an Africanist. It did not escape me that he styled himself as president but under military rule. I was not about to debate the legitimacy of his office or title – certainly not when I needed funds to keep the wolves from the PAC's door. Babangida sermonised me about peace and democracy, and about why the PAC should lead the charge in disbanding apartheid and inducting democratic rule. I agreed. He was yet to tell me whether the money would be forthcoming. He suggested that we be housed in a state guest house until he found an occasion to see me again. Seriti and I lived in a plush, all-expenses-paid mansion with a butler and a gourmet chef. On the sixth day or so, the president's office summoned us. Babangida pulled out a cheque-book from his desk drawer. He wrote out and gave me a personal cheque of around 600 000 pounds sterling drawn on a British bank and payable to the PAC. The cheque was not crossed and thus was also payable to its bearer. Seriti and I quickly started our journey home, via London.

The evening we landed in South Africa, Mlamli Makwethu arrived at my home in Atteridgeville. He asked for the cheque. I gave it to him. He drove off. He did not wait to hear that Babangida thought that the PAC should enter the transition fray and that he had offered scholarships for the immediate training of young pilots and agricultural extension officers.

A few days later, it came to my attention that the cheque had not been cleared through the Johannesburg PAC bank account but through a bank account in Lesotho. This meant the head office in Johannesburg remained in financial ruin. That was the last straw. I was furious. I stormed into our bedroom and screamed to Kabonina, my wife and partner in the struggle since my release from Robben Island: 'Da, I have had it! I've had it! I can't take this dithering, thoughtless, indecisive and incompetent leadership of this party. Kabo, I am out of there! I am a practising advocate. I must focus on my legal career and we have young children to bring up. In any event, I don't want to be a backbencher, Da. I am not a politician. I am a freedom fighter. I am out of there!'

I immediately sent my letter of resignation to Makwethu and later released it to the media. Then Kabo and I packed our bags, and took Dudu, Sedise and Botshelo with us to two undisclosed holiday destinations until mid-January 1993. I ignored all media enquiries. The media storm raged and died down.

It must be said that the sudden unbanning of liberation movements, the release of political prisoners and the return of exiles spawned considerable uncertainty within the PAC in exile and at home. It is not unkind to observe that the PAC was outflanked by the rapid milestones towards negotiations. Its representatives sat in the OAU, NAM and UN, but could not rubbish or derail the ANC-sponsored resolutions supporting negotiations. The PAC's global allies supported the various international declarations that held that conditions existed for ending the armed struggle and engaging in a peaceful settlement. This meant that the Frontline States and the Liberation Committee of the OAU would alter their roles. The former harboured liberation armies and the latter funded their upkeep. These were obvious menaces to a continued armed struggle. The PAC's conversations on the way forward should have taken full notice of the change of sentiment amongst its armed-struggle allies.

Ordinarily, a call for peace over violence has an inherent and universal appeal. The moral and utilitarian force of peace over armed conflict is irresistible. It is illogical to prefer armed conflict when there is a reasonable opportunity to resolve a conflict by non-violent means. It would not avail one to assume a posture that says: I don't even want to try a peaceful resolution. I won't engage in talks about talks. It is tantamount to saying: I won't even look to see if there are reasonable prospects of peace. People valorise champions of peace and, for good reason, demonise sponsors of war.

The internal PAC debates were varied and rigorous, but were invariably inconclusive. In some instances, the debates ran aground on conventional slogans. Foremost was whether the minority government meant what it had promised. Another deep concern was the wisdom of suspending the armed struggle and winding down the internal uprising in favour of a negotiated settlement. There was a risk of demobilising revolutionary forces and the international solidarity. Should the negotiations come to nought, it would be difficult to rekindle their fervour to fight on. The third bother was whether the balance of forces favoured a useful and progressive settlement. Many within the party thought the state appeared to have all the aces in the pack. That was simply not true. Apartheid had run out of runway. It was a monumental error for some inside the party to see De Klerk's regime as an indefatigable monolith. On all reckoning the regime needed a negotiated settlement more badly than met the eye.

The other argument against negotiations was that it was unlikely that the regime would concede the proprietary advantage and privilege of their constituency. The economic power relations were expected to elude the settlement and remain unaltered. Some Africanist diehards quickly added that one could not resolve the land question over the negotiating table. The line ran: 'Land is grabbed by conquest. It cannot be repossessed by dialogue.' The line rang true and was hard to contradict.

It was indeed reasonable to predict that a negotiated transition would be half-baked. Absent an outright conquest by the liberation armies, a negotiated settlement would hardly alter the ownership of the means of production or reverse the historically uneven social relations between the oppressor and the oppressed. That was an important ideological anxiety that the PAC had to keep in focus. But it was not the pressing and immediate question the PAC had to confront.

The question was stark. It was neither doctrinal nor ideological. It was tactical. What should the PAC do when the two other important actors in the same conflict opted for discussions to end the contest? One response would have been to stay away from the deal-making and pursue all forms of resistance, including the armed struggle. That would have been a plain election to continue fighting and not to talk. That option would have been a clear notice to its members and all other supporters that the struggle goes on – *Aluta continua*. Everyone would have had to reckon with that strategic choice. The PAC itself would have had to arrange its affairs as an insurgent force whatever the outcome of the negotiated transition. That may have meant assuming a warring stance even after a democratic transition, I hesitate to say, like, that of RENAMO (the Mozambican National Resistance) or UNITA (the National Union for the Total Independence of Angola). The merits of that choice would have been a different matter and one to be judged by history.

The other option was to take a place around the negotiating table as the third most influential party. At the table, the PAC would have been able to form a negotiating coalition with the ANC on matters of mutual interest. It could have cried foul if the transactions between the ANC and the regime did not measure up to the broad interests of the people. It could have tilted the tenor of the conversations towards its ideological passion. It could have made compelling submissions around core issues such as spatial and land redress, racism, historical privilege, amnesty and reparation, economic inclusivity, social equity, the form of electoral representation and account-ability, worker rights and gender justice.

Instead, the PAC made no clear election – this despite a further flurry of vital interventions aimed at curbing spiralling violence within the country and persuading the PAC to join the multi-party negotiations. The concerns over violence were fuelled by the Boipatong massacre. On 17 June 1992, 40 people were killed in their homes in a dawn raid by unknown armed invad-ers. The widespread perception was that the massacre was engineered by the government, or that the government had failed to take adequate measures to prevent it. The ANC suspended settlement discussions amidst widespread criticism that it was negotiating with a murderous regime. This presented space to urge the ANC to resume talks and the PAC to join the multi-party negotiating forum.

In June 1992, the OAU ministerial council met hurriedly with the PAC and ANC to receive a briefing on the state-sponsored violence. The coun-cil called for a cessation of violence, but nevertheless urged the two parties to return to the negotiation table. Later, the secretary general of the UN, Boutros Boutros-Ghali, invited Mlamli Makwethu to a meeting in Dakar on 30 June 1992. At the same venue, he also met with Nelson Mandela. His bot-tom line was that negotiations must be resumed and both the ANC and PAC must be key participants. Within two weeks, on 15 July 1992, Mandela and Makwethu were invited to address the Security Council of the UN on the threat to peace in South Africa. In the end, both were enjoined as 'liberation movements and legitimate representatives of the people of our land' to resume the search for peace and democracy.

The PAC left its members and supporters guessing on its response to and position on the potential transition. They never knew whether or not to support a negotiated transition. The PAC refused to suspend the armed struggle. It scoffed at multi-party negotiations between the ANC and the regime. It insisted that negotiations be held at a neutral venue. That inflexible demand kept it out when the ground rules for negotiation were settled. The PAC resolved to join CODESA as late as June 1993, and then only agreed to halt hostilities. That was more than three years after its banning had been lifted in February 1990. It arrived at the multi-party negotiation forum as an emaciated party and distinctly junior to the ANC and the National Party, whose respective statures had grown in the meantime.

By then Mandela had adroitly sold the negotiations process to the masses. The talks were seen as a logical and final push for democracy. They bought into it, albeit with some scepticism amongst militant pockets within his party. The masses trusted him. Nelson Mandela would not agree to what was not in the interest of the people. Barring related mass violence, the entire media narratives were about and supportive of an agreed political settlement. By then all political parties, including small ones of the homeland variety, had joined CODESA III. It was the only game in town.

All parties round the table had a semblance of a voice. But deals were deals only if and when they were agreed to by the two big players. Sufficient consensus, as the phrase went, could never be reached in the negotiations when the ANC or the National Party was unhappy and disagreeable. The PAC had no such sway. In the transition to democracy, it was hamstrung by a flabby balance of forces, analysis, indecision and delay. By the time the PAC turned up at CODESA III, it was already wasting away, gaunt and emaciated. This is the image it carried into the first democratic elections of 1994. The malaise was mirrored in its meagre share of the electoral outcome. It garnered only 1.2 per cent of the national vote.

Shortly after his retirement as president of the republic, Mr Mandela and I had a good few breakfasts at his residence. Zelda or Thoko, his aides, would call saying Tata wanted to share breakfast with me. We lived in the same neighbourhood of Houghton. I told the aides I was honoured, but the breakfast would have to be between 8 and 9am because I had a sitting at the Constitutional Court at 10am. Tata would clear his throat and explain that he was grateful for sharing breakfast. 'You must excuse me now that you are a big, big judge and I am a retired old man.' He said he looked forward to the breakfast because, as the Russians say, 'You have breakfast with your family; lunch with your friends; and dinner with your enemy.'

On one of those occasions, Mr Mandela looked at me sombrely and said: 'You know, Dikgang, I had remarkable respect and admiration for Robbie. He had clarity of thought and was an ideological giant.' I asked, 'Tata, who is Robbie?' 'Oh Dikgang, I meant Robert Mangaliso Sobukwe,' he replied. 'It is therefore sad that the PAC has performed so lowly in the elections.' I asked him why the PAC had attracted so few votes. He replied: 'You see, in my view, the PAC behaved like a pine tree. A pine tree is tall and firm even when there is strong howling wind. It stands erect until it is felled down and broken by the wind. We, in the ANC, were like the willow tree [*isihlahla somyezane*]. It bends in the face of headwinds. It sometimes hangs downwards to find water. You see, Dikgang, tactics are sometimes more important than principle.'

Let it suffice to observe that tactics and strategy are important in pursuing a goal. Wonderful goals call for efficient and smart means. This does not mean, however, that expedient strategy always trumps the courage of principle. There are moments when it is more appropriate to be a pine tree than a willow tree. It all depends on the kind of concessions one makes. There must always be an appropriate balance between principle or ideology, on the one end, and the tactics that are necessary to achieve the ideological purpose, on the other.

CHAPTER 28

A few detours during transition

The years of the initial transition – 1990 to 1994 – were nearly all-consuming. This had to be because, for the first time, the goal of a genuine democratic rule was in sight. We all had to fix our gaze on the potential goal. And yet the progression was linear towards dismantling colonialism and apartheid. The regime was on a path of apparent repentance, but it had not rolled over. It insisted on negotiations precisely because it wanted to salvage vital interests of its constituency. This meant many twists and turns awaited us.

The country experienced unheard-of levels of so-called black-on-black violence. People were killed on trains and in hostels and informal settlements by unidentified assailants. In areas like the KwaZulu-Natal Midlands and the Eastern Cape, violence was attributed to political rivalry sometimes within the broader liberation movement. Some state operatives continued to target and kill activists. Usually innocent grassroots people continued to be hurt or killed and their assailants, for the most part, were faceless. They were sometimes given opaque identities like the 'Third Force'. This connoted groupings that were bent on derailing the dialogue towards a new democratic constitution.

The De Klerk government denied sponsoring the violence against the people and set up the Goldstone Commission to get to the bottom of the violence and to find its sponsors. The violence became a severe obstacle to peaceful negotiations. It was not conducive to a climate within which peace and stability could be brokered. Peace accords of many varieties were concluded, but the violence persisted. The three phases of multi-party negotiation forums were called off or suspended as many times over the three years. Even so, by June 1993, CODESA announced that it had reached consensus that elections based on a universal franchise would be held on 27 April 1994. Soon thereafter, in July 1993, CODESA announced an agreement on a two-phased transition led by an interim constitution and followed by a final constitution that would be drafted and adopted by elected parliamentary representatives that sat as a constituent assembly.

During the transition, death – violent or natural – intruded. Jafta Kgalabi Masemola died on 17 April 1990 in a mysterious motor collision. The truck that collided with his car fled the scene. He had been released from Robben Island on 15 October 1989 after serving nearly 27 years of imprisonment. He enjoyed that limited freedom for a mere few months before his premature and violent demise. Nobody has been held to account for the circumstances of his death. None would have been more suited to lead the PAC in the transition than him, at a time when its president, Zephania Lekoane Mothopeng, was ailing and ageing.

Masemola is reputed to have met with Nelson Mandela at Victor Verster on the eve of his release on 11 February 1990. The meeting was at Mandela's request. There is no known record of their conversation. And yet Masemola's public position on negotiations in the six months of his life out of prison was known. He steadfastly refused to engage in any negotiations with the regime, except if it was to result in the return of land to the dispossessed African majority, and to the establishment of a free and just society.[34]

Zephania Lekoane Mothopeng died on 23 October 1990 at the age of 77.[35] He had been president of the PAC since 1986. He had been released a little before the end of his fifteen years' imprisonment term on Robben Island. His response to Nelson Mandela's invitation to negotiations with the regime was that the power and control of institutions of the state were not matters for negotiations. They must be surrendered to the African majority.

Martin Thembisile 'Chris' Hani was assassinated on 10 April 1993. He was the general secretary of the SACP and commander in chief of MK. Hani had returned home from exile following the unbanning of the ANC in 1990, and took over as head of the SACP in December 1991. He supported the suspension of the ANC's armed struggle in favour of negotiations. Hani's cowardly assassination brought the country to the brink of widespread racial violence. Commentators have often remarked that the parties to the negotiation process were jolted into action. They deliberated with due haste and, in June 1993, agreed that democratic elections would take place on 27 April 1994, a little over a year after Hani's assassination. Chris Hani's convicted assassins, Janusz Walus and Clive Derby-Lewis, were sentenced to death in October 1993.

Andries Petrus Treurnicht was a white supremacist of a kind. He was the leader of the Conservative Party from 1982 until he died on 22 April 1993. He vehemently opposed the ending of apartheid and democratic rule. His party was the official opposition in the whites-only parliament. Derby-Lewis, who was convicted for the murder of Chris Hani, was a member of parliament of his party and a close ally of Treurnicht. A commentator suggests that the heart ailment that led to Treurnicht's death was worsened by the arrest of his close ally for Hani's murder.[36] It is reported that at the point of his death, he had persuaded his followers to join the multi-party negotiation forum to demand a carve-out of a separate Afrikaner state. In effect, the Conservatives wanted to secede from the greater country in order to form an exclusively 'Boer' republic.

In December 1990, Oliver Reginald Tambo returned home from exile, where he had been for over 30 years. He was president of the ANC for just over 25 years, from 1967 to 1991. Much has been written about his sterling stewardship that kept the ANC together in torrid times in the diaspora. On 24 April 1993, OR Tambo succumbed. It is fair comment that he was the originator of the position that conditions existed for exploring a peaceful end to apartheid, and the induction of a non-racial democratic state. He never saw the day to cast his first democratic vote. Just as Treurnicht was spared the detested land, OR never saw the Promised Land.

As I have intimated, the transition was not all that life was. Many aspects of normal living continued. One was the raising of my teenage daughter and two sons, although Kabo was far more hands-on than me. She woke up very early in the morning, set up the breakfast table, and had the children bathed and dressed for school before she went off to her work as a lecturer at a nursing college. In spite of my own heavy workload, I managed to make and find space to share meaningful time at home with my children. I monitored their progress at school like a hawk. I raided their school bags and inspected their school books. And I drove the boys to school virtually every morning before the daily treadmill run. During these trips to school, I wanted to know everything about their schooling and I would ask them to tell me about the previous day at school. I attended as many school cricket, rugby and soccer matches as I could, cheering my sons on to the touch-lines, and I was there at athletics meets as well. Kabo and I went to the school drama evenings; we cheered, whistled and gave our kids deserved standing ovations. As a family we also managed to squeeze in regular winter and summer holidays. We visited Kabo's parents and mine with the children often and to the joy of their grandparents. Unlike my father, who generally sneered at and avoided bear hugs, I had learned to hug my children and tell them how much I loved them. Those warm embraces stood me in good stead when I was away from home on struggle-related chores. This was not a zero-sum game, I believed. My contribution to the transition to freedom and democracy need not translate to an equivalent loss to my children. They had to understand my, and our, collective dim past, but also, they had to be ready to take full advantage of the free space their forebears had created for them with blood and sweat. Not many things can provide that readiness for children better than a warm, love-filled home and a sterling education.

Another show that had to go on was my practice as an advocate. It was embedded in my personal and public identity. It had been cultivated within the apartheid state and was likely to survive the transition. Throughout the twists and turns, I kept my chambers open with the secretarial and other support staff. I paid my rental and other Bar Council dues. I received a continual flow of briefs and instructions to perform court and other legal work. I appeared in court frequently side by side with my role within the political space. For the upkeep of my family I earned from my practice and drew no salary or stipend from the movement. If anything, I made constant contributions to social and political causes. I suspect that my lawyer persona was somewhat stubborn. It overshadowed my political role.

Nelson Mandela played an indispensable role in the Groote Schuur and Pretoria minutes of 1990. He led his party towards an early and firm commitment to negotiations. Despite all that, in October 1990, the state charged his wife, Winifred Nomzamo Mandela, in the High Court, Johannesburg, for the death of Moeketsi 'Stompie' Seipei on 1 January 1989.

Seipei was a UDF child activist from Parys in the Free State and he was murdered when he was barely fourteen years of age. He was detained by the security police several times from the age of twelve. He fled his home for refuge in Soweto. Around October 1990, my chamber phone rang. My personal assistant came hurrying into my chamber. Normally, she would put calls through from her office – not this time. She was visibly excited. 'Mr Mandela is on the line, Advocate,' she said. I asked: 'Who?'

Mandela made quick small-talk and then moved on to the purpose of the call. 'Comrade Zami has been charged in the High Court. Will you please defend her? If you agree to defend my wife, the legal team will be George Bizos SC, Pius Langa and you.'

For a moment I was breathless. It was a big ask, but it was also one which I might not turn down. I did not know why Mandela thought I should be part of the legal team. This wasn't a question of whether I had the expertise to see the trial through, but rather what strategic considerations had led him to pick this particular team. Perhaps George Bizos and Pius Langa were more predictable choices than me. The hearing was likely to be long, tricky and a matter of great public interest. Quite apart from her husband, Madikizela-Mandela was a renowned freedom fighter in her own right and arguably more militant than he was.

Our brief was limited to Mrs Mandela, who was charged together with John Morgan and Xoliswa Falati. They faced similar charges. The co-accused were represented separately. The state's case was that, on 29 December 1988, Mrs Mandela had ordered the kidnapping of four young men from the Methodist Church manse in Orlando, Soweto, where they had lived with Reverend Paul Verryn, and their subsequent assault at her residence. The young men were Stompie Seipei, Kenneth Kgase, Pelo Mekgwe and Thabiso Mono. Seipei was accused of being a police informer. At the time, that was a serious and ill-fated accusation. The kidnapped boys pleaded, saying that Stompie was not a police informer. Stompie was led into a room at Mrs Mandela's residence and stabbed in the throat. He died.

Jerry Richardson, a member of the Mandela Football Club and who some-times served as Mrs Mandela's bodyguard, was convicted, in a separate and earlier trial, of the murder of Seipei.

The trial lasted six months before a courteous but irascible judge. Mr Mandela attended court most days. Mrs Mandela, Mr Mandela and Dali Mpofu, then an assistant to Mrs Mandela, met up with George Bizos and me in his office in Innes Chambers on court days. Predictably, a large throng of onlookers gathered to have a look at two national icons. Mr Mandela's body-guards had their hands full as people were on the lookout for one of those quick handshakes that Mr Mandela was known to dish out. The entourage would walk across Pritchard Street to the courthouse every morning, after lunch and at the end of each day's proceedings. The mayhem seemed never to abate. The media houses and *paparazzi* set up near the point of street-crossing for months on end. Radio and television ran nightly cross-overs or inserts on the trial. Many gathered in the street in genuine admiration of and sympathy with the Mandela couple. Many others came to bare the primor-dial, if not bloodthirsty, lust for fallen heroes and soiled icons. For reasons that are obscure, humans bay for giants with clay feet. The mighty must fall.

Pius was often away or detained elsewhere and so the legal work rested on George Bizos and me. I took detailed statements of Mrs Mandela's version of events and responses to state testimony. For this, I had to follow up at her home in Soweto over weekends. Thereafter, I had to have the statements typed up for George's cross-examination in the new week. That took up most weekends. On occasion I relieved George of the cross-examination chore. At the end of a gruelling trial, Mrs Mandela was found guilty on four charges of kidnapping and four of being an accessory after the fact to assault. Her co-accused were convicted along the same lines. In May 1991, she was sentenced to six years' imprisonment, partially suspended. The Appeal Court intervened and suspended the entire imprisonment sentence.

I spent many hours with Mrs Mandela during the trial. We developed a bond that saw her call me up many times for legal and familial advice. In time, she asked me to act for her as counsel in a good few other court cases. I have had the benefit of listening to her life story told by herself. When she was arrested and tried in the Stompie Seipei case, the state produced proof (which lawyers call SAP69) that she had a previous conviction. She had been convicted for assault. Before I could ask her what the previous conviction was about, Mrs Mandela laughed heartily, flickering her big brown eyes and showing her full set of teeth and dimpled cheeks. She narrated how one night policemen had raided her home of banishment in Brandfort. She woke up to the shouting of 'Police! Police!' Before she had time to put on her dressing gown, one of them kicked down her bedroom door and rushed in. 'What are you doing in my bedroom before I am properly dressed?' she demanded angrily. She laughed, remembering how she had hit the cop flush and hard on the jaw. He fell instantly to the ground, scrambled to his feet and left. At the ensuing trial the cop who was standing in the witness box was in a neck-brace. She refused to plead to the charge of assault on police. 'Dikgang, I don't plead before illegitimate courts, kaloku!' In fact, from the dock she promised the cop more if he ever intruded into her private space again. She was sentenced to a suspended jail term.

Mrs Mandela is a odd mixture of courage and fearlessness. She is indeed a remarkable revolutionary. She cares for downtrodden and vulnerable people. Her patriotism and sacrifice are not open to any doubt. She carried the full brunt of the wrath of our oppression. She supported internal uprisings decade after decade. Later in her life, she provided refuge and sustenance for many MK cadres. She brought up her children and grandchildren single-handedly. She stood by her husband for the full duration of his incarceration. Her political and personal lives were not without blemish. (If yours is, throw the first stone.) On balance, there is much to celebrate in the life of Nomzamo Winifred Madikizela-Mandela.

Her marriage fell victim to the hectic transition. On 13 April 1992, Mr Mandela announced his separation from Mrs Mandela and he moved out of the common home in Orlando West, Soweto. I continued to minister to Mrs Mandela's legal needs until the beginning of the divorce proceedings, a matter to which I revert later.

Another sequel of the transition was the hunger strike amongst political prisoners on Robben Island. As we have seen, since 1988 the repentant apartheid regime started freeing political prisoners seemingly on its own motion. The releases were unconditional. The legal mechanics for the releases were neither obvious nor transparent, but the freed activists did not care one bit about the legal fiat that got them out of jail. Most reasoned that they should not have been there in the first instance.

However, the mechanics for release of political prisoners was a matter of vital interest to activists who remained jailed long after their political movements had been unbanned and after Nelson Mandela had been released from jail in February 1990. Unsurprisingly for the ANC, the two critical impediments to negotiations were the release of political prisoners and the indemnity from prosecution of political exiles who choose to return home. The ANC could not afford merrily to engage the regime while its comrades languished in jail or were in exile. The government's preconditions were a commitment to negotiate a new constitution and to forswear armed resistance. Minutes of the early engagement with the ANC reflected their respective anxieties. As early as in the Pretoria Minute, a joint task team was to report on protocols and guidelines to manage the speedy release of prisoners and return of exiled citizens.

Political inmates on Robben Island thought all that took too long. They demanded their immediate release. They backed up their demand with the ultimate act of resistance of a prisoner – a hunger strike. They drew a collective list of legal counsel to unearth the reasons for the delay to their release. The chosen team was Dullah Omar, George Bizos, Arthur Chaskalson and me.

The Cape morning was sunny and the sky was blue and cloudless. The breeze over the Waterfront embankment was slight and gentle. The legal team got onto the boat to Robben Island. I was wearing a suit and carrying a pretentious briefcase, the kind that lawyers yank around with them to look important. I thought I looked the part. The morning may have been routine for Dullah, Arthur and George, but it was not routine for me. My recollection of the same embankment was of a cloudy, cold and wet day, with howling winds over the leaping Atlantic. I was foot-chained and hand-manacled. I was hurled down a narrow staircase from the deck headlong into the belly of *Dias*, the prison boat.

I had not returned to Robben Island since my release seventeen years earlier. I had never wanted to and so I did not. But here I was, standing on the deck of the *Dias* and feeling like the monarch of all I surveyed. The embankment looked smaller and more pathetic than when I first saw it as a prisoner. So did the *Dias*. The boat looked tiny now and the prison wardens tending to it greeted and deferred to Advocate Dikgang Moseneke no end. I declined to go down into the hull, choosing instead to savour the full trip from the deck. I had no words to describe my sense of triumph. I had the 'I will be back' swagger – not unlike Arnold Schwarzenegger's famous promise, rather than threat, in *The Terminator*.[37] The moment was even sweeter because the ruling elite of the apartheid state were hard at work to undo their bankrupt tyranny.

On the island, we met up with a delegation of prisoners reflecting diverse political tendencies. They included Naledi Tsiki, Tokyo Sexwale and Jeff Radebe. They were gaunt and famished but militant. They needed certainty about the process and dates of their release. Their demand was anything but irrational. As we have seen, scores of political prisoners, including very senior leaders of the broad liberation movement, had been released unconditionally. However, the pick of prisoners and their dates of releases were decided by the state unilaterally. A joint framework for the release of political prisoners was yet to be agreed. The Groote Schuur Minute agreed to a task team to resolve the very matter.

The delegation was strident and demanded their freedom from jail forthwith. We, the legal team, made a few telephone calls from Robben Island to the minister of justice, Kobie Coetsee. We instantly procured his commitment to furnish the inmates with a timetable of releases. The hunger strike ended amidst shouts of '*Amandla! Izwe Lethu!*' and '*Kuyahanjwa*, comrades!'

By the afternoon, I was back on the deck of the *Dias*. This time I could not suppress the swagger. I placed my sunglasses carefully on the ridge of my nose. Again I surveyed the leaping tide of the tempestuous Atlantic. I felt even more triumphant. The mission had been accomplished. At last, the now rueful government had become responsive. I could not but remember how little they had cared when political prisoners nearly dropped dead in our eighteen-day hunger strike at the same facility.

CHAPTER 29

Negotiations and an interim constitution

After December 1992, my focus was unbroken. By then it was obvious that all the stars were aligned to produce a negotiated settlement that would lead to democratic rule. At the opening of parliament in February 1993, President De Klerk vowed to do everything within his grasp to reach an inclusive negotiated settlement in that year. He shared that resolve with Mr Mandela, the ANC and its allies. By then many other political parties had chosen the same path to the unstoppable destination. On 5 March 1993 a new multi-party negotiating forum was convened (CODESA III). All political entities, except for AZAPO and the right-wing Afrikaner Weerstandsbeweging (AWB), signed up. 'Uncle' Barney Desai and Patricia de Lille signed up for the PAC. The train left the station irreversibly.

From January 1993, I looked inward and put my head down. I resolved to pursue the enterprise of a practising advocate with rigour. Soon, I gave the Bar Council notice that I sought to assume silk status. In those days, I was obliged to give notice of my intention to apply for silk to every other advocate who was my senior at the Bar. None of my seniors objected. Pound for pound, I had prosecuted a vigorous, diverse and complex practice at the Bar, despite the apartheid margins. I had litigated against or side by side with most of my peers for over a decade, after a five-year stint as a partner in an attorneys' law firm. Add three years of apprenticeship as a candidate attorney and I had a solid eighteen years of exposure to legal practice. I had fearlessly presented cases of vulnerable individuals and communities, as well as of political activists of the widest variety. Whatever limited business law cases emerged from black businesses, I was briefed in most. I had appeared in all courts of the land, including the Appellate Division. I was ready for a new phase in my career.

Members of the Bar Council conducted a peer review of sorts to satisfy themselves of my suitability to earn senior counsel status. They supported my silk application and forwarded it to Judge President Frikkie Eloff. In turn, the judge president was obliged to assess the forensic skills and experience of counsel who craved silk status. He gave me the nod and soon I had letters patent appointing me senior counsel of the republic, signed by Kobie Coetsee, the minister of justice, and FW de Klerk, the state president.

It was then that the irony of my appointment as silk hit me. A state that I fought and sought to destroy with every sinew of my being had conferred on me the treasured professional status of silk. The security killer-squad of the same state had conspired to murder me at least twice, as TRC records would later reveal. The paradox did not end there. I was a senior counsel without a vote. I remained subject to the horror of the state's racial antipathy and economic exclusion. There was a saving grace, however. When I took silk, the regime had begun to totter and was on a route of forced penitence. It was poised to agree to the demise of its unwelcomed rule.

Two vital developments occurred at the multi-party talks. In June 1993, the parties agreed to hold national and provincial elections on 27 April 1994. Shortly thereafter, in July 1993, a ground-breaking compromise was struck. There would be an interim constitution. Under it the minority government would end and elections would be held. The resultant parliament, at times, would sit as a constituent assembly that would draft and adopt a final constitution. That compromise would give legitimacy to the constitution as a progeny of 'we the people'.

One afternoon, my telephone rang. It was Thabo Mbeki, enquiring whether I would serve on the technical committee tasked with drafting the interim constitution. If I were so minded, he said, I should call Arthur Chaskalson, who would furnish me with the mandate of the drafting committee.

I was quietly excited, but careful not to imperil my resolve to preserve my law practice and to stay outside of the political space. In my mind, there is a firm line between a freedom fighter and a politician. The former is the bearer of revolutionary and moral idealism. The latter, barring a few notable exceptions, vends the possible and expedient. Often the expedience degenerates to power and not service, to self-interest and not public good.

Happily, the mandate of the technical committee was neutral. Its members were nominated by negotiating parties but approved by the assembly of all parties for which the technical committee worked. It was co-chaired by Francois Venter, a professor of constitutional law from Potchefstroom University, and Arthur Chaskalson SC. Its members included Bernard Ngoepe, a member of the Pretoria Bar, who in time became the judge president of the Gauteng High Court; Firoz Cachalia, an attorney and activist; and George Devenish, a professor of constitutional law at the University of Natal. We were expected to work full-time on the task and well beyond the call of duty. The technical committee's relationship with the multi-party negotiation forum was one of agency. The committee worked for the collective of the parties in the plenary assembly. Its primary task was to convert the political consensus of the negotiating chamber into a constitutional text. Every draft, usually in the form of a chapter or discrete clauses, was first circulated to all the parties and thereafter debated in an open plenary assembly.

The technical committee remained in attendance in the assembly during the debates on its drafts. We made amendments agreed to by the assembly. When the drafting committee could not agree on a text to place before the assembly, we produced more than one text reflecting the divergent drafts. The assembly would choose the one it preferred or ask the committee to revise its proposed drafts. By and large, the drafts of the technical committee were highly regarded and altered only marginally. In some instances, the assembly would request a constitutional law opinion from the technical committee on a discrete issue. I worked closely with Arthur on the research.

The plenary assembly agreed on most provisions of the draft interim constitution. But there were hefty differences. The most raucous divergence was whether the envisaged republic would be a federal or unitary state. Parties from the left were anxious to establish a competent unitary state capable of effective transformation. The National Party, former homeland entities and others on the right pushed for a loose and decentralised federation in which the provinces held the bulk of the executive and legislative competences, while national centre held limited and defined residual power. The compromise to this trenchant contest between federalism and unitarism was to split the difference by formulating complicated schedules of exclusive and concurrent national and provincial competences. The schedules resurfaced in the final constitution.

Another sore point was the character of the final constitution after a majoritarian election. Once the National Party and other like-minded parties had conceded a two-stage constitution-making process, their concern was to agree with the minimum principles that would gird the final version of the constitution. They insisted that the new Constitutional Court must certify whether the final constitution was in harmony with the pre-set constitutional principles. That compromise set up a delicate balance between outright majoritarianism in constitution crafting and the anxiety of minorities about the character of the final text.

Agreeing on the wording and reach of the constitutional principles was trying. Our drafts were scrutinised finely. Proposed changes in the wording of our draft constitutional principles were many and indicative of the core differences and concerns of the parties from left to right along the political scale. Parties that were likely to be electoral minorities preferred ample constitutional principles that were worded to constrain the exercise of public power.

The bill of rights chapter did not stoke up as much difference as one would have expected. Surprisingly, except for the right to basic education, there was no big push for the inclusion of socio-economic rights as properly justiciable. Thankfully, justiciable socio-economic rights were inserted in the final constitution. No constitutional principle in the interim constitution outlawed socio-economic guarantees. Also, those parties opposed to the inclusion of socio-economic protections had no proper answer to the proposition that the social devastation of apartheid called for a state-led 'Marshall Plan'. In the end, the inclusion may not have mattered much, because the burden of reconstruction and development fell squarely on the new democratic government.

The property clause in the interim constitution was perhaps the biggest give the liberation movement had to tolerate to go over the democratic winning line. The first part of the property clause in the interim constitution seemed to concern itself with future acquisition and disposal of property. It promised everyone the right to acquire and hold rights in property or dispose of it. Its thrust was clearly futuristic. Historical rights in property that had vested were protected by the assurance that 'no deprivation of any rights in property shall be permitted otherwise than in accordance with a law'. The property clause recognised that certain laws may regulate, limit or deprive the use or enjoyment of property. Also, the state may expropriate a right in property in accordance with a law, provided it is for a public purpose only. Expropriation must be against payment of compensation agreed to with the affected person or determined by a court. The property clause, in effect, sanitised historical dispossession and entrenched proprietary benefit and privilege of an unequal past.

Perhaps the stickiest part of the interim constitution came right at the end of the negotiations and drafting process. It related to truth and reconciliation. We came to learn that the securocrats in the police and army would not support the transition unless two matters had been resolved: a constitutionally sanctioned process of amnesty for past crimes that were politically inspired, and pensions. At that point the formal task of the technical committee had come to an end. I was more than happy to be relieved of the task of formulating a constitutional text that would address a matter so complex. The postamble of the interim constitution was the outcome of that intractable debate. It sought to find a balance between the truth and retribution, on the one end, and forgiveness and reconciliation, on the other. The upshots of the twin debate were the TRC and sunset clauses that were dressed up as obvious deal-makers without which the transition would stall. Arthur and Francois were seized with that intractable final stage.

The final draft of the interim constitution was completed and adopted by parliament by the end of 1993 and assented to on 25 January 1994. But it only took effect on 27 April 1994.

My role in the technical committee in Kempton Park meant that I had to be away from practice for six months. I was pleased to be back in chambers. It was December 1993, and I was going to find a moment to go on holiday with Kabo and my Dudu, Sedise and Reabetswe. We chose Malelane Lodge on the doorstep of the Kruger National Park.

CHAPTER 30

'Dikgang, I am glad I have found you ...'

That early morning, Mpumalanga promised to be searing hot. In December the temperature along the banks of the Sabi River easily rises to 40°C. The only right place to take refuge is under the shade of a big tree. Nothing shields one from the scalding African sun better than an indigenous tree's shade. We found reclining chairs around the pool but moved them under the trees. We had no business to dare the sun like other holidaymakers in constant search for a suntan. My daughter and sons were going to live in the pool no less than crocodiles do in the Sabi River. As for me, I was planning a combination of the casual reading of a novel and an occasional dip.

Just as we were settling into a relaxed morning, a man in wildlife ranger attire walked up to me and tilted over while holding a walkie-talkie in his hand.

'Excuse me, sir, there is somebody on the line who would like to talk to you,' he said.

'But nobody knows I am here,' I replied. 'Who could that be? I am here to rest. I really do not want to field calls here.'

'I think, sir,' he persisted, 'you want to take this call.' Then, in a quivering voice, he added: 'It is Mr Mandela, sir.'

The ranger was right. I jumped off the reclining chair and stood erect, as if Mr Mandela himself was in sight. I wondered how he had come to know where I was. I still do not know, up to this day, how he tracked me down. The obvious suspect is Tiego, my younger brother, who may have very well leaked my secure hideout.

'Dikgang, I am glad I have found you.' His distinct, hesitant but firm voice came through. 'Mr De Klerk has nominated Judge Kriegler to chair the Electoral Commission, which will run the April 1994 elections. I have nominated you to become the deputy chairperson. You have to accept this nomination. The role you have to play is of great importance to all of us.'

I remained dead silent. I had just completed a six-month stint of helping to write the interim constitution. Now I would obviously have to give up another six months to see the elections through.

'Are you there?' Mr Mandela interrupted the silence.

'Yes, Tata,' I replied.

Frankly, I did not know how one says no to Nelson Mandela. And yet at the same time I knew how historic and momentous his invitation was. He was, in effect, inviting me to oversee the transition to democratic rule on behalf of millions of people in our land. I had hardly finished telling him that I accepted the nomination when he added: 'Tomorrow at Tuynhuys in Cape Town, there will be a meeting which must be attended by you and me and Mr De Klerk and Judge Kriegler. The meeting cannot be delayed further because the Government Gazette appointing the chairperson and the deputy chairperson of the IEC must be published tomorrow evening.'

There was nothing else for it. I was immediately to relocate my entire family to Cape Town. We abruptly terminated our booking at Malelane Lodge and by midday we were in Pretoria. Kabonina, the kids and I quickly repacked for a different holiday destination.

By late afternoon, I had found my way to Tuynhuys. I had never met Mr De Klerk before, but he must have known who I was. He had signed my letters patent in order for me to become the first and only African senior counsel in my province. I had appeared before Johann Kriegler as a judge. The meeting of the four of us was brief and businesslike. After giving me a bearhug, Mr Mandela remained largely quiet throughout the meeting.

FW de Klerk chaired the proceedings. Kriegler and I formally accepted our nominations and the terms of the Government Gazette that confirmed our respective appointments were finalised for publication later that day. The historic import of the meeting did not escape me. Kriegler and I set a date for our first meeting in Johannesburg in early January.

I had never run elections before; nor had Johann Kriegler. In no time, the rest of the members of the Independent Electoral Commission (IEC) were nominated and appointed. They included a wonderful spread of South Africans who brought diverse skills to the fore. Commissioners included Dawn Mokhobo, a prominent executive director of Eskom; Frank Chikane, who had served as the secretary general of the South African Council of Churches; Helen Suzman, who had served for decades as the only member of the opposition in the all-white and virtually all-male parliament of the time; Zac Yacoob, a senior counsel from the Durban Bar; Charles Nupen, a renowned activist and labour lawyer; and Oscar Dhlomo, a former Inkatha Freedom Party (IFP) member and KwaZulu homeland government cabinet member.

Several distinguished international commissioners were also added to the panel. They included Gay McDougall, a human rights activist lawyer from Washington DC; Professor Eklit, an elections expert from Scandinavia; Professor Tekle from Somalia; and Professor Ron Gould, an electoral expert from Canada.

The elections were to be conducted in terms of an ambitious legislation, the Electoral Act of 1993, which places vast powers in the hands of the chairperson, deputy chairperson and the rest of the commissioners. The election date, 27 April 1994, was already known. This meant that, in effect, the commission had less than four months in which to set up office from scratch, appoint executive and field staff, and set up voting regions, districts and polling stations within districts. There had never been an election that was truly nationwide in South Africa before, one that included every adult South African citizen. This meant that the operations of the IEC had to be rolled out to every nook and cranny of the country. The implications and demands of setting up an operation of this magnitude are best left to the imagination. Suffice it to say, we had our work cut out for us. At an instant, we were to establish a full-scale human resources division with a nationwide reach, replete with employment contracts, a payment system and internal disciplinary processes. We established a full-scale electoral division to set up all physical and managerial resources for conducting an election. As we were entitled to anticipate, there would be objections, complaints by political parties and individuals, as well as compliance issues. A national monitoring and compliance division had to be set up post-haste.

Kriegler and I set up a head office in Kempton Park, which housed all the commissioners and the heads of all the executive decisions that were necessary. We appointed a CEO, Dr Renosi Mokate, who was tasked with forming a complete executive and management system, including financial officers who would have to manage the hundreds of millions of rand that had been appropriated to ensure a complete and smooth running of the elections. We needed massive procurement capabilities to secure the resource needs of our entire national operation. At a certain point we may have hired every single car on hire in the country and issued hundreds of petrol and maintenance cards right across the land.

In order to ensure that all our objectives were achieved, all commissioners had to assume full-time executive roles and be on duty well up to eighteen hours a day. They assumed accommodation around the IEC headquarters in Kempton Park and had to work every day of the week. Johann Kriegler and I lived side by side in the same hotel facility for a solid four months with little or no respite.

Once the infrastructural and administrative challenges were in hand, we lifted our heads to deal with the obvious obstacles presented by a country that had been carved out to fulfil the apartheid spatial design. The homeland states of Bophuthatswana and Ciskei and the homeland government of KwaZulu were unlike the other homeland governments: these three had not allowed the IEC to set up full infrastructure in their territories. From early March 1994, it became clear that we had to procure the cooperation of these homeland states in conducting electoral education, setting up district and regional offices, and, more importantly, setting up actual voting stations and making firm arrangements for their security before and on voting day.

Johann Kriegler and I met with Mr De Klerk and Mr Mandela at the Union Buildings. We provided them with a status report on preparations for elections. The report showed that we had not been able to roll out electoral infrastructure in Bophuthatswana and KwaZulu. The upshot of the meeting was that the Transitional Executive Committee (TEC) would continue to engage these entities at a political level. We also agreed that Kriegler and I would approach both governments with a formal request to permit us to conduct electoral training, appoint electoral staff, and set up voting districts and stations.

We agreed to visit the president of Bophuthatswana on 10 March 1994. While we knew that he, President Lucas Mangope, in his parliament publicly refused to surrender authority to the TEC, which resulted in mass protests across Bophuthatswana, we were still duty-bound to make a formal request to set up electoral facilities in that territory.

We came to know, during the course of 10 March, of the events that led to the shooting and death of a number of AWB right-wingers who, it seemed, were attempting to quell the uprising in Bophuthatswana. The army also confirmed with Kriegler and me that President Mangope had retreated to his traditional home in Motswedi. The army, at the request of Mr De Klerk, arranged for the two of us to be conveyed to his residence by army helicopter. The trip was to commence at Waterkloof military base. Shortly before our departure, Mr De Klerk's jet landed at the base and he wished us well on our difficult mission. For reasons which I cannot remember now, Kriegler and I left the base in the late evening in two massive army helicopters. The leading helicopter heading towards Zeerust carried several special unit soldiers who were visibly heavily armed. The helicopter in which Kriegler and I travelled was also well populated with special unit operatives, who seemed to be carrying weapons of war on virtually every part of their bodies.

The trip took a good three hours. There was constant radio communication with the North West military bases about the exact location of President Mangope's home in the vicinity of Zeerust. I must say I was puzzled that they did not have the exact coordinates. The radio cross-overs also revealed that there was a concern about an army battalion that appeared to be located at President Mangope's residence. Johann and I could only sit haplessly in the copter. From all that I heard, it sounded like a full military operation that needed a full reconnaissance before war. Our mission was civilian and peaceful. We wanted to persuade the president to permit his uprising people to rejoin the republic and participate in the upcoming elections.

We reached the sprawling residence and its vast grounds after midnight. Our helicopter remained in the air while its bright searchlights scoured the property. The first helicopter moved lower and lower until the troops on it started jumping off with automatic rifles fully drawn as they landed on the ground. Within minutes, I could hear our pilots relay the feedback: *'Die plek is beveilig'* (The place has been secured). Only then did our massive helicopter touch down. Johann Kriegler and I were helped out of it and we walked into the residence.

Someone called President Mangope from his bedroom. He found Johann Kriegler and me perched on his grand sofas. (We had avoided the one that looked obviously imperial.) I did not know the affinity between Mr Mangope and Johann Kriegler. He greeted Johann first, saying, *'Goeie môre, Johann'*, and Johann replied, *'Goeie môre, Oom Lucas.'* It turned out that Johann had acted as counsel for the president many times. *Rre* Mangope then turned in my direction and said: *'Dumela, Mokwena. Le ntlela bosigo, Mokwena, jaaka mabana. Le dikgogo, le dikgomo tsame di a lela'* (You approach my home like an enemy. Even my chickens and cows are running amok). It was indeed so. When the big army helicopters floodlit his property and blew up a storm, his chickens and cows became very upset.

Time was running out and it was crucial that we set up an electoral infrastructure in Bophuthatswana, and so Johann Kriegler wasted no time in outlining our mission. We did not refer at all to the ongoing uprising within the territory nor the fatal shooting of right-wing rag-tag army operatives that had been flashed across TV screens all over the country. President Mangope assumed a sombre mood and started making his point.

'We are an independent state,' he began. 'Sovereignty once conferred can never be revoked. You two are asking me to surrender the rights of our people to selfdetermination and nationhood. Allow us to retain our sovereignty and to merge with Botswana, which is closer to us than the rest of South Africa.' He turned towards Johann Kriegler and said, in Afrikaans: 'The Afrikaners betrayed the Batswana people. They seem to have forgotten that when the Great Trek led them to amongst the Batswana people, unlike others, we did not fight and kill them. We gave them land, cattle and women.'

Mr Mangope then turned to me and switched to Setswana. '*Mokwena, o mosimane wa Motswana o botlhale! Fela o direla matabele bo M-a-n-t-e-l-a lebo S-i-s-u-l-u. Mme go siame*' (Mokwena, you are a very smart Motswana, young man! And yet you are in the service of Nguni people like Mandela and Sisulu. But that is fine).

In a tirade of remarkable oratory, President Mangope had, in sum, told Kriegler and me that we were traitors. At that point, he asked his son, Kwena Mangope, who carried the rank of brigadier, to join the discussion on whether to sign off a draft undertaking that would permit the IEC to set up its operations within Bophuthatswana. Kwena said they wanted to study the document overnight; they would see that it was delivered to our offices in Kempton Park the following morning.

As they say, the rest is history. We put up a full electoral machinery in Bophuthatswana, and the people of that territory cast their much cherished votes on 27 April 1994.

The other frontier threatening to jeopardise the pending elections was the Bantustan government of KwaZulu led by Chief Minister Mangosuthu Buthelezi. He had made several public and private declarations to the effect that people of his territory would not participate in the elections. Kriegler and I were aware that there were continuous attempts by a variety of people to persuade him to agree to the people of KwaZulu participating, amongst them Mr Mandela and Mr De Klerk. To this end they had met with Chief Buthelezi as well as with the Zulu king. We, however, understood our brief to be narrower. We sought to interact with Chief Buthelezi and members of his cabinet and of his legislature for an outright consent to make all the preparations necessary for the electoral process. It was important to appoint and train voting and counting officials and to set up district offices in KwaZulu. There was a significant concern about free electioneering within the territory as there were known 'no-go zones' in which only one party would be permitted to have access to potential voters.

Kriegler, Helen Suzman and I made our way to Ulundi, the capital of KwaZulu. We had arranged meetings with the chief minister. He, however, chose to convey our request to set up an electoral infrastructure in KwaZulu to his entire legislative assembly. Johann Kriegler was given the opportunity to address the assembly, whose members were for the most part traditional leaders. Judge that Johann was, he told the assembly that they must allow the IEC to set up its operations in that territory because the law on elections said so. The chief minister did not have to say a word. Several of the traditional leaders took serious offence. One after the other, in indignant and bellicose isiZulu, they reminded us that they were not bound by the laws Kriegler was talking about. They would allow voting in their territories only if they decided to. In effect, they showed us the door.

Over the years, I had developed a warm rapport with Prince Buthelezi. I have already related how he received me on a visit to his royal residence at Phindangene, when he took me to the highest point of the homestead, which looked out over hundreds of beautiful undulating hills. After a traditional ritual, he pointed at a cow and instructed his aides to slaughter it in honour of me, his guest. In time, the prince arranged that the processed hide be delivered to my residence in Pretoria. Our relationship was cordial and mutually respectful. The cordiality extended well beyond the elections. When his son made his way to Gauteng after 1994, Prince Buthelezi alerted me to Zuzifa's presence and asked me to play the role of elder brother to Zuzi. So I was quite comfortable when the commission asked me to lead a task team of commissioners to oversee the preparation of the actual elections for all of Natal and KwaZulu. From mid-March to election day, Gay McDougall, Charles Nupen and I were given that task. It was arguably the toughest geographic area in which to deliver elections. Rivalry between the ANC and IFP was real and led to several deaths and many injuries. There were 'no-go zones' within both the broader Natal province and in KwaZulu. While we had succeeded in setting up an electoral infrastructure in Natal, none of the IEC functionaries could gain access to KwaZulu. This meant that the IEC had no effective presence on the ground.

In order to resolve this impasse, Gay, Charles and I made several trips to Ulundi. We had several helicopter and fixed-wing flights into Ulundi and held numerous meetings with the chief minister and sometimes together with other cabinet ministers. Buthelezi supported, in principle, my efforts to set up IEC infrastructure, but never gave any outright consent. It was clear from the discussions that he had bigger fish to fry before his people joined in the elections. On occasion, he would express dismay at how Mr Mandela and Mr De Klerk had not included him in the major decision making related to the transition. He always condemned the so-called no-go areas and violence related to political party rivalry.

On one evening, around mid-April 1994, deputy minister of justice Danie Schutte and I were summoned to a hurried meeting in Ulundi in the trust that Prince Buthelezi might agree to his territory participating in the elections. The meeting was an odd mixture of tough political exchanges between Danie Schutte and the chief minister and prayer sessions led by a famous pastor. We flew back on a charter from Ulundi to Pietermaritzburg well after midnight, but still with no firm agreement on whether the IEC might be functional within KwaZulu.

A few days before the elections, Prince Buthelezi announced that the IFP would participate. The ballot papers had already been printed in a secured printing environment in the United Kingdom. The IFP, its party logo and the face of its leader were not on the ballot papers. Voting stations were yet to be identified and proclaimed in the Government Gazette. Voting and counting officers had to be identified, employed and trained within days. We in the IEC task team in Natal had to arrange for all-round electoral security in KwaZulu. Urgent and intense meetings with the police and the army ensued. For the work at hand, days were too short and the evenings even shorter. I remember too well how Charles Nupen, Gay McDougall and I criss-crossed KwaZulu, sometimes by road but mainly in army helicopters, to check on the quality and effectiveness of the hurried electoral infrastructure.

It became obvious that we had to adapt the provincial and national ballot papers to include the IFP. Charles Nupen took charge of that treacherous operation. In no time, he found out what the private printing capacity in Durban was and he commandeered their printing presses. The instruction was to do no printing other than print little narrow strips carrying the IFP, its logo and the face of its leader. What was more, Charles had to ensure that the strips were carefully pasted onto the bottom part of the ballot papers.

On the morning of the elections, just a little after 7am, my Durban hotel phone rang. It was Prince Buthelezi. He was polite but clearly very angry. He told me that he had seen the ballot paper with the little strip pasted at the bottom. His image was flattened and looked like the cartoon character 'Jojo', he announced. Then he added angrily: 'Advocate, how could my people vote for me when I look like *itokoloshe*?' I remained silent while he talked. Then I expressed deep regret, although I myself had not seen the pasted strips. I pointed out that it was so late in the hour that I would not be able to do much to rectify the unsatisfactory printing. I enquired at which place he would be voting and undertook to be present there and to pay my respects. It was an easy promise to make because the day before we had heard that Mr Mandela had chosen to cast his vote at Inanda and Prince Buthelezi would cast his vote in Umlazi. Gay McDougall was required to be at Inanda when Mr Mandela voted. Up to this day, she appears in the frame of the shot captured when Mr Mandela cast his first vote ever. I dutifully observed Prince Buthelezi cast his vote.

Within the hour, the commissioners posted in Natal and KwaZulu had regrouped, and we were on helicopter flights to different parts of the province to observe the voting flow and to provide executive support where it was needed. In KwaZulu, teachers had hastily been appointed as voting officers. One of the difficulties was that it was not possible to appoint monitors, nor were there party observers in most of the stations in KwaZulu Natal. We had to resort to the ballot boxes that had been used by the KwaZulu government in the earlier Bantustan elections. We also had to rely on KwaZulu police to secure the voting stations and to transport the ballot boxes from the widely spread voting stations to the counting centre in Durban. Most of those trips lasted hours as ballot papers were conveyed from the north towards the provincial counting stations.

On voting day there were indeed several challenges facing the IEC. I have chosen not to detain you or me with the details here. The IEC extended the voting into an extra day. Thereafter, we all descended on the counting centre in Durban. Save for spoilt ballots, every ballot paper was counted. But here was the rub: there was no voters roll. And we, the IEC, had no idea how many people were eligible to vote. Of course, there was a valiant attempt to stop multiple voting by using indelible ink on each voter, but we could not exclude the real possibility of ballot stuffing.

After a count and another count and yet another count in the presence of all party representatives, the IFP won the majority of the votes cast in KwaZulu and Natal. In other words, they emerged the ruling party of KwaZulu and Natal. As inexplicable as that outcome might have seemed to many, that was the outcome that the counted valid ballots dictated.

Having mopped up the operations in KwaZulu-Natal, I returned to the IEC headquarters in Kempton Park. The critical task now was to audit and collate all provincial and national results. The entire commission was charged with this complicated task. Initially all district, regional and provincial totals were posted up on an electronic leader board, a service procured by the IEC from IBM. Within two days, the leader board displayed material adding and percentage irregularities. We had to shut down the electronic display. We had to resort to desktop spreadsheets to collate all the results. On 6 May 1994, Kriegler and I stepped up onto a televised podium at Gallagher

Estate in Midrand and announced the national and provincial results. In the press conference that followed, I was asked by a journalist whether I would be available to repeat this electoral feat. I remember it well. And I remember my answer, too – which was an emphatic 'No'. Unlike me, Johann Kriegler said he would consider doing it again. And as history showed, he became the first chairperson of the IEC after the 1994 elections.

The very day after we had read out the results, I was called from my office to Johann Kriegler's office. There were two matters to be discussed. One was a threatening court application by Tony Leon from the Democratic Party on the ground that there had been several irregularities at the main Johannesburg voting station and at the Nasrec counting station. The other matter related to the results in KwaZulu and Natal. Present in the office were Mr Jacob Zuma and Dr Nkosazana Dlamini-Zuma. My attitude in the meeting was straightforward. Yes, there may have been irregularities in certain aspects of the electoral process, but that was not the only question the law required the IEC to ask. The other question was whether the elections were substantially free and fair. I insisted that, despite the irregularities, the elections reflected the will of the people. They were not only free, but they were also substantively fair. If any of the parties were minded to litigate, the IEC would certainly resist the litigation. But the more important consideration was whether the litigation would sully or soil an electoral outcome which in substance reflected the voice of the people. I added that if the elections in KwaZulu and Natal were to be subverted, even by a court order, the country could be courting the bloodshed which we all had done so much to avoid by ensuring that everyone who wanted to participated in the elections.

Tuesday, 10 May 1994, was a propitious day. It was historic in the best senses of the word. The event meant our world would never be the same again. Nelson Mandela was inaugurated as president of the first democratic Republic of South Africa. It was a moment that no words can easily capture. When we arrived at the Union Buildings, Kabo and I were led along the red carpet to front-row seats just behind heads of state from virtually the whole world. We took our seats close to Johann Kriegler and his partner. Our prominent seats in the oval of the Union Buildings spoke to the privilege we had in conducting elections that led to Nelson Mandela's inauguration. At a personal level, I had an indescribable sense of vindication and achievement. It is not often that one embarks on a path of revolution and lives to realise a significant part of the idealised change.

CHAPTER 31

Back to the Bar, acting judge and Constitutional Court nomination

With the inauguration festivities behind me, I returned to my chambers at the Pretoria Bar. Despite my prolonged absence, word quickly went around amongst the attorneys that I had returned. Briefs started flowing in quick and fast. The kind of legal work I received became markedly different from what I used to do before the start of democracy. What was more, several of the briefs were from the office of the state attorney, which ordinarily acts for cabinet ministers and state departments. It felt strange. Throughout my career, I had always bowled from the other end. I had earned my professional joy from taking wickets of the government, but now I had to get used to acting for the ruling elite and well-resourced people in society.

Amongst the many briefs I received, I remember one from the state attorney to act on behalf of Prince Mangosuthu Buthelezi, who had become our minister of home affairs. My instructions were to defend a constitutional challenge against an old-order piece of legislation that prohibited the possession or other uses of pornographic materials. I told my instructing attorney that I thought the law was plainly invalid. He quickly came back to say that the minister thought not. And that the court, not me, should make the call. The matter went to the Constitutional Court, and we lost.[38] The legislation was found to offend the free expression guaranteed in our constitution.

In another matter, I was briefed to appear for the owner, Mr Andrew Phillips, of the Sleepy Hollow Hotel in Rivonia. He sought an interdict to

prevent rogue police from harassing his business operations and customers under the pretext that he was running a brothel. Mr Phillips must have
thought the world had changed. He seemed to think a competent black
counsel might be more suitable to pursue his case than otherwise.

The practice fun did not last long. During June 1994, my phone rang and
Judge President Eloff invited me to come and perform a stint as an acting
judge at the High Court in Pretoria from 25 July 1994. The convention then
was that it was not open to a senior counsel to turn down an invitation of
that sort. From July to September 1994, I served for one term as an acting
judge of the Supreme Court, as it was then known.

Serving as an acting judge was yet another irony in my life. I lived in a
democratic country. I was a senior counsel – of some repute, I might add.
Thus it was appropriate that I was offered an acting-judge stint on the High
Court bench at which I had practised for many years. But I couldn't help
but remember that I now sat as a judge in the very same court in which I
had been charged and convicted 30 years earlier. That portion of the irony I
could process more easily. I had long learned not to feel like a runaway slave
who would feel chained long after the shackles had fallen off.

But something still jolted me. One morning after a court sitting, I walked
into the judges' tea room for the 11:15am tea break. Seated on one of the high-
backed red leather chairs was an elderly gentleman with a full crop of white
hair. His rather ruddy, slightly chubby and sagging old face looked famil-
iar. It was Peet Cille – the judge who sentenced me to ten years on Robben
Island. He must have retired long before. In my years as counsel, I never
appeared before him as a judge in active service. I speculated that he might
have popped in for tea as nostalgic retired judges occasionally do. Perhaps
he was finishing off an innocuous commission he picked up before the end
of the old government. Nelson Mandela would probably have walked up to
him and given him a warm handshake and perhaps a bear hug. I did not
know how I would have come out on that encounter. I was saved by the gong.
Teatime ended and I hurried off to resume my court hearing at 11:30am.

I enjoyed my acting-judge stint. Most of the judges knew me from my long practice at the Bar. Judge President Eloff allocated me to sit with him in most appeals. At the end of the acting appointment, he asked me to consider accepting a nomination to be appointed permanently. I politely thanked him for the invitation, but was careful not to promise anything.

One morning my chamber phone rang. It was Nomzamo Winifred Madikizela-Mandela. She broke into a big infectious laugh, saying: 'Comrade senior counsel, *ndim*' (it's me).

'Are you well, Mama?' I asked.

'Jo! Jo!' came the reply. 'uMadiba, the president, has fired me. You must do something.'

I roped in Vincent Maleka as my junior and the following day we had an extended consultation with Mrs Mandela.

During May 1994, the president appointed Mrs Mandela deputy minister of social affairs. The president had issued a directive that no minister or deputy minister of state may travel abroad without his prior consent. The deputy minister accepted an invitation to travel to Ghana. She travelled without the prior consent of the president. The trip was widely covered in the public media, and when she returned home, the president called her in and fired her at point-blank range.

The interim constitution contained provisions on a government of national unity. The president was obliged to consult with the two deputy presidents – Thabo Mbeki and FW de Klerk – as well as Prince Buthelezi when he wanted to change the make-up of government ministers. In the haste to dispatch his defiant and estranged wife, Mr Mandela did not consult. Prince Buthelezi quickly confirmed on enquiry and was happy to say so on affidavit. That was enough for our case. It mattered not that the president might have consulted both his deputies.

There I was, called on to sue our brand-new president, one with whom I had more than a passing acquaintance at that. But there was no professional discomfort on my part. If I was available and I was offered a brief in any dispute, I was obliged to accept it, and so I did. Overnight, Maleka and I prepared the papers for an urgent application to the High Court. A short while after the papers were served on the presidency, counsel for the president called me and conceded that Mrs Mandela's dismissal was unlawful and invalid. She was thus entitled to resume her office as deputy minister and to be paid costs of her case. The victory was short-lived. Even before we raised our glasses, the president fired her again – this time lawfully.

Chief Justice Michael Corbett called for nominations to fill the new Constitutional Court judicial posts. Someone, or perhaps a lawyer organisation, nominated me. In a moment of weakness, I accepted the nomination. I must have been suitably flattered that someone thought I could be shot up to the top of the judicial pile instantly. The chief justice sent me an invitation to the interview. I developed a deep sense of discomfort. The evening before the interview, I faxed him a letter withdrawing my acceptance of the nomination. I did not want to be a judge at that time. It was too early. I was in my 40s. My children were at secondary school and a civil servant salary would not have seen them through. I thought a decade from then I would have acquired the thoughtfulness and demeanour the task called for. Also, there was no shortage of talent from which to populate the court. Lastly, I did not want to be fenced into a public office so early after the start of the democratic government. I was entitled the room to weigh carefully my options as a free person. I had cleverly eschewed political office. I felt unhappy to be caught in another version of public office immediately. I wanted to reclaim a personal and private space. If you like, after more than 30 years of unremitting struggle and activism, I wanted to take a short break and put my feet up.

I chose to stay on at chambers and continued to be blessed with fascinating legal work. I was ably supported by young junior counsel who had started to trickle into practice in Johannesburg and Pretoria and, on occasion, in Durban and the Eastern Cape. These included Ish Semenya, McCaps Motimele, Mojanku Gumbi, Kgomotso Moroka, Vincent Maleka, Modise Khoza, Soraya Hassim, Lindiwe Nkosi-Thomas, Nathan Ponnan and Dion Basson.

In 1992, Legoai Pitje was murdered in mysterious circumstances by a policeman. His killer was tried, convicted and sentenced to death. When

Legoai died, he was the first and longest-serving black member of the Johannesburg Bar. When I came to do pupillage at the Johannesburg Bar, he was my senior and he had mentored me on the ways of surviving in a fraternity that was, in many ways, alien. On almost every working day we had lunch together and we shared many after-work social activities. Our friendship flourished. His sudden and violent death left me not only distraught but also with a huge personal void – a jolting reminder of just how mortal we are.

Legoai's widow, Mrs Spatyana Pitje, sued the state and sought to hold it vicariously liable for the demise of Legoai – caused by an off-duty police officer known loosely as Rodney. The claim was ripe for trial in 1995. Four of us volunteered to appear for Legoai's widow. I led a team of sparky young advocates: Ish Semenya, Vincent Maleka and Kgomotso Moroka. Our unenviable challenge in court was to show that when Rodney murdered Legoai, he did so as a police officer who was acting within the course of his employment. Only the murderer, Rodney, could salvage our case. He should know why he murdered Legoai and whether it was in furtherance, albeit misconceived, of the mission of the police.

Ish Semenya and I went to consult with Rodney, who was being kept on death row in the maximum-security section of Pretoria Central Prison. I inferred from his quivering lips and staring eyeballs – they looked as if they were about to drop out of their sockets – that this might have been Ish's first visit to the terrifying place of death. I think I was calmer. I had been to the death row once before, when attorney Griffiths Mxenge had asked me to get Andrew Zondo to sign a power of attorney for an appeal against his death sentence. In 1986, Zondo had been found guilty for planting a limpet mine in Amanzimtoti that killed five civilians. He was sentenced to death by Judge Raymond Leon at the Scottburgh Circuit Court. He was nineteen years old at the time of the offence and 20 when he was hanged.[39]

Rodney was brought out of his death-row cell to the consulting rooms where Ish Semenya and I were waiting. He was emaciated and pale. His speech was incoherent and loud, and he seemed hard of hearing. His eyes were enlarged and he never blinked. He kept a piercing eye contact. He repeatedly asked whether talking to us would help spare his life, which wondrous promise we could not make. Months of waiting for one's death on a certain day will get anyone mindless and Rodney was raving mad. There was no way he was going to advance the course of Mrs Pitje's civil claim. We could not possibly put a madman in the witness stand. Even more importantly, we could not extract the truth of the circumstances in which Legoai died. Only Rodney knew and he was now mad.

Leveson J held against the widow and dismissed her claim for loss of support. The judge held that the policeman had killed Legoai 'whilst on a frolic of his own'. It hurt deeply. Legoai was a professional colleague, brother and friend to all four of us who were also his counsel. In time, the murderer escaped the noose. Unlike Zondo, his death sentence was not carried through, because, since 1990, the government agreed to a moratorium on hangings. In time, his death sentence was reprieved in light of the Constitutional Court ruling that declared the death penalty inconsistent with the constitution.[40]

I came out of Legoai's trial with a bleeding and twisted nose. Perhaps his nightmarish and abortive case was my parting shot from just over fifteen years of active and rewarding law practice.

CHAPTER 32

Telkom and NAIL

The phone at my advocates' chambers rang. 'Dr' Pallo Jordan had been appointed by Mr Mandela as the minister of posts, telecommunications and broadcasting, and it was he who was on the other end of the phone. By then Pallo and I had built a considerable friendship in arms. This began mainly in Harare on an evening at the sumptuous home of Dr Ibbo Mandaza. Pallo and I were attending patriotic-front meetings between the ANC and PAC in Harare in 1991. At the end of one of the days, Ibbo invited both of us to his home for dinner and drinks. Both Ibbo and Pallo were long-standing revolutionaries on the African continent. Ibbo had apparently fought in the army of Robert Mugabe's ZANU and Pallo had been exiled for decades while serving the ANC. So this was a marvellous evening, if you like, of three-cornered conversations about post-colonial Africa and a wide range of other socio-political trends on the continent and abroad. The food was good, as was the conversation. But the wine was even better. The evening crept up on us through to the early hours of the morning. That intellectual merrymaking probably halved Pallo's and my usefulness on the second day of the bilateral meeting. After Harare, Pallo and I met a good few times during the course of the 1991-to-1994 transition.

Today Pallo explained that the new democratic state had inherited Telkom, which had been recently severed from the Post Office. Telkom had been registered as a public company in which the state owned all the shares.

Pallo planned to reconstitute its entire board in order to make it more class-, race- and gender-diverse. He saw Telkom as a vital cog in modernising communication in the new democracy. He talked at a high level about the digital revolution, and about the urgent need for a major broadband infrastructure and a greater access to telephony by the previously marginalised people in communities. I wondered why I deserved this lecture on what Telkom could be. Then he popped the question and I said 'Yes' – but only after insisting that Pallo obtain a clear mandate from the president to appoint me.

That was how I became the chairman of Telkom. The point about the mandate was this: I wanted to be a presidential appointee. In that way, I would enjoy sovereign support in the work I was asked to do. Also, Pallo would not feel free to terminate my appointment without the nod of the president. Pallo and I went ahead to put together a collection of very talented and diverse South Africans to serve with me on the new board. They included Ms Wendy Luhabe (she was a new breed of entrepreneur – also founder and co-executive director of Wiphold); Ms Fatima Jakoet, a chartered accountant and auditor from the Western Cape; and Mr David Sussman, the executive chairman of the JD Group.

The initial understanding was that I would give Telkom two working days a week. After a few months, however, it was quite clear that although my role was that of a non-executive, there were many issues that required a resident chairman. Telkom had to be restructured into a new company in most senses of the word. Over 90 per cent of its management were white males. The balance of the workforce of nearly 90 000 technicians and labourers were black men and women. It was mainly a voice company in a world where revenues had to be derived increasingly from digital communication. It was a fixed-line company at a time when mobile telephony was knocking hard at the door. Its national infrastructure had to be reimagined in many drastic ways. The urgent task that was beckoning was to provide a massive fibre-optic roll-out in the fast-growing major metropoles across the country. The one big example was Sandton, where every street block seemed to be under high-rise construction. I quickly gathered that Telkom's profitability levels were compromised by operational and executive ineptness in a number of areas. The tender process – the purchase of goods and services – of the company occurred within well-formed patronages and to the benefit of a few boys of cosy clubs.

Very quickly the challenge of my new role as the supremo of Telkom became all-consuming. It was different from law practice. And yet, my legal experience afforded me the facility to learn new things fast and to implement them in a given regulatory framework. My new role was analytical as well as practical and goal driven. Telkom had the potential to make lots of money for the state and the people, but also for many corporates that depended on its telecommunications and digital solutions. Accessible and cost-effective communication could turn around the lives of residents and small-business people for the better. In my usual idealism, I could visualise a national telecommunications company that could become a significant catalyst for true social change. I was not naive. As I assumed the role, I knew that legislation entrusted Telkom with a duty to permit authorised interception of telecommunication for valid national security reasons for the fight against crime.

One of my prime key performance areas was to find a new chief executive officer. The board authorised a full-scale local and international search for a person who would help formulate and implement the new vision of the company. The search and subsequent interviews ultimately yielded Dr Brian Clarke, who before then was the CEO of the Council for Scientific and Industrial Research (CSIR). The marching orders of the company were uncomplicated. The company called for a radical restructuring in pursuit of transformation of the economy and heightened levels of profitability.

Within a few months of my joining the board, Pallo and I agreed that I would become a full-time chairperson. This meant that my practice at the Bar would be the casualty. The idea of giving up the practice of law was radical and frightening, but I was a citizen of a new world that called for fresh and bold ventures, which before then were simply out of reach for reasons that had nothing to do with talent or ability. The prospects of helping to direct a gigantic state enterprise thrilled me no end. It offered me a change from the arduous lawyering through the turbulent preceding two decades. I was excited by the promise of what the digital revolution could bring to the world. I knew nothing about the technical and engineering underpinnings of that revolution, but I saw no reason why I could not be one of the inspired front-runners.

My new task was poised to open up an entire world for me. And it did. Every other year I had to attend the international and regional telecommunications union conferences. I met and made acquaintances and friends with CEOs, chairpersons and presidents of mighty telecommunications companies from around the world. Senior management at Telkom took every effort to tutor me quickly on the fundamentals of the business and the broad technical trends. I began to sound like a real telecoms boffin. I even garnered the courage to deliver papers at a good few local conferences.

Kabo and I went to Davos as part of the South African entourage at the beginning of every year. In time Jay Naidoo became minister of posts, telecommunications and broadcasting, and with him we travelled the developing and developed world to study and examine their offerings, which might be suitable for the drastic transformation of Telkom. We were also in search of a strategic partner who would join us in the renewal of Telkom's technical operations. Brian Clarke, Jay Naidoo and I became locked into complicated negotiations structuring a transaction which would secure Telkom a strategic partner. We ended up signing up SBC Telecom from the USA and Telekom Malaysia.

Perhaps the most gripping tale that came out of my early years as chairman of Telkom was related to Vodacom, a virtual subsidiary of Telkom. Alan Knott-Craig was its CEO, and Telkom had a 50 per cent board participation through a shareholders' agreement with its partner, Vodafone. Mr Knott-Craig appeared before the board and sought to persuade us that Vodacom needed shareholder loans adding up to R1 billion. This meant Telkom had to advance R500 million. Before then, I had never heard of so much money let alone been called upon to approve its disbursement. The other shareholders would advance the balance.

Alan was a young and outstanding engineer who, shortly before my time, was hand-picked by Telkom to develop a mobile telephony business at Vodacom. In the boardroom, he sat towards the end of the horseshoe-shaped table. He had set up a projector earlier for his presentation. He looked rather young and very edgy. As a lawyer would do, I fired a question that I hoped went to the heart of the matter.

'Why must Telkom lend your company half a billion rand?'

'Mr Chairman, I plan to build base stations all along the N1, N2, N3 and N4 highways,' he replied.

'What are base stations?' I asked.

He pulled out a flipchart, put it up and frantically started drawing a series of intersecting circles, all the while explaining what a cell was and how a signal could be relayed from base station to base station built along a highway. Each would have a radius of transmission. The intersecting cellular pattern would allow motorists or passengers to make uninterrupted mobile calls during a road trip.

'Mr Chairman, I need the money to build base stations so that everyone on our roads may communicate wherever and whenever they choose to do so.'

I was simultaneously stumped and amazed by the thought. It sounded like over-the-top techy imaginings. Who would want to chat on the phone and drive a motor vehicle at the same time? Like a petulant lawyer out of his depth, I fired back.

'Mr Knott-Craig, are we going to spend so much money so that people could have the fun of chatting during motor-vehicle trips?'

'Yes, Mr Chairman. The more people use their mobile phones, the more Vodacom and Telkom will make money. So to speak, the till will never stop ringing, Mr Chairman.'

I was both naive and wrong. Alan Knott-Craig was spot on. He persuaded me and the rest of the board. I sponsored and supported the resolution to give Vodacom R500 million of Telkom's money, which converted in time to equity of nearly R100 billion due to Telkom.

My first term of appointment was for five years, starting from 1995. It was renewed in 2000 for a further five years. During the course of the first term, Dr Brian Clarke left the company and I acted as CEO for nearly two years while the board was in search of a new CEO. The search yielded Mr Sizwe Nxasana. At that point I assumed my role as a non-executive chairman.

I did not propose to beat any drums about the success of the company on many fronts while I was chairman of the board. That positive trajectory is well recorded in the annual reports of the company from 1995 through 2001. The reports were meticulously prepared and are filled with copious technical, operational and financial data. It gave me great joy that the company consistently paid shareholder dividends that ran into a few hundreds of millions each quarter.

The low point of my tenure, I think, was approving executive management plans to retrench a large number of workers for what was termed 'operational reasons'. SBC Telecom and Telekom Malaysia took the view that the workforce was way in excess of the actual operational needs of the company. They were unashamedly saying that with fewer working people the company would make more profit. The partial privatisation of Telkom certainly invited an unintended human cost. The board approved the retrenchment plans of management. The least the board could do was ensure that the retrenchment packages were as generous and palliative as they could be in order to soften the blow on workers. Still, it was painful. It was a big blot on my otherwise pretty corporate canvas.

My thrilling stay at Telkom suggested to me that I could develop a corporate career that would advance my personal and material interest. In law practice, you earn every cent through hard work and slog over late nights. Corporate leadership, too, demands diligence and intellect, but the financial rewards in business leadership are plainly much more than in legal practice.

Dr Nthato Motlana, whom I had known for many years throughout the struggle, asked to see me, and on an evening in 1995 he came to my residence in Atteridgeville. He was accompanied by a gentleman I had not met before named Jonty Sandler. Dr Motlana and I exchanged pleasantries in the Setswana language, which we share. Kabo came to the lounge to greet

Dr Motlana and Jonty. It turned out that Nthato's and Kabo's mothers both attended the same school – the renowned St Peter's High School. Dr Motlana quickly moved to the purpose of the visit. He let Jonty Sandler tell me about the vision of establishing a black-owned and black-controlled diversified and listed company. New Africa Investments Limited (NAIL) would be the vehicle for that vision. Dr Motlana joined in to explain the vision to set up a 'black Anglo American corporation' led by trusted and credible African leaders. He and Jonty were planning to put together an executive team that would ensure that NAIL procured a strong pipeline of corporate acquisitions. In short, the growth of NAIL would be both organic and by acquisitions.

They said they had approached Zwelakhe Sisulu, who was then the CEO of the SABC. In principle, he was agreeable to joining NAIL at the end of his contract with the SABC, with the portfolio of developing and running NAIL's media assets. NAIL had just acquired an overwhelming majority shareholding in the newspaper *The Sowetan*.

Dr Motlana explained that his dream team would also include Cyril Ramaphosa. At the time Cyril was a member of parliament and chairperson of the constituent assembly, which was entrusted with the duty to draft and adopt the final constitution. Jonty and Nthato had already held preliminary discussions with him and he had expressed his willingness to join the NAIL executive team when his constitution-making obligations ended in early 1996. Cyril was tipped to set up and run a significant mining and resources division at NAIL. The envisaged portfolio fitted rather well with his extended exposure to mining and resources when he led the National Union of Mineworkers (NUM) over a number of years.

Dr Motlana said he thought that I would complement that executive team. He would serve as group chairman while Cyril, Zwelakhe, Jonty and myself would serve as executive deputy chairmen, each responsible for a discrete division of the business. He suggested that my responsibility would be to look after the financial services assets of NAIL. By then NAIL had bought a small shareholding in Metropolitan Life from Sanlam Limited with a call-and-put arrangement to acquire up to 51 per cent of Metropolitan Life. Jonty explained that the suite of financial services would include a merchant bank and a retail bank. My role, he told me, would require me to relinquish any executive or full-time role at Telkom, and assume an executive role at NAIL.

The total vision and the plan to achieve it sounded most impressive. There was little doubt that I was being invited into a fascinating venture to create a dream corporation that would set the trend for black economic empowerment. After the discussion, I took time out to think about the invitation. In our second meeting, Jonty thought that the time had come to tilt the scales. He flipped open a chart, which showed the controlling corporate structure of NAIL. If I were to accept their proposal, I would be allocated a shareholding in the private company that controlled NAIL with a combination of ordinary and 'N' shares. The controlling company also tendered a restraint-of-trade payment and an attractive annual remuneration package. They explained that the offer would be in every way the same as the one that would be made to Cyril Ramaphosa and Zwelakhe Sisulu. I accepted.

By the end of 1995, I had started setting up office at the NAIL head office in Epsom Downs while I remained non-executive chairman of Telkom. In 1996 I went on a search for a professional assistant. This resulted in the appointment Ms Lesley Grobler, who was to become a central figure in my corporate career. Young as she was, she displayed incredible loyalty. She paid attention to detail. She took care of a great deal and managed my office with remarkable effectiveness. Her role was particularly important because I was still spending two days a week fulfilling my responsibilities at Telkom. In my absence, she held the fort admirably. When I ultimately canned my corporate career, I had no hesitation in inviting Lesley to join me in a comparable role at the Constitutional Court.

Between 1996 and 2001, much of the initial vision of NAIL was achieved. Zwelakhe went on to build a sizeable integrated media portfolio. He acquired more print media assets in addition to *The Sowetan*. He also bought radio assets. To them, he added Urban Brew, a reputable media and television production house. NAIL also bought, through New Africa Books, a controlling stake in David Philip Publishers.

In the portfolio I ran, we went on to acquire a majority shareholding in

Metropolitan Life Limited. In time I became the chairman of Metropolitan with the majority of board members appointed by NAIL. In 1997 NAIL founded African Merchant Bank (AMB), which it also controlled. I also chaired that board of directors. Within a year of its formation, under the stewardship of Rob Dow and a skilful team, which included transaction experts such as Andrew Sprague, Zenzo Lusengo, Carel van der Merwe and Chris Vosloo, NAIL took AMB to the Johannesburg Stock Exchange. The initial listing was a roaring financial success. The share price rose to many multiples of its listing offering. Not long thereafter, using NAIL's highly rated paper, through a share swap we acquired a majority shareholding in Theta Group. We instantly re-baptised it as 'African Bank Limited'. Thereabout, the NAIL market capitalisation had grown to a staggering R14 billion.

The good rarely comes without the ugly. Cyril Ramaphosa's stay at NAIL was short-lived. He had a falling-out with Jonty Sandler and chose to leave. Cyril and I had become good friends and it was truly sad to see him tender his resignation from NAIL. He left together with his support staff, which included people like Ms Donné Cooney. Then a crisis of a different kind struck. It was unpalatable and led to the departure of Jonty Sandler from NAIL. Dr Motlana chose to tender his resignation in support of Jonty's departure. The crisis was about share options issued by the board to the executive team. When the share options were issued, they carried a rather modest value given the level of the NAIL share price. The value of the executive share options rose through the roof. It was tracking the highly enhanced market rating of the NAIL share that was seemingly propped, by the sharp rise of the AMB and Metropolitan share prices.

Of course the share options were disclosed in the company's final accounts. Institutional shareholders objected to the size of the share options and their enhanced value. The institutions demanded that the options be given up or reduced. Jonty's attitude was that the share options had been properly allocated and accrued, and should not be relinquished. Zwelakhe and I, in the executive committee deliberations, took a different view. We acknowledged that the share options had become very rich and, although

331

they were properly and lawfully issued, that they should be relinquished. Shareholders were entitled to raise their disapproval. Zwelakhe and I relinquished the share options. Jonty Sandler and Dr Motlana left the company against payment to them of an agreed sum.

The NAIL dream team was dealt a severe, if not mortal, blow. The market rerated the share price downwards. Some of the gloss had been taken off that fairy tale and, going forward, the corporate enterprise needed a rethink. One such effort happened when Marinus Daling, the chairman of Sanlam, and I agreed to explore a possible merger of the life houses of Sanlam and Metropolitan to create a transformed financial services behemoth. Sadly, Daling died before the negotiations were brought to fruition.

In 2001, Zwelakhe and I sold our controlling stake in NAIL to Wiphold and Safika Holdings controlled by Saki Macozoma and Moses Ngoasheng. Shortly thereafter, NAIL was delisted and its assets were sold off.

CHAPTER 33

The bench beckons again

On 30 October 1999, I was in Twickenham, London, watching a rugby Test match between South Africa and England. Unsurprisingly, nearly half the people in the stands were wearing Springbok jerseys. Those who weren't wore our scarves or were certainly waving our new multi-coloured flag. Cheers in Afrikaans from row to row were loud and combative: '*Vat hulle, manne, vat hulle!*' Alwyn Martin, a good friend who then was chairman of Vodacom, loved rugby and was making many bellicose cheers for the Springboks. Another friend, Nazeer Camroodien a travel agent, was sitting next to Alwyn.

Alwyn's phone rang and he left his seat to take the call. When he came back his face was sombre. He turned to me and said, 'You have to go home immediately. Your father has taken seriously ill.' Instantly, my navel sank tightly into my belly. I developed a yawn and a cold tremble. My sixth sense was adamant that my father was not only ill, but had died. I flew home overnight and I arrived at his residence to find many cars on the street. My worst suspicion became fact. My father was 77 years old but played golf regularly. On the fateful day he had played with Tiego, my brother, at Pretoria West Country Club. Tiego told me that our father had hit a remarkable shot towards the eighteenth green. Then he walked slowly over to a big tree off the fairway, lay down under its shade and passed on. We have marked that hallowed ground under the shade with a little stone memorial. To this day, when I play at Pretoria West Golf Club, I walk up to the memorial in humble awe.

I evoke the passing on of my father because he often said to me: 'I wonder why you left law for business. It does not become you. You, my son, are a lawyer to the core. You should have stayed on as a judge after your acting-judge stint. That is where you belong. You are likely to make a bigger difference there than in business.'

When the bench started beckoning again, my father was no longer there. It would have pleased him no end to know that I was seriously considering accepting a permanent appointment on the bench.

Even before I sold my stake in NAIL at the beginning of 2001, Mojanku Gumbi invited me to an informal meeting with President Mbeki. At the time she was serving as the legal adviser to the president. I had met with the president a good few times throughout my stay in business as chairman of Telkom. I regularly presented Telkom's corporate plans to him and Minister Ivy Matsepe-Casaburri, who represented the majority shareholder in Telkom. The meeting Mojanku arranged was of a different timbre. President Mbeki said he thought that I would better serve the people by assuming the role of a judge.

I was guarded. I did not make any undertaking to him that I would quit corporate life. The decision whether to become a judge was mine alone. Mbeki must have sensed my reticence, so Arthur Chaskalson joined the fray. He called me into his judge's chambers at the Constitutional Court and made the argument that I was required to do my bit to advance a diverse and representative bench. Not long thereafter, Mr Mandela weighed in, insisting that I go onto the bench. For his part, he said, I should have been a judge from 1994.

I resigned from the board of Telkom. I left NAIL, having sold my control equity, and I resigned from all other corporate appointments. At the invitation of Judge President Bernard Ngoepe, I started my stint as an acting judge at the High Court in Pretoria from 30 July 2001. As the news became public, the media speculated far and wide that I had been tipped to become chief justice in due course. That was news to me. No one had made that undertaking, nor could it be lawfully made. Mr Mandela attended one of the three farewell gala dinners organised by various entities to see me off from the business world. He was asked to say a few words. Totally out of turn, he chuckled and blurted out a remark, which had no factual foundation: 'Dikgang will be our next chief justice.' He stunned his audience. Everyone knew, however, that he could not make good his fanciful wish. He was a retired president and a 'jobless pensioner', as he often wryly referred to himself.

My acting-judge stint at the High Court was uneventful. After a friendly interview before the Judicial Services Commission (JSC) chaired by Chief Justice Chaskalson, on 29 September 2001 I was appointed by President Mbeki as a permanent judge of the High Court. At the interview, Arthur disclosed his efforts to get me to accept a nomination for an appointment. So did Advocate Marumo Moerane SC.

What stood out during my short stay at the High Court was an assignment in Zimbabwe in 2002. The president appointed Judge Sisi Khampepe and me as a judicial envoy to investigate and report on the legal framework for conducting elections in Zimbabwe, and whether the framework had been complied with. The chief justice called me and said the envoy of judges was highly unusual, but that he had been consulted and he approved. Alongside our envoy, the president appointed a much larger and diverse delegation of eminent South Africans led by Dr Sam Motsuenyane.

Sisi and I stayed in Zimbabwe for a few weeks leading up to the national elections. We produced a report and handed it to the president. In it, Sisi and I held that the electoral regulatory framework had been breached in many material ways and that the elections were not free and fair. The president chose not to make our report public. The majority report of the Motsuenyane Commission held the elections to be free and fair. Its findings were made public. Sisi and I declined to disclose our report and directed the public media to the presidency. Both the Mbeki and Zuma administrations chose not to disclose the report to the public. Litigation followed and lasted for nearly ten years, during which the *Mail & Guardian* newspaper sought to compel the disclosure of our report. The report saw the light of day on the order of the Supreme Court of Appeal in 2014.[41]

The Zimbabwe report stress-tested our independent-mindedness, even though I was a new and junior judge. Sisi and I kept the appropriate judicial aloofness and distance even when we knew well what outcome in our report the president preferred. Dr Nkosazana Dlamini-Zuma, who then served as the minister of foreign affairs, and Mojanku Gumbi summoned Sisi Khampepe to a meeting and made plain their unhappiness about the report. She came back and assured me that our report remained unchanged. We were unanimous in our findings and she had not been persuaded to alter her stance. A decade later, when the report was revealed, I felt a deep sense of pride. We had done the right thing even in a closeted report. I was grateful for my judicial sense of right and wrong. I had the steadfast facility to make the call I considered correct even in the face of displeasure at high places of government. Sisi and I 'spoke truth to power' even when it was inexpedient and might have narrowed our career progression.

Within a year of my stay at the High Court, I was nominated for elevation to the Constitutional Court. The JSC recommended me, and President Mbeki appointed me a judge of the Constitutional Court on 1 November 2002. Clearly, he did not think that our difference on the legal validity of the Zimbabwe elections was a ground to resist my judicial progression. It may well be that he was enchanted by my judicial distance and forthrightness. He must have understood that I meant to be a good judge for all our people, and a good judge doesn't suck up to authority or to anyone else. A good judge neither solicits nor doles out favours. The single obsession is to pursue judicial truth, to dog only just outcomes in all causes.

In 2005, Chief Justice Chaskalson announced his retirement. Arthur left earlier than his term of office permitted, which meant he took a smaller pension. He was anxious to secure a stable and credible succession arrangement at the court. Had he seen out his full term, Pius Nkonzo Langa, his likely successor, would have served a short and ineffective stint as chief justice. After

Arthur's departure, President Mbeki announced his intention to appoint Pius Langa as chief justice (he was the deputy at the time) and to appoint me as his deputy. I was thrilled. I felt up to the new task and was fully committed to it. The JSC unanimously endorsed my nomination, and the president appointed me deputy chief justice on 1 June 2005.

I occupied this post, to my mind, with humility and pride for more than a decade, serving under three different chief justices. An intriguing tale is yet to be told as to why I was overlooked as many times and never became chief justice. That little yarn belongs in another book – my judicial memoir – and will be told when the time is right.

CHAPTER 34

My family hits a deadly patch

From the beginning of 2003, I began settling into my judicial chores at the Constitutional Court. Gradually, I began to appreciate the sheer size of the task and the enormous responsibilities it carried, but I felt well equipped to tackle the chores at hand. The Bar had hard-wired me into long hours and high-order industry. The endless tomes of reading I tackled with much gusto. Early in my career at the Bar, I had taken a crash course in speed reading. I had mastered discerning and comprehension skills that saw me glide past the unimportant detail towards the core issues. The judicial work demanded more than a hard slog. It imposed an intellectual rigour tempered only by the normative and equitable considerations of our first law. Every case was difficult to resolve. Each raised fresh societal and legal questions yet to be resolved. Correct answers were hard to come by. Only a few precedents of the past were useful. We had never had constitutional supremacy within a genuine democracy before. New law was meant to reimagine society. Often there was huge public interest in every pending decision.

Arthur Chaskalson had helped give me a soft landing at the court. He spared no moment to affirm and validate me. He was a brilliant lawyer without even a tinge of lawyer-like arrogance. He had a humble disposition that made him a compassionate leader who cared unstintingly for the democratic project. He was brilliant, modest and compassionate. His sound insight into legal rules was matched only by his humanism.

It was Arthur who allocated the first case in which I had to write a judgment for the court. *Thebus and Another v The State*[42] was a monster of a case to a new judge. It harked back to a dim past and yet had continued relevance. It raised the intricate question of whether the common-law doctrine of common purpose in criminal liability was still good law under the new constitutional order. The doctrine teaches that the criminal conduct of one or more perpetrators in the commission of a crime may be attributed to another accused if he or she is shown to have acted in furtherance of the same objective or common purpose. I hated the doctrine. It was a thinly disguised form of vicarious liability and had wreaked havoc in political trials of the recent past. The accused, known as the Sharpeville Six, were sentenced to death on common purpose. Many other activists had fallen foul of this legal rule. And yet, outside an emotive political setting, the doctrine still had social usefulness in combating violent group or organised crime. Arthur visited my chambers regularly and encouraged me to write as well as I could and, in time, I would benefit from the comments of the rest of the bench. With Arthur's careful nurturing, the common-purpose part of the judgment carried a unanimous vote of the court. It felt a little like a near-perfect drive off the first tee of a treacherous golf course. What woe that may lie ahead may be impossible to foretell, but even so, being decently off the first tee calls for a passing celebration.

Pius Nkonzo Langa was a quiet man – certainly less talkative than me – and he was a patient listener. He was also supportive and welcoming. He was blessed with quiet wisdom and judicial temperament. I did not know then that we would spend so many years together on the bench and that my judicial life and fate would be so closely tied to his.

Justice Johann Kriegler had just left the court and I inherited the vacancy, as well as his green judicial gown and court chambers. We had run the first democratic elections of 1994 together. For six months we had battled the demons of the democratic transition and emerged on the other side, after numerous skirmishes, rather fond of each other. He was the quintessential and coldly bright jurist yielded by the imperfect past regime. I was a child of our revolution. Now our different worlds but identical public tasks converged at the court again. His cutting blue eyes peered into my brown ones as he handed me his green gown and said: '*Kleinboet, veels geluk! Jy moet nou nie nonsense aanvang nie. Sterkte!*' (Little brother, congratulations! You must not go down the wrong alley. Best wishes!)

Other than Justice John Didcott, whose death, sadly, was rather untimely, and Justice Ismail Mahomed, who had moved on to head the Supreme Court of Appeal, the full complement of the justices appointed by President Nelson Mandela was still there. Laurie Ackermann and Richard Goldstone left within a year or two of my arrival. Colleagues such as Tholi Madala, Albie Sachs, Yvonne Mokgoro, Kate O'Regan, Zac Yacoob and Sandile Ngcobo had a long haul ahead and I had all the time to get to know them better.

Just when I thought my judicial life was placid and on track, excruciating personal loss was hovering. Pondering over death, African folklore cautions that death within a family never strikes once only. The ancestors rarely call up only one of their kith and kin. Bereavement tends to put up its tent at one family location for a while as one after another succumbs. Talking about this lived fear of multiple deaths, my mother, the matriarch of our family, would say: '*Bakwena! Modimo o re etetse*' (My people! God has paid us a visit).

Within a year of my stay at the court, Kabelo Moseneke, my brother, died. He passed on during October 2003, after a small surgical procedure and left a young widow, Merrikie, and a daughter, Boipelo. Losing him hurt deeply. My mother thought we had reason to fear because Kabelo passed on during the month of October. She drew much meaning from my father having succumbed during the month of October only a few years earlier.

Within six months of Kabelo's death, my wife's stepfather died. Daddy Mash, as I affectionately called him, addressed me as 'Yes, my boy' to his grave. My mother-in-law would admonish him to remember that I was a judge of a very, very big court. He would reply: 'Well done, my boy.' He was in his mid-80s when he succumbed, but it still hurt. His passing left my mother-in-law vulnerable, lonely and sickly. Both my mother- and father-in-law were not on the conventional hate list. I cared for them very much indeed, and they loved our children and their grandchildren without bounds. They were the very first circle of the village that brought up Kabo's and my children. When Kabo and I built our professional careers, the grandparents were always there to house, feed and look after the children. They were a big part of bringing up our children. In their old age, Kabo and I did everything we could to tend to their every need. We bought them a home near our own. We resisted putting them in an old-age home. It is not a done thing. Our common custom requires us to nurse elderly parents until they slip through our fingers. You forget at your peril what folklore teaches. Once they have passed on, your parents become your ancestors – your spiritual guardians. Who in his or her right mind wants to incur the wrath of looming ancestors?

On 31 October 2005, our second son, Botshelo 'Bo' Gabaiphiwe Moseneke, stopped breathing while in an intensive care unit. He gave his last breath in my full view. Every machine and gadget connected to his body went lame and quiet. All lights, measures, blips and indicators died. His body lay there, warm but lifeless. I shook him violently, pleading with him to rise and live again. The nurses quickly screened him off from the rest of the immediate world. My son Sedise and I stood inside the screen around Bo and wailed mindlessly. Kabo had opted to stay home during Bo's one-month stay in the ICU. How was I going to tell her of our common tragedy? It hurt to the bone.

Bo had been born with child-onset diabetes and he was fully insulin dependent. He fought the disease with remarkable valour and candour. He quickly knew all about the disease and managed it superbly. He went through a boarding high school at Christian Brothers College in Pretoria and he ran in school athletics. He played rugby and cracked the second team. He became the school tennis champion. He joined the school dramatic society and won several acting awards. He lived a full and wholesome life. After matric he took a gap year in Spain, where he attended an intensive tennis camp trying to qualify for junior Wimbledon. When he came home he went to Wits School of Drama, where he studied film, theatre and television. He worked as an intern at Radio 702 and later, still in his teens, became a TV presenter at Urban Brew. He was recruited into SuperSport, where he became a regular national sports anchor specialising in covering Grand Slam tennis tournaments and soccer matches. He also did many voice-overs on SuperSport's promotional content.

Bo travelled the world with me and Kabo. We spent two weeks at the Atlanta Olympics as a family. We spent time in New York – where Bo wanted nothing less than to dine at the Waldorf Astoria. Why? Well, he saw Eddie Murphy dine there in the movie *Coming to America*. He and Sedise came along with Kabo and me to London for nearly two weeks. Bo spared no moment to live fully as he and Sedise explored every corner of that sparky city. He came along to Switzerland and Germany and pried, asked, searched, wondered and marvelled. He went up the Austrian mountains and skied to his heart's content. He laughed heartily, wide-mouthed with narrowing eyes. He lived life to the hilt. He assured Dudu, Kabo, Sedise and me how much he loved us. A premonition perhaps?

On one fateful evening, I saw my son on TV present a SuperSport wrap-up after a football match in Cape Town. It was a cold, inclement evening and the rain was pouring down. He managed to put in his signature closing lines: 'May the good gods of Afrika bless and keep you wherever you may be on this beautiful continent. I am Bo Moseneke signing off. Good night.'

Bo contracted pneumonia the following day. In ICU, it became double pneumonia. His immune system could not fight back. He succumbed. It hurt then. It hurts now. It will hurt for ever. Kabo and I have made a little shrine in our home. It bears all things about Bo. Even more than ten years later, the little shrine stays lit and we pray and trust that the light will never set on our son, Botshelo.

My mother-in-law, Gertrude Nozizwe Masikwane, heard of Bo's passing on. She died within two weeks of Bo's death. Again it hurt. It hurt deeply. I do not think we have overcome the trauma. But closer to home, my life partner and soulmate, Kabonina, has never been the same again. We ask, pray and plead that in time she will find her sprightly stride once more.

CHAPTER 35

'What matters is what is good for our people'

My father despised birthday celebrations. He thought they were a fetish for those who needed an emotional crutch. He used to say birthdays come and go and no effort and money should be wasted on them. A little early morning happy birthday, greeting ought to be enough. Perhaps he owed this stoic lifestyle to his sparse upbringing during the Great Depression, but in our home we never celebrated birthdays. When Kabo was married into our family, she was quite stunned that we sometimes forgot each other's birthdays while she remembered all the birthdates of her inner and extended family members.

I turned 60 years of age. I thought there was magic in the number 60, although subjectively I thought I felt closer to 45 years. How quickly the years had gone! Not long before then, I was a little revolutionary and later a frail prisoner. Thereafter, I was a dashing young attorney followed by a highly geared practice as an advocate at the Bar. Also, in quick succession I became a husband and a father. And now there I was, a justice of the Constitutional Court and the deputy chief justice of the republic. I thought to myself, rather smugly, that even if my father turned in his grave I was going to mark my 60th birthday with a little party, surrounded by family and friends. Kabo supported the idea. In no time, the idea moved on to a joint party with Peter Vundla, who turned the same age at the same time as me. The venue was to be at Zimbali Coastal Resort, where we had a holiday home. The evening was truly well appointed. Peter and I invited friends in equal numbers and shared the costs. My family turned out resplendent and friends came from far and wide. It was a grand evening.

To much applause and shouts of 'Speech! Speech!' I rose to my feet. I started by going down memory lane. I recalled my upbringing and the meandering road since then to the point when I was elevated to the bench. I reiterated my gratitude of occupying public office as a judge and said that I had thought carefully about that choice before accepting an appointment. That was plainly so because I had a number of options in law practice, business and politics which were open to me. And yet in the end I turned my back on all of them to focus on a judicial role (which was still to unfold for close on another ten years). I made it quite clear that despite my sometimes tormented past and role in the revolution, I meant to be a good judge to the very core. Referring to the ruling party of the day, I made my position quite clear that when I perform my judicial role, what is important is not what the ANC or its delegates want, but what is good for all our people. In this context, the ANC meant no more than the ruling elite or those who wielded public power, whoever they may be. As I spoke, I said no more than to repeat the credo of every judge in our land.

There are laws in our constitutional democracy, starting with our first and supreme law, which is the constitution. We are all citizens, politicians and judges alike, compelled to obey the law. Judges do not make the law. Once a law is democratically adopted, it binds all. The primary function and duty of judges is to interpret and enforce the law. This they must do in relation to all in an even-handed and dispassionate manner. When it comes to the exercise of public power, judges must hold to the law those who wield such power. This is particularly important in order to ensure good governance, but also to advance a good and better life for all our people, irrespective of their vast, celebrated and well-protected diversity.

My address to the guests at my private party was reported in the *Sunday Times* newspaper the following morning, seemingly by an unknown and uninvited news reporter. Just about then the ANC was holding their annual conference in Polokwane, at which Thabo Mbeki lost the vote as president of the ANC to Jacob Zuma. Some, or many of them read into my statement much more than it was intended to convey. The ANC was a political party in turmoil, and some of its members were sniffing around for those who were supporters of Jacob Zuma or supporters of Thabo Mbeki. None of those divisions interested me in the least. It mattered not to me who was at the helm of the ruling party. I had a job to do and my business was to describe its content and how I intended to execute it – fairly and without fear or favour.

The Monday following the article in the *Sunday Times*, Kgalema Motlanthe and Mathews Phosa sought an urgent meeting with me and Pius Langa at the court. I explained to them what I had said and what it had meant. They assured me that they understood and were well satisfied with the discussions we had. They went off to make a press statement saying so.

Some people within the ruling party continued to cast aspersions at the statement. Throughout, I truly ignored insinuations that the declaration I had made at my birthday party was meant to be a mark of support for Thabo Mbeki or of opposition to Jacob Zuma. As my memoirs show, I have worked with both leaders in a variety of contexts, in circumstances of mutual respect and appreciation of our respective roles in the long struggle to free our people from debilitating oppression. The irony was this: I knew Jacob Zuma far better and longer than I knew Thabo Mbeki. I spent a decade with him on Robben Island. When Kabo and I went on honeymoon to Durban in 1975, it was Jacob Zuma who met us at the airport, hosted us and thereafter handed us over to comrades Griffiths and Victoria Mxenge. During the transition in the 1990s, Jacob Zuma and I did a lot to try to establish a patriotic front.

In contrast, I met Thabo Mbeki only in the 1990s, after his exile years. Each of them, alone or together, has made tremendous contributions, particularly in the days leading up to the transition to democracy. Both men wanted political power. I had no interest in their contestation. I had no business to take sides over who might suitably lead the ruling party. I have always seen myself as a freedom fighter and not a politician. My revolutionary zeal would have died under the rubble of expedient foot shuffling. I have made the point that politicians crave for power and influence and sometimes absolute control. They deal in expedience only in order to extend their power. A freedom fighter is animated by ideals of social and political justice. A freedom fighter is enthused by the prospect of a real and salutary alteration of power relations in society. And their conduct ought to be properly aligned to the pursuit of the ideal of liberation in its best senses.

In the judicial role I had chosen to play, it mattered not who led the ruling party. As my judicial mantra went, it was not what the ruling party, for the time being, wanted that mattered to me. Rather, it was always what was good for our people. That sometimes nebulous or perhaps tenuous public good is cordoned off by our chosen common ideals, which are sourced in great part from modern African humanism and finds an echo in our supreme law. If anyone, however powerful or weak, deviated from that grid of public good as encrusted into law and the values of the constitution, I was duty-bound to make that call. Our common convictions and ideals are meant to give space to the full potential of each of us and to maximise our common good

In the years that followed, I did my damnedest to stay true to my judicial credo. As I came to the end of my term of office, I looked back with gratefulness at the many decisions I had had the privilege to make and the many judgments that were meant to give effect to the common wishes of our people. I continue to live in hope that what I said at my 60th birthday party will be the article of faith of every patriot worthy of judicial office in our land.

Epilogue
Was it all in vain?

Mine is a long tale. I have written it up and am relieved that I managed do so. But in doing so, I have also told the story of our nation seen from my unique but narrow view point. I have related how we as a collective sought to a halt colonial oppression and its minion, social exclusion. So, the question whether it was all in vain has an inevitable duality. The first and easier answer would be limited to my personal journey, but the second and more pressing enquiry is whether the process of altering power relations in society and inducting a genuine democracy and freedom is on good course.

I start with the easier answer. My tale meanders from the dusty streets of Atteridgeville through to my secondary tuition and my untimely residence on Robben Island. Then I had no idea that my perilous experiences were to set me up for a life of remarkable challenge and fulfilment. The pain and adversity in my childhood prepared me for a lifelong commitment to conduct that hopefully would bring true and full liberation of our land and all its remarkable people.

'So I knew when I came out of Robben Island that I had to make a choice either to go into exile or to remain a combatant in the domestic struggle. I chose to do things the way I knew best: to become a lawyer of remarkable excellence, of unfailing integrity and of commitment to the broader struggle of our people in all their kinds, shapes and colours for an equal, inclusive and just society.

To that end, I wanted to become an attorney, even if I was a convicted 'terrorist'. I did everything possible to achieve that. I litigated against the Law Society to let me in. I went on to the Bar Council, which had a race clause that excluded black people. There, too, I kicked the door open. In our troubled past and in difficult times, I was very determined to become a spokesperson for our people.

Before the democratic transition had gained traction, I made a conscious choice not to be a politician but to remain a freedom fighter and a revolutionary. This I thought I could best achieve by resigning from all political formations and by concentrating on being a full-time legal practitioner. Aside from a little digression into business, I concentrated on becoming as good an activist lawyer and later a judge as I could be.

I defended every activist you care to remember. I searched for and found Umkhonto weSizwe cadres in solitary confinement. I saved a number of the Azanian People's Liberation Army combatants from state execution. I appeared in trials of Azanian National Liberation Army fighters. I had the privilege of defending Dr Fabian Ribeiro, Titus Mafolo, Smangaliso Mkhatshwa, Winnie Madikizela-Mandela, Jan Shoba, Clement Zulu, Achmad Cassiem, Nkosinathi Nhleko, Ingoapele Madingoane, Zwelakhe Sisulu, Thamsanqa Mkhwanazi, Thami Mazwai, Mathatha Tsedu, Ronnie Mamoepa, Don Nkadimeng and scores of other activists, as well as numerous trade union formations.

I had the blessing of a vast, varied and progressive law practice which was aligned with my personal and collective mantra that I was my own liberator and that our people are their own liberators. But more keenly, the sojourn on Robben Island set me on a course of constantly asking, what are the features of a good society?

Out of all this two cardinal lessons emerged. First, you cannot merely dream about your revolutionary ideals. You have to take real and concrete steps to pursue legitimate goals. The second lesson was that I was my own liberator. The phrase is copied from the inimitable revolutionary thinkers Anton Muziwakhe Lembede and Robert Mangaliso Sobukwe. They, in turn, must have borrowed it from Amílcar Cabral. These public intellectuals in essence were urging young people like me to pursue *inkululeko nge xesha lethu* – freedom in our lifetime.

As my mother often says, *di tshegofatso tsa Modimo ga dina tekanyetso* (the blessings of the Lord know no limit). The first of the blessings for me was near-perfect health in a young body. This allowed me no end of energy. I prosecuted a vigorous law practice across the length and breadth of our country amidst a people's revolt. For that, apartheid securocrats almost murdered me, not once but twice. In the fifteen years of my judicial service, I never once took sick leave; the only time I was away from work for a week was when my beloved son Bo succumbed. So a lifetime's dedication of hard work was what I brought to my judicial obligations.

The second blessing was the love I have and continue to have for our people, and foremost for those who live on the edges of society. They are entitled to live in a just and socially inclusive society where their dignity and self-worth are intact and cherished. They must have access to quality education, universal health care, water and sanitation; they deserve to have a place they can call home, an environment that is well preserved and, in all this, the space simply to be human. This explains why, at my 60th birthday party, I made the point and I make it again here: it is not what the ruling party wants, it is not what any other political elite wants, but rather it is what is good for our people that is important. That is what made me wake up in the morning and be a good justice of our highest court to the extent that all my faculties permitted me.

What a privilege it was to serve our people, and I am grateful that I was able to do my part. I have had the space to work, to think and to write to my heart's content. I have had the pleasure of writing on virtually every big political, social and commercial dispute in our land. I have delivered academic papers at law and justice conferences across our country and elsewhere. I have had the joy of going to law schools in this land and in other lands only to find extensive passages of what I have written taught to young lawyers in training. I have also had the privilege of training young people about the contours of our struggle history and their ever-present duty to guard over the genuine freedom of the people. I have been blessed with extraordinary colleagues, who made judicial collegiality appear natural and inbred. We kept together a remarkable apex court in the marvellous tradition started by Arthur Chaskalson, Pius Langa and the inaugural justices of the Constitutional Court.

My third blessing was the affection and support shown to me by many people of our country across social class, gender, race, religion or other lines of distinction. At funerals and functions, airports and supermarkets, at sports events and many other places and occasions, people have walked up to me to proffer a compliment or express their gratitude for my public duties. On my retirement I received hundreds of emails complimenting me on my career and contribution. Barring a few exceptions, most of the media, including a vibrant social media, have been as complimentary.

Outside my profession, I drew much satisfaction from community work – were this in my capacity as chancellor of Wits or for fifteen years as chairperson of the Nelson Mandela Children's Fund, together with other trustees and the wonderful stewardship of Sibongile Mkhabela, or by offering a couch and an ear to young people seeking support, career guidance and bursaries. I have enjoyed addressing grassroots and other social formations of a wide variety on our constitutional transition and debating their questions of deep disbelief or mistrust about whether the constitution meant anything for them.

Small personal joys were ample. I single out one. I remember well how a retired Mr Mandela would often invite me to breakfast or tea. I lived a few streets away from his residence in Houghton. Most visits turned out to be only a light chat about various things – except for one particular day. On that day he asked me if I would look after him in his absence. When he saw my expression of surprise, he cut to the chase. He said it was a fair question from an old man to a younger man. Tata went off to write his last will and testament and appointed me, together with George Bizos SC and Themba Sangoni JP, an executor of his deceased estate.

The day after Tata's sad demise it fell on me, armed with the will in my possession, to meet with President Jacob Zuma and to let him know of the extensive provisions in the will on the form of burial Tata had directed. The president readily assured me without demur that the burial provisions would be observed. As I went through the chores of giving effect to Mr Mandela's will, his words rang in my head again and again: 'Dikgang, will you look after me when I am not here?' It has been a rewarding privilege to serve him in his absence and a task I continue to carry out.

As I end, going back to where I started, I saw myself as my own liberator. Our people are their own liberators. In the last instance, the people are the bedrock of our democracy. It is they who matter and we, along with the institutions that wield public power, such as our courts, are in their service. This to me was the ultimate statement of personal and collective agency. We have to identify worthy causes that might change our lot and our communities and country. Immediately thereafter, we must ask the question that Lenin famously posed, 'What is to be done?' And then we must get up and do things – things that will move our personal worlds and bring us closer to our idealised collective condition of genuine freedom.

So my life journey has not been in vain, I want to think, and I am grateful for the space my nation favoured me to have, love, cherish and use, and for all the blessings my little efforts brought to me, my family and, hopefully, my country.

The more difficult question to answer is this one: was our democratic transition all in vain? There is no single and simple answer. I choose to start with the good news. We have managed a treacherous transition and set up ground rules that underscore our democratic ethos, public morality and governance. We have inducted a representative democracy premised on proportional representation and a closed party list. We have established and maintained a functional democratic state with all the customary markers, including multi-partyism, regular elections, and rule of law and separation of powers. Our parliamentary system functions more certainly at an elective than at a participatory level. In some parts of our country, local government functions and renders the basic services the law commands. Our fiscal and state treasury functions are not shabby and our revenue collection is world-class. Our courts are independent and effective. Our institutions meant to police our democracy – the auditor general, the electoral commission, the human rights commission and the public protector, to name a few – have teeth and often they do bite. We boast a robust civil society that takes up social causes around just about every social concern: for instance, campaigns on land inequity, on defence of the constitution and the rule of law, on private and public corruption, on electoral probity, on HIV/AIDS and access to health care, on gendered violence, on access to quality education, on free expression and access to public information, on funding of higher education, on public transport and road tolls and, most recently, on the use of taxes. We have more than our fair share of open and public dissent and street protests by mainly the unemployed and poor and worker formations. We have a strong labour movement, although now hobbled by economic stagnation and the large-scale laying-off of workers. Our press is free, prying, fearless and unbending. None of our citizen has been jailed only for political, religious or other beliefs. Our levels of violent crime are tormenting, but we are not pitted against one another in an open civil war or genocide or terrorist attacks. Our transition has indeed yielded a measure of democratic dividend.

But now here comes the bad news – the wrinkles of our democratic transition. When the constitution was negotiated, the parties skirted around the need for social change. The negotiators did not stare in the eye the historical structural inequality in the economy. There was no pact on how to achieve the equality and social justice the constitution promised. Instead, the constitution imposed qualified duties on the state to facilitate access to social goods such as health, housing, water, education and social grants. But these socio-economic entitlements were premised on and limited to state transfers as and when funds were available. On the face of it, the protections were praiseworthy and they promised a state-sponsored reduction of poverty, but in practice socio-economic rights did not speak to how to restructure the economy in a way that rendered it more productive and inclusive.

The absence of a social pact was a far-reaching omission given the inequality embedded in the social structure of the country at the start of the transition. I am, however, not debating whether at the time of negotiations, given the balance of forces, a radical social pact was feasible. Short of an outright military conquest, probably it was not. I am simply observing the plain fact that an existing and insular economic arrangement survived the transfer of political power. This simply meant ownership of productive assets (plainly including investment to grow the economy) and management prowess by and large remained unaltered.

In a compelling study *A Manifesto for Social Change*,[43] the authors provide a graphic representation of the social structure our country inherited. The economic elite continue to own productive assets and to control skilled management; they are focused on maximising profits and retaining ownership. The political elite remains propertyless. Their prime strength is control of the state and its revenues. Their consumption is funded by the state coffers and not by profits garnered from productive activity or investments. The political elite seeks to retain power by increasing the consumption of the middle class and of the underclass of the poor and unemployed, on whose vote they depend to retain political control. But the political elite cannot themselves create jobs or invest in or expand the economy. They must earn the collaboration of the economic elite to do so. While the blue-collar workers form part of the formal economy, they, as the economy stagnates, face ongoing retrenchment, loss of membership and loss of influence on the political power elite.

On the other end of the scale, the underclass has neither productive assets nor management skills. They operate outside the formal economy. They are unskilled, unemployed, poor and dependent on social grants. Social grants, like the salaries and benefits of the political elite, are state transfers only for consumption and not for investment or expansion of the economy. The only assets of the underclass are large numbers and their vote. The authors explain that intermittently the underclass, and so, too, blue-collar workers, resort to violence to express social grievance. The state, in turn, responds with coun-ter-violence to quell the uprisings. That, the authors argue, explains in great part unfortunate incidents such as the Marikana shootings of August 2012 and other acts of violence on protesters by the police.

After a cutting analysis, the same authors seek to explain the present economic stagnation by reference to a collection of causal and interrelated factors, the first being rapidly declining manufacturing. As they put it, the production machine has gone quiet. This deindustrialisation of society must be contrasted with accelerated private household and state consumption. They suggest that the country and its people are caught up in a capitalism of consumption rather than of production. The second factor would be declin-ing capital investment spawned by the reluctance of investors to commit to what they perceive as relative insecurity caused, in part, by an uncertain regulatory framework, misgovernance and corruption, and the ironic risk of deepening social inequality. The commodity-boom retreat is also cited as having a material part in the economic stagnation. The low growth, in turn, has led to growing government debt expected to be 50 per cent of GDP at the end of the financial year 2015/16; blue-collar workers losing jobs; one in four able-bodied people being unemployed; and one in two youth unemployed. The authors conclude that stagnation inevitably leads to the onset of insta-bility pushed back now mainly by government transfers to the unemployed and poor.

This is a terrifying diagnosis. I am not an economist, but this time around, although not always, I follow what they are saying. The spectre of a stagnant economy yielding widening social inequality, stubborn unemployment, and a growing and poorer underclass is not only stressful but also deeply at odds with our notions of a just society. This threatens to wipe out our democratic dividend.

Of course, the rule-of-law framework imposed by the constitution is important. It continues to represent the minimum agreement and common convictions of our people. It has drawn heavily from and is well aligned with minimum international standards of human rights and human decency. It has created a valuable framework for holding the ruling elite to act within the law and in the best interest of the people. It has been a valuable regime to arrest autocracy, to flush out bad governance, to demand openness in public affairs and to enforce executive accountability. It bears repetition that our democratic framework is deeply intolerant of abuse of public power. It requires us to weed out all corruption, and wasteful and unauthorised expenditure at all levels of the state and by and within independent private capital. Patronage and inept and incompetent public appointments, corrupt tender practices and so-called state capture all strike at the heart of fundamental features of our law, our democratic ethos and the mortal fight to equalise society.

The people, courts of law, civil society and all democratic institutions ought to ensure meticulous compliance by all, and by the political elite in particular. In all this, democratic accountability is all-important. Not the judiciary, not the public protector, not other constitutional watchdogs, but the people are the final arbiters of who, how and for how long a party or person may act in their name and in their stead in public office. I am stating the obvious: the real guardians of our democracy are the citizenry. In the space that representative democracy affords, citizens ought not to hesitate, if warranted, to hold the feet of any ruling elite to the fire. Ordinarily, democracy is premised on insecurity of tenure. Elected representatives hold office only at the pleasure of the people (provided the electoral system is credible). For that reason, regular elections and a limited term of office are vital features of democratic accountability. They are the means of how the people and not the political elite govern. And yet, often on our African continent leaders subvert popular accountability by evading limited terms and staying in power for decades. Some go so far as to fiddle with the electoral process. Many overturn the democratic prism by making the people subservient to the leader. In that low scenario, personal and public agency of the people wilts, economic growth stalls and the political elite feed off the only material resource – national treasury, which is made up mostly of loans, foreign aid and meagre revenues.

Going back to our constitutional arrangements, it is well and good to have the near-perfect normative standards, but they are not a panacea. Even if they were, they are sometimes observed in the breach. So the normative standards tell us little about how to achieve inclusive growth in a way that overcomes structural economic inequality and resultant low growth. This must surely mean that the national conversation, particularly with the youth, must urgently concentrate on what is hurting the people of our country most – economic inequality and stagnation.

Should we not be pointing our young people to some obvious and burning questions? For example, how, within the discipline of our constitution, do we collectively reconfigure the social structure of our country? What structural changes to the economy are necessary to create a wider spread of access to productive existing and new assets? Where would the access to and use of land be located in that debate? Closer to home, and crucially, how might the unemployed and poor underclass escape the constraints of capital and management skill and join economic production? What stance should the working class assume to push back retrenchments and increase their numbers? Is it true that we need to industrialise again? If so, how do we get the production machine to hum again – and sustainably? Put more simply, what plans do we need to create new captains of industry, entrepreneurs, new jobs and new economic output? How do we shift the national paradigm from consumption to savings, investment and manufacture? How do we, in time, convert the consumption of social grants to production and excess? What should the ideal regulatory framework be within which domestic and foreign direct investment would be ratcheted up?

The next complex question is by which fiat should the economic debate be kick-started again and in earnest? Should all social classes be drawn around the table to fashion a restructuring plan? I can almost hear the murmurs saying that all this has been tried before. Yes, but it is far more urgent now than ever before in the 22 years of democracy South Africa has had. The political elite alone are unlikely to achieve that fiat despite their perennial claim that they can fix the economy and create jobs. History has shown us differently.

The economy, not the political elite, yields jobs.

We should also disabuse young people of the fallacy that joining and worshipping the political elite is the only valuable path to personal reward or national growth. Their campaigns must refocus from a bid to access political favours to productive roles that will in time reduce the social distance and deficit our nation is staring in the face. We must shift the paradigm away from political party bigotry and contestation towards models that emphasise hard-nosed economic skills. Businesses matter. New goods and services are primal. Economic activity has everything to do with destruction of the social burden. Our youth must look to themselves alone or collectively to enter economic activity. We must again remind the youth of the indispensable place of learning and acquiring useful skills. Let us restore hard work and determination to their rightful places.

But above all, we must assure our youth that honesty matters. Integrity, particularly in public life, in business, at the workplace and in all social interactions, is indispensable. Truthfulness and honest dealing in the public space must never be sacrificed at the altar of convenience or self-benefit.

Each young person must search for her or his chosen field and then work it hard. In time, this will add to the domestic product. No true success comes easily. Young people must strive for a day of decent work, whether this is in the formal sector or, even more importantly, outside it. Let's urge our young citizens along a path of newness, of creativity and of self-reliance. The youth must shun patronage. They must turn their backs on mindless consumption and instant gratification. I urge them to embrace the difficult fact that resources, whether private or public, are scarce. Bluntly, beyond the defined public obligations of the state, nobody is entitled to have their private needs fed or to being dissatisfied when they don't get this and more. The better social ethic is not always to demand and demand that one's needs are met but rather to go out there and help to find real, fair and lasting solutions. To borrow from the Great Trek pioneers, although in a different context, who reminded themselves: *'n boer maak a plan*. Go out there. Make a plan.

For instance, it is vital that we introduce a fresh ethic on how we make space for the ever-growing underclass of the unemployed and poor to gain access to productive resources. Should the state not devise models in which homeless people, appropriately supported with public resources, build their own homes, clinics, roads and public facilities? Why can't the model be extended to planting their own trees and producing their own food? Why can't we have, with appropriate and patient training and financial support, villagers building their own boreholes, dams, piped water, sewerage, roads and irrigation facilities? Why is it necessary always to call for state tenders on areas of development well suited to be executed by the people who are otherwise jobless and dependent on social grants? When we do this, are we not, in effect, directing resources to the already productive class and only deepening the hopelessness of those on social margins? What I am suggesting is that, carefully and thoughtfully, social grants could be converted from consumption to productive spend. Similarly, a reduced state salary bill could also be directed towards development. We must think hard about how we free our marginalised people from only waiting and waiting for the delivery of something by the state. Let the tender moguls step aside and let the people develop their countryside and informal urban settlements. Why not? It would surely go some way to restoring their sense of self-worth. In my parlance, the people must again urge towards their personal and public agency.

You may have sensed that I am pleading that our country finds the ingenuity to resolve its social injustice, because no one should be called upon to fight two revolutions in one lifetime. It comes back to my swansong: each one of us is his or her own liberator and together people are their own liberators.

God bless.

Acknowledgements

I owe a number of people a debt of gratitude.

My wife, Kabo, and the children gave up on me in joining family fun. As timelines became pressing, I wrote even on holidays.

Lesley Elworthy-Grobler, my executive assistant of nearly 20 years, took dictation and typed significant chunks of the manuscript and did much in its initial layout. Without her it would have been near impossible to complete the manuscript within the set time lines. In my judicial chamber I had a number of law clerks and researchers who were very impressive, clever and diligent over the years of the writing project. They were curious to be let into my life story through the manuscript. The bargain with yearly intakes was that they would work through the manuscript chapter by chapter to eradicate obvious spelling, grammatical or formatting errors. I would, in turn, recognise their useful work by acknowledging them by name: Molebogeng Kekana, Maha Hussain, Jenalee Harrison, David Kora, Lebogang Makgwale, Carolene Kituku, Michelle Toxopeus and Zizipho Ncontsa. I am thankful and hope your young legal careers will flourish.

Many people over the years have urged me to record my life experiences and I am grateful to all of them. However, I single out my brother Tiego, who kept up interest and to whom I have sent intermittent texts of the manuscript in embryo. Peter Vundla's autobiography *Doing Time* was not only an excellent read but also reminded me that it can be done and should be done soon. I am equally indebted to Vincent Maleka SC, who regularly spared time to enquire after the progress of the manuscript. Another friend, Nita Lawton-Misra, cared much about the progress I made in my writing. She drew attention to the importance of the book and unselfishly supported and urged me on to complete my writing, I am grateful.

At the start of my writing of this book in 2012, while on sabbatical, I was a distinguished visiting fellow at Georgetown University Law Centre at the invitation of Dean William Treanor. My schedule of occasional lectures on comparative constitutional law was designed to be light. That allowed me to start writing my memoir while resident on the campus. The Law Centre provided me with the space to write with little interruption. I remain grateful.

The Pan Macmillan team led by Terry Morris have been wonderful partners in the project. They were appreciative of and gentle with my writing. Andrea Nattrass urged me on gently on logistics while Alison Lowry did a superb and meticulous job with the editing.

I am grateful to former president of the republic, Thabo Mbeki, for composing the Foreword. In doing so he has not only honoured me, but he also added the value and thoughtfulness we are used to expecting from him. At a sentimental level, his life and my life, in war and in peace, have criss-crossed in quiet but meaningful ways. It is so that we have never displayed public affection, considerable as it may be. On the other end, it would be surprising if we agreed on every public issue past or present. About one thing we agree: Africa must rise and its people flourish. Only fleeting glimpses of our comradely affinity and common paths, particularly on Africa, are reflected in the manuscript.

Dikgang Moseneke
Tshwane
16 August 2016

Notes

1. See http://en.wikipedia.org/wiki.Mfecane as well as:

   JD Omer-Cooper, *The Zulu Aftermath: A Nineteenth-Century Revolution in Bantu Africa*, Longmans, 1978; an outstanding example of the traditional view.

   Norman Etherington, *The Great Treks: The Transformation of Southern Africa, 1815–1854*, Longman, 2001; refutes accounts of the Mfecane.

   Carolyn Hamilton, *The Mfecane Aftermath: Reconstructive Debates in Southern African History*, Indiana University Press, 1995.

2. See J Whiteside, *The Story of the Century, 1823–1923*, www.ebooks.read.com/authors_eng/j.whiteside.

   James T Campbell, *Songs of Zion: The African Methodist Episcopal Church in the United States and South Africa*, Oxford University Press, 1995.

3. For a historical account of the Wesleyan missionary project in South Africa, see J Whiteside, *The Story of the Century, 1823–1923*, www.ebooks.read.com/authors_eng/j.whiteside.

4. Bennie A Khoapa, Mangena M Mokone, '1851 to 1936 – Ethiopian Church/African Methodist Episcopal Church', http://www.dacb.org/stories/southafrica/mokone_mangena.

5. James T Campbell, *Songs of Zion: The African Methodist Episcopal Church in the United States and South Africa*, Oxford University Press, 1995.

6. South African History Online, http://www.sahistory.org.za/topic/timeline-sefako-mapogo-makgatho.

7. See http://www.allatsea.co.za/shipwreck/mendi.

8. John S Mojapelo, *The Corner People of Lady Selborne*, Unisa Press, 2009.

   Jane Carruthers, 'Urban Land Claims in South Africa: The Case of Lady Selborne Township, Pretoria, Gauteng', www.unisa.ac.za/default.asp.

   SA History Online, 'Pretoria the Segregated City', www.sahistory.org.za/article/segregated-city-2.

9. John S Mojapelo, *The Corner People of Lady Selborne*, Unisa Press, 2009.

10. Zeke Mphahlele, *Down Second Avenue*, Faber and Faber Ltd, 1971. First published in 1959.

11. Years later, and during Jacob Zuma's role as president of the republic, he was always delighted to take time off his full schedule to open chess competitions and encourage young chess combatants.

12. *Bantu Callies Football Club (Also known as Pretoria Callies Football Club) v Mohtlhamme and Others* 1978 (4) SA 486.

13. See http://clarkcunningham.org/PR/Mandela3a.htm; http://criticallegalthinking. com/2013/12/06/nelson-mandela-lawyers-ideal/.

14. See http://www.sahistory.org.za/people/godfrey-mokgonane-pitje.

15. See https://en.wikipedia.org/wiki/A._Leon_Higginbotham,_Jr.

16. See https://en.wikipedia.org/wiki/Julius_L._Chambers.

17. *Ex parte Moseneke* 1979(4) SA 884(T): [1979] 4 All SA 891.

18. See https://en.wikipedia.org/wiki/Duma_Nokwe.

19. See http://www.sahistory.org.za/topic/ black-consciousness-movement-timeline-1903-2009.

20. See https://en.wikipedia.org/wiki/United_Democratic_Front_(South_ Africa)#Relationship_with_the_Black_Consciousness_Movement.

21. See http://www.cosatu.org.za/show.php?ID=925.

22. See https://en.wikipedia.org/wiki/National_Council_of_Trade_Unions.

23. See https://en.wikipedia.org/wiki/United_Nations_Security_Council_Resolution_591.

24. See http://www.africacrime-mystery.co.za/books/fsac/chp23.htm.

25. See http://www.blacklooks.org/2006/08/the_long_journey_of_clement_zulu.

26. See http://www.sahistory.org.za/people/johannes-maisha-stanza-bopape.

27. See http://www.sahistory.org.za/dated-event/ anti-apartheid-activist-dr-david-webster-assassinated.

28. See https://www.google.co.za/?gws_rd=ssl#q=kwame+nkrumah.

29. See http://www.britannica.com/biography/Julius-Nyerere.

30. See https://www.google.co.za/?gws_rd=ssl#q=leopold+senghor.

31. See https://www.google.co.za/?gws_rd=ssl#q=tafawa+balewa.

32. See https://en.wikipedia.org/wiki/Patrice_Lumumba.

33. See http://www.sahistory.org.za/people/john-nyathi-pokela.

34. See http://www.sahistory.org.za/people/jafta-kgalabi-masemola.

35. See https://en.wikipedia.org/wiki/Zephania_Mothopeng.

36. See http://www.independent.co.uk/news/world/andries-treurnicht-dies-in-cape-town-hospital-right-loses-strong-stabilising-force-writes-john-1456851.html.

37. See https://www.google.co.za/?gws_rd=ssl#q=i+will+be+back.

38. *Case and Another v Minister of Safety and Security and Others* [1996] ZACC 7; 1996 (3) SA 617 (CC); 1996 (5) BCLR 608 (CC).

39. See https://books.google.co.za/books?id=tdHYbwJbGeEC&pg=PA41&lpg=PA41&dq
    =death+penalty-+Zondo+judge+Leon&source=bl&ots=Jrs6BhKW_Q&sig=0_evGz_
    nmBLXpN4gdPonZMiofHA&hl=en&sa=X&ved=0ahUKEwjan5aNmvLKAhXIPBoK
    HWFVD1MQ6AEINjAF#v=onepage&q=death%20penalty-%20Zondo%20judge%20
    Leon&f=false.

40. *State v Makwanyane and Another* [1995] ZACC 3; 1995 (3) SA 391 (CC); 1995 (6) BCLR
    665 (CC).

41. *President of the RSA v M & G Media Ltd* [2014] ZASCA 124.

42. *Thebus and Another v The State* [2003] ZACC 12; 2003 (6) SA 505 (CC); 2003 (10)
    BCLR 1100 (CC).

43. Moeletsi Mbeki and Nobantu Mbeki, *A Manifesto for Social Change: How to Save
    South Africa*, Pan Macmillan, 2016.

Index